Robert G. Watson

A History of Persia

from the beginning of the nineteenth century to the year 1858, with a review of the

principal events that led to the establishment of the Kajar dynasty

Robert G. Watson

A History of Persia
from the beginning of the nineteenth century to the year 1858, with a review of the principal events that led to the establishment of the Kajar dynasty

ISBN/EAN: 9783337287160

Printed in Europe, USA, Canada, Australia, Japan

Cover: Foto ©Andreas Hilbeck / pixelio.de

More available books at **www.hansebooks.com**

A
HISTORY OF PERSIA

FROM

THE BEGINNING OF THE NINETEENTH CENTURY TO
THE YEAR 1858,

WITH A

REVIEW OF THE PRINCIPAL EVENTS THAT LED TO
THE ESTABLISHMENT OF

THE KAJAR DYNASTY.

BY

ROBERT GRANT WATSON,

FORMERLY ATTACHED TO HER MAJESTY'S LEGATION AT THE COURT OF PERSIA.

Ἔστι μὲν ἡμῖν ἡ ἀρχὴ ἡ πατρῴα πρὸς μὲν μεσημβρίαν, μέχρις οὗ διὰ
καῦμα οὐ δύνανται οἰκεῖν ἄνθρωποι, πρὸς δὲ ἄρκτον, μέχρις οὗ διὰ χειμῶνα·
XENOPHON's *Anabasis*, I. 7.

LONDON:
SMITH, ELDER AND CO., 65, CORNHILL.
1866.

TO

CHARLES ALISON, Esq., C.B.,

HER BRITANNIC MAJESTY'S ENVOY EXTRAORDINARY AND MINISTER

PLENIPOTENTIARY TO THE COURT OF PERSIA,

ETC., ETC., ETC.,

THIS WORK IS RESPECTFULLY INSCRIBED.

CONTENTS.

CHAPTER I.

INTRODUCTION.

PREFACE.

—◦◦◦—

IT was suggested to me to continue the history of Persia from the period at which Sir J. Malcolm's work ends to the present time ; but it appeared to me to be desirable to include in this volume a *résumé* of the leading events which paved the way for the establishment of the Kajar dynasty. As, however, I can throw little or no new light upon the events of that period of Persian history, I have not devoted much space to it ; and refer the reader to the eloquent pages of Sir John Malcolm for fuller details.

From the death of Aga Mahomed Khan to the present time—an interval of about seventy years—the history of Persia has not, I believe, been written (excepting by Persian chroniclers) in any continuous form, although the events of certain periods have been described with sufficient accuracy and fulness.

With regard to some portions of the history of modern Persia, I have had to trust to such information as was to be derived from Persian sources. The English reader may be disposed to look with mistrust on information coming from such authorities ; but in all that refers to what has taken place in Persia in relation to any European state, I have availed myself of every opportunity of testing the accuracy of Persian statements by comparing them with the accounts given by European authorities.

With regard to the incidents of the wars between Russia and Persia, I have preferred to trust to the impartial statements of Europeans who took no part in the struggle, but who derived their information from Russian officers and Russian prisoners as well as from the Persians.

Those portions of this narrative which rest solely on Persian statements, refer to the internal affairs of the country, and to the dealings of its government with the Affghans, the Oozbegs, and the Turkomans.

Having indicated in foot-notes the authorities upon which I have chiefly drawn, I need not enumerate them here; but in acknowledging my obligations to those writers, and to others whose names I may have omitted to mention, I also beg to express my thanks to Mr. Glen, British Vice-Consul at Tehran, and to Meerza Ibrahim, for the assistance they have kindly afforded me in preparing this work.

R. G. WATSON.

St. James's Club, London, *October* 20*th*, 1865.

A HISTORY OF PERSIA,

&c. &c.

CHAPTER I.

INTRODUCTION.

Population of Persia—Cultivated Portion of the Country very small—
Supply of Water—Artificial Irrigation—The Elburz Mountains—
Attachment of Persians to their Native Country—Persia inhabited
by Men of various Races—The wandering Tribes—The Turkish and
the Persian Languages—Two classes of People in Persia—The Per-
sians a robust Race—The Persian Character—Estimate formed of it
by Europeans—Persian Government—Checks on the Royal Authority
—Court of the Shah—Education in Persia—National Religion of the
Persians—The Persian Army—Labourers and Villagers—Mendicants
—Trade and Produce—Climate—Prospects of the Country.

A HISTORY of Persia under the Kajar Princes may be
appropriately prefaced by an account of the general
condition of that country and of its inhabitants during
the reigns of the kings of that dynasty. Such an account,
however, may be the more suitably condensed in this
work, inasmuch as a full description of the manners and
the religion of the people of Persia at the beginning
of this century has been already written by an English
author,* and as it may be said of the customs of the

---

* Sir J. Malcolm.

Shah's subjects, as it was of the laws of the Medes and Persians of old, that they alter not.*

The dominions of the Shah are inhabited by a population variously estimated at from five to ten millions of souls. As no census is ever taken in Persia it is impossible to obtain correct information on this point. Seeing that the superficies of the country is three times as great as that of France, even the larger of the above figures would give a very small number of inhabitants in proportion to the extent of the land. That such should be the state of things cannot be considered surprising when one reflects that the cultivable, and even the cultivated, portion of the kingdom is but a small portion of the total area. The salt desert is a waste which supports only the wild ass and the gazelle, and in many of the provinces of Persia the extent of cultivated ground is limited by the supply of water, no land being capable of producing crops except such as receives artificial irrigation. A very much greater extent of ground might be cultivated if water were forthcoming for the purpose, and much of the vegetation of the table-land of Iran owes its existence to the water that has already been brought to the gardens and fields by artificial means. All that has, up to the present time, been done in this respect has been done by the Persians themselves, and it is, therefore, needless to remark that much more might be done to secure an abundant supply of water by bringing European skill

---

* The admirable work of the Chevalier Chardin contains such a correct, detailed description of the customs, religion, and productions of Persia, that it is unnecessary to enter into a minute examination of these. I shall in this chapter confine myself to the endeavour to give the English reader a general idea of the state of society amongst the modern Persians, and of the conditions of life in that country.

and energy to bear on the solution of the problem. Water is procured in the district of Tehran by digging a series of deep pits, and establishing an underground communication from the higher to the lower. After a certain distance the water appears on the surface of the ground, and it runs in an open channel to its destination. These water-courses are called " kanats," and the whole plain of Tehran is covered with them. The earth taken up where the shafts are sunk forms little mounds at the mouths of the pits, and rows of these can be traced in all directions. Besides these artificial streams there are many small natural rivulets which continually flow down from the slopes of the Elburz mountains, but which of themselves would be far from sufficient for supplying the wants of a large city. At the distance of twenty-four miles to the west of Tehran the river of Kerij bursts through a mountain gorge into the plain, and a portion of its waters has been turned from its natural course and brought eastwards to the city by means of a canal. Where this canal joins the river a large body of water flows into it from the latter, but ere the water has traversed its course of four-and-twenty miles its bulk has diminished to one-seventh part of the original volume. The porous soil it runs over absorbs the remaining six parts, with the exception of what escapes by evaporation. A more energetic race to whom water was as precious as it is to the inhabitants of Tehran would long ere this have constructed a covered water-tight aqueduct to replace the open canal, which would increase the supply of water sevenfold. There are other means which might be adapted for supplying the element that is wanted to turn so many square miles of desert into fertile fields

and gardens where, instead of the thorn, should come
up the fir-tree, and instead of the briar the myrtle-tree.
The most obvious of these is to construct strong barriers
at the foot of some of the lower ravines of the Elburz
mountains, the chain of which lies ten miles to the
north of Tehran.   The whole chain is covered with
snow each year from top to bottom, and from October
till April the whole of the upper part for a height of
thousands of feet remains white.   In April and May this
precious snow melts and flows down through the ravines,
and inundates the plain, which at that season is in no
want of an extra supply of water.   But were a series of
reservoirs constructed, as they very easily might be, at
the foot of the rocky ravines, the precious fluid would be
saved and would be available for use in the succeeding
months.

Means might be had recourse to for supplying the
district of Tehran with water even on a larger scale than
would be yielded by the adoption of the plan indicated
above.   The country to the north of the Elburz mountains happens to be as abundantly supplied with streams
of water as the plain to the south of that chain is
destitute of them.   If the course of one of these rivers
could be diverted towards the south a great boon would
be conferred on one district and no loss inflicted on the
other, and it is the opinion of engineers that, by cutting
out a new channel for one of these streams from a point
sufficiently high, a river might be turned, by the aid of
some tunnelling, into the plain of Tehran.   Every drop
of water that is brought supplies the means of extending
the cultivation, and thus of attracting a greater fall of
rain.   It is observed that the yearly fall of rain in the

plain of Tehran greatly exceeds that of former times, when the amount of cultivation was much less. In the district to the north of the Elburz chain, where the whole face of the earth is covered with forests and jungle and crops, the amount of rain which falls is excessive. If, therefore, the Persian Government were to plant trees along the edges of all the watercourses in the plain of Tehran, and were to sow fir-cones along the southern slopes of the Elburz, which are moistened all the summer through by melting snow, it might be reasonably anticipated that in a few years' time their labour would be rewarded by a greatly increased fall of rain each year. In the meantime the general aspect of the country in which the modern Persians live may be best described as a vast desert, in which many fertile oases are scattered here and there; but from this description must be excepted the district between the Elburz mountains and the Caspian Sea, as well as the fertile province of Azerbaeejan. The country, such as it is, and uninviting as it seems to the eye of a stranger, is the object of the admiration and the love of every true Persian. I do not mean to assert that love of country, as Europeans understand the term, is pre-eminently a Persian's quality. A Persian is perhaps prepared to do as little for his country as any man on earth, but while he holds his country's interests as of no moment whatsoever in comparison with his own, he yet thinks in his heart that there is no land in the world at all comparable to the land of Iran. I believe most Persians who should be sentenced to perpetual exile, and warned that they would be liable to be condemned to death if again found upon their native soil, would, like Shimei, be unable to resist the temptation of viewing once more what is as dear to them as Jerusalem was to the descendant of Judah.

By the way in which Persians in other lands talk of their own country one would imagine that Persia was the most charming region of the whole world. Its climate, its water, its fruits, its houses, its gardens, its horses, the shooting it affords, its scenery, its women, are all the subjects of the most unqualified praise on the part of the Persian in Europe or in India. In the midst of the evidences of European splendour and luxury he boasts how superior in every respect is his native land, and while partaking in European society and dissipation, he longs to drink once more at the fountainhead of the wine of Sheeraz, and to listen once more to the recitation of the odes of Hafiz.

Persia is peopled by men of various races. A very great proportion of the population of Persia is composed of wandering tribes, that is of a large number of families who pass a portion of the year in the hills. It is in this sense only that they can be considered wanderers. They invariably occupy the same pasture-grounds one year after another. Their chiefs are possessed of great authority over the tribesmen, and all dealings between the government and the tribes are carried on through the heads of these divisions. Through the chief the taxes, whether in money or in kind, are paid, and through him the regiments which his tribe may furnish are recruited. The office of chief is hereditary. The tents in which the tribesmen dwell are for the most part composed of a light framework of the shape of a bee-hive. This is covered with a coating of reeds, and above it is placed a thick black-felt. It has but one

door, and no window or chimney. This is the Turkoman tent, which is used by the Shahsevend and other
tribes, but the Eelyats in central Persia make use of
tents of another construction, with flat or slightly-
sloping roofs.

The provinces near the Persian Gulf contain many
Arabs and men of Arab extraction. Such are for the
most part the inhabitants of Laristan, and of the country
lying to the left of the Shat-el-Arab and of the lower
part of the Tigris. The Bakhtiari mountains, between
the valley of the lower Tigris and the plain of Ispahan,
are the dwelling-place of tribes of another race, and of
whom and their country very little is known. The
mountains of Kurdistan give birth to a warlike people,
who are attached to their own tribe-chiefs and who never
go far from the borders of Turkey and of Persia, sometimes proclaiming themselves subjects to the Porte and
sometimes owning allegiance to the Shah. At the foot of
one part of these mountains, on the borders of the lake
of Uroomiah, there is a plain on which dwell twenty-
five thousand Christian families, who hold the tenets of
Nestorius. At Ispahan, at Tehran, at Tabreez, and in
other parts of Persia, there is a more or less considerable
population of Armenians. At Hamadan, at Ispahan, at
Tehran, at Meshed, at the town of Demavend, and
elsewhere in Persia, Jews are found in considerable
numbers. The province of Gilan is inhabited by a race
of men peculiar to itself, the descendants of the ancient
Gelae. The people of Mazenderan speak, as do the
Gileks, a dialect of their own. The province of Astrabad is partly inhabited by Turkomans ; and in the districts
claimed by Persia, which border on Affghanistan and

Beloochistan, the Affghan and Belooch elements are prominent in the population. At Kerman a few Hindoos reside, and at Yezd there are about two thousand families of the original fire-worshippers of Iran. But the two principal races to be met with in Persia are the Turks and the Persians or Mongols. The former are, as a general rule, spread over the northern provinces; the latter over the southern. The Persians of Mongol extraction for the most part speak only the Persian language, while those of Turkish race speak the Turkish language in preference to the Persian.

The inhabitants of Persia may be divided into two classes—those who inhabit the towns and villages, and those who dwell exclusively in tents. The former class remain stationary during the greater part of the year, the richer orders only leaving the towns for two months during the summer heats, when it is possible to obtain cool air in the hills or upper grounds close by. The tribes who dwell in tents move from place to place with the varying seasons of the year. In the spring time they drive their flocks and herds to their accustomed pasture-grounds, and if they have a right to the pasture of mountains which are inaccessible in spring they move up to their summer quarters as soon as the snow disappears. Winter finds them on the plains prepared, in their black tents, to brave its utmost rigour. These Eelyat tribes serve each a separate chief. For the Eelyats of Fars there is a hereditary chief called the Eelkhani, to whom they all owe allegiance; from whom they receive the laws that rule their conduct; and to whom they pay the revenue imposed upon them. They contribute a certain number of soldiers to the

Shah's army. Very little is known as to the numbers and the peculiarities of these nomads. The Eelyat tribes of Turkish descent have an Eelkhani appointed by the Shah. Besides these tribes there are wanderers who are less numerous and who occupy a less prominent position —the gipsies common to so many countries.

The Persians of almost all the denominations I have mentioned form a healthy and robust population. Probably the comparatively small amount of chronic or hereditary diseases amongst the adult inhabitants may be principally owing to the fact that all children in Persia are, when very young, exposed to a mode of treatment which must tend to put an end to the weak and unhealthy amongst them, as effectually as if the Spartan law were in existence by which all deformed children were not permitted to be brought up. The climate of the northern part of Persia is in winter exceedingly severe, but with all its rigour little children are dressed in an attire which leaves the stomach entirely unprotected. The mortality amongst children is, I suppose in consequence thereof, very great; and the infants who survive this rough treatment grow up for the most part to be healthy and vigorous. After they have passed the tender years of infancy and early childhood, their education and training are not such as to impede the free development of their youthful bodies. Most of the Persians go through some sort of education, but that their learning is not pushed to any great length may be gathered from the fact that reading the Persian language fluently is still a rare accomplishment in Persia. The Persians grow up both ignorant and superstitious, believing for the most part in Mahomed and Ali and Hussein; believing in the pre-

dictions of their soothsayers and astrologers, in lucky
hours and the evil eye, and in the occult science which
derives its name from the Magi. Persians are, as a
general rule, not devoid of intelligence ; but their cleverness is too often allied to want of honesty and moral
rectitude. The children amongst the ancient Persians,
we are told, were taught to ride, to speak the truth, and
to draw the bow. The chief thing impressed on the sons
of their representatives would seem to be that which
was taught to the children of the Spartans—namely,
never to allow themselves to be found out in telling a
falsehood. This lesson they certainly take to heart.
Nothing is more difficult than to convict a Persian of
telling an untruth, and nothing at the same time less
common than to hear the plain facts of a case from the
lips of an inhabitant of that country.

Like their ancestors, the modern Persians are taught to
ride. They make use of high-peaked saddles, and wedge
their feet into flat iron stirrups, and lean well forward, so
that when their horses fall they not only come with great
violence to the ground, but generally find their feet
entangled. Nevertheless, they ride courageously at full
speed over the very worst ground, and by the very brinks
of the most appalling precipices. They are utter strangers
to the fear that comes of physical nervousness. When
their courage fails them, as it too often does, the fact is
to be attributed to moral causes. They are skilled in
the knack of throwing the *jereed* and catching it again
without once having checked their speed ; and like the
Parthians of yore, these with their bullets as those with
their arrows, can check the pursuit of their enemies by
deliberately turning round in their saddles and aiming

steadily and firing, while all the time they are galloping before the face of the foe. A skilled Persian horseman, too, can avoid the blow of a spear thrown after him by swinging himself over the saddle and suspending himself by his legs until the danger be past.

The Persian character does not seem to have, for the most part, produced a favourable impression upon Europeans.* But as the character of no nation is without its defects, so is there no people whose character can be said to be wholly bad. Many good qualities are to be found side by side with the crimes and vices that defile the land of Persia. The people in general are patient and easily governed. The poorer classes are frugal and respectful. The poor are not allowed by their rich countrymen to starve for want of food.

---

* Of the many authors who have described the modern Persians, I shall only here quote from two—the late Sir H. Pottinger, and the late Sir J. Macdonald. The former writes:—"Among themselves, with their equals, the Persians are affable and polite; to their superiors, servile and obsequious; and towards their inferiors haughty and domineering. All ranks are equally avaricious, sordid, and dishonest, when they have an opportunity of being so; nor do they care for detection when they have once reaped the benefit of their superior genius, as they term it. Falsehood they look upon in all cases where it facilitates their ends, not only justifiable, but highly commendable, and good faith, generosity, and gratitude are alike unknown to them. * * * * In short, to close this outline of the Persian character, I shall add, without the fear of confutation, that from my own observation, I feel inclined to look upon Persia at the present day to be the very fountainhead of every species of tyranny, cruelty, meanness, injustice, extortion, and infamy, that can disgrace or pollute human nature, or have ever been found in any age or nation."

Sir J. Macdonald observes:—"The Persians are a remarkably handsome race of men, brave, hospitable, patient in adversity, affable to strangers, and highly polished in their manners. They are gentle and insinuating in their address, and, as companions, agreeable and entertaining; but, in return, they are totally devoid of many estimable qualities, and profoundly versed in all arts of deceit and hypocrisy. They are haughty to inferiors, obsequious to superiors, cruel, vindictive, treacherous, and avaricious, without faith, friendship, gratitude, or honour."

Fathers of families, as a general rule, make a suitable
provision for all their offspring, whether born in lawful
wedlock, or illegitimate.   All classes own willing allegiance to their lawful sovereign, and men conduct
themselves towards each other with good nature and
with the outward forms of respect.   On the other
hand, one cannot live amongst Persians without becoming aware of the absence from their character of many
of the qualities that make human life most pleasant,
and of the presence, in their stead, of many of the
habits and vices that are held elsewhere to disgrace
humanity.   If there be any beauty in truth, in honesty
in dealings between man and man, in uprightness and
independence of character, in wedded love, in family
life and family affection, in readiness to sacrifice fortune
or life, if necessary, for the public good, in tolerance
towards others in points relating to religion, in fair
play towards others, in gratitude for past kindness, in
modesty, in a consistent endeavour to provide for the
well-being of posterity—such beauty it would be vain
to expect to meet with in Persia.

*   *   *   *   *

Two hundred and fifty-three monarchs have in succession mounted the Persian throne,* and the theory of
the Persian constitution is to the effect that the King is
the state, and that all men live for the king.   The
authority of the Shah, however, is kept in check by the
precepts of the Koran; by the courts established for
the administration of justice, according to the Sherra, or
written law; and by those in which decisions are given

* *See* Chardin.

according to the Urf, or customary law. All appointments to offices throughout the kingdom are made by the Shah or by those to whom he delegates his authority.

The King of Persia is constantly attended by a set of gentlemen who are denominated *peishkhidmets*, or waiters in the presence. They correspond in rank and title to the lords and gentlemen in waiting at the courts of Europe. They are not only contented, like them, to assume the denomination of household servants, but they perform the actual duties of domestic retainers. The Shah's dishes at breakfast and at dinner are placed upon the tablecloth by men holding a high position in the country, some of them being the sons of his ministers, and others being themselves governors of provinces. The Shah's *kalean*, or pipe, is held by a nobleman, when his Majesty thinks proper to smoke ; and when he leaves the room the royal slippers are placed before his feet by a man who may, perhaps, any day be chosen to represent the majesty of Persia at a foreign court. Indeed, some of the favoured aides-de-camp and gentlemen-in-waiting would scarcely care to exchange their position, in which they bask continually in the sunshine of the royal presence, for a mission to a foreign court, which they would consider at best as a sort of honourable banishment. Those of the Shah's personal attendants who have been appointed to be governors of provinces seldom or never care to proceed to their respective governments. They appoint deputies to rule in their place, whilst they continue to stand in the presence of the king, subject though they be to those little inconveniences that arise from the sudden ebullitions of temper to which even the mildest of men occasionally give way. A *peishkhidmet* who may be unfortunate enough to arouse the royal anger is adjudged, without appeal, on the spot to the punishment of the bastinado, which, however, can generally be modified by a little adroit bribery.

The terms of flattery with which a king's ears are in Persia besieged from infancy, might be supposed sufficient to destroy much of the original goodness of a prince's disposition. The sons of the Shah are in their childhood surrounded by an establishment of ceremonious adulators, and the heir-apparent is usually named at a very early age to be the titular governor of the principal province of Persia. He goes to reside at Tabreez, and is thus removed from the guardianship of his mother, who is probably the only person in the world who cares sufficiently for his best interests to correct him when he ought to be corrected, and to check him when he ought to be checked. He receives thus an artificial education, and by being forced at so early an age to take a prominent part in public ceremonials, he becomes prematurely a man, when it would be better for him to be still a boy. At the age of fourteen or fifteen he is married to a wife, of whom, the chances are, he soon grows tired. He then marries another, and then a third, and his anderoon goes on increasing. Up to the present time no prince royal of Persia has ever had the good fortune to travel abroad. Were the king or the heir-apparent to do so, many of the arts of civilization might, to some extent, no doubt, be introduced into Persia on his return; but the risk of finding his throne threatened by others is at all times too great to admit of the Shah venturing to leave Persia.

The King of Persia chooses his wives not exclusively from amongst the princesses or the highly-born ladies of the land, but equally from amongst the whole of the daughters of his subjects. Any peasant, if she be beautiful, may become the favourite wife of the Shah, and the mother of the heir-apparent. The son of the present King, who was first designated to be his successor, was born of the daughter of a peasant. The boy died, as did his only full brother, and in his place the son of a princess was named the King's heir. It is probably to the free admixture of stranger blood in the royal family of Persia that the healthiness and the unusually great personal attractions of the princes and princesses are chiefly to be attributed.

*   *   *   *   *

The Persian Government, as I have said, is formed upon the principle common to all independent Mussulman nations, namely, that the head of the state is an absolute King, who is expected to rule according to the laws laid down in the book containing the decisions of the successors of Mahomed.

In all dubious cases the Koran forms the authority to which both sides can appeal, and the meaning and application of the Koran are expounded by the men of the law, who make it the business of their lives to prepare themselves for explaining the sacred texts, and to point out and apply the decisions of the fathers. This is the law of the country, and though the Shah has power over the law insomuch that in cases not coming within circumstances specified in the written or traditionary Mahomedan code he may exercise his own discretion, yet as being a Mahomedan the Shah is under the same law as his subjects, and Mahomedanism has too much force in Persia to render it safe for any king to interfere with the dispensation of law according to the principles laid down for the observance of the disciples of Mahomed. But the learned doctors are only the expounders of the law, and merely give their opinions upon points referred to them. They have no authority to see their precepts put into practice, or to insist on their decisions being carried out. The enforcement of the law is the province of the Shah, and of the ministers and governors in authority under him.

The sovereign in Persia has unlimited power to name his own Vizeers, and afterwards to degrade them when it suits his views to do so. The normal state of things in all Mahomedan governments is that there should be a Grand Vizeer ; but this post has remained vacant in Persia for the last six years, since the disgrace of the late Sedr Azem, who is one of the very few eastern Grand Vizeers who have lost their place without at the same time losing their life.*   The Prime Minister, when such a functionary exists, is the *alter ego* of the Shah—the superintendent of every branch of the administration, and the referee on every disputed question. In the absence of a Grand Vizeer, many of the functions proper to such a post devolve on the Shah himself. There are several Vizeers in office, each at the head of a department, but although one of them is president of the council of ministers, they do not, out of the council chamber, owe obedience to any one save to the Shah, to whom such matters are at present referred as used in former days to be settled by the Grand Vizeer.   The President of the Council is the *Mostofi-el-Memalek*—the

* Written before the accession to power of the Sepah Salar, in March, 1865.

Secretary of State—who is Minister of Finance. The other Vizeers, or secretaries, are the Minister of the Interior, under whom are all the provincial governors; the Minister for Foreign Affairs; the Minister of Justice; the Minister of Public Works; the Master of the Mint; the Minister of War, who is also Commander-in-Chief of the Army; and the Comptroller of the Privy Purse and Private Secretary of the King. Each of the Vizeers has a large number of secretaries and clerks under him, to attend to the duties of his particular department.

The Persian Government cannot be said to be a very efficient or an energetic one. Great confusion prevails in almost every branch of the administration. The Ministers retain their power during the Shah's pleasure, and it is believed that one of the chief objects of securing office in Persia, next to that of gaining the royal favour, is to amass as much money as the direction of a department is capable of affording. Almost everything in Persia is a question of money. The Vizeers have not only to pay for their posts on their first being appointed, but they have afterwards from time to time to pay for the privilege of continuing in office. In return, they, as a matter of course, think it right to apply the same rule to their subordinates and clients, and the result is that justice is a thing to be bought, rather than claimed as a right, and that a man who is rich enough to compound for his offences may do almost what he pleases.

All governors of provinces and of towns must pay for their appointments, which they hold not for any special period, but during the king's pleasure. They do not, as a general rule, exercise the power of life

2

and death over those they govern; but this authority is delegated to the rulers of the chief provinces of the empire at a distance from the capital, such as Azerbaeejan, Fars, and Khorassan.   It is found that, as a rule, men remain in office much longer than would be supposed, seeing that dismissal does not follow incapacity, but depends chiefly on the caprice or the necessities of the head of the State.   It is no uncommon thing for a man to remain five or even ten years at one post, and when an official personage quits one government or office, it is, as a general rule, only to go to another, for no Persian makes such poor use of his time in office as not to be rich enough when it is over to purchase for himself another post.   The authority of the governor of any province or district at a distance from the capital is so great, that few of those under it care to subject themselves to the effects of his anger by making representations against him at Tehran; but when a notoriously bad governor is named to a town or district, the people occasionally send a present to the Shah, with a request that the dreaded ruler may be transferred to another post.

     *   *   *   *   *

There is no system of national schools in Persia. All the towns and villages are provided with *moollahs,* or priests, who give instruction to children; but the terms upon which they do so are arranged between the masters and the parents of those they instruct. Boys of all ages attend these schools, where they are taught to read the Koran, to read the Persian writing, to add and multiply figures, to write, &c.   The schoolmaster generally receives a present from a boy's father on the son's being able to prove that he can read any part of the Koran. The terms upon which a youth is taught the slender amount of information which the village instructor can convey to him are very moderate ; but, notwithstanding this, education is still so far behind-hand in Persia, that a man who can read and write prefixes the word *meerza* to his name by way of an advertisement of his acquirements. Girls are allowed to attend a *moollah's* class up to the age of seven years, after which their education is confided to the care of a learned woman. Children of high rank are instructed in their father's house by persons hired for the purpose. Girls are taught to read, and to write, and to sew, and occasionally their education includes some instruction in Persian music. But the range of their ideas is by no means wide, and a man more instructed than a Persian generally is would not, probably, find their society very engaging.

An exception to the rule by which education in Persia is left to private persons, is in the case of the college which has been established by the Government at Tehran. The pupils in that establishment are maintained at the Shah's expense during the course of their instruction. The college is placed under the direction of the Minister for Public Works, and amongst the professors there are several Europeans. The French language is taught to those who wish to study it, and the English language is professed and taught by a Frenchman. The other branches of an ordinary country education in Europe are also more or less provided for.

Of late years the Shah has been in the habit of sending a certain number of youths to France to be there instructed in medicine and in the different other branches

2—2

of ordinary learning. Several of these have come back to Persia, but they are looked on with an eye of distrust by the majority of their less instructed countrymen, who take care to do all in their power to prevent them from having the opportunity of putting in practice anything they may have learned, and thereby throwing others into the shade. Whether any material results will in time follow this movement no one can as yet pretend to have sufficient grounds for knowing.

     *   *   *   *   *

The national religion of Persia is Mahomedanism of the Shceah sect. The Persians maintain the inalienable right of Ali to the immediate succession to the throne and mantle of Mahomed. The ministers of religion enjoy great influence amongst all classes of the people, and it may be observed, as being illustrative of the respect felt by Persians for the Mahomedan religion, that, though they are notoriously untruthful, they do not dare to take a false oath if it be administered by a *Mujtehed*, or high priest. Indeed, these functionaries are very loth to administer oaths, for fear of entangling a true believer in falsehood. The peculiar feature with regard to the religion of the Persians is the extreme veneration which they feel for the memory of Hussein, the son of Ali. That Imam does not seem to have done anything which merited the honours that are yearly paid to his shade. Ten successive representations are devoted to the exhibition of his sufferings and death, and each year, on the first day of the month of Mohurrem, most Persians appear clad in the sombre garments of mourning. During that month each quarter of a Persian town has a theatre for this religious representation, in which the impassioned beholders sit in long rows regarding the performance on the stage. The interior decoration of these theatres is sometimes very gorgeous. Each *takeah* has a patron, who takes care, for the sake of his own reputation, that the interior be suitably arranged. The one whose patron is the Shah, is, as might be supposed, the most magnificent of all. His Majesty assigns to the merchants of Tehran the honourable task of decorating the different portions of the royal *takeah*, and the merchants gladly respond, at their own cost, to the invitation.

His majesty and all the court are present at the different representations, and no cost is spared for the dresses of the actors or the illumination of the stage. So dear is this performance to the Persians that all classes contribute willingly of their wealth or their labour to render it successful. The experienced *moollahs* who are employed as stage managers may be seen hurrying through the town on their mules, going from one *takeah* to another to give the benefit of their experience. Singers lend their voices to swell the mournful chant. Little children are brought on the stage, and repeat their parts with surprising correctness, and with much feeling. The owners of the finest armour lend their glittering helmets and burnished coats of mail to deck the warriors of Yezeed. Carpenters work for nothing in constructing the tiers of seats for the audience, and soldiers come forward gladly to represent the contending hosts on the Arabian plain. If by any accident a man be killed during the performance of the Tazeeah-it is considered that his soul goes directly to the regions of eternal bliss. If anything go wrong during the representation it is

considered to be a sign of the displeasure of the Almighty.
In this year, 1864, a violent storm took place during the
holy days at Tehran.   Before the fierce volume of dust
and wind tent after tent went down, inflicting death and
injury on those within, and destroying a countless
amount of property.   So dire a calamity must have
followed a special offence, and the priests and holy men
were not long in finding out the reason of this display of
the wrath of heaven.   There is among the priesthood of
Tehran a *moollah* whose remarkable gifts entitle him
to be numbered among the sons of thunder.   He was
the favourite divine of the capital, and his brethren
were sufficiently jealous of his acquirements and of
his popularity.   He was admitted to preach in the *ande-
roons*, and was supposed to be a man altogether immacu-
late.   It came to be known, however, that, like the rigidly
virtuous Cato, he was not insensible to the charms of
wine, and his enemies took care that he should be one day
publicly discovered in a state of drunkenness.   He was
brought before the chief priest to receive a sentence,
which was proportioned rather to the scandal that had
been created than to the rarity of his offence.   He was
condemned to a cruel and degrading death ; a penalty
which, however, on the eve of the days of the festival,
was remitted by the Shah, who is a lover of the highest
attribute of kings.   His Majesty furthermore commanded
the eloquent *moollah* to preach on one of the days of
Mohurrem, which day was followed by the occurrence of
the storm that swept away the royal Tazeah, and thus
the other priests had no difficulty in divining the cause
of the hurricane.

Ere the royal tent had fallen, a last effort was made

by a saintly man to avert the coming calamity. This fanatic, who was willing to show his faith by deeds, declared to the bystanders that the tent could never fall which contained so holy a thing as himself. He therefore spurred his horse into the midst of the arena, from whence he invoked the mercy of Him on whom he called. But all was in vain. A fresh gale at that instant hurled the tent from its base, and buried horse and rider under its folds.

Many pious *sheeahs* disapprove of the holy subject of the death of Hussein being represented on the stage. In some parts of the Shah's dominions, no theatrical exhibition takes place, but priests read in families the same mournful story during the appointed days of *Mohurrem*. During these days the whole nation is moved to hysterical sorrow to a degree scarcely to be credited by those who have not witnessed it. Not only do women and children, but bearded and aged men, sob and cry as if their hearts would burst, when under the influence of the actor's performance or of the preacher's eloquence. Nor is it only when at the theatre or the mosque, or the prayer-meeting, that Hussein's mournful story is present to their thoughts. They carry to their houses the impression of the preacher's words, and it is no uncommon thing to meet in those days in the streets of the city a band of young men chanting a dirge-like song, the burden of which is—"Alas! alas! for Hussein."

*   *   *   *   *

The military force of Persia consists, in theory, of a hundred thousand men, infantry, cavalry, and artillery; the greater proportion of this number being

regular infantry. The cavalry is nearly all irregular, and is in general only called on for local service
under the chiefs of the particular district where it is
raised. The Shah's body-guard consists of two regiments of regular cavalry, of about 800 men each. One
of these bodies of horsemen are called gholams, or
slaves, of the Shah, and are considered to hold a very
honourable station in society. There has been lately
raised another small troop of body-guards known by
their accoutrements of silver. The irregular cavalry
are variously habited, according to the custom of the
country whence they are drawn. One small troop in Kurdistan is clad in mail and complete armour. There are
about 5,000 artillerymen in the Persian army, and this
branch of the service is by no means badly organized.
It is their artillery that gives to the Persians the advantage
in their contests with the Turkoman tribes.

The Persian soldiers afford excellent material for an
army, but the military system of the country is such as
to neutralize the good qualities of the private sentinels.
Persian soldiers are naturally and individually sufficiently
brave. They are remarkably hardy, patient, and enduring.
They require scarcely any baggage, and can march thirty
miles a day for many successive days, while living on
nothing but bread and onions. They patiently endure
almost any treatment, however hard. Their pay is always
kept in arrears, generally for two or three years. When it
is issued the men do not receive it in full. The lieutenant-
colonel of a regiment exacts a certain contribution from
the captains, who in turn demand a sum for themselves
from the soldiers, and so on. Enlistment is compulsory,
each district and each tribe being obliged to furnish its

quota of men. For this service there are no volunteers, as the hardships of a Persian soldier's life are too well known throughout the country to induce the peasants willingly to encounter them. Each regiment is recruited from the district where it was raised, and the men serve not for any specified period, but until they are no longer capable of serving. In their old age they may obtain their discharge and find other occupation for themselves, or be thrown on public charity. The Persian regiments are not generally provided with a surgeon, but the hospital arrangements of each corps are under the superintendence of the commanding officer, and they are bad or not, according to his honesty or capacity.

There is no commissariat department in the Shah's army, and all baggage is carried by asses. The troops are armed with percussion muskets, which are now supplied from the Persian arsenals. As the soldiers are generally without any ready money, and get no rations, they receive permission to work as labourers in the fields, or as mechanics. It is on the proceeds of such labour that a large portion of the army mainly subsists. The officers, excepting those in the higher grades, occupy a very modest position in a Persian social point of view. An officer below the rank of major is not considered to be a gentleman. All grades in the army are filled up from favour or from bribery, and consequently there is much incapacity to be met with amongst the officers in command. As a general rule they have little or no knowledge of military affairs, and they have as little reliance on themselves as their men have confidence in them. They are not wanting individually in physical courage, but their moral deficiencies neutralize in the hour of battle any physical good qualities of which they may be possessed.   The chiefs have not patriotism sufficient to induce them to face death, willingly, for their country's sake, and the soldiers, believing that the chiefs have neither skill nor courage, generally take to flight before a determined opponent.   The Persian regiments are trained after the European manner: they are taught by a number of instructors of different European nations, but these officers hold no command in the Persian army.   Their labours are in a great measure thrown away, owing to the habit which prevails of granting a whole regiment leave of absence for six or eight months together—a boon which is often conceded to a corps on condition of its relinquishing its claims to arrears of pay.

*   *   *   *   *

The conditions to which working men in Persia are subjected vary to a certain degree in the different provinces of the kingdom.   I shall endeavour to state what their life often is in the districts near the city of Tehran. The *faleh*, or labourer, is ready to undertake almost any description of occupation.   He works in the city as an assistant to a mason, mixing lime or carrying bricks, or, if he be wanted, he is equally ready to give aid in the cultivation of gardens or fields in the country. His working hours are from sunrise to sunset each day of the week except Friday, which is generally observed as a day of rest.   About ten o'clock he has an interval of half an hour for breakfast; and from one to two o'clock he rests again to take food, to say his prayers, and sometimes to sleep for a little while. He generally works in a lazy manner, and requires to be

kept under the eye of an overseer. For a day's labour
he receives, in Tehran, a sum varying from $5\frac{1}{2}d.$ to $11d.$,
according to the season of the year, and in the country
he generally receives rather more than at Tehran. In
the winter he is often out of work, and in the spring-
time his labour is cheaply bought; but as summer
advances he is more in request, and in the autumn his
wages are at the highest point to which they reach. Of
the sum which he daily earns he spends generally about
one-half or three-fourths for his breakfast and dinner
and clothing, and he lays by the rest against the winter,
when he will have nothing to do; or else he sends it to
his wife. The Persian labourer is, as a general rule, a
married man. If he have to go forth from his native
village in search of work he usually leaves his wife
behind him. If his wife have children she does not go
out to service, but if she be unencumbered she often
takes employment in the household of some gentleman.
The wife of a labouring man in Persia, although she
seldom does any work in the fields, can assist her husband to some extent in earning the bread of the family.
She can undertake the making, or the mending, or the
washing, of clothes, and she can utilize her spare time in
preparing cotton-twist and in various other ways. Her
clothes, and those of her children, if she have any, are
the reverse of costly; her husband wears but one suit of
garments in the year; and the house-rent they pay is
light. The staple of a labouring man's food is bread,
which commodity is usually sold at Tehran at the rate of
one mān (or $6\frac{3}{4}$ lbs.) for 8 shahis, or $4d.$ Beef is cheap
and abundant in winter, but it is not eaten at other seasons
of the year. As a general rule Persian peasants eat

meat three or four times a week, if they cannot afford
to eat of it every day.   In the autumn they salt
mutton for the winter consumption.   They enjoy a
plentiful supply of milk, cheese, and rice.   Mutton is
usually sold at from twopence to threepence to the
pound.   Rice is the article of food most in demand; *
vegetables are cheap, and of various kinds; and fruit,
including grapes, mulberries, melons, and water-melons,
is in the summer and autumn months exceedingly
abundant, and to be had at the lowest imaginable prices.
Sherbets and ice are within the means of the poorest
people, and, altogether, in respect of diet, the condition
of the labouring man in Persia can bear a favourable
comparison with that of the peasant of most other
countries.

Much has been said and written regarding the
oppression to which the country population in Persia are
subjected from those placed in authority over them, or
from powerful personages who may pass through their
districts.   But, whatever may be the case in other parts
of the country, in the immediate neighbourhood of the
capital the rural population are not subjected to much
habitual tyranny.   They pay their contributions towards
the support of the Government, and supply their proportion of soldiers for the army, and if any one attempt to
put exactions upon them they can make their voice
heard by their landlords, or, if necessary, by the Shah
himself, who has recently established a way for receiving

---

* The potato is not esteemed by the Persians.   That vegetable, it
may be remarked, does not, as some writers have been led to believe, bear
the name of *Alu-i Malcolm.*   The Persian word for potato is *Seeb i zameen,*
which is an exact translation of *pomme de terre* or *erd-apfel.*

petitions direct from any one whomsoever. The occasions on which Persian villages suffer most are when governors or princes pass through a district on their way to their posts, accompanied by a numerous train of exacting followers. A royal progress, too, is a source of no small loss to the population of those parts of the country through which the king passes. His Majesty, it is true, pays liberally for all the provisions supplied to his numerous travelling establishment, but it is to be feared that the money so given by the king never finds its way into the pockets of those whom he intends to be its recipients. The king is for ever on the move, and it occasionally happens that when he announces his intention of honouring some particular province with a visit the inhabitants, so far from feeling elated, send his Majesty a large present in money in order to induce him to spare them the intended honour.

The Persian peasants' recreations are the yearly-recurring festivals, when work is wholly or partially suspended. These are the new-year, the gathering of the harvest, and the seasons appointed for observance by the religious authorities. Every village in Persia is supplied with a bath, which is a source of great enjoyment to the villagers. An ice-house is attached to each village. The houses occupied by the Persian peasantry are sufficiently comfortable, and generally contain felts or carpets, and such articles of domestic furniture as are necessary for the use of a family. Although slavery exists in Persia all field-labour is free, the slaves being only employed in domestic service. Persian Mahomedan peasants are not even tied down to one spot, but can go from one village to seek work in

another, according to their own convenience. Each
village, however, has a patron, or feudal-lord, at whose
expense the peasants are all entertained on the recurrence of the yearly feasts. All Persians of any consequence maintain a large number of idle retainers about
them, who contribute nothing to the general wealth of
the country.

The class of men who obtain their daily bread by
the charity of others is also very numerous in Persia.
There are no poor-laws or workhouses, and, therefore,
to private charity is left the task of relieving the wants of
the indigent. If such relief were only extended to the
diseased, the aged, and the infirm, the calls upon the
charitable would be comparatively slight ; but I believe
the greater proportion of the beggars of Persia to be composed of able-bodied men, who lack no means, except the
will, necessary to enable them to earn their own bread.

The fraternity of *dervishes* or religious mendicants is
spread over the country. They are for the most part an
entertaining set of men, who enjoy the good things of
this life, and who appeal for charity, not to any physical
claims to it, but to their religious character solely. These
useless members of society are of two classes,—those who
reside in towns and live at their ease in the midst of
their families, and those who make a vow of celibacy,
and who wander about the country. The distinguishing
badges of the first of these two classes are the *dervish's*
cap, the peculiarly shaped axe carried over the shoulder,
and the water-cup slung over the arm. There are hundreds of these jovial beggars scattered over Persia, and
many of those in Tehran find their employment so
lucrative that they are enabled by it to live in well-

appointed houses, and to eat of the fat of the land. They have a chief who disposes to a certain extent of their gains, and who assigns to each *dervish* the post he is to occupy on the annual occasion when the house of each wealthy person in Tehran is besieged by a member of this brotherhood, who refuses to quit his position outside the door until he has received his contribution. The *dervish* pitches a small tent or covering for himself in the street, and makes a small plot of garden beneath it, and there he sits from morning till night, and nearly all night through, until he has received his money. When he has been suitably paid he retires at once, and there is no fear of another taking his place. But if the master of the house be indifferent to the inconvenience of having a spy constantly at his gate, whom there is no dislodging, the *dervish* after a time has recourse to other measures than the mere display of patience. In the dead of night he blows his horn under the windows of his victim, and the sound of this blast is considered so peculiarly unlucky, that the master of the house is at once beset by all within it, and entreated no longer to defer giving his contribution. The *dervish* does not have recourse to this extreme measure until he has allowed a suitable time to elapse. He probably thinks it his duty to earn his money by remaining at the gate for some days, and it is also a sign of import-ance to have a *dervish* at one's door, and therefore the house-owner is in no hurry to remove him, so long as he abstains from using his horn.

The *dervishes* who take a vow and roam about the country may be supposed to be influenced by motives of religion. They are often thinly clad, and if they receive much in charity they do not seem to indulge in many luxuries. Their heads are bare, and their aspect altogether such as to open the hearts of the charitable.

Besides the dervishes, there are many professional beggars in all the towns of Persia. In Tehran they had so increased in numbers, that in the year 1863 all beggars were prohibited from asking for charity in the city. Many of these are real objects of mercy—the halt, the maimed, and the blind—but many of them also are strong men who only put on the appearance of blindness in order to draw down pity. But what they want in real claims they generally make up for in the eloquence and loudness and perseverance with which they ask for alms. There is no hour of the day, and no day of the week, that does not, according to them, seem to afford a special reason why people should at that particular time be charitable. It would seem to be held by them as being almost beyond question, that a mendicant who demands alms on the night of Friday is entitled to receive relief. A still more cogent reason is the recurrence of any feast-day, such as that of the birth of Mahomed, or of Ali, or of Hussein. One is asked for the sake of God, and for the sake of the holy Prophet, for the sake of the blessed Ali, and of the martyred Imam, or for that of the revered Zeinul-Abedein, to take pity on the poor, and to relieve their necessities.* A little flattery, too, is generally applied to the passers-by. A domestic servant is called a khan; a syed is loudly reminded that he is the descendant of the blessed Prophet; and a respectable

---

* If a European pass, they will appeal in the name of Hezret Eesa, the Lord Jesus, or in that of the Virgin Mary.

Persian gentleman is boldly addressed as a prince. The mendicants often sit in groups of twos or threes, and while the one makes an eloquent and touching appeal to the feelings of the passers-by, the others emphasize it by the words "*Illahi ameen!*"—"Oh, God! amen!"

*   *   *   *   *

Within the last thirty years an extensive and flourishing trade has sprung up between Persia and various European nations. Cotton, silkworms, silk, wool and other raw produce, are exported to England, France, and Russia, and in return Persia receives manufactured goods and articles of luxury from Europe. As the imports exceed the exports, Persia is each year drained of a very considerable amount of gold or of silver to make up the balance. The quantity, indeed, of precious metals which must have been collected in Persia must have been very considerable in order to have withstood for so long the drain which has been now going on for years. It is the opinion of some European merchants that money will soon become so scarce in Persia as to reduce the imports to the measure of the exports. Money bears in Persia a value beyond that which it has in almost any other country. The legal rate of interest is twelve per cent., but no money, as a general rule, can be obtained on such easy terms. Twenty-four per cent., with ample security, is easily obtained for a loan, and sometimes as much as sixty per cent. a year is extorted by usurers in contributions of five per cent. a month. Were the Persians given to taking thought for the morrow, they could very easily either provide in their own country many articles, —such as sugar—which are now imported from abroad ;

3

or, on the other hand, they could, by making means of communication between the interior and the seaports, pave the way for an indefinite increase of the exports from their country. But political economy is not as yet studied in Persia, and things go on year after year from bad to worse, the experience of the past leaving little room for hope of any amelioration in the future.

It may seem strange that there should be a very large consumption of wines and of spirits in a country the bulk of the people of which are Mahomedans. Such, however, is the case in Persia. Wines are valued for their intoxicating qualities and not at all for their flavour, and therefore the inferior wines of the country are more in demand than the costly produce of the grapes of Europe.

Persia, on the whole, is an unusually healthy country, but there are certain diseases which are more prevalent amongst Persians than amongst many other nations. When one bears in mind the great elevation of the table-land of Persia, the numerous chains of mountains with which the country is intersected, and the consequent variation of temperature to which the people, living as they do in a sunny land, are exposed, one learns without surprise that fevers prevail to a great extent amongst the Persians. For another reason this complaint prevails in the low-lying provinces of Persia, namely, because they are overrun with moisture and with vegetation, and the hot sun produces malaria. This could in a great measure be remedied by draining. Consumption is rare amongst Persians, although it is not altogether unknown. Dysentery is a common disease amongst them, and cholera and small-pox have at intervals made great ravages in that country. Diseases of the eye are also exceedingly frequent, the glare everywhere being very strong in summer, and dust-storms being constantly encountered.

During the last two thousand years, whose history we possess, Persia has been repeatedly overrun by foreign conquerors, and the sequel of each conquest has been the same,—namely, that the influence of climate and of luxurious Persian habits has relaxed the energies and the original virtues of the invaders, and disposed them in turn to fall victims to another conquering people. No truth is more plainly written on the page of universal history than that a foreign race loses its distinguishing qualities unless continually reinforced by recruits from its native land. The last complete invasion of Persia occurred sufficiently long ago to admit of time having softened down the enthusiasm and the energy of the conquerors. The races who at present inhabit Persia have become habituated to the climate, and are as much the growth of the soil as are the castor-oil plant and the pomegranate. The dry, rarefied climate of the high table-land of Persia redeems its inhabitants from sluggish dulness of the imagination, but it does not redeem them from the listlessness produced by the Eastern sun.

The inhabitants of Persia are contented with their condition and dead to all desire of progress, to which indeed their religion is a sufficient bar. Under these circumstances it is in vain to look for the dawn of a brighter day over the realms of Iran until a fresh element be introduced into its population. A demand for foreign luxuries may be generated by the perseverance of foreign traders, and some barbarous practices may fall into disuse through the influence of European missions, but neither the Persian people nor the Persian Government possesses the energy requisite for any real progressive movement in the path of civilization. The impulse necessary to produce such a movement in Persia, if it ever be given, must, as in the case of Hindustan, be given by a race of foreign conquerors, and until the course of time bring round a fresh settlement of energetic peoples in Persia, that country must linger on in its present condition of semi-stagnation.

CHAPTER II.

IN order rightly to understand the history of the accession to power of the princes of the Kajar dynasty in Persia, it is necessary to go back to the revolution, which was brought about in that country by the Affghan invasion early in the eighteenth century, and by the subsequent successes and conquests of Nadir Shah. Never did a line of kings rule with more full consent of their sub- jects than did the Sefaveean Shahs of Persia.* They were endowed as a house with every claim which could command the obedience and the reverence of the people. They followed the Moslem faith, and were of the national Sheeah sect. They were, moreover, sprung from a descendant of the lawgiver of Mecca ; and to the advan- tages belonging to a descent from the Prophet, from a saint, and from kings, several of them added the attribute of distinguished personal merit. For the hundred years

---

* " L'autorité des Sophis est sans bornes ; ils ont droit de vie et de mort sur leurs sujets, et il n'est point de souverains qui soient si absolument et si promptement obéis."—*Mémoires de Perse.* Amsterdam, 1749.

See also in the historical portion of CHARDIN's *Persia.*

which immediately preceded the outbreak of the storm
that ended in the destruction of this royal house, the
greatest tranquillity had prevailed throughout the realm
of Persia.

It was under the weak administration of Shah Hussein,
that the authority of the government first ceased to be
felt at the extremities of the empire, and that at length
the Affghan tribes threw off the Persian yoke. After a
strife, in which fortune was for some time divided betwixt
the combatants, the Affghans, under Mahmoud, invaded
the dominions of the Shah, and laid siege to his capital,
Ispahan. After a protracted blockade, during which the
inhabitants had to endure every species of hardship and
suffering, the city fell into the hands of the invaders,
whose monarch, Mahmoud, made himself master of the
crown and the throne of the Sefaveeans. But this
warlike Affghan was not possessed of the qualities necessary to establish and perpetuate a foreign rule in Persia.
His career of ferocity was brought to a close by the
conspirator's dagger, and his relative Ashraff, who succeeded him, profited so little by the warning that he and
all of his nation were driven out of the country within
six years from the date of the conquest of Ispahan.
This release was brought about by the energy and perseverance of Nadir, who from being a petty robber in
Khorassan had risen to command the armies of Persia,
and to replace on the throne the heir of the Sefaveean
kings. It was, however, by means of the spell which
the name of that famous race carried with it, that the
unknown soldier of Khorassan was able to effect such
mighty deeds. All that he did was done in the name of the
rightful heir to the throne; and had Tahmasp possessed

either judgment or abilities, not all the services which Nadir had rendered to the State would have sufficed to make it safe for him to supplant the family which were considered, and are by many Persians still considered, to be the Agas, or masters, of the country. Even when Tahmasp, by his errors and incapacity, had given Nadir the opportunity of dethroning him, the wary general did not yet venture himself to take the vacant seat. The infant son of the late king was put up as a puppet, under the guardianship of the general, and he continued to be the titular Shah until such time as the new victories of Nadir had given that ambitious man a surer hold on the affections of the army and on the fears of the nation. Even then his characteristic caution was not lost sight of. Instead of openly seizing the regal power, he preferred the manner of acquiring it by the consent of the deputies of the people, whom he assembled on the plain of Moghan.

There, like Cæsar, he went through the form of refusing a proffered crown, which he at last agreed to accept, as it were against his inclination, and solely for the public good. This sagacious politician made it a rule, while usurping the possessions of monarchs who were unable to hold them, to ally his own family with those whose descent and position commanded the deference of men. His eldest son was married to the sister of Shah Tahmasp. His second son espoused the daughter of the Emperor of Delhi, with whose hand he obtained the sovereignty of all the provinces of that empire which lay to the west of the Indus. His nephew contracted an alliance with the daughter of the King of Bokhara, the descendant of Genghis Khan.

Nadir, in his last years, laid aside the prudence by the practice of which he had found his way to the throne. Turning on his most faithful friends in quick succession, he made it impossible for any of his subjects to have the slightest security for life and property, and from such a state of things it followed, as a matter of course, that, sooner or later, those who feared for their own lives would rid themselves of an inhuman tyrant. The blow which the conspirators struck was approved of by all the nation, excepting the followers of an Affghan chief, named Ahmed Khan, who commanded 10,000 Oozbegs and Affghans, and who determined to avenge the death of his friend. Ahmed Khan, however, was over-matched, and he returned with his force to Kandahar, where he founded a kingdom of his own. The empire of Persia was thus shorn of all the conquests of Nadir, and reduced to the limits of the ancient realm of the Sefaveeans, without the province of Affghanistan. I fear that the narration of the events which followed the death of Nadir Shah, may somewhat perplex the reader; but in order to enable him to appreciate the present state of things in Persia, it is necessary that he should have some idea of the chaos out of which it was evolved.

Nadir was succeeded by his nephew Ali, who took the name of Adel Shah. The first act of this prince on acquiring power was to put to death the whole actual and possible progeny of his uncle, with the exception of one boy, named Shahrukh Meerza, who was the son of the eldest son of Nadir, by Fatima, the daughter of Shah Hussein, and who was, therefore, at the same time, the heir of the Sefaveeans and of the conqueror who had supplanted them. Adel Shah gave out that this lad, too, was dead : indeed, his only object in sparing Shahrukh's life was that he might make him a nominal king, in the event of the people demanding a ruler sprung from their former sovereigns. Adel Shah was dethroned by his brother Ibraheem, who was, in turn, defeated by the adherents of Shahrukh. This youth then mounted the throne, and put to death the destroyer of his father and of all his house, save himself.

It might have been predicted that Persia would now, under an amiable king, enjoy a reign of peace; but there was to be no peace as yet for the unhappy land. Besides the youthful Shah, there remained another descendant of the Sefaveean kings, and one who had in his veins none of the Suni blood of Nadir. A sister of Shah Hussein had been married to the custodian of the shrine of Imam Reza at Meshed, and her son conceived that he had a better claim to the throne of Persia than had the descendant of Shah Hussein's daughter. His creatures raised the cry that Nadir's grandson intended to renew the efforts made by that conqueror for substituting in Persia the faith of the Sunis for the Sheeah doctrines which are so dear to the nation. By these means he collected a party with which he was able to defeat the army which the king led in person against him. Shahrukh was taken prisoner and at once rendered incapable, as was supposed, of remounting the throne, by being deprived of his sight. His successor was very soon afterwards in turn defeated by Shahrukh's general, Yoosuf Ali, who first deprived the rebel of eyesight, and then put him and his two sons to death.

Yoosuf replaced the blind king on the throne, and proposed to act as regent, but he soon found himself

under the necessity of trusting once more to the chances
of battle.   Meer Alum Khan and Jafer Khan, two chiefs
who commanded respectively a corps of Arabs and one of
Kurds, joined together for the purpose of overturning the
newly-constituted government.   On gaining a victory,
they consigned the king once more to prison, and deprived
the regent of eyesight.   But it was not to be expected
that the two victorious chiefs would long continue on
friendly terms with each other.   A fierce battle was fought
between them, and Meer Alum remained master of the
field, and caused the eyes of his enemy to be torn from
his head.

The supreme power in Persia, in those times, when
once obtained was anything but secure.   Two enemies in
opposite directions were prepared each to contest with
Meer Alum the prize ; to lose which was, at the same
time, to lose the light of day.   One of these two was
Ahmed Shah of Affghanistan, who, after having conquered
Seistan, laid siege to Herat towards the close of the year
1749.   Shahrukh had sent Yoosuf, his general, to the
relief of this place, and it was while absent on this expedition that that chief had heard of his master's defeat.   By
his retirement, Herat fell into the hands of the Affghans,
whose king advanced from thence to try with Meer Alum
the fortune of battle.   The event of the contest was
decided by a lance which transfixed the breast of the
Persian, and the Affghan king forthwith laid siege to
Meshed, a place which was defended by a garrison of
nearly 8,000 Sheeahs.

During this time there was in the field in Mazenderan, at the head of a considerable force, another
pretender to power, whose name demands especial notice.

Mahomed Hassan Khan, Kajar, was the hereditary chief of the lower branch of that portion of the great tribe of Kajar which was`established near the south-eastern corner of the Caspian Sea. His father, Fetteh Ali Khan, had espoused the cause of Shah Tahmasp, and had afforded to that prince effectual shelter from the Affghans in his native domain in Astrabad. He was a soldier of experience and reputation, and he shared with Nadir the command of the army by the aid of which Tahmasp sought to regain the throne of his fathers. Nadir, jealous of so meritorious a rival, put Fetteh Ali Khan* to death, and he afterwards, in order to cause jealousy in the tribe, appointed to the government of Astrabad the chief of the upper branch of the Kajars. The son of Fetteh Ali Khan took refuge with the neighbouring Turkoman tribes, by whose aid he captured Astrabad, which city, however, he was unable to hold. Returning to the desert, he remained with the Turkomans until the death of Nadir, when he raised the standard of revolt in Astrabad and Mazenderan. In the course of a few months, he was at the head of a force with which he was enabled to oppose the progress of Ahmed Shah, of Affghanistan. He defeated a body of troops sent against him, and succeeded in extending his authority over the three provinces which lie between the Caspian Sea and the Elburz Mountains ; namely, Astrabad, Mazenderan, and Gilan.

In the meantime, Ahmed Shah compelled Meshed

* " This chief left two sons, Mahomed Hassan and Mahomed Hussein. The younger died, and the elder took refuge with the Turkomans."— Translated from the *Rauzat-es-Sefa*.

Sir J. Malcolm makes Mahomed Hussein to have been the survivor.

to surrender; but in sight of the anarchy which prevailed over Persia, he did not think fit to pursue his
conquests further, or even to retain all he had taken.
Herat and Seistan were joined to the Affghan kingdom,
to which by their position they naturally belong, but
Khorassan was formed into a separate state, to be
governed by Shahrukh, the blind grandson of Nadir.

The important province of Azerbaeejan was at this
time held by an Affghan chief called Azad, who for some
time carried on a war with the Czar of Georgia, but who
afterwards agreed to a treaty of peace with him by which
the frontier between their respective possessions was to
be the river Araxes. The southern part of Persia, also,
was not without its pretenders to the vacant seat of
government. Ali Merdan, a chief of the Bakhtiari,
produced a real or pretended grandson of Shah Hussein,
in whose name he raised a force with which he was
enabled to lay siege to Ispahan. After a time that city
opened its gates to the besiegers, and the young Ismail
was put on the throne under the guardianship of Ali
Merdan. This state of things continued for a year,
Persia being divided into four governments; the south
obeying Ismail; Azerbaeejan, Azad; the Caspian provinces, Mahomed Hassan; and Khorassan, the blind
Shahrukh.

But it ought to be observed that the authority of
Ismail over the south of Persia was never more than
nominal. The two men who ruled in his name were
Ali Merdan and Kereem Khan. The latter was a
young chief of the Zend, a tribe of Kurds, and it
was to his coöperation that the success of Ali Merdan
was mainly due. So long as these two chiefs remained

on good terms with each other all went well; but
at length Ali Merdan issued orders for the arrest of
Kereem, and on the same day he was himself assassinated by one of the many admirers of the young
Zend chieftain. After this event Kereem assumed the
sole direction of affairs, and by his justice, moderation and activity, he soon acquired the confidence of
the people. The harmless grandson of Nadir was now
left undisturbed in his principality, while the three
rivals, Kereem, Azad, and Mahomed Hassan, proceeded
to settle, by means of the sword, the question as to
which of them was to be the sole master of Persia. A
three-sided war then ensued, in the course of which
each of the combatants in turn seemed at one time
sure to be the final conqueror. Kereem, when he had
arranged matters at Ispahan, marched to the borders
of Mazenderan, where the governor of that province was
ready to meet him. After a closely contested battle
victory remained with Mahomed Hassan; who, however,
was unable to follow up the foe, as he had to return in
order to encounter Azad. That leader had invaded
Gilan, but, on the news reaching him of the victory
which the governor of Mazenderan had gained, he
thought it prudent to retrace his steps to Sultaneeah.
Kereem re-united his shattered forces at Tehran, and
retired to Ispahan to prepare for a second campaign.
When he again took the field, it was not to measure
himself once more with the Kajar chief, but to put down
the pretensions of Azad. That wary Affghan, however,
shut himself up in Kasveen, a position from which he
was enabled to inflict much injury on the army of
Kereem, while his own troops remained unharmed

behind the walls of the town. Kereem retired a second time to Ispahan, and in the following spring advanced again to meet Azad. A pitched battle took place between them, in which the army of Kereem was de-feated. He retreated to the capital, closely pressed by the foe. Thence he continued his way to Sheeraz, but Azad was still upon his traces. He then threw himself upon the mercy of the Arabs of the Germeseer, or hot country, near the Persian Gulf, to whom the name of the Affghans was hateful, and who rose in a body to turn upon Azad. Kereem, by their aid, once more repaired his losses and advanced on Ispahan, while Mahomed Hassan with fifty thousand men was coming from the opposite direction, ready to encounter either the Affghan or the Zend. The Affghan did not await his coming, but retired to his government of Tabreez.

The Zend issued from Ispahan, and was a second time defeated in a pitched battle by the Kajar. Kereem took refuge behind the walls of Sheeraz, and all the efforts of the enemy to dislodge him from there were ineffectual. Mahomed Hassan Khan in the following year turned his attention to Azerbaeejan. Azad was no longer in a position to oppose him in the field, and he in turn became master of every place of importance in the province, while Azad had to seek assistance in vain— first from the Pasha of Baghdad, and then from his former enemy, the Czar of Georgia. Next year the conquering Kajar returned to Sheeraz, to make an end of the only rival who now stood in his way. It appeared, indeed, that the struggle between them was too unequal to last long. On the side of the Kajar were eighty thousand men, commanded by a general who had twice defeated the Zend chief on an equal field. Kereem was still obliged to take shelter in Sheeraz, and to employ artifice in order to supply the place of the force in which he was deficient. Nor were his efforts in this respect un-attended with success : seduced by his gold, many of the troops of the Kajar began to desert their banners. In the meantime the neighbourhood of Sheeraz was laid waste, so as to destroy the source from which Mahomed Hassan drew his provisions ; by degrees his army vanished, and he had finally to retreat with rapidity to Ispahan with the few men that remained to him. Finding his position there to be untenable, he retreated still further to the country of his own tribe, while his rival advanced to Ispahan, where he received the submission of nearly all the chief cities of Persia. The ablest of Kereem's officers, Sheikh Ali, was sent in pursuit of the Kajar chief. The fidelity of the commander to whom that chieftain had confided the care of the pass leading into Mazenderan, was corrupted ; and, as no further retreat was open to him, he found himself under the necessity of fighting. The combat which ensued resulted in his complete defeat, although he presented to his followers an ex-ample of the most determined valour. While attempting to effect his escape, he was recognized by the chief of the other branch of the Kajar tribe, who had deserted his cause, and who had a blood-feud with him, in pur-suance of which he now put him to death.

For nineteen years after this event Kereem Khan ruled with the title of Vekeel, or regent, over the whole of Persia, excepting the province of Khorassan. He made Sheeraz the seat of his government, and by means of his brothers put down every attempt which was made

to subvert his authority.   His brother, Zeki Khan,
presented the complement of his own character, being as
resolute and unsparing as Kereem was wanting in that
quality.   The rule of the great Zend chief was just and
mild, and he is on the whole, considering his education
and the circumstances under which he was placed, one of
the most faultless characters to be met with in Persian
history.   He died at Sheeraz, in the year 1779, at a
very advanced age.   It is probable that Kereem thought
that from the great services which he had rendered to
the country, and from his unceasing endeavours to
administer justice and to encourage commerce and
industry, the succession to his authority would without
question be secured to his eldset son—a youth who is
said to have shared the amiable qualities possessed by
Kereem himself.   But it was to be regretted that the
regent should have made no more definitive settlement
for carrying on the administration of the country in case
of his demise—an event which, from his advanced age,
could not have been expected to be very long deferred.
Kereem left behind him two brothers.   The younger of
these, Zeki Khan, while governor of Ispahan, had been
guilty of the folly and ingratitude of revolting against
his eldest brother.   The revolt was soon quelled, and
Kereem, not contented with saving his brother from the
fate which his crime deserved, had carried clemency to
the mistaken length of raising him to as high a position
as the one he had forfeited.   The result was that that
ungrateful man, on the death of his benefactor, seized
his two sons, and usurped the government.   He next
massacred many of the chief inhabitants of Sheeraz,
including a number of officers who had taken possession

of the citadel for the son of Kereem, and who had only surrendered it to the usurper on the solemn promise that their lives would be spared. Zeki Khan, however, found that he would have to contend with two enemies before he could reign in peace. One of these was his elder brother, Sadek, whom he found means to put to flight; the other was his cousin, Ali Murad, against whom he advanced with an army. Ali Murad had been beforehand with him in levying the taxes due by the city of Yezdikhast; and when the inhabitants declined to pay their duties a second time, the tyrant was so inflamed with rage that he ordered a number of the principal citizens to be thrown from the rock on which that city stands. These and other equally inhuman orders were the means of bringing the tyrant's career to an abrupt close. His guards cut the ropes of his tent at night, and whilst he was encumbered beneath the folds of the pavilion, they despatched him with their daggers. The son of Kereem was now for a second time placed upon the seat of power, but he did not long enjoy it in peace. He was soon doomed to experience the ingratitude of his other uncle, Sadek, whom he treated with favour, and who in return caused him to be arrested and placed in confinement. But Ali Murad once more took up arms in his cause. After fighting for some time with varied fortune, he pretended to the kingdom in his own name, for Sadek, by way of putting an end to one cause of the war, had deprived the sons of Kereem of their eyesight. Ali Murad after a time advanced on Sheeraz, and after a protracted siege obtained possession of the city, while Sadek took refuge in the citadel, which he was soon obliged to surrender,—an act of submission which was

4

followed by his being deprived first of his eyesight, and later, of his life. His sons and grandsons, with one exception, shared the same fate. The only one of the family who was spared was Jafer, the half-brother of Ali Murad by his mother. He had disapproved of his father's ambitious designs, and he lived to fill his throne.

In the time of Kereem the government of Damghan had been confided to Hussein Kuli Khan, the second son of Mahomed Hassan Khan Kajar, who had taken advantage of a favourable opportunity to revolt. He was defeated by the brother of Kereem, and forced to fly to the Turkomans, by whom he was seized and put to death. At the death of Kereem, Aga Mahomed Khan, the eldest of the nine sons of Mahomed Hassan Khan Kajar, made his escape from the city of Sheeraz, where he had been detained as a hostage.

The following is the manner in which this escape was effected. The sister of Mahomed Hassan Khan, after the death of that chief, became the wife of Kereem Khan. This lady, Khadeejah Begum Khanum, was the mistress of the harem of the Zend chief and was consequently in a position to befriend her nephew, Aga Mahomed, with whom she was in the habit of communicating through his page, Soleiman Khan Kajar. When her husband was at the point of death* she sent a message to her nephew that if he remained in Sheeraz he would, after the demise of Kereem, be put to death by the chiefs of the Zend. Aga Mahomed, upon learning this, left Sheeraz on a hunting excursion in the neighbourhood. When news was brought him of the death

---

* Rauzet-es-Sefa.

of the regent he returned at sunset to the Ispahan gate of Sheeraz in order to learn the confirmation of the event, which he did from the officers of the guard. As he was entering the city he allowed the falcon which was on his wrist to fly away as if by accident, and this gave him a pretext for galloping after it to the spot where his favourite steed was in readiness. The gate was then closed and his flight was not suspected until the following day. Returning to the country of the tribe of which he was now the chief, his first enterprise was to expel his younger brother from Astrabad, and to seize the government of that province. He then raised a force of Kajars and of Turkomans sufficient to enable him to conquer the adjoining province of Mazenderan, and he further gained over the governor of Gilan, so that the whole of the country between the Caspian Sea and the Elburz Mountains soon owned his authority alone. Ali Murad, while laying siege to Sheeraz, sent a force of twenty thousand men against Aga Mahomed, but this army was unable to force the pass in the Elburz which was defended by the Kajar's troops. After this success Aga Mahomed advanced from behind the mountains and obtained possession of the cities of Tehran and Kasveen. On news of this reaching Ali Murad at Sheeraz he immediately despatched his son with a force of thirty thousand men in order that he might effect a junction with his other troops and compel Aga Mahomed to retire. Ali Murad himself at the same time removed to Ispahan, to which place he transferred the seat of government. Aga Mahomed, unable to make head against the large force sent against him, once more retired behind the mountains, while Sheikh Veis the

4—2

son of Ali Murad attempted to force an entrance both into Mazenderan and into Gilan, but was unsuccessful in both cases and was constrained to retire upon Tehran for the winter. Ali Murad in the meantime succeeded in persuading the governor of Gilan to desert the cause of the Kajars, and Aga Mahomed's next efforts were directed to punishing his unstable adherent. The town of Resht was taken by him and the governor's palace reduced to ashes, but that functionary himself had time to escape by sea. In the following year * the troops of Ali Murad succeeded in penetrating into Mazenderan and in compelling Aga Mahomed to shut himself up in the city of Astrabad, in which he had collected his treasures. It seemed as if he would be soon reduced to the last extremities when a sudden change of fortune once more set him at liberty. A mutiny occurred in the invading army, and the son of Ali Murad, in order to save his life, retreated to Tehran, while his disbanded troops set out for Ispahan. Ali Murad left his son Sheikh Veis Khan at Tehran and marched with another army to overtake and punish the insurgents, and to encounter his half brother, Jafer, who had revolted; but the severity of the weather during this march was more than he could support, and he expired before the army reached Ispahan. After this event that city once again became the scene of the wildest anarchy. The soldiers who had quitted their ranks at Astrabad plundered the capital at their discretion, and the troops who had been under the immediate command of Ali Murad found themselves at his death without a leader. The governor of Ispahan attempted by largesses to win the support of

* 1784.

these mercenary and unprincipled troops, but his schemes were disconcerted by the arrival of Jafer, the son of Sadek and the nephew of Kereem Khan. That chief was requested by the inhabitants of Ispahan to take upon himself the task of restoring order, and having done so he wrote to invite Sheikh Veis, the son of Ali Murad, to come and to assume command in the place of his father. Ali Murad and Jafer had been half-brothers, and in full confidence in the good faith of the latter, the son of Ali Murad outstripped his soldiers and came on almost alone to Ispahan. But on his alighting at the palace-gate he was seized by order of Jafer and loaded with chains; and, seeing that his father had put Jafer's father and brothers to death, it seems unaccountable that Sheikh Veis should have so far trusted Jafer. He paid for his temerity by the loss of his liberty and of his eyes.

The pretenders to the vacant Persian throne were now reduced in number to two; namely, Jafer Khan of the Zend tribe, the nephew of Kereem, and the persevering Aga Mahomed, the Kajar chief, who had so far repaired his disasters as to be able to penetrate with a considerable force to Kashan, from whence he threatened Ispahan. Jafer sent against him an army commanded by one of his officers, and which included many of the troops that had abandoned their ranks at Astrabad. These Kurds for the second time played into the hand of Aga Mahomed. They deserted their standards and retired towards their mountains, leaving their comrades unable to make head against the Kajar, who was thus enabled to march on without opposition to Ispahan, from which city Jafer fled to Sheeraz. Aga Mahomed next turned his attention to bringing into subjection the mountainous countries inhabited by the Bakhtiari and Loors. Having obtained some successes over these tribes, he treated them with such severity, and permitted his soldiers to be guilty of such barbarities towards them, that the revengeful feelings of the mountaineers were deeply stirred, and a new army was raised to act against him. The soldiers composing this force were animated by the wrongs of men whose wives and daughters had been the prey of those they now stood against in the field. Their ardour carried all before it, and Aga Mahomed fled in disorder to Tehran, in which city he intrenched himself, and from which point his future operations were directed. This struggle in one part of Persia gave time to Jafer to recruit his strength in another part of the country. On hearing of the rout of the army of the Kajar, the Zend chief quitted Sheeraz and once more took possession of Ispahan, the garrison of which place, who had been left by Aga Mahomed under the command of a trustworthy partisan, retired to the citadel where they defended themselves with courage to the last extremities. Jafer was next employed in endeavouring to reduce to subjection his cousin Ismaïl, who raised an army in his interests in the Bakhtiari mountains. This force was defeated by Jafer, but Ismaïl, with the aid of fresh levies, compelled his cousin to seek safety in flight, though he was himself soon afterwards deserted.

While the Zend tribes were thus wasting their strength in fighting against each other, a contrary policy was inaugurated on the side of the Kajars, who had at one time been arrayed under the hostile banners of Aga Mahomed and of two of his brothers, but who consented at length

to own allegiance to the head of the family alone. Aga
Mahomed was thus enabled to advance with an overwhelming force to Ispahan, from which city Jafer once
more fled to Sheeraz. When Aga Mahomed, after
having passed some time in arranging the administration
at the capital, at length followed his enemy to Sheeraz
he found that place impregnable; and, failing in all his
attempts to reduce it, he returned to Ispahan. Jafer in
the following spring directed his efforts to the acquisition
of the city of Yezd. This object was not effected, and
during the months that it occupied his arms his enemy
had time to establish his authority over all the North of
Persia. Jafer next sent his son, Lutf'ali, to subdue the
Germiseer, and that gallant youth after a siege of three
months took the almost impregnable citadel of Lar,
from whence he passed into Kerman. At the same
time Jafer himself was making a final effort to re-
establish the Zend domination over the Northern part
of Persia. Having taken Yezdikhast, Abada, and
Koomeshah; he saw the way open to Ispahan, which city
was evacuated by the brother of Aga Mahomed. But
Jafer only regained this capital to abandon it for the
third time on account of a rumour of the advance of a
Kajar army, and on his return to Sheeraz he was
assassinated in the month of January, 1789. The
murderers of Jafer usurped the inheritance of his son,
and Lutf'ali was obliged to flee from his own army and
to take refuge with the Arab chief of Abooshehr, a place
which is better known under the abbreviated name of
Bushire. There this young hero raised an army with
which he speedily marched to Sheeraz, where, after
having defeated the force sent against him, he ascended

the throne of his father. Aga Mahomed Khan saw with well-grounded apprehension the progress of a young soldier who was beloved by his adherents and who had shown himself to be so well fitted for command. The Kajar chief had been invited by a certain number of the principal men of Sheeraz to advance to that place and drive his rival from his government. He accordingly left Tehran in the early part of the summer following the period in which had occurred the death of Jafer, at the head of an army of fifty thousand men, but finding that the Zend chief was firmly established in Sheeraz he did not take any active measures against that city. Lutf'ali, however, found himself strong enough to be able to attack Aga Mahomed in the field. The battle which ensued would in all probability have ended in the defeat of the Kajar had not a portion of Lutf'ali's troops retired towards their native mountains before the rout was complete. This unforeseen conduct, while it dispirited the remaining Zend soldiers, gave Aga Mahomed the opportunity of rallying the Kajars, who eventually obliged Lutf'ali to retire with precipitation to Sheeraz. Aga Mahomed, after this action, remained for six weeks before the city, but, finding that he was not able to produce any impression upon it, he returned to Tehran for the winter.

As Aga Mahomed thenceforth continued to be the master of the north of Persia, and as Tehran was fixed upon by him as the capital of his dominions, it is now time to give some account of the Kajar tribe which supplied the dynasty that took the place of the Sefaveeans; of the city which was selected to supersede the ancient metropolis of Persia; and of Aga Mahomed Khan.

CHAPTER III.

IF we give credit to the Persian historian of the Kajars
we must believe that that tribe can trace its origin as far
back as to the time of Terek, the son of Japhet, the son
of Noah. But without referring to remote antiquity, it
is sufficient to state that the tribe of Kajar has been
known to exist for the last several hundred years. It is
of Turkish origin, and was early divided into three
branches, the Suldoos, the Tengkoot, and the Jelayer.
The Suldoos never came to Persia. The Tengkoot
branch, which only consisted of thirty or forty families,
became incorporated with the Moghul tribes. The
Jelayer became settled in Iran and Turan, and seem
at first to have given their name to all the tribe.

A Kajar or Jelayer chief, called Sertak Nooyan, was,
under the Moghuls, naib, or deputy-governor, of all the
country from the Oxus to Rhei. He, himself, we are told,
resided near the banks of the Goorgan River, and from
this circumstance dates the connection of the Kajar tribe

with the province of Astrabad. At his death his government was made over to his son Kajar Nooyan, who gave his name to the whole of his tribe ; and his offspring became illustrious in Persia, and in the neighbourhood of the Goorgan. After the downfall of the descendants of Genghis Khan, the Kajars united with a Turkoman chief called Hassan Beg, who took service with the Sefaveean Shahs. The mother of Shah Ismaïl was of the Kajar tribe, which circumstance secured to them much influence during the reign of that sovereign. Shah Tahmasp deputed a Kajar on an embassy to the Sublime Porte, who concluded a treaty between the Sultan and his master.[*]

In the Persian annals of the year of the Hejira 969, it is recorded that the provinces of Karabagh, Genja, Khorassan, Merve and Astrabad, were ruled over by the two great branches of the Kajars, called Zeeadloo and Kavanloo. Their influence seems to have rendered Shah Abbass somewhat apprehensive ; and, in order to make it innocuous, he divided them into three branches. Of these, one was sent to Merve and Khorassan ; another was established in Karabagh ; and the third was settled at Astrabad, and on the banks of the Goorgan. In these exposed situations the Kajars soon became greatly reduced in. strength, on account of their losses in the frontier wars with Lesghis, Turks, and Turkomans.

The branch of the Kajar tribe which was settled on the Goorgan and in the province of Astrabad, became subdivided into two sections, which, from the relative position of their pasture-grounds, received the distin-

---

[*] A.H. 969 : A.D. 1561.

guishing names of Yukhari-bash, and Ashagha-bash, or
the upper Kajars, and the lower Kajars. Another
account states that the origin of this distinction arose
from the circumstance that at the fort of Thebarekabad,
the upper part was assigned to one branch, while the
lower was given over to the other. The chief of the
upper branch was considered to be the head of the whole
division of the tribe until the time of Shah Tahmasp,
the son of Hussein ; but when Fetteh Ali Khan, who
was the chief of the lower division, became one of the
two generals of that prince, his position gave him a pre-
ponderating influence in his tribe, of the whole of which
he then became the chief.* When he was put to death
by Nadir, the influence of that general was employed in
favour of the chief of the upper branch of the Kajars,
whom he made governor of Astrabad, while the son of
Fetteh Ali Khan had to take refuge with the Turkomans.
It has been already stated that Mahomed Hassan Khan
by their aid at one time obtained possession of the city
of Astrabad, and that in his final struggle with the
general of Kereem Khan he was deserted by the chief
of the upper division of the Kajars, and in his flight was
recognized by the same person, and put to death.

After this event his sons took refuge with the
Turkomans, but they yielded themselves later to Kereem
Khan, who assigned Khasveen† as a place of residence
for the family. The two eldest sons, who were complained of by the inhabitants of that city, were removed
to Sheeraz.

---

* To avoid confusion I shall, in the succeeding pages, speak of the
Astrabad Kajars as if they formed the whole tribe.

† Rauzat-es-Sefa.

This branch of the Kajar tribe was settled near Astrabad. That province lies along the south-eastern extremity of the Caspian Sea. It is of limited extent, being in length not more than a hundred miles, while its breadth varies from four to forty miles. It possesses great natural resources, which are for the most part left undeveloped. Attached to the government of Astrabad are the nomad Turkoman tribes of Yemoot and Goklan, the latter of which is bound to contribute one half of the revenue. Only one town now exists in the province, but many ruins attest its superior prosperity in the time of Nadir. Ak-kaleh, Giour-kaleh Perez and Shahrek appear, from what remains of them, to have each greatly exceeded in circumference the present city of Astrabad. That place is now in a state of dilapidation, and its walls are in so ruinous a condition that parties of plundering Turkomans have often passed through the gaps into the city. Astrabad is about twelve miles distant from the sea, is situated on rising ground, which commands a view over a lovely plain, and is backed by wooded hills and snow-clad mountains. No landscape could be fairer than that presented by the neighbourhood of Astrabad; but no district has ever witnessed a more constant succession of deeds of blood and violence. The Persian peasants are at all times liable to be called from their out-of-door labour to take part in the defence of their villages, against parties of ruthless marauders who live on spoil, and who carry away with equal indifference either the produce of Persian rice-fields for their maintenance, or the inmates of the peasants' cottages to be sold as slaves in the marts of Khiva and Bokhara. Under no circumstances can a Persian ever venture to go unarmed from one village of the province of Astrabad to another ; and even an escort is no sure protection, as the robbers come, for the most part, in numbers sufficient to enable them to combat any force which they are likely to encounter.

Ak-kaleh, near Astrabad, was the seat of government of Mahomed Hassan Khan, and from thence he gradually established his power over the whole region which lies between the Elburz mountains and the Caspian Sea. When the fortune of his son, Aga Mahomed Khan, had made him master not only of these provinces, but also of all central Persia from the frontier of Khorassan to the uttermost limits of Azerbaeejan, that chief was mindful of the events which had transpired in Persia in his own time. He had seen his father again and again obliged to retreat to Astrabad and fall back upon the support of his own tribe, and, on the death of Kereem Khan, he had seen the seemingly well-established power of the Zend princes successfully disputed by himself. However firmly, therefore, the Kajar rule seemed under him to be planted, experience did not warrant him in assuming that there would be no further changes in the line of the rulers of Persia. He or his successors might, like his father, have to retreat behind the Elburz, and trust to the assured fidelity of their clansmen. He did not, therefore, venture to establish his seat of government at a spot so far removed from the pasture-grounds of the Kajars, as was the ancient capital of Persia. Two hundred and fifty miles to the north of Ispahan, there was a town which, though before the time of Aga Mahomed it was comparatively a place of small account, yet possessed the advantage of lying at the foot of the Elburz mountains. The plain of which it was the chief city had in turn boasted of the very ancient town of Rhages,* and of the modern Mahomedan city of Rhei, which is said to have contained a population of 1,500,000 souls,† and to have been, after Babylon, the largest city the East ever saw. Of Rhages all that now remains is the name of Erij, and near where it stood are the fortifications of a Greek camp, supposed to have been constructed by Seleucus. Of Rhei we can still trace the walls, which enclose an enormous space; and two towers, with cufic inscriptions engraved on their bricks, still attract the attention of the traveller.

The earliest mention of Tehran ‡ occurs in the writings § of an Oriental author of the twelfth century. At that time its inhabitants, like Troglodytes, had their dwelling-places entirely under ground; a state of things which continued until the fifteenth century of the Christian era. The people of Tehran of those times are said to have lived in a constant state of insurrection against their sovereign, waylaying those who passed by the neighbourhood, and retiring to their caves when pursued. There were no means of dislodging them from their subterranean city. The first European traveller who visited Tehran,‖ describes it as being, in

---

* "Et interim tradidi in manū Gabeli fratris mei, qui erat in terra Medorum in urbe Rages, decē talenta argenti."—TOBIAS, cap. i. v. 14. Editio Sebast. Munsteri.

† CHARDIN: vol. ii. p. 411.   ‡ *Notice sur Thehran.* Par LANGLES.

§ The *Moadjemel Boldan.*

‖ "Taheràn è città grande, più di Casciàn, ma poco popolata, e poco habitata, per esser tutta piena dentro di grandissimi giardini, con infinità di frutti d'ogni sorte; i quali, principiando molto a buon' hore, per esser quella città in aria calda assai, si mandano a vender, per tutto 'l paese intorno, più giornate lontano. E sede di Chàn, e capo di provincia; . . . Son di più le strade ombrate tutte da Platani; di maniera che io chiamo Taheràn la città dei Platani."—*Viaggi di* PIETRO DELLA VALLE. Roman edition of 1658, p. 306.

the year 1618, a spacious town which contained few inhabitants, and which was chiefly devoted to gardens. From the chenars which shaded nearly all the streets, he called it the city of plane-trees. In the time of the Sefaveean Shahs it was the chief city of a province, and it was at different epochs honoured by being the place of a temporary residence of those kings. It did not lie along the routes frequented by the chief caravans, and its industry was purely agricultural. Shah Tahmasp, the son of Hussein, took refuge with his harem at Tehran, during the Affghan invasion. That prince there received an embassy from the Ottoman Porte. The city was besieged by the Affghans, and was almost entirely destroyed by those ruthless invaders; but Tahmasp, whom they wished to secure, was able to effect his escape. From this period onwards the name of Tehran[*] appears frequently in the annals of Persia. Nadir Shah, on his return from India, ordered the priests of all the professions of faith of the peoples of his dominions, to meet him at Tehran,[†] in order that he might come to an understanding with his subjects regarding the adoption of a reasonable religion. It was at Tehran that that tyrant caused his son Reza to be deprived of his eyesight; and the unfortunate prince was subsequently massacred in the same town, by order of his cousin, Adel Shah. It was to Tehran that Kereem Khan retreated with the remnant of his shattered forces after his first defeat by Mahomed Hassan Khan.[‡] It was from Tehran that the

---

[*] Chardin speaks of Tehran as being " une petite ville du pays que les anciens geographes appellent *la comisène*, entre la Parthide, l'Hyrcanie et la Sogdiane."

[†] *Voyage en Perse.* Par OLIVIER. Vol. v. p. 418.

[‡] *Voyage en Perse.* Par OLIVIER. Vol. vi. p. 47.

general of Ali Murad attempted to put down the revolt of
Aga Mahomed Khan.　That town was then, for the first
time, taken by the Kajar chief, who, however, was quickly
driven out of it.　On again obtaining possession of it,
he made it the base of his future operations, and finding it
conveniently situated for communicating with the central
and western districts of Persia, while at the same time it
was within a short distance of the habitation of the Kajar
tribe, he determined to make it the capital of the country ;
a position which it has ever since continued to hold.

　　A French traveller, who visited Tehran in the reign
of Aga Mahomed,* gives a minute description of the
appearance which that city then presented.　From
the fact that the bazars and the mosques, as well as the
houses of the people and the palace of the king, were all
new, it appeared that the place must, at a previous period
not long past, have been almost completely destroyed by
the Affghans.　Aga Mahomed, having chosen Tehran as
his capital, erected in it, for the convenience of travellers
and merchants, commodious caravanserais and places for
transacting business, which made the former provincial
town one of the handsomest cities in Persia.　Tehran was
surrounded by a square wall of earth, and by a broad
ditch.　The extent of the walls was about seven miles,
but only a small portion of the area therein inclosed
was inhabited in the time of Aga Mahomed.　Large
vacant spaces and extensive gardens occupied a great
part of the ground, and nearly a fourth of the city was
devoted to the ark, or citadel, which contained only the
palace of the king.　In each of the four faces of the
wall there was a gate, defended by a large round tower,

* M. OLIVIER.

three hundred yards in front of it, which towers were made to contain two or three pieces of cannon. But notwithstanding all the endeavours which Aga Mahomed made to people his new capital; notwithstanding the aid which he held out to the merchants and artisans who came to settle in it; the population which it contained towards the end of his reign did not exceed fifteen thousand souls, including the household and troops of the king, who amounted to three thousand.

Aga Mahomed Khan was the eldest of the nine sons of Mahomed Hassan Khan, Kajar, who lost his life, as we have seen, by the hand of the chief of the rival branch of the Kajars. It has been stated that some time after his death his family came to Kasveen, a city which lies ninety miles to the west of Tehran. At first only two of the sons were brought to Sheeraz; but it appears that other members of the family afterwards followed them to that place, where, though they were detained as prisoners at large, they were treated with the greatest kindness by the chief of the Zend. The second brother, Hussein, was afterwards entrusted with the government of Damghan. He rebelled, and on being defeated by the brother of Kereem, who was sent to put down his revolt, he fled to the Turkomans, and was put to death. He left two sons, the elder of whom, Fetteh Ali Khan, afterwards became king of Persia. This Hussein Khan was the only full brother of Aga Mahomed. Notwithstanding his revolt, the Zend chief conferred upon a younger member of the family the government of Astrabad; but he continued to detain Aga Mahomed and two of his other brothers as hostages at Sheeraz.

Aga Mahomed had in his early years fallen into the

5

hands of Adel Shah, the nephew and successor of Nadir, against whom the Kajar chief maintained himself in revolt. Adel Shah had the cruelty to order that the boy should be reduced to the condition of an eunuch, and this atrocity turned all the victim's thoughts to the pursuit of his ambitious views. He accompanied his father, while still a boy, upon journeys and in various campaigns, and was left by him in charge of the important government of Azerbaeejan. When by his father's death he became the chief of his tribe, had he seen any chance of succeeding, it is probable that he would not have laid aside his efforts to establish the supremacy of the Kajars; but he had the sense to see that the power of Kereem Khan was too well established to admit of the slightest hope of success in such an undertaking during the lifetime of the Zend chief. He accordingly gave himself up with his brothers, and resolved to wait until a more favourable opportunity should present itself of realizing his dreams of ambition. While enjoying the favour and kindness of Kereem, he was used to vent his spite against the triumphant foe of his house by cutting, with a knife which he concealed beneath his robe, the rich carpets of the regent; not reflecting that he hoped that those same carpets would one day come into his own possession. At the death of Kereem he made his escape, along with two of his brothers, from Sheeraz, and raised the standard of revolt in the province of Mazenderan. After a protracted struggle, in which fortune at one time was with him and at another against him, he finally succeeded, as we have seen, in establishing his authority over the centre and the north of Persia, from the borders of Khorassan to the frontier of the Ottoman empire.

Aga Mahomed had still one rival to encounter, Lutf'ali,

the grand-nephew of Kereem Khan. No contrast could be greater than that which these two men afforded. Lutf'ali was still a youth, but already he owed his power as much to the fame of his own achievements as to his descent from a race of rulers. He was a model of manly beauty, and was for the most part as just and generous as he was brave and energetic. Aga Mahomed was a man of mature years, and it was to the circumstance of his being the eldest son of his father that he was indebted for being able to overcome the almost insuperable obstacle presented by the fact of his being cut off from the possibility of transmitting his power to the offspring of his body. In person he was miserable to behold; and though he must be admitted to have been possessed of personal courage and of extraordinary energy, yet those qualities were stained by his injustice and ingratitude, his vindictiveness, his suspiciousness, his avariciousness and his cruelty. He owed his success in a great measure to the coöperation of two of his brothers, to whom he solemnly promised the governments of Ispahan and of Kasveen respectively; but when he had gained his object he deprived one of the two of his eyesight and the other of his life. It is revolting to read all the atrocities that are recorded of this monarch. One example will suffice to show the reader the extent to which tyranny and cruelty were carried in his reign. The French writer above referred to* mentions that he was at Tehran at the time of Aga Mahomed's return from Meshed, when the king signalized his arrival by the following act of punishment:—At Meshed he had consigned a picture to the care of one of his officers, and on his reaching Tehran he

---

* M. OLIVIER.

ordered it to be unpacked and brought into his presence. In the course of its transport on a mule or camel over six hundred miles, the glass of the frame had been broken, and the painting itself slightly damaged. For this the eyes of a deserving officer were torn from his head, and, after having been deprived of all he possessed, he was expelled from Tehran.*

When Aga Mahomed, after his first victory over his rival, had retired from before the walls of Sheeraz, Lutf'ali conceived the project of rendering himself master of Ispahan by a dashing movement which would take that city by surprise. He set out from Sheeraz towards the end of the month of November, at the head of ten thousand cavalry, unencumbered by tents or baggage, or other provisions than a small quantity of rice which each soldier was ordered to carry with him. But the severity of the season rendered this bold enterprise abortive, and after having made but two marches the force returned to Sheeraz. At this time all the south of Persia, from the united streams of Euphrates and Tigris on the west, to the confines of Yezd and Kerman on the east, acknowledged the authority of Lutf'ali. During the following winter he employed himself as well in raising an army for operations when the weather should relent, as in putting in order the different branches of the administration at Sheeraz, and in holding out encouragement to

* " Mehemet était dans l'usage, à l'égard de ses serviteurs qui avaient le malheur de lui déplaire, de leur faire ouvrir le ventre, et arracher les entrailles. Il avait même poussé, à l'égard de quelques-uns d'entre eux, l'atroce barbarie jusqu'à leur mettre les entrailles autour du cou, et les exposer dans cet état, encore vivans, à la dent des animaux carnassiers." . . . " Cruel, féroce, au-delà de toute expression, il faisait également ouvrir le ventre à ceux de ses sujets Musulmans qui étaient accusés de boire du vin."—*Voyage en Perse*, par OLIVIER. C. v. p. 135.

those who wished to extend their commercial transactions. In the following year, as Aga Mahomed did not again advance against Sheeraz, Lutf'ali Khan marched to Kerman, to compel the governor of that province to surrender the city to his authority. Declining to accept the advantageous compromise offered by that chief, he laid siege to Kerman at the beginning of winter, but was unable, owing to the weather, to make any impression upon the place. In the following spring, Lutf'ali Khan determined to advance upon Ispahan, and rescue that city once more from Kajar domination. He had not made more than a few marches from Sheeraz when an event occurred which had the effect of deciding the destinies of Persia.*

The person to whose aid both Lutf'ali Khan and his father had been mainly indebted for the partiality displayed towards them in misfortune by the citizens of Sheeraz was the Kelanter, or civil governor, of Fars, who was named Haji Ibraheem. That magistrate —who was the descendant of a converted Jew—had been appointed to the high post he held by Jafer Khan ; and, influenced by gratitude, he had greatly contributed to placing Jafer's son upon the throne. Lutf'ali Khan selected Haji Ibraheem to be his minister, and at first he seemed disposed to place every confidence in him. In view of the services rendered by the Vizeer, it is not extraordinary that his master should have regarded him in the light of his most faithful subject; for it is obvious that had he entertained any views of seizing the government, he would have taken advantage of the opportunity of his prince being destitute and a wanderer. But it is dangerous in Persia for a subject to render too

* A.D. 1701.

great services to his king : if the latter be at all of a
suspicious disposition, evil tongues are not wanting to
misrepresent even the greatest services ; and such was
the case on this occasion.   The head of Jafer Khan
was said to have been mutilated after his assassination
by a man whose ears Jafer had caused to be cut off.
This man, however, obtained a full pardon from Lutf'ali,
on the intercession of Haji Ibraheem, and he was afterwards included in a list of persons who received robes
of honour from the prince.   This latter circumstance so
enraged the widow of Jafer, that she sent for her son, and
violently reproached him with the baseness of his conduct.
In Persia, it is considered to be a point of honour to
avenge the blood of a relative ; and it may be well
imagined that this reproach from his mother stung the
young prince to the quick.   Sending at once for the man
he had pardoned, he demanded of him what punishment
a person should receive who had behaved badly to his
sovereign and benefactor.   The unhappy man is said to
have replied that such an one deserved to be burnt alive ;
and Lutf'ali Khan, forgetful of his princely word, had
the barbarity to order that this sentence should be forthwith executed on him who had pronounced it.   This act
caused him the loss of his crown and his life.

Haji Ibraheem, who had obtained the man's pardon,
afterwards told the English historian of Persia,* that from
that moment he had lost all confidence in Lutf'ali Khan.
Satisfied, by what followed, that his own existence was at
stake, he took the resolution of removing the crown from
the head on which he had placed it, and making over
Sheeraz to Aga Mahomed Khan.   For this end he took

* Sir John Malcolm.

his measures so well that, without any blood having been shed, Lutf'ali was driven to seek safety by fleeing from his own camp with a handful of men, and retreating to the shore of the Persian Gulf. There, by the aid of an Arab chief, he raised a small force with which he appeared before the walls of Sheeraz. The deeds of heroic daring ascribed in Persian story to Rustem and the fabulous heroes of old were now surpassed by the real achievements of Lutf'ali Khan. Aga Mahomed sent a force under one of his generals to the support of Haji Ibraheem; but Lutf'ali, with his band of Arabs, attacked, and after a severe struggle put to flight, this numerous corps. The Kajar prince, on hearing of this defeat, sent another army against his rival, whose troops it outnumbered in the proportion of ten to one. Lutf'ali left his entrenchments on the approach of the enemy, and by his example so animated his men that they again gained a complete victory over the Kajars.

Aga Mahomed now advanced in person at the head of his main body, which was so numerous that we are told the soldiers of Lutf'ali were to it scarcely more than as one to a hundred. The Zend chief attacked and defeated the advanced guard of the enemy, and following up his advantage in the dead of night, he carried confusion and dismay into the camp of the Kajars. He had penetrated to the royal pavilion, where Aga Mahomed awaited him at the head of his guards, when he was assured that the Kajar prince had fled, and entreated not to permit his soldiers to plunder the treasure which his tents contained. Aga Mahomed awaited in calmness the approach of dawn, when the muezzin, by calling the soldiers to prayer, assured them that their king had never deserted

his post. The small numbers of the Arabs, who were
employed in plundering, were of course discovered by the
daylight, and Lutf'ali Khan was compelled to seek safety
in flight, which was continued until he reached the province of Kerman. Passing from there into Khorassan,
he raised a force with which he was enabled to defeat a
corps sent against him, and to lay siege to Darabjerd.
On the approach of a Kajar army he raised the siege,
and, after having sustained a defeat, once more took
refuge in Khorassan. His last exploit was, with the aid
of a few followers, to take possession of Kerman.

The city of Kerman, which was the place of refuge of
the last Sassanian kings on the Arab invasion of Persia,
is situated on the eastern side of a wide plain about half
a mile from the foot of some heights, which, crowned
by the ruins of an ancient castle,* called the Kalla-i-
Dokhter, or Virgin Fortress, extend for a short distance
west of a range of high and rocky hills bounding the
plain on the east. As seen from these heights the town
presents the following appearance : It is enclosed by a
mean wall and dry ditch, both ruinous, and measuring in
circumference about two and a half, or three, miles. On
the western side stands the citadel, called Bagh-i-Nazar,
which contains the residence of the governor and a few insignificant huts. On the eastern side the citadel has a gateway and seven towers on the walls ; on its western side a
gateway opening into the plain ; on its southern face there
are five towers, and it is surrounded by a dry ditch.† The

* Mr. Abbott's *Notes on the Cities of Southern Persia.*
† "In the ditch," says Mr. Abbott, "I found three brass field-pieces
and one brass howitzer. One of the former bore on it the initials of the
East India Company. An old gun in a ruinous state lay near, with a crown
and cross on it, and the figures £3.3.4. It is probably of Portuguese make."

town possesses a gateway on each of its four sides. In point of population, Kerman was formerly the second city in Persia. Owing to the scarcity of timber, almost all the houses have arched roofs. The place and the surrounding scenery have a dreary aspect, which is the effect of the absence of trees, the little cultivation, and the few villages which the plain possesses. The space between the present town and the Kala-i-Dokhter was either the site of a former city, or a portion of one.

The heights command the place at a long range, and on these a Kajar army, led by Aga Mahomed Khan in person, took up its position, and set about the task of driving Lutf'ali from his last stronghold. The attack was opened on the western side ; but the gallant Zend prince withstood, during a period of four months, all the efforts which the genius and experience of the Kajar chief could suggest for the purpose of compelling Kerman to surrender. It is said that during this time two-thirds of the besieged troops and of the townspeople perished from want of food and water. But the brave Lutf'ali was destined once again to be the victim of treachery. The chief to whom he had confided the charge of the citadel opened its gate to give admission to the Kajar troops, who poured in overwhelming force into the place, and defied all resistance. As the gates of the town were watched by bodies of men sufficiently numerous to prevent the passage of Lutf'ali, the hero threw a few planks over the ditch, which were removed as soon as he and three of his attendants had crossed it. Then, with his wonted impetuosity, he burst through the lines of the enemy, and he succeeded in reaching the town of Bem, in the district of Nermansheer, on the borders of Beloochistan. The brother of the chief of Nermansheer had been with Lutf'ali in Kerman, and three days having elapsed without his appearance, the chief became convinced that, if alive, he must be in the hands of the Kajars. In the hope of being able to save him,* he basely determined to violate the laws of hospitality. Lutf'ali was warned of his danger, but he was loth to give credit to the report of intentions on the part of his host which were so much in contrast with the common practice of the Eastern nations. His few followers, finding him obstinate, consulted their own safety by. taking to flight; and when armed men came to seize him, he was unable, alone, effectually to make head against them, notwithstanding a momentary panic which the influence of his presence caused. He had gained the back of his Arab charger, when the blow of a sabre brought the noble animal to the ground, and the rider fell wounded into the hands of his assailants.

In the meantime, Aga Mahomed Khan, by the vengeance which he was wreaking on the inhabitants of Kerman, was teaching other cities the consequences of giving shelter to his foes. He issued orders to deprive all the adult males of their life, or of their eyesight; and the females and children, to the number of twenty thousand, were granted as slaves to the soldiers. But when news reached the conqueror that his enemy had been captured, a stop was put to the slaughter; which had been dictated as much by policy as by cruelty. The vengeance of the royal eunuch was now partly diverted from the citizens of Kerman to be concentrated for the moment on his captive rival. The unsurpassed courage displayed by

---

* In this hope he was disappointed.

that ill-fated prince, and the constancy with which he had supported every reverse of fortune, might have been expected to inspire some gleam of pity in the breast of a soldier who had himself known adversity. But no trait of mercy was to be discovered in the conduct of the triumphant Kajar. The eyes of his wounded foe were torn from his head,* and the further treatment to which he was subjected was such as could only have been conceived in the mind of a brutal barbarian.† Aga Mahomed could not at first resolve to renounce the pleasure of knowing that his rival still lived in misery; Lutf'ali was, therefore, sent to Tehran, where, after a time, he suffered, by the bowstring, that death which he had so often braved in battle.

To commemorate the final downfall of the Zend dynasty, Aga Mahomed Khan is said to have decided on forming a pyramid of skulls on the spot where Lutf'ali Khan had been taken; and for that purpose, (according to the authorities I follow,) he decapitated six hundred prisoners, and despatched their heads to Bem, by the hands of three hundred other prisoners; forcing each man to carry the skulls of two of his former comrades. On arriving at Bem, the three hundred survivors met the fate of the other six hundred. The pyramid said to have been thus composed still existed in the year 1810; affording to an English traveller‡ a horrid evidence of

* "It is stated that Aga Mahomed himself put out the eyes of his rival."
—POTTINGER's *Travels*.

† "An old man whom I met at Sheerauz, who had served under Lootf Alee Khan in his youth, informed me of this. He had been an eye-witness of the dreadful treatment to which his unhappy master was subjected."—BINNING : *Two Years' Travel in Persia.*

‡ The late Sir Henry Pottinger.—(With reference to this horrid monument, which was seen by Sir H. Pottinger, I have followed the generally

the implacable and bloodthirsty disposition of the first
Kajar Shah. It is beyond question that the city of Kerman
was given up for three months to the incessant ravages
and plunder of an exasperated army, which, under the
sanction of its chiefs, committed the most unheard-of
enormities. The wives and daughters of the citizens—
some of the latter being children of tender years—were
publicly exposed to the brutality of the soldiers in the very
presence of their husbands and fathers, who were afterwards forced to receive them thus dishonoured, or to
destroy them with their own hands on the spot. All the
fortifications and the elegant structures with which
Kerman had been beautified by the Affghans during
the period of their possession of this part of Persia, were
razed to the ground, and the famous city that had been
the emporium of wealth, luxury and magnificence, was
doomed to lie desolate for many years, to expiate the
crime of having afforded a last shelter to the heroic rival
of Aga Mahomed Khan.

---

received account—that of the above-mentioned traveller and of Fraser ; but
I observe that Mr. Abbott, in his *Notes on the Cities of Southern Persia,*
of which he has kindly allowed me to make use, throws some doubts upon the
correctness of the story which attributes the erection of this pillar of skulls
to Aga Mahomed Khan, as he could find no verification of this tale when
he visited Kerman. It is to be presumed, however, that Pottinger, who
travelled in that country nearly forty years earlier, had good grounds for
the statement he makes.)

CHAPTER IV.

No sooner did Aga Mahomed Khan find himself absolute
master of the Persian empire than he set about the task
of re-establishing the relations which had formerly sub-
sisted between the Czars of Georgia and the Shahs of
Persia. When the latter were sufficiently powerful, they
had always exacted tribute from the former : Abbass the
Great received this contribution punctually during the
whole of his reign. It consists of a certain number of
children of both sexes, who became household slaves.*
During the long period that Persia was torn to pieces by
domestic wars after the death of Nadir, the sovereign of
Georgia was not called upon to acknowledge the suze-
rainty of any of the chiefs of his Mahomedan neighbours ;
but, in the meantime, the countries lying between the
Caucasus and Persia were fast falling under the ascendancy of another government, whose grasp they found it
impossible to shake off. As the rise and spread of the
Russian power in Georgia has exercised a permanent

---

* CHARDIN : *Voyage en Perse.* Vol. i. p. 332.

influence over the destinies of Persia, it may be useful here to trace the connection between the two countries from its commencement. It was after Russia had finally triumphed over Sweden that the arms of the Czar Peter were, for the first time, turned against Persia.

In the city of Shumakhi, which, at that time, formed part of the Persian empire, a Russian mercantile company was established under the protection of the Shah.* The neighbouring mountaineers surprised and sacked the town, and caused a heavy loss to these Russian subjects.† This occurred during the siege of Ispahan by the Affghans, when Shah Hussein was powerless to render justice, and when Mahmoud, the invader, was in no humour to attend to the reclamations of a sovereign of whom he had, probably, never heard the name. Tahmasp, the son of Hussein, who was sent by his father to endeavour to raise an army at Kasveen, the native seat of the Sefaveeans, besought from thence the armed assistance of the Czar of Russia for ridding Persia of the Affghans. The proposal suited the views of Peter, whose capacious mind was already occupied with the scheme of making the Caspian Sea a Russian lake, and of endeavouring to attract to that country the transport of the commodities sent to Europe from Asia. He had already caused soundings to be made of the Caspian Sea, and charts to be drawn up of its coasts, and in the month of May, 1722, he set out in person for the Shah's dominions, accompanied by the Empress Catherine. They descended the Volga to Astrakan, from which place the Czar moved his army

---

* *Histoire de Russie sous Pierre le Grand,* par VOLTAIRE, p. 510.

† " Trois cents marchands Russes avaient été assassinés à Chemakha, et le commerce avait éprouvé une perte de 4,000,000 de roubles d'argent."— *La Russie dans l'Asie Mineure,* p. 83.

of 40,000 men southwards to Daghestan, partly by land, but chiefly by sea. The chain of the Caucasus terminates to the eastward at a place called Derbend, a word meaning a gate in a pass. It is so named because there existed at that spot a natural opening in which there was a gate in the famous wall which was built from sea to sea to prevent the ingress of the Scythian horsemen. This sea-washed fortress, which lies on the side of a beautiful hill that rises from the shore, might have been defended against all the power of the Czar ; but the governor preferred, by a timely submission, to secure the protection of so redoubtable an enemy. Thus ended the first Persian campaign of Peter the Great, who returned in triumph to Moscow.

Mahmoud, the Affghan, fearing lest Shah Hussein should find in Peter a supporter capable of restoring the Shah's fallen power, endeavoured to induce the Ottoman Porte to declare war against Russia. In the last campaign in which the armies of these two nations had been pitted against each other, the advantage had remained with the troops of the Sultan. It was the campaign of the Pruth, in which the army of Peter had only been saved from utter destruction by the tact and coolness of Catherine. Turkey, in turn with Persia, claimed obedience and tribute from the petty kings who ruled the country lying between the Caucasus and the dominions of the two great Mussulman powers, and Mahmoud strove to excite the jealousy of the Porte at the interference of the Czar in the affairs of that region, —an interference which was justified by the expressed desire of Shah Hussein. The Turks saw the armies of Peter already in Daghestan, and, naturally fearing lest they should advance into Georgia, the Porte determined to declare war against Russia. From this design the Turks were, however, diverted by the advice of the ambassadors of Germany and of France. The emperor declared that if Russia were attacked Germany would defend her,* and the French representative pointed out that it was not for the interests of Turkey to encourage a successful rebel such as Mahmoud.

In the meantime the Russian army in Daghestan received reinforcements and prepared to advance to the southward. At the extremity of the peninsula of Absharon, which juts out from the western shore of the Caspian Sea, stands the fortress of Badkooba, or Bakoo, a place cele-brated chiefly on account of the everburning fires of naphtha in its vicinity, which attracted the adoration of the fire-worshippers of old, and which are to this day constantly tended by a succession of priests from India. Bakoo yielded to the Russian general Matufkin, and immediately after its capture a treaty was concluded at St. Peters-burg between the Czar Peter and the ambassador of Tahmasp (who acted for himself, as his father Hussein was a captive), by which the former engaged to take up arms for the restoration of the Sefaveeans, on condition of the cession to him in perpetuity by the latter not only of Derbend and Bakoo, which were already in his possession, but also of the three provinces of Gilan, Mazenderan, and Astrabad. This treaty met with the approval both of Tahmasp and the Ottoman Porte,† and

---

* *Histoire de Russie sous Pierre le Grand*, p. 514.

† " Les conquêtes (de Pierre) sont reconnues de la Perse et de la Turquie par les traités de 1723 et de 1724."—*La Russie dans l'Asie Mineure*, p. 85.

" Pierre-le-Grand a reconnu que la difficulté de l'occupation serait aussi

until after the death of Peter the southern coast of the Caspian Sea remained nominally in the possession of Russia ; the native Khans continuing, however, to rule in their respective states. The Caspian provinces of Persia were restored to that power in the time of Nadir,* and they still remain a portion of the Persian empire ; but the idea of Peter the Great of making the Caspian Sea a Russian lake has never been abandoned, and much has been done by his successors towards its realization.† Nadir obtained the submission of the ruler of Georgia, and he not only recovered the whole of the Persian possessions to the west

---

grande, à cause de la perfidie du climat et du défaut de communications, que les victoires avaient été promptes et peu disputées. Aussi se borne-t-il à jeter des garnisons dans quelques places fortes ; l'administration du pays est conservée, les différens Khans restent souverains dans leurs états. Sa sollicitude est seulement éveillée par la situation de la Géorgie qu'il veut soustraire définitivement au joug Turc. . . . Ses successeurs, justement effrayés par la consommation d'hommes qu'entraînait l'occupation, évacuèrent successivement les pays conquis."—*La Russie dans l'Asie Mineure*, p. 85.

  "La Russie, par les traités de Rechte et de Gandja (1732 et 1735), retrograda d'abord jusqu'à Baku, et ensuite se retira derrière la ligne du Térék."—*La Russie dans l'Asie Mineure*, p. 86.

  * " A treaty to this effect was concluded in the year 1735. Mazenderan and Astrabad had been already restored to Persia by a treaty concluded at Resht." [The Treaty of Resht was made in the year 1732.]—*Blackwood's Magazine*. Vol. xxi.

  † " Dominer donc la mer Caspienne, c'était ouvrir à la Russie le commerce de toutes ses côtes, et rétablir, à son profit, cette ancienne route commerciale de l'Inde, que nous avons vue exploitée tour à tour par les Grecs et les Romains."—*La Russie dans l'Asie Mineure*, p. 82.

  " IX. Approcher le plus près possible de Constantinople et des Indes. Celui qui y regnera sera le vrai souverain du monde. En conséquence, susciter des guerres continuelles, tantôt au Turc tantôt à la Perse ; établir des chantiers sur la mer Noire, s'emparer peu à peu de cette mer, ainsi que de la Baltique, ce qui est un double point nécessaire à la réussite du projet ; hâter la décadence de la Perse ; pénétrer jusqu'au golfe Persique ; rétablir, si c'est possible, par la Syrie, l'ancien commerce du Levant, et avancer jusqu'aux Indes, qui sont l'entrepôt du monde."—Extract from the document known as the *Political Testament of Peter the Great, Czar of Russia.*

of the Caspian Sea, including Derbend and Bakoo, but he also undertook an expedition against the Lesghis of Daghestan, and made some impression on those hardy and intractable mountaineers. While the eastern portion of the country which lies between the lofty range of the Caucasus and the mountains of Lazistan and Eastern Armenia passed, as we have seen, from the possession of Persia to that of Russia, and was again recovered by the former power, the central and western districts of that portion of the globe remained under the sway of several petty princes, who owned allegiance at different times to one or other of their powerful neighbours. The country extending from the eastern shore of the Black Sea to the borders of Persia on the one hand, and from the frontier of Turkey to the foot of the mountains of Circassia on the other, is one of the very fairest portions of the earth. It contains the famous realms of Ea and the classic Phasis, of which we early read in the voyage of

> The wonder'd Argo, which in vent'rous peece,
> First through the Euxine seas bore all the flowr of Greece.

It was divided into several principalities, three of the most considerable of which bore respectively the names of Mingrelia, Imeretia and Georgia. These countries were inhabited by races of people whose rare beauty is proverbial over the world. Their children, who for ages have been brought in large numbers into Persia and into Turkey, have, by their intermarriages with the people of those lands, been the means of changing tribes, at first remarkable for their ugliness, into handsome and pleasing-looking people ; and at the present day the Georgians and Mingrelians are to a great extent doing for the Russian

nation what their ancestors did for the followers of Alp-
Alsran and of Timur.

This fair country and its fairer inhabitants were for
hundreds of years a prey to all the evils that spring from
and follow a system of weak and barbarous government.*

---

* " Les gentilshommes du pays ont pouvoir sur la vie et sur les biens
de leurs sujets, ils en font ce qu'ils veulent.   Ils les prennent, soit femme,
soit enfant.   Ils les vendent, ou ils en font autre chose, comme il leur
plait."—*Voyage du Chevalier Chardin.*   Vol. i. p. 172.

" Quand les seigneurs sont eux-mêmes en différend, la force en decide :
celui qui est le plus fort gagne la cause.   Voici comment ils s'y prennent :
ils fondent à main armée sur les bestiaux de leur ennemi, sur ses vassaux,
sur ses maisons, sur ses terres, pillant, brûlant, abattant tout ; et enfin,
lorsqu'ils ne savent plus à quoi s'en prendre, ils arrachent les vignes, les
mûriers et les arbres aussi utiles ; que si les parties viennent à se rencontrer
durant ces actes d'hostilités, ils se combattent d'une manière sanglante.   Le
plus foible et le plus maltraité ne manque jamais de recourir au prince, qui
sans cela ne prendrait point connoissance de la querelle."—*Idem.*   Vol. i.
p. 174.

" La Mingrélie est aujourd'hui fort peu peuplée, elle n'a pas plus de
vingt mille habitans. Il n'y a trente ans qu'elle en avait quatre vingt mille.
La cause de cette diminution vient de ses guerres avec ses voisins, et de la
quantité de gens de tout sexe, que les gentilshommes ont vendus ces
dernières années.   Depuis longtemps on a tiré tous les ans, par achat ou
par troc, douze mille personnes de Mingrélie."—*Idem.*   Vol. i. p. 183.

" C'est une chose qui n'est pas croyable que l'inhumanité des Mingréliens, et cette cruauté denaturée qu'ils ont tous pour leurs compatriotes, et
que quelques uns ont pour leur propre sang.   Ils ne cherchent que l'occasion
de s'emporter contre leurs vassaux, pour avoir quelque prétexte de les
vendre avec leurs femmes et leurs enfans.   Ils enlèvent les enfans de leurs
voisins et en font la même chose ; ils vendent même leurs propres enfans,
leurs femmes et leurs mères, et cela non par provocation ou motif de vengeance, mais uniquement par l'impulsion de leur naturel dépravé.   On m'a
montré plusieurs gentilshommes qui ont été dénaturés jusqu'à ce point.
Un d'eux vendit un jour douze prêtres . . Ce gentilhomme devint amoureux
d'une demoiselle ; il résolut de l'épouser, quoiqu'il eut déjà une femme.
. . Le gentilhomme ne savoit où prendre ce qu'il avait promis pour obtenir
sa maîtresse, et ce qui lui fallait pour la noce, qu'en vendant des gens.   Ses
sujets qui apprirent son dessein, s'enfuirent et emmenèrent leurs femmes
et leurs enfans.   Reduit au désespoir, il s'avisa de cette perfidie tout à fait
outrée.   Il invita douze prêtres à venir chez lui dire une messe solennelle
et faire un sacrifice.   Les prêtres y allèrent bonnement.   Ils n'avaient
garde de penser qu'on les voulût vendre aux Turcs, ne s'étant jamais rien
vu pareil en Mingrélie.   Le gentilhomme les reçut bien, leurs fit dire la

6—2

There was no security for life or for property, and no check was placed upon conduct which was at variance with the plainest dictates of religion and of humanity. The people of the country were as deficient in every pleasing moral quality, as they were abundantly endowed with physical excellences. They were barbarous,* ignorant,

---

messe, leur fit immoler un bœuf, et les en traita ensuite. Quand il les eut bien fait boire, il les fit prendre par ses gens, les fit enchainer, leurs fit raser la tête et le visage, et la nuit suivante il les mena à un vaisseau Turc, où il les vendit pour des meubles et des hardes ; mais ce qu'il en tira ne suffisant pas encore pour payer sa maîtresse et pour faire sa noce, ce tigre prit sa femme et l'alla vendre au même vaisseau."—*Idem*, p. 184.

"Lorsque je passai à Akalziké, on disait que les Turcs voulaient se mettre en possession de ces pays là et y mettre un pacha, ne sachant point d'autre moyen de rémedier aux guerres continuelles qui les detruisent et les dépeuplent notablement."—*Idem*, p. 330.

" Les Géorgiens ont naturellement beaucoup d'esprit ; l'on en ferait des gens savans et de grands maîtres si on les élevait dans les sciences et dans les arts ; mais l'éducation qu'on leur donne étant fort méchante, et n'ayant que de mauvais exemples, ils deviennent très ignorants et très vicieux. Ils sont fourbes, fripons, perfides, traîtres, ingrats, superbes. . . . Ils sont irréconciliables dans leurs haines et ils ne pardonnent jamais. . . . Les gens d'église, comme les autres, s'enivrent et tiennent chez eux de belles esclaves, dont ils font des concubines. Personne n'en est scandalisé, parceque la coutume en est générale et même autorisée."—*Idem.* Vol. ii. p. 41.

* " Elles (the women of Mingrelia) sont civiles, pleines de cérémonies et de complimens, mais du reste, les plus méchantes femmes de la terre ; fières, superbes, perfides, fourbes, cruelles, impudiques. Il n'y a point de méchanceté qu'elles ne mettent pas en œuvre pour se faire des amans, pour les conserver et pour les perdre.

"Les hommes ont toutes ces mauvaises qualités encore plus que les femmes. Il n'y a point de malignité à quoi leur esprit ne se porte ; ils sont tous élevés au larcin ; ils l'étudient, ils en font leur emploi, leur plaisir, et leur honneur. Ils content avec une satisfaction extrême les vols qu'ils ont faits ; ils en sont loués ; ils en tirent leur plus grande gloire. L'assassinat, le meurtre, le mensonge, c'est ce qu'ils appellent les belles actions. Le concubinage, l'adultère, la bigamie, l'inceste, et semblables vices, sont des vertus, en Mingrélie. L'on s'y enlève les femmes les uns aux autres. On y prend sans scrupule en mariage, sa tante, sa nièce, la sœur de sa femme. Qui veut avoir deux femmes à la fois, les épouse ; beaucoup de gens en épousent trois. Chacun entretient autant de concubines qu'il veut ; les femmes et les maris sont réciproquement fort commodes là dessus. Il y a entre eux très peu de jalousie. Quand un homme prend sa femme sur le fait avec son galant, il a droit de la contraindre à payer un cochon, et

superstitious, debauched and debased, also idle and devoid of good faith.

The country of Mingrelia, the ancient Colchis, was in a great part covered with wood, which spread so fast as to threaten to engross the whole face of the land. Rain fell almost constantly, and in summer the hot sun acting on the moist earth, produced fevers and other diseases, which reduced the number of the population and cut short the duration of the life of man. In order to counteract, in some degree, the evil influence of such a climate, the Mingrelians spent a great portion of their time in taking open air exercise ; the nobles occupied themselves chiefly in hunting. There were no towns, nor anything similar, in the country, with the exception of two villages on the

d'ordinaire il ne prend pas d'autre vengeance. Le cochon se mange entr'eux trois. Ce qui est surprenant, est que cette méchante nation soutient que c'est bien fait d'avoir plusieurs femmes et plusieurs concubines, parcequ'on engendre, disent-ils, beaucoup d'enfans qu'on vend argent comptant, ou qu'on échange pour les hardes et pour les vivres. Cela n'est rien toutefois au prix d'un sentiment tout à fait inhumain qu'ils ont, que c'est charité de tuer les enfans nouveaux nés, quand on n'a pas le moyen ou la commodité de les nourrir, et ceux qui sont malades quand on ne les saurait guérir."— *Voyage du Chevalier Chardin.* Vol. i. p. 170.

" Les Mingréliens et leurs voisins sont de très grands ivrognes."— *Idem*, p. 179.

" Ces peuples sont paresseux et lâches au-delà de l'imagination."— *Idem.* Vol. i. p. 160.

" Presque tous les Mingréliens, hommes et femmes, même les plus grands et les plus riches, n'ont jamais qu'une chemise et qu'un caleçon à la fois. Cela leur dure au moins un an. Pendant ce temps, ils ne les lavent que trois fois."—*Idem*, p. 177.

" Je m'arrête aussi longtemps à la peinture des avantages physiques des Géorgiens et de leurs princes, parcequ'il n'y a malheureusement pas grand éloge à faire de leurs avantages intellectuels."—*Les Peuples du Caucase.* Par J. BODENSTEDT.

" Sonò anchè, a dire il vero, le più belle donne di tutta l'Asia ; sono le Giorgiane gigantesse di statura : hanno quasi tutte capelli neri e occhi pur neri, grandi e belli ; carnagion bianca, e coloritissima, mercè, come io credo, il liquor di Bacco, che a loro è molto familiare."—*Viaggi di* PIETRO DELLA VALLE. Vol. ii. p. 15. Roman edition.

sea coast. The houses, which were built on posts driven into the ground, were scattered in twos and threes all over the principality, and in case of civil war or invasion from without, the people retired into one or other of ten castles, placed in the midst of a forest so dense that it could only be penetrated by those who possessed the clue and who were unopposed from within.

Georgia is furnished by nature with everything that can contribute to render a population prosperous and happy. The climate is dry and very cold in winter, and if for a part of the summer the heat is excessive, a refuge from it may be found in the neighbouring mountains. The ground has to be artificially watered; but this element is abundantly supplied by the river Kur, the stream which gave his name to Cyrus, the conqueror of Persia. The earth when watered produces grain in abundance, and excellent fruit of almost every kind. Cattle and game abound in the country, and the river Kur and the Caspian Sea supply fish of fresh water and of the ocean. The vineyards of Khakheti yield the best wine of Asia, and at a price so moderate as to bring it within the reach of the poorest people. Such a country might well excite the cupidity of its powerful neighbours, and accordingly we find it passing under the protection of one of these after another. Shah Ismaïl of Persia compelled the Czar of Georgia to pay him tribute and to send him hostages. This tribute was continued to his son, Tahmasp; but after his death, the Georgians threw off the Persian yoke : * which, however, was soon again re-established, and was confirmed by Abbass the Great, who marched to Tiflis, and sent the Czar of Georgia a prisoner to Mazen-

---

* CHARDIN. Vol. ii. p. 49.

deran,* and afterwards caused him to be put to death at Sheeraz. When Abbass was no more, the Georgians again attempted to throw off the Persian yoke; but the general of Shah Sefi defeated them in several engagements, reduced the country to its former condition, and built the fortress of Gori to overawe Tiflis.

That city, the capital of Georgia, lies at the foot of a mountain, and is built at the present day, on both sides of the river Kur. Up to a late period, Tiflis was surrounded by strong and handsome walls, excepting on the side on which it was bounded by the stream. On the south it was commanded by a large fort placed on the slope of a mountain, into which only Persians were admitted. This fort was erected in the year 1576,† at a time when Georgia was in the possession of the Turks, who in like manner built nearly all the fortresses which exist in the principality. The Persian authority was never so firmly established over this country as to enable that government to act independently of the wishes of the Georgians. We read that, under the Persian domination, wine and the flesh of the forbidden animal were openly sold in the streets, and that not a single mosque was to be found in the city of Tiflis. Within the walls of the fortress the conquerors ventured to erect a small place of worship, where the Moslem might bow their heads towards the Keblah.. The Georgians could not penetrate into the fort, and the mosque was therefore finished; but when the muezzin dared to ascend the minaret and with a loud voice to summon all men to prayer, the indignation of the Christians was roused, and from without they hurled such a shower of stones at the turret of the

obnoxious building, that the muezzin, to save his life, was
forced to descend, and he never again repeated the same
experiment.   Such being the state of religious feeling, it
might be supposed that no Georgian would have ventured
to apostatize from the faith of his fathers, and yet we are
told on indisputable authority* that the greater part of
the Georgian nobility professed outwardly the Mahomedan
religion.

The royal family of the Bagratides asserted its descent
from King David of Israel,† and sat on the throne
of Georgia from the sixth century of the Christian
era, the conquerors of the principality respecting the
claims of the reigning house, and merely requiring
tribute.   Under the Turks, the princes of Georgia were
allowed to maintain the profession of the Christian faith,
and the same liberty was at first accorded to them by
their Persian masters.   But on the death of a Georgian
Czar, his two sons disputed his succession, and appealed
for assistance or arbitration to the Persian Shah.   The
demand of the younger brother came first to Ispahan,
and he was promised the inheritance of his father on the
condition of his becoming a Mussulman.   On these terms

* Sir JOHN CHARDIN, Plenipotentiary of King Charles II. to the Dutch
States.

† *Transcaucasia*, by Baron HAXTHAUSEN, p. 121.

"In the year 575 of our era, the first of the Bagratide family ascended
the throne, and his successors retained the government until 1800, when
they ceded it to Russia."—*Idem*.

"The Bagratians were descended from Abraham by the line of Isaak.
The first of this family who came to Armenia was Shumbat, during the
captivity by Nebuchadnezzar.   One of his posterity was the celebrated
Bagarat, who lived in the reign of Valarsaces; and, in consequence of his
exalted virtue and eminent services, ennobled by that prince by the title of
Bagarat the Bagratian.   All members of his family from this time were
universally known by the title of Bagratians."—*History of Armenia*. By
Father M. CHAMICH.

he became governor of Georgia, and so long as that
country remained under Persia, a prince of the royal
house of the Bagratides who professed Mahomedanism
was the viceroy, or vali, of the Shah. The heir-apparent
was kept as a hostage at Ispahan, and enjoyed the
honourable post of governor of that city. Tiflis under
these princes was a handsome and populous town, where
merchants and strangers from many countries were at all
times assembled. The Czar of Georgia made it his
place of residence, and maintained a court suitable to
his rank.

The troubles that ensued upon the death of Nadir
Shah had afforded to the vali of Georgia the opportunity
of freeing himself from the Persian yoke, and even of
acquiring a portion of the territory of Persia. But the
Czar Heraclius foresaw that this act on his part would
draw down upon him a heavy retribution, when the
day should arrive that would see Persia again united
under a single ruler ; accordingly, he prepared himself
against such an event by entering into a close alliance,
offensive and defensive, with the Empress of Russia. In
the year 1783, a treaty was signed by which the Georgian
prince renounced all connection with Persia, and
declared himself the vassal of the Empress Catherine ;
who in turn bound herself and her successors to protect
Heraclius, the son of Timuras, and to guarantee the
possession not only of all the actual dominions of the
Georgian Czar, but also that of all the lands which
might in future be acquired by him.

When Lutf'ali Khan, the gallant rival of Aga
Mahomed, had perished, and when the Kajar chief had
received the submission of the southern provinces of

Persia, the hour had arrived when he was free to punish the rebellious Czar of Georgia. Before setting out for that country, he summoned Heraclius to return to his duty, to pay the accustomed tribute, and to appear at his court to do homage, and take the oath of fidelity. The reply of Heraclius was that he acknowledged no suzerain but Catherine the Second of Russia. Aga Mahomed was unwilling to give up the rights of his country over Georgia, and he was also unwilling to suffer the encroachment of Russia. He accordingly collected a large force, and in the spring of 1795 set out from Tehran for Ardebeel, at the head of sixty thousand men. At Ardebeel he divided his force into three corps. One of these was despatched by the plain of Moghan in the direction of Daghestan, to exact the required oath of fidelity from the chiefs of that quarter, and to levy the arrears of tribute. This force met with no opposition, and executed the services required of it. The second corps marched upon Erivan, which place acknowledged the authority of the Czar of Georgia, and was defended by fifteen thousand Georgians under the command of the son of Heraclius. The third corps was under the immediate orders of Aga Mahomed himself. With it he marched to undertake the siege of Sheeshah, a hill fort near the Araxes, in the province of Karabagh ; at which place he met with a stubborn and unexpected resistance. Failing alike in his efforts to reduce this stronghold and to corrupt the fidelity of the governor, Ibraheem Khaleel Khan, he contented himself with leaving a force to invest the fort, whilst he himself proceeded to join his second *corps d'armée* at Erivan.

That city, which is the capital of the province of

Armenia, stands in an extensive and well-watered plain, at the distance of a few miles from the base of Mount Ararat. Its fortress, which was built by the Turks in the year 1582, was in the old style of defence. It had three walls of earth, or of clay bricks, flanked by towers and strengthened by narrow ramparts. It overhung a deep and abrupt precipice, along which a river ran, and on the edge of which stood the palace of the governor of the province. In this stronghold only Persians were permitted to reside, the Armenians who worked or trafficked in it in the day-time being obliged to return at even to their houses in the city. The usual garrison of this fort was two thousand men, and the city of Erivan lay within the range of its guns. This place had fallen into the hands of the Persians in the year 1604, and had been fortified by them. Nine years later it had successfully withstood a siege of four months from the Turks ; but that people afterwards held possession of it for a short period. They lost it in the reign of Shah Sefi, and again took it from the Persians during the troublous time that followed the downfall of the Sefaveean dynasty. It was regained to Persia by the arms of Nadir, and seized by Heraclius the Czar of Georgia, after the assassination of that conqueror.

Aga Mahomed's army was not furnished with a battering train, and he was therefore unable to make any impression upon Erivan. Under these circumstances he determined to disregard the rule of warfare which forbids an invading general to leave a fortified place behind him. He left a portion of his army to blockade the capital of Armenia, and with his remaining forces he marched to Genja, the modern Elisabetpol, at which town he effected a junction with his first *corps d'armée*, which had by this time accomplished the duties assigned to it in Sheervan and Daghestan. The aged Czar of Georgia advanced to meet the Persian army with a force that did not exceed in number a fourth part of the invading host. The Georgians fought with great valour, but they were encountered by the Persians with equal bravery and were finally compelled to give way. The Czar then retreated to Khakheti, to which place he was followed by the greater portion of the citizens of Tiflis. The Kajar king then entered that city, where his troops met with no resistance. Of the inhabitants who had remained to await his approach, the infirm and the aged were massacred, and the youth of both sexes, to the number of fifteen thousand, were taken as slaves. The city was given over to be pillaged, the houses were set fire to, and the citadel was demolished. After this, the Persian army retired from the place, and marched on Tehran, taking the route of the valley of the Kur and the plain of Moghan. On the news of the fall of Tiflis reaching Erivan, the governor of that place surrendered it to the Persian commander; but the high-spirited governor of Sheeshah continued to defy the power of the Shah. On his route Aga Mahomed found Shumakhi, the chief city of the province of Sheervan, which he contributed to ruin. This city had formerly been the capital of an independent state, and an European writer* has left us a description of the handsome appearance which it presented in its flourishing days. The attacks of the neighbouring Lesghis, and the frequent recurrence of earthquakes, did much to destroy Shumakhi; but the

---

* OLIARIUS.

city continued to be the chief town of a government until the year 1860, when it was supplanted by Bakoo. Shumakhi now presents to view the melancholy spectacle of an immense collection of ruined houses, amidst which a few of its former inhabitants continue to linger. From here the Kajar king pursued his way to his capital, where he at length consented to undergo the ceremony of being publicly crowned as Shah of Persia at Tehran.* According to the Persian historian, he had been crowned ten years before at Astrabad.

In the meantime, the power with which the Czar of Georgia had chosen to ally himself, was taking measures to reassert his authority. Heraclius had not failed to apprise the Russian governor † of the adjoining province of the demand made of him by the Shah of Persia; but that functionary was not prepared to see Aga Mahomed's threats so soon followed by acts, nor to find him advance upon Tiflis while Sheeshah and Erivan still held out behind his army. When the Empress Catherine was made aware of what had taken place, she gave orders to the officer in command of the troops on the frontier to attack the town of Derbend, which place was accordingly invested. Before its walls the Russian army passed the winter of 1795-96, and in the spring of the latter year Count Valerian Souboff crossed the Terek with reinforcements. This Russian general, who had performed distinguished services under Potemkin at the siege of Bender, had now under his orders an army of thirty-five thousand men ; and after having made himself master of some of the outworks of Derbend, he summoned the

---

* A.D. 1796: A.H. 1210.
† See *Progress of Russia in the East.*

city to surrender, threatening, if it should refuse to do so, to take the place by storm. Having become possessed of Derbend, the Russian troops marched to Bakoo, while a flotilla, with four thousand men on board, established itself on the small island of Sari, near Lenkoran, from which position it threatened the province of Gilan. An attempt, however, which it made to get possession of Enzelli, the port of Resht, was successfully withstood. After the surrender of Bakoo, the Russian army retired for the summer to the highlands in the vicinity of Shumakhi. In the month of October, Count Valerian Souboff took possession of that city, from which he despatched a force up the valley of the Kur, with orders to occupy Genja, and to advance from there upon Tiflis. But sufficient time had not elapsed to admit of these commands being carried into execution, when the army received the news of the death of the Empress, which was followed by an order to retire. The Russian general accordingly recalled the advanced division of his army, and gave up all his conquests, with the exception of the important fortresses of Bakoo and Derbend.

Aga Mahomed Khan had re-asserted the right of Persia to claim tribute from the Czar of Georgia, and there now remained but one portion of the ancient kingdom of the Sefaveeans, with the exception of Affghanistan, which did not belong to his dominions. Shahrukh Meerza, the blind grandson of Shah Hussein and of Nadir, since he had been placed by Ahmed Shah the Sedozye on the throne of the principality of Khorassan, had been allowed by the various pretenders to the government of Persia to remain in the quiet possession of this one small portion of the dominions of his grandfathers. Mahomed Hassan the Kajar, Azad the Affghan, and Kereem the Zend had all fought with each other, but had never interfered with the fourth ruler of Persia. Nor had the blind prince been disturbed during the seven years of war in which Aga Mahomed Khan disputed with the Zend princes for the mastery in Persia. His hour, however, was now come, and without having received from him the smallest offence, Aga Mahomed marched against him, on the pretence of wishing to make the pilgrimage to Meshed. So eager was the Kajar Shah to complete the reintegration of Persia that he would not postpone his Khorassan expedition even to enable him to oppose the advance of the Russian army on the western shore of the Caspian Sea. At the very time that Count Valerian Souboff was crossing the Terek, Aga Mahomed set out from Tehran for Astrabad, where he remained for some time before marching on Meshed, being employed in inflicting a signal punishment on the Turkomans. Prince Shahrukh was not in a condition to resist the invader of his dominions, and he therefore advised his sons to consult their own safety, while he himself came out two stages to meet the Kajar king, bringing with him rich presents by which he hoped to appease him. The Kajar Shah limited himself at first to requiring that his army should be furnished with all that it needed in money and in provisions; but on arriving at Meshed, he demanded to be at once put in possession of the seals of state as well as of the royal treasure, and he required that prayers should be offered up in his name in the mosques.

Meshed, the capital of Khorassan, is chiefly famous for containing the mosque of Imam Reza, which is visited

by more than fifty thousand pilgrims in the course of
each year, and from the revenues of which eight hundred
persons are fed daily. The quadrangle of this mosque
is about one hundred and fifty paces square,* and is
paved with large flagstones, having in the centre a
beautiful kiosk, which was built by Nadir Shah, and
which is covered with gold and raised over the reservoir
of the water for ablutions. A range of alcoves extends
round three sides of this quadrangle at some ten feet
from the ground. A wall of considerable height surrounds
the court, having on each side a gigantic archway covered
above the entrance with blue tiles and with inscriptions in
white and gold. Over the western archway is a white cage
for the muezzin, and outside of it is a very high minaret,
the beauty of which cannot be exaggerated. The capital
is exquisitely carved, and the shaft below it, for about
twenty feet, is covered with gold; as is a light pillar of
about half that height above it. This portion of the
mosque was built by Shah Abbass. In the centre of
the eastern side of the quadrangle, two large doors
admit the pilgrims into the inner mosque, which contains the marble tomb of Imam Reza, surrounded by a
silver and golden railing. Beyond these two doors, are
two smaller ones encrusted with jewels of great value.
The inner mosque is capable of containing three thousand persons, and over it rises a dome entirely covered
with gold, with two minarets at the sides, likewise gilded
all over. Beyond the golden dome is a smaller one of
bright blue, which marks the beginning of another
mosque, the quadrangle of which is larger than that of

---

* *Journal of a Diplomate's Three Years' Residence in Persia,* and
FERRIER's *Caravan Journeys.*

Shah Abbass.   At the eastern side of this enclosure rises an immense blue dome, having in front two lofty minarets covered with blue tiles of Kashan.

The general state of lawlessness and misgovernment throughout the province of Khorassan made the invasion of Aga Mahomed at this time a public boon.

Shahrukh was willing to do everything that Aga Mahomed required of him, excepting to furnish the money wanted, and to give up the jewels of his family. But to obtain the possession of these was one of the chief objects of the Kajar king's invasion of Khorassan, and he was not the man to hesitate as to the employment of any means which seemed likely to bring about this end.   Aga Mahomed felt convinced that the blind prince must be in possession of the greater part of the jewels which Nadir Shah had brought with him from Delhi, and the robbery of that conqueror was now to be visited upon his descendants to the second and third generation.   Shahrukh was seized by the ferashes of the Kajar king, and received the punishment of the bastinado ; but this not proving sufficient to overcome his love of his treasure, hot irons were applied to different parts of his person.   Yielding at length by degrees, under the influence of a burning fever, he discovered his largest ruby to his torturer, who at once ordered the jewels to be packed up for transmission to Tehran.   The Kajar Shah had received the submission of the whole of Khorassan, and taking with him the blind and aged prince, as well as a number of other hostages, he set out on his return to Tehran, having left in Meshed a garrison of twelve thousand men.   On the way, death relieved the still suffering Shahrukh from the fear of

further indignities at the hands of his barbarous de-
spoiler.

On his arrival at Tehran in September, 1796, Aga
Mahomed dismissed his troops to their homes for the
winter, requiring them to reassemble under his banners
in the spring of the following year. During his Georgian
campaign the Kajar Shah had put to death all the
Russians whom he had taken in Tiflis ; and he had given
orders for seizing all of that nation who were to be found
at Enzelli, Saleean, Bakoo and Derbend. The result was
that twenty-seven sailors were sent loaded with iron chains
to Tehran. The first punishment inflicted on these men
after their arrival at the capital was to force them to put
out the eyes of forty Persians who had been condemned
to be blinded for not joining the army. They were then
suffered to wander about the town, living on such charity
as they could obtain from the few Armenian inhabitants
of the town. A week after his return from Khorassan,
Aga Mahomed vented upon these helpless sailors the
rage with which he had been inspired by the successes of
Count Valerian Souboff. They were all seized and
strangled.* We are told by the French traveller who
was at Tehran at the time of this execution, that he
expressed to Haji Ibraheem, the prime minister of Aga
Mahomed, his surprise that the Shah should limit his
reprisals on the Russians to this act, and should delay to
march in person to repair the disasters of the war. The
reply was that there was no hurry in the matter ; that
orders had been issued not to undertake anything of
importance during the winter ; and that on the return of
spring a few months would suffice to chastise the Musco-

---

* *Voyage de M. Olivier.* Vol. ii. p. 141.

vites for their audacity.   This speech was a boastful
evasion ; the truth being that the Kajar Shah could not
afford to keep on a war footing, during the winter, an army
amounting to nearly 70,000 men.   Apart from this, his
troops were in no condition to repulse those of Russia ;
had they come to close quarters, the Persians would
have been compelled to give way before the veteran conquerors of Bender and of Ismaïl.

The above-mentioned traveller * was charged with a
mission from the French Republic to the minister of Aga
Mahomed.   The object of this mission appears to have
been twofold : in the first place, to ascertain whether or
not a profitable interchange of commodities could be
established between France and Persia ; and, in the
second place, to endeavour to unite the Persians with
the Ottoman Porte in a combination against Russia.
Satisfactory replies were given on both points by the
prime minister, but the difficulties which lay in the way
of the establishment of a trade between Persia and
France appeared to be too great to be overcome.   Two
treaties had at an anterior period been concluded between
the two countries ; but it did not seem worth while to the
French negotiator to propose to renew them, nor to
obtain protection as formerly for French establishments
at Ispahan and Sheeraz and on the shores of the Persian
Gulf.   The troubles through which Persia had passed
had been of too long duration, and were too freshly
imprinted on men's minds, to warrant the assumption
that European merchants, or their trade, could meet with
efficient protection in so unsettled a, country.   With

---

* M. Olivier.

respect to the second object of the mission—that of endeavouring to unite Persia with Turkey against Russia —the Persian minister listened to and agreed with the arguments of the Frenchman, and promised on the part of his master that an ambassador should be sent to Constantinople.

Aga Mahomed Khan had now re-established order throughout his dominions; the roads were secure for travellers and for caravans; the taxes were paid with regularity; and hostages were ready to answer for the continuance of the distant chiefs in their duty to the sovereign. But under this apparent calm, a feeling of discontent was spreading at the idea of being governed, and even made to tremble, by one whose physical condition ought, according to the customs of Persia, to have excluded him from the throne. These feelings were only natural, but they might not have led to any practical result had it not been for the tyrannical folly of Aga Mahomed himself. Unwarned by all the lessons which the history of his country afforded, that the patience even of the Persian people had a limit, and that when men were kept in terror of their lives they took the remedy into their own hands, the infatuated monarch went on in his career of cruelty and tyranny until it was brought to a close by the dagger of the midnight assassin.

In the spring of 1797, Aga Mahomed quitted Tehran for the last time, and led his army towards the Araxes. When within a few miles of that river he learned that the governor of the fortress of Sheeshah, in the province of Karabagh, had been compelled by the inhabitants to abandon his post, and that he had only to take possession of the place. With this object in view he hurried on in light marching order to the river's side. The stream was deep and rapid, and the boats could contain only a few men at a time. The king had given the order that his army should pass the Araxes. The soldiers who should brave the current's force ran a great risk of being drowned; but a watery grave was less terrible in their eyes than to have to face the wrath of their ruthless monarch : they did not hesitate a moment, and a sufficient number gained the further bank to enable Aga Mahomed to take possession of the fortress of Sheeshah. Here his earthly career was destined to end. For a slight offence he condemned two of his domestic servants to death, but as it was the night of Friday,* he consented that they should be spared until next morning. One of these was his personal attendant, and we are told that this man was permitted to perform his usual duties while he was under sentence of death. At midnight this servant, whose name was Sadek,† entered the monarch's tent, accompanied by the other servant who was to have suffered with him next morning, as well as by another man, and the three put an end to the life of the king.

We are told by the Persian historian‡ that Aga Mahomed's last words were uttered in reproach to his murderers for having killed him under such circumstances that not a soldier of his army could escape from the enemy. The murderers then seized the crown jewels, and handed them over to Sadek Khan Shekaki, one of the generals of the army, who afforded the assassins protection.

Aga Mahomed, at the time of his death, was fifty-

---

* The Mahomedan holy-day of the week.
† The two accomplices were named Khodadad and Abbass.
‡ Rauzet-es-Sefa.

seven years of age, and, counting from the death of
Kereem Khan, which occurred in 1779, he had ruled
over a great part or the whole of Persia for a period of
eighteen years and ten months.

In reviewing this monarch's life and character, due
allowance must be made for the circumstances under
which he was placed, and for the character of the people
he had to deal with. He was the hereditary chieftain of
one of the most powerful tribes of Persia, and the first
object of his existence was the exaltation of the Kajars.
His earliest and his strongest impressions were all
associated with hatred of the rival tribe of Zend, and
so little were such feelings obliterated by all the kindness which he and his father's family had received from
Kereem Khan that, when he had finally planted his
foot upon the necks of his hereditary enemies, he caused
the remains of Kereem to be exhumed and placed under
the portal of his palace at Tehran, so that he might have
the satisfaction of treading upon them every time he
passed it. With Richard of York, he would have liked
to see his sword shed purple tears for all that wished the
downfall of his house. Nadir Shah had put his grand-
father to death; and Nadir's nephew, Adel Shah, had
inflicted the most cruel injury upon himself. The last
offence would, in the minds of most persons, be likely to
rankle the longest; but if we can form an opinion from
the fact that Aga Mahomed caused the bones of Nadir
to be brought to Tehran and laid beside the remains of
Kereem Khan, while those of Adel Shah were permitted
to rest in peace in the holy city of Meshed, it would
appear that he hated the memory of the great enemy of
his family more than that of the person who had irre-

parably injured himself. His whole life was devoted to one all-engrossing object—the establishment of his family upon the throne of Persia. To that one end everything else was made subordinate.

Perhaps the greatest piece of self-denial that could have been required of such an one as Aga Mahomed was to abstain from avenging the blood of his father, who was put to death by the chief of the rival branch of the Kajars ; but he had the wisdom to see that a house divided against itself cannot stand, and, in order to secure the cordial support of the whole united tribe, he freely forgave the rival family, and throughout his reign continued to employ many of its members in some of the highest offices in the kingdom. This prudent conduct was productive of the best results ; the example set by Aga Mahomed in this respect has been followed by his successors, and, at the present day,* the army of the King of Persia is commanded by the chief of the upper branch of the Kajar tribe. Aga Mahomed Khan found Persia in a state of anarchy, and he saw that it was only by a strong hand that order could be restored to his country. The first Kajar king was inordinately avaricious, but money was with him only as means to an end. The eagerness which he exhibited to become possessed of all the jewels that had formerly belonged to the crown can be well understood, as their possession by his heir would be likely to tend to the consolidation of his power. The activity and perseverance displayed by this extraordinary man throughout his long career merit a meed of praise, and the proof of his foresight and wisdom is to be found in the fact that the kingdom which

* 1864.

he handed over to his heir has ever since maintained its integrity under Kajar princes; with the exception of some outlying provinces which have been conquered by Russia, and a small island in the Caspian Sea, which has fallen into the possession of the same power.

Aga Mahomed Khan had, as has been said above, only one full brother, the same who revolted against Kereem Khan and was slain by the Turkomans with whom he took refuge. That brother's blood was avenged by Aga Mahomed in his expedition against those tribes; and the blood feuds of those times between Kajars and Turkomans have gone on multiplying to the present day: a Persian army is now in the field to endeavour to punish and subdue those refractory neighbours. Aga Mahomed's natural heir was the eldest son of his next brother, and accordingly Fetteh Ali Khan was early designated to be his uncle's successor. He was employed by him to command armies, and afterwards to rule over the provinces of Fars, Kohghiluyeh, Laristan, Yezd, and Kerman.

Aga Mahomed feared lest, after his death, his nephew's authority might be disputed by his half-brother, Jafer Kuli Khan, whose bravery and experience gave him great weight in the tribe. The means he adopted to remove all apprehension on this account, were as follows:—He sent his mother to induce his brother to come to Tehran on his way to Ispahan, of which city he had promised to appoint him governor. He further swore on the Koran that he would not detain him longer than one night at Tehran. Having by these means got the object of his fears within his power, he posted assassins to waylay him next morning as he was on the point of leaving Tehran for Ispahan. By this atrocious proceeding he violated the dearest ties of kindred, of faith, and of hospitality ; and yet his purpose would have been equally well attained by a less flagrant crime, since Jafer Kuli, had he been only detained in confinement, could not have troubled the future repose of the kingdom. As it was, Aga Mahomed was enabled to keep the oath that he had sworn, by sending his brother's corpse out of the city on the day of his death.

Before setting out from Tehran for the last time, Aga Mahomed had instructed Meerza Mahomed Khan, the governor, in the case of anything happening to the sovereign, not to open the gates of the city to any one excepting Fetteh Ali Khan. The different chiefs of the dispersed army made their way by various routes to the capital, and encamped on the plain of Doulab to the eastward of the city. The governor, assisted by the vizeer, Meerza Mahomed Shefi, acted strictly in accordance with the instructions of the late king, turning a deaf ear to all the entreaties of the pretenders to power, and placing a strong guard at all the assailable points of the city until the arrival of Fetteh Ali Khan. That prince had been engaged in looking on at a representation of the martyrdom of Hussein, when the news of his uncle's death reached him. After the customary delay of three days, which were devoted to lamentation for the late Shah, and to taking precautions for the safety of the south of Persia, he set out for Tehran. On the twelfth day he reached Kinarigird, twenty-four miles from the capital, where he was met by his younger brother, and by the Itimad-ed-Dowleh, Haji Ibraheem Khan, who had not yet been permitted to enter Tehran. From thence he sent an angry remonstrance to Ali Kuli Khan, the

brother of the late Shah, who had remained at Kasveen ;
and he further despatched his own brother to punish
him for his remissness, and to bring him to the royal
presence.

The young king then set out for his capital, and on
the way he was met by his ambitious uncle, whose
adherents had dispersed at Kasveen, and who had no
alternative but to throw himself upon the royal clemency.
We are told by the Persian historian that, before setting
out on his last expedition, Aga Mahomed Khan had sent
for his heir, and had given him certain instructions,
which might guide his conduct in the event of his
suddenly being called upon to assume the reins of power.
One of these charges was that in the case of Ali Kuli
Khan's disputing the throne with his nephew, and the
latter overcoming him, he should beware of listening to
the intercession of the queen-mother in his favour ; and
accordingly we read that the first act of the young king
after his arrival at Tehran, was to refuse the petition of
the aged sultana for mercy to the prince, and to cause
the eyes of his uncle to be put out, and his person to be
conveyed to Balferoosh. After this, on the 4th of the
month of Sefr, 1212, Fetteh Ali Shah ascended the
throne of Persia.

CHAPTER V.

THE assassins of Aga Mahomed Khan had possessed
themselves of the two famous diamonds, the Taj-Mah,*
and the Derya-i-Noor,† and of the other royal jewels,
which they handed over to Sadek Khan Shekaki. That
general being thus the master of one of the chief roads
to power in Persia, set out, on the breaking up of the
camp at Sheeshah, in pursuit of the dispersed bodies of
men who were proceeding towards Tehran. An Oriental
army, on the death of its chief, becomes like a rope of
sand, and Sadek Khan found no resistance to his own
compact division, which he was soon able to increase
to the number of fifteen thousand men. This aspiring
general seems then to have begun to assume the attributes of royal power. He appointed his eldest brother

---

* Crown of the moon.   † Sea of light.

general of Karachadagh, and his younger brother darogha of Tabreez, while he himself marched towards Kasveen, where his family had been left. It was necessary for the young Shah to take immediate measures for putting down so formidable a rival, and accordingly a council was held at Tehran for the purpose of deciding on the steps which should be adopted for this end. In view of the fact that the king could not oppose the rebel general with a force so numerous as that under his orders, the majority of the royal advisers were of the opinion that the risk of the enterprise was too great to be allowed to fall upon the Ṣhah, and that the service should be entrusted to one of his officers. The news of the arrival of Fetteh Ali at Tehran had made it more necessary for Sadek Khan to make himself master of Kasveen; but the governor of that city resisted his endeavours to enter it, and his distress was increased by hearing that his two brothers had been overcome by the governor of Khoi, and reduced to seek safety in flight.

The young king first despatched a servant to encourage the people of Kasveen in their efforts to defend themselves; but on the following day he declared that Aga Mahomed had appeared to him in a dream during the night, and had reproached him for not doing battle in person for the possession of his crown. He accordingly marched to Kasveen four days after he had ascended the throne, taking with him a force of seven thousand men. The rebel general, on the approach of the king, drew up his force in battle array, and, clothing himself in armour, prepared to abide the issue of the contest. The engagement, which lasted for two hours, ended by Sadek Khan having to abandon the field, from which he contrived to proceed in haste to Sarab in Azerbaeejan ; his army being totally defeated, and his camp equipage falling into the possession of the Shah. The news of this victory had the best effect throughout Persia, as it discouraged men from taking part in'any schemes of rebellion which may have been entertained. The Shah entered Kasveen in triumph, and thanked the citizens for their devotion to his cause. That city, celebrated as being the birthplace of Lokman, stands on a broad plain, about ninety miles to the west of Tehran, and dates its origin from an early period in the history of the nations. It was the point to which the Emperor Heraclius penetrated in his third expedition into Persia. It was the capital of the earlier Shahs of the house of Sefi, and in connection with that name it has been immortalized in the page of Milton.*

For services rendered in the battle at Kasveen, the Shah appointed his brother to be governor of the province of Fars. As this was the most important post in the kingdom, it may be thought not out of place to give at this point a short account of the province in question. Sheeraz, the capital city of Fars, is situated towards the centre of a narrow, fertile plain, shut in by mountains on the north-east and south-west.† The circumference of its walls is about three and a half miles. They are surrounded by a wide ditch, partly filled from underground springs and from ruinous canals ; the water having no outlet, stagnates round the city,—a circum-

---

* " Or Bactrian Sophi from the horns
Of Turkish crescent, leaves all waste beyond
The realm of Aladule, in his retreat
To Tauris or Casbeen."
† Mr. Abbott's *Notes of the Cities of Southern Persia.*

stance that accounts for its periodical unhealthiness. The form of the city is very irregular, the walls presenting numerous faces. On the northern side stands the citadel, a small, well-built inclosure, with towers at the angles, and a ditch around it. The citadel was constructed by Kereem Khan. Sheeraz, like most towns in Persia, gives the traveller the impression of being a city in decline. Its houses are crowded together, and they are built on a smaller scale than those of most Persian towns. The dwelling-places belonging to the more wealthy citizens are handsomely ornamented within with gilding and painting. The streets are remarkably narrow and uneven, and loop-holed turrets and barricades are frequently seen on the walls and roofs of the houses; indicating the presence of insecurity and danger. The habitations are built for the most part of burnt-brick, an improvement on the general style of Persian houses. The roofs are flat, and in spring they are covered with a growth of grass. The court-yards and gardens are planted with orange, lemon, and sycamore trees. The population of the city is estimated at thirty-five or forty thousand souls, and it is composed of Mahomedans, Jews, Armenians, and Guebres. The people of Sheeraz bear the reputation of being turbulent and prone to insurrection. Once a week, on Friday, the inhabitants of the two divisions of the population called Hyderi and Neametali, repair to the open ground beyond the city walls, and engage in a skirmish with slings and stones; an exercise which is not unfrequently followed by a close fight with swords and daggers.

Fars is one of the largest provinces of Persia, and it includes several dependencies, such as Laristan, Kohghiluyeh, and the districts subject to Bunder-Abbass. The province of Fars extends northwards to Yezdikhast; to the north-west it extends beyond Ram-Hormuz. The province embraces the whole of the Chāb country to the Karoon river; although that district is now attached to the government of Shuster. On the west and south, Fars is bounded by the Persian Gulf; and the south-east beyond Bunder-Abbass, by the mountains of Beshakird. The districts of Shehr-Babek and Seerjan, belonging to Kerman, form its eastern boundary; while in the direction of Yezd the limit of the country is at Aberzoo.

There are three regions in Fars, each of which possesses a distinct climate. North of Sheeraz is the Serhad, or cool region, while to the south of the parallel of Fessa is the Germiseer, or hot region, which possesses two very different degrees of temperature—the withering heats on the shores of the gulf, and the cooler atmosphere of the higher plains, which are denominated the Serd-seer. The face of the high country is for the most part occupied by mountains, between which lie vast cultivated plains. Some parts of the province are sparingly wooded, more particularly the hilly tract between Servistan and Fessa; while Desht-i-Arjin possesses its forests of oak. To the south of Fessa, the palm-tree is found in abundance, and the high country to the south of Sheeraz produces a variety of trees and other vegetable productions; including amongst the former, the cherry-tree, the apple-tree, the pomegranate, the plum-tree, the apricot-tree, and almost all varieties of those producing nuts; and, amongst the latter, wheat, barley, cotton, and gum-plants, besides tobacco and rice, the finest grown in Persia. The face of the country is diversified by some small lakes of salt water in the vicinity of Sheeraz, and by a fresh-water lake near Kazeran. This fine province contains also much mineral wealth, including copper and lead; but in this respect its riches have been but partially explored. The inhabitants of Fars are divided into the settled occupants of the towns and villages, and the wandering tribes, or Eelyats, whose chief resides in the city of Sheeraz.

Such was the government the Shah bestowed upon his brother. Sadek Khan, who had carried the crown and the royal jewels away with him from the field of Kasveen, was enabled by their means to make his peace with the king, who appointed him governor of a province.

Ibraheem Khaleel Khan, the chief of Sheeshah, caused the body of Aga Mahomed to be placed in that fortress until the Shah's orders should be received for its disposal. An officer was despatched for the purpose of bringing it to Tehran, and it was placed temporarily in the holy shrine of Shah Abdul Azeem. In this sanctuary his father's ashes reposed; but Aga Mahomed had more to answer for than his father, and it was therefore necessary that his corpse should be removed to a holier spot. From the shrine of Shah Abdul Azeem, it was conveyed with great state to Baghdad, and was finally deposited at Nejjef, in Arabia, at the shrine of Ali. The three assassins, Sadek, Khodadad and Abbass Ali, were, one after another, captured; and when they had been put to death with torture, their bodies were consumed by fire.

On the first of the month of Shaval, 1212, it being the 21st of March, or Nowroz, and also the feast of Bairam, Fetteh Ali Shah was crowned king of Persia.

Mahomed Khan, the son of Zeki Khan, and nephew of Kereem Khan, had been for some years in exile at

Baghdad, but, on hearing of the death of Aga Mahomed, he returned to the south of Persia, and, in the district of Nermansheer, he contrived to raise a force sufficient to enable him to possess himself of Ispahan. His army was soon afterwards defeated by the troops sent against him by the Shah, and he himself narrowly avoided being made prisoner in a garden, from whence he contrived to make his escape to the Bakhtiari mountains. An officer of rank was sent by the Shah to reprove the people of Ispahan for having yielded to the usurper, and with orders to put to death all those in the place who had taken an active part in the insurrection; a fate from which the Imam-i-Jumah had influence sufficient to save his fellow-citizens.

The celebrated city of Ispahan was no longer what it had been in the days when it contained the court of the Sefaveeans, and its decline was the more marked from the enormous space to which, in the time of its splendour, its streets and buildings had extended. It stands near the southern extremity of a vast plain, covered with a fine, light soil, and which is terminated in this direction by low mountains and rocks. It now occupies a space of about six miles from east to west, whilst its breadth is about one-third of its length. It is, however, difficult to determine where its limits lie, as its gardens, groves, and buildings, blend with the neighbouring villages. It is no longer a walled city, but open on all sides; its ancient defences, mentioned by an European traveller * as being twenty thousand paces in circumference, having been destroyed by the Affghan invaders more than a century ago. The fort, however,

* CHARDIN.

which was afterwards built by Ashreff, and which encloses the centre of the town, is still standing. The river Zenderood skirts the city on its southern side, and is traversed by three bridges. Its waters, after fertilizing several fine districts, flow eastwards, and are, after a comparatively short distance, lost in the ground. When viewed from a height, the scene presented by this great city, embosomed in umbrageous gardens and vineyards, is one of much beauty; the surface of the plain in its vicinity is also diversified by large and picturesque villages, and dotted with pigeon-towers. The population of the place has been estimated by an observant modern traveller,[*] as not exceeding a hundred thousand souls; its bazaars and parishes are of great extent, but a large portion of them being ruinous and uninhabited, gives one the impression that it is thinly populated. The seemingly interminable extent of its lofty, arched bazaars, gives an idea of the former grandeur of this once proud city. The surrounding country affords in abundance all the requisites of life; provisions, therefore, are cheap. The fruits are of the finest description; amongst them are to be found melons, peaches, pomegranates and pears, and grapes of no fewer than thirty-nine varieties: thirteen pounds of the last-mentioned fruit are procurable for the equivalent of fourpence sterling. The wine of Ispahan is considered to be the best in Persia.

The once flourishing Armenian colony of Julfa is now reduced to about three hundred and fifty families, the result of a long course of oppression and of the consequent decay of commerce.

It was to be expected that on the death of Aga

---

[*] Mr. Abbott, her Majesty's Consul-General at Tabreez.

Mahomed some effort would be made by the chiefs of the tribes of Zend to recover their paramount influence in Persia; and therefore it is not surprising to read of the attempt made by Mahomed Khan to dispute the peaceable accession to power of Fetteh Ali Shah: but that monarch had also to encounter rivalry from far different quarters.

Sadek Khan, Shekaki, with Jafer Kuli Khan, the Beglerbegi of Azerbaeejan, and Mahomed Kuli Khan, the governor of Uroomeeah, formed a conspiracy against the king, and appeared in the field at the head of twenty thousand men. Suleiman Khan, Kajar, was despatched against them with twelve thousand men, and he was followed by the king in person. Suleiman Khan, however, contrived to sow dissension in the councils of the conspirators. Mahomed Kuli Khan went to Uroomeeah, and Jafer Kuli to Khoi, while Sadek Khan came to throw himself at the king's feet at his camp of Nekpeh, where he made over to his majesty the last of the crown jewels, which he had detained, and where he once more obtained the royal pardon. Mahomed Kuli Khan sent his Georgian page to the Pasha of Baghdad, and demanded assistance, which the Pasha positively refused to give him. He then attempted to escape from Uroomeeah, but, finding himself intercepted, he returned to that place and shut himself up in the citadel, where he remained a prisoner until the Shah's arrival, when he was taken to Tehran and put to death.

At this time the Shah received the submission of the chiefs of Genja, Derbend, and Koobeh, - and also that of Goorgeen Khan, son of the late Czar of Georgia, who addressed a petition stating that his father Heraclius, although from his years he might have known better, had been very foolish to rebel against the Shah of Persia, and had received the due reward of his crime in seeing his city pillaged and twenty thousand of its inhabitants put to death or made slaves. The petition went on to say that although the father had been a stone, yet the son was a jewel,* and that in accordance with the lessons of history and the traditions of the Sefaveeans, he, Goorgeen, considered Georgia as belonging to the possessor of the crown of Persia, and himself as one of the officers of the Shah, under whom he held his government, and whose orders he was ready to obey. In reply Goorgeen received a royal firman expressive of the king's satisfaction.† The rebel conspirator, Jafer Kuli Khan, fled from Khoi at the approach of the Shah, and took refuge with the Pasha of Byazeed; and his majesty the king, having thus restored order in Azerbaeejan, returned to Tehran.

Mahomed Khan, the Zend chief, who had fled from Ispahan to the Bakhtiari mountains, there found the means of once more raising the standard of rebellion against Fetteh Ali Shah. The Kurdish tribes of Bajelan, Beeranah, and Nednez, elected him their chief, and he was joined by a number of bandits. The Shah issued orders to the governors of Malayer, Nehavend, Looristan and Burujird, to act in concert against him. After several engagements, Mahomed Khan was once more obliged to take refuge in the mountains, where he raised another force, with which he attempted to surprise the camp of Mahomed Veli Khan, the Shah's general, who was sent against him with 12,000 men. Being again

---

* Rauzat-es-Sêfa.
† A.H. 1213: A.D. 1798.

defeated, he attempted to reach Bussora, near which place he was made a prisoner and blinded.

The list of rebellions against the authority of the young Shah was not yet made up. The next person he had to contend against was no other than his own brother, Hussein Kuli Khan, whom he had appointed to be governor of the province of Fars. It is hard to conceive what could have induced the young prince to forget his duty to his sovereign and his brother, for, whilst he saw the king obliged to contend in so many quarters with envious rivals, we are assured by the Persian historian* that the governor of Sheeraz passed his time in peace and in the enjoyment of unbounded luxury. His garments were said to be of cloth of gold; his board was furnished with all that Oriental magnificence could devise; his stable contained the finest steeds that the breeds of Nejd and Aneysa could produce; and the loveliest women of Sheeraz beguiled, with dance and song, the tedium of his harem hours. His manner of living was reported to the king, and as his majesty probably did not think that such a governor was very likely to consolidate Kajar influence in the south of Persia, he relieved him of a portion of his charge, and appointed an experienced general to be chief of the province of Looristan and of the troops of Fars. Upon this the prince sent for some counsellors, and put to them the question whether or not they would advise him to attempt to secure for himself the sovereign power. Three of these had the honesty to show him the folly and wickedness of such an attempt; but their candour was ruinous to themselves, for they were instantly deprived of sight. The prince then

---

* Reza Kuli Khan.

marched to Ispahan, where he gave out that he was going to wait upon the Shah; hoping by this tale to induce the nobles of the province to go with him in his train.

Information of these proceedings reached the royal camp as the Shah was on the point of setting out from Khoi in the direction of Sheervan and Daghestan; the news caused a change of route to be adopted, and the king returned to Tehran. On his way he was met by the blinded prisoner, Mahomed Khan of Zend, whom the Shah ordered to be handed over to some soldiers of a tribe which had suffered much at the hands of Mahomed's father. Contrary, however, to the savage Persian usage of rigorously exacting the rights of retaliation, these men thought the blind man unworthy of being despatched by their daggers, and they therefore set him at liberty. We are told that he begged his way to Bussora, displaying in his person the baneful results of blasted ambition. The young Shah must have been utterly at a loss whom to trust. On his way to Tehran he received intelligence of the defection of two of the generals in whom he had till then reposed the utmost confidence. One of these was Mahomed Veli Khan, who had put down the rebellion of Mahomed Khan, Zend, and who now espoused the cause of the Shah's rebel brother. The other was the chief, Suleiman Khan, whom the king had left in charge of the government of Azerbaeejan. This Suleiman Khan, who was the Shah's first cousin, despatched his force in the direction of Tehran, with the intention of first allowing the two brothers to fight and afterwards attacking the victor. The two brothers drew near to each other in the plain of Taraghan, and by the influence of their mother an interview was brought about between them, at which the prince set forth that the revenues of the province of Fars were insufficient for his expenditure, and demanded to be appointed governor of Kerman also. The Shah did not refuse this request, and the prince on returning to his camp made the further stipulation that he should be invested with the government of the whole of Irak, and in addition that he should share the royal dignity with his brother. To these extravagant demands no answer was returned, and the prince proceeded to draw up his forces in order of battle. The Shah, while preparing to oppose his brother, sent repeated messages exhorting him to return to his duty. These, however, were disregarded, and the two hosts met face to face. But there was one privileged person whose influence was at the last moment sufficient to prevent the bloodshed that had been about to ensue. This was the mother of the two youths, who rushed between the opposing ranks, and with tears and cries forbade the soldiers to be partici-pators in this unnatural strife. The prince by this time had had leisure to perceive that his forces were not sufficient to enable him to contend successfully with the army of the Shah, and he therefore sent to implore the royal clemency. This was granted upon the sole condition that the traitor, Mahomed Veli Khan, should be given over for the purpose of being put to death ; a stipulation to which the prince acceded.

Suleiman Khan, who had been awaiting on the borders of Azerbaeejan the news of the result of the expected engagement between the Shah and the prince, was completely disconcerted at the turn events had taken, and, being in fear for his own life, he came on to Tehran and took sanctuary in the royal stable. From thence he wrote a petition, in which he stated that he had been the victim of circumstances, and the Shah was generous enough not only to forgive him his act of treason, but further to restore him to the dignity he had forfeited. He further displayed his royal clemency by appointing his brother to be the governor of Kashan, and by sparing the life of the traitor, Mahomed Veli Khan.

The Affghans at this time took advantage of the troubles in Persia to invade the province of Kerman from the direction of Seistan, but they were expelled from it by Hussein Kuli Khan.

Another of the aspirants who disputed with Fetteh Ali the possession of the crown of Persia was Ishak Meerza, the great-grandson of that Ismaïl, the pretended descendant of the Sefaveeans, in whose name Kereem Khan had originally fought. He was, however, quickly overcome, and his subsequent treatment afforded a further instance of the generous disposition of Fetteh Ali Shah.

Previously to this, Prince Mahomed, the brother of Zeman Shah of Cabul, and the grandson of the founder of the Affghan kingdom, had taken refuge in Persia. He now wrote to ask for help in recovering the government of Herat, which province he offered to hold under the orders of the Shah, whom he further offered to serve in extending his dominion in the direction of Turkestan. The Shah accordingly gave him the troops he required, and with their aid he succeeded in establishing himself at Herat.

The Shah's arms were also victorious in another quarter, where Persia had been invaded by a force collected by that Jafer Kuli Khan who had taken refuge

with the Pasha of Byazeed, and whom the Shah forgave
and appointed governor of Khoi. The king showed his
gratitude to Heaven for these successes by repairing the
golden domes of Kerbela and Kazemain, and by furnishing a door of the same metal for the mosque of Fatima
at Koom.

The Shah had now put down the rebellions of Sadek
Khan; that of his own brother; that of his cousin;
that of one of his generals; those of a chief of the Zend,
and that of a pretended descendant of the Sefaveeans.
It remained for him now to crush yet another pretender
to sovereign power. This was Nadir Meerza, the son of
Shahrukh, and the great-grandson of Nadir Shah. That
prince, on the occasion of the visit of Aga Mahomed to
Khorassan, had taken refuge with the Affghans, and on
the death of the first Kajar Shah he had returned to
Khorassan, and assembled troops about his person.
Fetteh Ali sent to warn him of the consequences of his
conduct, and, misdoubting the effect of his remonstrance,
prepared to proceed to Khorassan with an army sufficient
to enable him to enforce obedience to his wishes. On
his way to Meshed he took by storm the town of Nisha-
foor, the governor of which place shut its gates against
him. He also took the town of Turbat, whose chief
refused to attend at the royal camp. On the army
reaching Meshed, the Sheiks, the Syeds, and the Ulema,
sent to implore the king to respect the sanctity of the
town, and of the shrine of Imam Reza. The discontented prince tendered his submission, received the
Shah's pardon, and gave his daughter in marriage to a
Kajar general; by which alliance the feud between the
two princely houses was put an end to.

The Shah then made haste to return to Tehran, and on the way there occurred an incident which shows that he was not unworthy of the exalted post which he had been called on to fill. In the vast desert between Bastam and Shahrood, comprising a distance of nearly sixty miles, the different divisions of the royal army were obliged to march in small parties, on account of the scarcity of water. On arriving at his encampment of the day, the king found to his great distress that the ladies of his harem, who had preceded him, had lost their way. Tired as he was after his day's journey under the Persian sun, the monarch, taking with him five thousand horsemen, set out to search for them in the desert. But his search was unavailing, and the hot sun caused so much distress amongst his troops, that the soldiers were forced to assuage their thirst by drinking the last of the water which they had brought with them in their bottles. They continued their march, and their sufferings increased. One small piece of ice only remained, which was reserved to cool the lips of the Shah; but the sovereign showed himself on this occasion to be capable of heroic self-denial. Like the Macedonian conqueror, in the desert of Gedrosia, he declined to drink whilst his warriors were still parched with thirst. With his dagger he broke the little lump of ice into fragments, and with his own hand he placed them one by one in the mouth and on the temples of a youthful chief who had fainted, and who, by these means, was sufficiently revived to be able to continue the ride with his comrades towards the encampment; where they had the satisfaction of finding that the ladies of the harem had already arrived.

Shortly after the return of Fetteh Ali Shah from Meshed, he was informed of the coming of an envoy who had already opened diplomatic communication between the British authorities in India, and the court of Persia. This envoy was named Mehdi Ali Khan, and he had been deputed to Tehran by the Governor of Bombay. The object of his mission was to endeavour to persuade the Shah to attack Affghanistan, and thereby relieve, for the time being, the minds of the European rulers of India from the apprehension under which they laboured lest India should be invaded by Zeman Shah. The envoy entered upon his task with a mind free from the restraint of a too scrupulous adhesion to truth. He took care to inform the chief minister of the court of Persia that the English authorities in India were not at all afraid of the Shah of Affghanistan, but that, on the contrary, they rather wished him to put into execution his repeated threat of invasion, in order that they might show how easily he could be defeated. The envoy tells us that, in his correspondence with the Persian Government, he artfully avoided pledging the name of the Honourable East India Company, but that he represented unofficially the ravages of the Affghans at Lahore, and mentioned that thousands of the Sheeah inhabitants of that quarter had fled from their cruelty, and had found an asylum in the East India Company's dominions; and he added that, if the King of Persia possessed the ability to check the career of such a prince as Zeman Shah, he would be serving God and man by doing so. He further endeavoured to hurry the advance upon Affghanistan of Prince Mahmoud and Prince Ferooz-shah, two brothers of the monarch of Cabul, who were at that time refugees

seeking the aid of Fetteh Ali against their relative.
Mehdi Ali Khan seems to have been by no means backward in incurring responsibility. He had been entrusted
by the Governor of Bombay with a letter to the King of
Persia, by which he was empowered to conclude any
arrangement he might choose to enter into. But had
the contents of these credentials reached the eyes of the
Shah's ministers, they would have led them to believe
that the English authorities were willing to purchase
their aid against the Affghans. Mehdi Ali Khan found
the Shah sufficiently disposed to attack the Affghans
without the inducement of an English subsidy, and he
therefore determined to suppress the letter by which he
was accredited, and to substitute in its place another
document, purporting to come from the Governor of
Bombay, in which that officer offered to the Shah his
condolence on the death of his uncle, and his congratula-
tions on his accession to the throne. The mission of
this envoy met with full success, and he returned towards
Hindostan, exulting in the assurance he had received
regarding the king's schemes of conquest in Affghanistan, and in the orders that had been issued for seizing
the persons of any Frenchmen who might venture to
show themselves in Persia.

Zeman Shah about this period caused his vizeer to
send an officer to Haji Ibraheem, the prime minister
of Persia, with a request that Fetteh Ali would make
over to Affghanistan the province of Khorassan. Such
a suggestion could not fail to draw out an explanation
from the king as to the policy he intended to pursue.
He instructed his minister to reply that it was his
intention to restore the south-eastern limits of Persia

to the condition in which they had existed in the time
of the Sefaveean Shahs : that is, he proposed to overrun, and to retain possession of, Herat, Merve, Balkh,
Cabul, Candahar, Thibet, Kashgar and Seistan.   Nor
was this meant to be an idle threat ; for orders were at
once given for the royal forces to assemble at Tehran.
These orders were punctually obeyed by all the tribes,
with the exception of that of the former rebel Sadek
Khan Shekaki.   That chief seems never to have fully
relinquished the dream of obtaining the supreme power
in Persia, and he held back until the army should
have quitted Tehran.   One of his followers conveyed
to the Shah the intelligence that it was the chief's
intention then to proclaim himself king.   The royal
clemency had been already stretched to the utmost limit
in favour of this general, who was strongly suspected of
having instigated the murder of Aga Mahomed Khan,
and who had undoubtedly afforded protection to the
actual assassins ; and the long-pent-up flood of vengeance was now to be poured forth on the head of the
infatuated rebel.   He was sent for to the presence of the
king, and was condemned to be bricked up in a room at
Tehran, and there left to starve to death.*

Fetteh Ali Shah proceeded to Sebzewar and Nishapoor, where his army was engaged for some time in the

---

* The room in which this sentence was carried into execution is now a
portion of the house provided for one of the secretaries to the British
Legation at Tehran.   An old servant who has lingered about the premises
for the last sixty years, informed me that on the fifth day after Sadek Khan
had been walled in, he was found to have pulled up the cement of the flooring
of the room in his despair.

The Shah's reason for adopting this cruel mode of punishment was a
superstitious dread of breaking an oath which he had formerly made, never
to shed the blood of Sadek Khan.

task of punishing the insurgent governors of those places. While in Khorassan the king received an ambassador, laden with presents, from Zeman Shah, who requested him, on the part of his master, to return to Tehran; this Fetteh Ali agreed to do, on the condition that the Princes Mahmoud and Ferooz should be received back in Affghanistan in a manner suitable to their rank.

In the meantime various reasons induced the English authorities in India to despatch to the Court of Persia a mission of a more imposing character than that which had been entrusted to Mehdi Ali Khan. The success which had attended the negotiations of that envoy in his endeavours to prevail upon the Shah to attack the Affghans, had not been known at Calcutta when the Earl of Mornington selected Captain Malcolm for the purpose of proceeding to the Court of Tehran. No English diplomatist had until this time been employed in Persia since the reign of Charles the Second.* Captain Malcolm was charged to make some arrangement for relieving India from the annual alarm occasioned by the threatened invasion of Zeman Shah; to counteract any possible designs which the French nation might entertain with regard to Persia; and to endeavour to

---

* " L'envoyé de la compagnie Françoise ayant eu avis qu'un agent de la compagnie Angloise, qui était à Ispahan, devait aussi avoir audience, et qu'il avait de longue main ménagé secrètement les ministres, pour la préséance sur lui. . . il représentait que le droit de la nation Françoise etait d'avoir la préséance sur toutes les nations chrétiennes,"—CHARDIN. Vol. iii. p. 168.

" L'agent Anglois disoit qu'ayant une lettre du roi d'Angleterre à rendre. . . une lettre de roi devait aller devant celle d'un corps de marchands."—*Idem.*

Mr. Kaye, who has overlooked this mission, will excuse me for correcting the statement in his *Life of Sir John Malcolm* that no English envoy had visited the Persian court since the reign of Queen Elizabeth.

restore to somewhat of its former prosperity a trade which had been in a great degree lost. The mission landed at Bushire on the first of the month of February of the year 1800, but it was not until the month of November of the same year that it reached the presence of the Shah. As a preliminary measure the envoy distributed presents to the various Persian officers with whom he was thrown in contact on the route from Bushire to Tehran, and on arriving at that city he laid at the feet of the king a costly offering of watches, arms, mirrors and jewels.

Two months later a commercial treaty and a political treaty were concluded between the envoy from India and the prime minister of Persia, the observance of which was made binding on all Persians by a firman from the Shah. This firman contained orders to the rulers, officers, and writers of the ports, sea-coasts, and islands of the provinces of Fars and Khuzistan, to take means to expel and extirpate any persons of the French nation who should attempt to pass these forts or boundaries, or desire to establish themselves on these shores or frontiers. By the commercial treaty it was stipulated that English and Indian traders and merchants should be permitted to settle, free from taxes, in any Persian seaport, and should be protected in the exercise of their commerce in the Shah's dominions. The English were likewise to be at liberty to build and to sell houses in any Persian port or city, and English iron, lead, steel, and broad-cloth were to be admitted into Persia free from duty, while the existing imposts on other goods were not to be increased. By the political treaty the Shah engaged to make no peace with his Affghan neighbour excepting upon the condition that the latter should agree to renounce all designs of attacking the Anglo-Indian possessions. On the other hand, the treaty bound the English authorities to furnish warlike stores to the Shah in the event of his majesty being attacked by the French or by the Affghan nation. After this the British envoy returned to India, leaving behind him in Persia, as we are assured by the Persian historian, a well-established reputation for common sense and justice, and knowledge of the world.

Shortly after this period there occurred in Persia one of those examples of the exercise of despotic power, which show at the same time the strength and the weakness of an Oriental monarchy. The Itimad-ed-Dowleh, Haji Ibraheem, the prime minister of Persia, had acquired such a degree of influence throughout the country as gave his enemies' statements the appearance of reasonableness, when they whispered to the Shah that it was the intention of his minister to depose him. There is no ground for believing that Haji Ibraheem actually did harbour any such design, but in justice to the character of Fetteh Ali Shah it must be remembered that he had been again and again betrayed by those in whom he had placed the utmost confidence, and from whom he had least reason to expect the conduct of which they had been guilty. He had shown clemency in so many instances that he cannot be suspected of having wished to shed needlessly the blood of one who had performed signal services to his family. A tradition is current in Persia, that Aga Mahomed Khan charged his heir not to allow the grey head of Haji Ibraheem, who had betrayed his first master, to go down in peace to the grave; but for such a statement I can find no authority. When, however, Haji Ibraheem was accused to the king of harbouring the design of displacing his master from the throne, it must have weighed heavily against him in the mind of Fetteh Ali that he had once shown himself to be sufficiently powerful to displace a Zend prince from his government, and to substitute a Kajar in his stead. His treason to Lutf'ali Khan was now to be avenged by the heir of Aga Mahomed. But Haji Ibraheem was too powerful to be openly attacked. Nearly the half of Persia was governed by his sons or other relatives, who would at his command have at once raised the standard of revolt against the Shah. An order was therefore issued that, on a given day, the prime minister and all his kindred should be seized or put to death. Two of his youngest children were brought from Sheeraz to Tehran, to share the fate which had overtaken the other members of their family. Of these one was a handsome and spirited boy, and when his life was interceded for, the stipulation was made that he should be reduced to the condition of an eunuch : the other child was considered to be so little promising that his life was conceded without its being thought necessary to take the same precaution as in the case of his brother. He lived to perpetuate the race of the king-maker of Persia ; and is at the present hour the guardian of the shrine of Imam Reza, at Meshed.

Fetteh Ali Shah determined to send a mission to India, in return for that which had recently visited his court. Haji Khaleel Khan was selected as his envoy; but this nobleman was unfortunately killed at Bombay, in a scuffle between his servants and the guards who were appointed to attend him. This event, which caused

a profound sensation in India, seems to have been looked
upon in Persia as an accident which had happened in the
usual course of things.   The steps taken by the Government of India to make what reparation was possible to
the family of the deceased envoy, more than satisfied the
Shah, who is said to have observed that the English were
at liberty to kill as many of his ambassadors as they
might have a mind to dispose of, provided they should
always pay as liberally as they had done on the present
occasion.   Mahomed Nebi Khan was selected to proceed
to Hindostan, in the room of the deceased nobleman.

  The hurricane of rebellion which had, as we have
seen, swept over Persia after the downfall of the Sefaveean
dynasty, had not yet expended all its force.   Rest-
less spirits were still striving to upset the authority of
the Shah, and they gathered round the king's brother,
whom they proposed to set up as the head of their conspiracy.   That prince had been, as I have said, appointed
governor of Kashan, a city not more than 130 miles
distant from the capital.   Kashan is situated on the
skirts of a great desert, on the high-road between the
northern and southern provinces of Persia.   It lies about
six miles away from a range of mountains, bounding the
level country on the south, and it stands on a plain,
which is in some parts extremely fertile, while in others
it is stony and perfectly sterile.   The walls of Kashan
are stated to be about three-and-a-half miles in circumference, and they are, now at least, in a ruined state.   The
large area within them is but imperfectly occupied, and
ruins meet the eye at every turn.   All the houses have
arched roofs, rafters being objectionable on account of
the ravages of the white ant; and the habitations are

usually situated much below the level of the streets. The population may probably amount to 30,000 souls. The bazaars of Kashan are extensive, and their principal street is well-built, lofty, and closed in with a domed roofing; but the shops, though numerous, are mean in appearance. Indeed, Kashan is more a manufacturing than a commercial town. Its fabrics of silks, velvets, printed cottons, copper utensils, &c. have long been known, and the present prosperity of the place depends upon them. The climate, notwithstanding the excessive heat of summer, is said to be extremely salubrious.* Those who can afford at that season to quit their occupations retire to the neighbouring hills, and those who remain in the city take refuge in the underground cellars. The city was in a great measure destroyed by an earthquake in the reign of Kereem Khan. The men of Kashan have the disgraceful reputation of being more effeminate and cowardly than those of any other town of Persia. On this account troops are very seldom raised from amongst them.† In the midst of such a population, the king's brother may have been thought to be but little likely to renew his attempt to establish himself on the Persian throne. The prince, however, did not trust to the men of Kashan for success in his ambitious undertaking. Furnished with a forged royal order, appointing

---

* Mr. R. E. Abbott's *Notes.*

† The following circumstance, which, I am informed, actually happened, illustrates the proverbial cowardice of the Kashis, as the men of Kashan are called : A hundred recruits from that city were brought to Tehran, but they there gave signs of such incapacity for military service that it was decided to send them back to their native place, and there to disband them. On receiving the order to return, this company demanded that a sergeant's party should be sent with them to Kashan for the purpose of protecting them from violence by the way.

him to be governor of Ispahan, he proceeded to that city, and assumed the authority which was made over to him by the former governor. By these means he made himself master of the provincial treasury, and extracted much money from the citizens. He then shut up his treasure in the fortress of Ispahan, and proceeded to the Bakhtiari mountains, to endeavour there to raise an army.

When the report of these proceedings reached Tehran, the Shah took immediate steps for crushing this new rebellion. Leaving his son at the capital, the king proceeded to Ispahan, travelling almost incessantly, and performing the march of 250 miles in the exceedingly short space of four days. There he detached one of his officers for the purpose of reducing Ispahan, while he himself set out in pursuit of his brother. It would appear that such prompt measures had not been anticipated by the prince; for the Shah, on reaching Gulpaeegan, received the intelligence that his brother was making for Kermanshah, with the purpose of reaching the Turkish dominions. Upon this the king despatched one of his generals, with orders to proceed to Kermanshah by forced marches, and to throw himself between the frontier and the followers of the prince. This movement, which was promptly executed, had the desired effect of driving the rebel into submission. He fled to the sanctuary of Koom, where, upon the Shah's arrival, he placed a drawn sword upon his neck in token of repentance, and once more received the royal forgiveness. This was his last attempt at rebellion; and he soon afterwards died in retirement, in the vicinity of Tehran.

After the suppression of this revolt of his brother, the Shah once more turned his attention to the affairs of

Khorassan.* Nadir Meerza, the son of Shahrukh, had
been left in the government of that province, and he had
sent his brother Abbass to Tehran, to be a hostage for his
good behaviour. The Shah was disposed to treat these
princes with lenity, on account of their illustrious descent;
but a petition which was addressed to him by the chieftains of Khorassan, imploring his protection against
Nadir Meerza, obliged him to interfere. He accordingly
despatched his son-in-law to Meshed, at the head of twelve
hundred horsemen, and he himself prepared to follow
with a more considerable force. On arriving at Meshed,
he at once closely blockaded the city, but he was prevented by religious scruples from permitting his artillerymen to open fire upon the holy place. This state of
things continued during a whole month, at the end of
which period the people of Meshed were reduced to a
state of considerable suffering. They would have yielded
the place to the Shah, had not the gates and the citadel
been occupied by the troops of Nadir Meerza. Under
these circumstances the chief priest of Meshed was
deputed to wait upon the king, and to intercede for his
fellow-citizens. The Syed came to the royal camp, and
won from the Shah a declaration that he wished no evil
to the citizens of Meshed, and was only desirous of
securing the person of Nadir Meerza. It was arranged
that the Shah was to retire from before the city, while the
chief priest, on the part of his fellow-citizens, engaged
that the prince should be seized and brought to the
presence of the king. Orders were accordingly given to
raise the blockade, and the royal forces returned to
Damghan, from which town they marched to Mazenderan.

---

* A.D. 1802.

The news of the massacre of the Persians at the sacred city of Kerbela by the Wahabi Arabs,* recalled the king to Tehran. The Shah at first proposed to march with his army to avenge this wanton proceeding, but reflecting on the grave import of invading the Sultan's dominions, he contented himself with despatching a special envoy to the Pasha of Baghdad, who promised to exterminate the whole nation of Wahab. The Shah's presence was then called for at Astrabad, to put down the incursions of the Turkoman tribes of the Attreck and the Goorgan districts. These he completely defeated, after which exploit he returned to Tehran. In this year † also the Affghans of Seistan invaded the province of Kerman from Bem and Nermansheer.

In the meantime, one of the king's officers had been left before the walls of Meshed, with a corps of observation. This general, seeing that Nadir Meerza was not delivered over to him as had been stipulated, called upon the Shah to furnish him with reinforcements

---

* For an account of the events that led to the attack on Kerbela by the Wahabis, see Palgrave's *Journey in Central and Eastern Arabia.* Vol. ii. pp. 41-43.

" A fanatic of Ghilan offered himself for the work of blood. He received suitable instructions in Tehran, whence he journeyed to Meshed Hoseyn, the authentic Mecca of Shiya'ee devotion. There he procured a written pardon for all past and future sins, and a title-deed duly signed and sealed, assuring him the eternal joys of paradise, should he rid the earth of the Nejdean tyrant ('Abd-el-'Azeez). . . . He one day took his stand in the ranks of evening prayer immediately behind 'Abd-el-'Azeez, went through the first two reka'as of Islamitic devotion, and, at the third, while the Sultan of Nejed was bowed in prostrate adoration, plunged his sharp Khorassan dagger in his body. . . . These events took place, so far as my informants could supply a date, about 1805 or 1806. . . . 'Abd-Allah marched northward against Meshed Hoseyn or Kerbelah, the main object of his hatred. Here the impetuosity of his onset overcame all resistance ; the town was stormed, and a promiscuous massacre of garrison and inhabitants appeased the manes of 'Abd-el-'Azeez.'

† A.D. 1803.

to renew the blockade of the city. One of the king's sons accordingly marched to his aid, and pressed the men of Meshed to open their gates to the king's lieutenant. But Nadir Meerza was determined to hold out so long as he might have a chance of being able to resist the Shah's authority. Familiarity with the shrine of Imam Reza seems to have removed from his mind the superstitious dread with which even the most hardened Persians would contemplate an act of sacrilege against so holy a mosque. In order to enable him to defray the expense of maintaining troops for the defence of the walls, he boldly proceeded to the sacred precincts where the priests chanted the song of praise of the Imam whose ashes were there entombed. Entering the Holy of Holies at the head of a band of men as unscrupulous as himself, he hewed away the silver bars that kept off the crowd of devotees from pressing on the tomb of the Imam. The dome of the mosque itself, before which, as it glitters in the Eastern sun, thousands of pilgrims from the utmost parts of Asia bow their heads in silent awe,—the dome itself was stripped of its golden splendours to supply the demands of the lawless soldiery. After the commission of an act so entirely in defiance of public feeling, Nadir seems to have become utterly reckless. The infuriated crowd rushed upon the band of despoliators, and, by superior numbers, forced them to desist from further aggression on the holy places.

Nadir attributed this resistance to his authority to the promptings of the venerable Syed Mehdi, the priest who a few weeks before had been the means of delivering his fellow-citizens from the blockade that had been established by Fetteh Ali Shah. This descendant of the lawgiver of Mecca was seventy years of age, and was, from his remarkable piety, considered to be the foremost saint in Persia. To this man's house the ruthless prince forced his way at dawn on the morning succeeding the day of his attack on the shrine. Not finding him in his outer chambers, the intruder was not to be deterred by the imperious custom of the East, which forbids strangers to penetrate into the apartments of the women. There the Syed was found kneeling on his carpet, in the act of addressing the appointed morning prayer to the Deity. But neither his character nor his occupation was sacred in the eyes of Nadir, who with his battle-axe hewed the aged man to the ground. A general outburst of horror was excited by this act, and the people with one accord opened the city gates to admit the troops of the Shah. Nadir Meerza made his escape through the public drain, but he was closely pursued, and was taken at the distance of four parasangs from Meshed. Chains were placed on his arms and legs, and he was conveyed in that condition to Tehran, and brought to the presence of the Shah. Public opinion demanded that he should receive the utmost punishment which it was in the king's power to give, and the summary way in which this punishment was inflicted was in accordance with Persian custom. When asked what excuse he had to offer for having slain the saint of God, he could only deny having committed the act attributed to him. Upon this the Shah ordered that his tongue should be torn from his head, and that his hands should be cut off. A red-hot wire was then drawn across the culprit's eyes, and those who had abetted him in his sacrilegious acts received the punishment of death. It is illustrative of the peculiar tenacity with which Persians follow up blood-feuds, that the historian of the Kajars remarks with complacency that by this affair the Shah avenged the fate of his great-grandfather, Fetteh Ali Khan, who had been put to death by Nadir Shah.

Fetteh Ali Shah was now at the zenith of his power and glory. He had put down all the internal insurrections that had disturbed his reign, and he had done much to maintain the integrity of the ancient kingdom of Persia. From the shores of the sea of Oman and the borders of Beloochistan, the wide extent of Iran to the waters of the Caspian obeyed his undivided sway. The young Czar of Georgia, though he had since yielded to Russia, had formally acknowledged him as his rightful paramount lord, and he had been encouraged by a powerful foreign government to extend his empire in the direction of Affghanistan. The monarchs of Persia had adopted the proud title of Shah-in-Shah, or king of kings, from the circumstance of their having claimed allegiance from four Valis, the hereditary rulers of Affghanistan, Georgia, Kurdistan, and Arabistan. Of these four subordinate Shahs, one—that of Affghanistan, as we have seen—had for ever thrown off the Persian yoke. The territories of the Vali of Arabistan had been incorporated with the country of Persia proper ; but as the Shah still claimed allegiance from the remaining two subject-kings, he might still lay claim to the title of Shah-in-Shah. He was surrounded by a family of sons, one of the most promising of whom had been named crown-prince * and

---

* " Abbass Meerza was not the eldest son of Fetteh Ali Shah. He had been selected to be the prospective heir to the throne by Aga Mahomed Khan. His elder brother, when a mere child, was asked by his grand-

heir-apparent of Persia. The Shah's revenue at the time
I write of, was computed by an English author * as
amounting to little less than six millions sterling. The
crown jewels of Persia in the possession of Fetteh Ali
have been estimated as being of more intrinsic value
than those of any contemporary prince of Christendom.†

But a dark cloud was gathering in the north, which
soon overshadowed this fair prospect, and which in due
time poured forth its violence over the kingdom of
Persia. The events of this period shall be recorded in
a separate chapter.‡

---

uncle what he would do if he were Shah ; when, with more candour than
prudence, looking on the hideous face of the eunuch, the child replied, " I
would put you to death." The answer had nearly cost him his life, and it
lost him his chance of a crown.

* Sir J. MALCOLM.

† The author of *Monarchs Retired from Business* makes a statement—
the incorrectness of which is proportionate to the confidence with which it
is advanced—to the effect that the modern Shah of Persia, like the shrine
of the three kings at Cologne, is surrounded by tinsel, glass, and false
jewelry. This well-informed author further tells his readers that the Shah
is bullied by Russia, cajoled by France, and not treated with over civility
by England.

‡ The following descriptions, by two modern travellers, give us some
idea of the Oriental splendour of which the Court of Fetteh Ali Shah was,
on festive occasions, the scene :—

" The first ceremony of the festival of Norooz was the introduction of
the presents from the different provinces. That from Prince Hossein Ali
Meerza, governor of Shiraz, came first. The master of the ceremonies
walked up, having with him the conductor of the present and an attendant,
who, when the name and titles of the donor had been proclaimed, read
aloud from a paper the list of the articles. The present from Prince Hossein
Ali Meerza consisted of a very long train of large trays placed on men's
heads, on which were shawls, stuffs of all sorts, pearls, &c. ; then, many
trays filled with sugar and sweetmeats ; after that many mules laden with
fruit, &c. The next present was from Mahomed Ali Khán, prince of
Hamadan, the eldest-born of the king's sons, but who had been deprived by
his father of the succession, because the Georgian slave who bore him was
of an extraction less noble than that of the mothers of the younger princes.
His present accorded with the character which is assigned to him : it consisted of pistols and spears, a string of one hundred camels and as many

mules. After this came the present from the Prince of Yezd, another of the king's sons, which consisted of shawls and the silken stuffs, the manufacture of his own town. Then followed that of the Prince of Meshed; and, last of all, and most valuable, was that from Hajee Mahomed Hossein Khan, Ameen-ood-Dowlah. It consisted of fifty mules, each carrying a load of one thousand tomans."—MORIER's *Travels in Persia.*

" The royal procession made its appearance. First, the elder sons of the king entered, at the side on which we stood, Abbass Meerza taking the left of the whole, which brought him to the right of the throne. His brothers followed, till they nearly closed upon us. Directly opposite to this elder rank of princes, all grown to manhood, their younger brothers arranged themselves on the other side of the transverse water. They were all superbly habited, in the richest brocade vests and shawl-girdles, from the folds of which glittered the jewelled hilts of their daggers. Each wore a robe of gold stuff, lined and deeply collared with the most delicate sables, falling a little below the shoulder, and reaching to the calf of their leg. Around their black caps they also had wound the finest shawls. Every one of them, from the eldest to the youngest, wore bracelets of the most brilliant rubies and emeralds, just above the bend of the elbow.

" At some distance, near the front of the palace, appeared another range of highly revered personages—mollahs, astrologers, and other sages of this land of the East, clothed in their more sombre garments of religion and philosophy. There was no noise, no bustle of any kind ; every person standing quietly in his place, awaiting the arrival of the monarch. At last, the sudden discharge of the swivels from the camel corps without, with the clang of trumpets, and I know not what congregation of uproarious sounds besides, announced that his Majesty had entered the gate of the citadel. But the most extraordinary part of the clamour was the appalling roar of two huge elephants, trained to the express purpose of giving this note of the especial movements of the great king.

" He entered the saloon from the left, and advanced to the front of it, with an air and step which belonged entirely to a sovereign. I never before had beheld anything like such perfect majesty ; and he seated himself on his throne with the same indescribable, unaffected dignity. Had there been any assumption in his manner, I could not have been so impressed. I should then have seen a man, though a king, theatrically acting his state : here I beheld a great sovereign, feeling himself as such, and he looked the majesty he felt.

" He was one blaze of jewels, which literally dazzled the sight on first looking at him ; but the details of his dress were these :—A lofty tiara of three elevations was on his head, which shape appears to have been long peculiar to the crown of the great king. It was entirely composed of thickly-set diamonds, pearls, rubies, and emeralds, so exquisitely disposed as to form a mixture of the most beautiful colours in the brilliant light reflected from its surface. Several black feathers, like the heron plume, were intermixed with the resplendent aigrettes of this truly imperial diadem, whose bending points were finished with pear-formed pearls of an immense size. The vesture was of gold tissue, nearly covered with a similar disposition of jewelry; and crossing the shoulders were two strings of pearls, probably the largest in the world. I call his dress a vesture, because it set close to his person, from the neck to the bottom of the waist, showing a shape as noble as his air. At that point, it devolved downwards in loose drapery, like the usual Persian garment, and was of the same costly materials with the vest. But for splendour, nothing could exceed the broad bracelet round his arms and the belt which encircled his waist; they actually blazed like fire when the rays of the sun met them; and when we know the names derived from such excessive lustre, we cannot be surprised at seeing such an effect. The jewelled band on the right arm was called 'the mountain of light,' and that on the left, ' the sea of light.'

" The throne was of pure white marble, raised a few steps from the ground, and carpeted with shawls and cloth of gold, on which the king sat in the fashion of his country, his back supported by a large cushion, encased in a network of pearls. The spacious apartment in which this was erected is open in front, and supported by two twisted columns of white marble, fluted with gold. The interior was profusely decorated with carving, gilding, arabesque painting, and looking-glass, which latter material was interwoven with all other ornaments, gleaming and glittering in every part, from the vaulted roof to the floor. Vases of water-flowers, and others containing rose-water, were arranged about the apartment.

" While the great king was approaching his throne, the whole assembly continued bowing their heads to the ground, till he had taken his place. A dead silence then ensued, the whole presenting a most magnificent and, indeed, awful appearance; the stillness being so profound among so vast a concourse, that the slightest rustling of the trees was heard, and the softest trickling of the water from the fountains into the canals.

" In the midst of this solemn stillness, while all eyes were fixed on the bright object before them, which sat, indeed, as radiant and immovable as the image of Mithras itself, a sort of volley of words, bursting at one impulse from the mouths of the mollahs and astrologers, made me start, and interrupted my gaze. This strange oratory was a kind of heraldic enumeration of the great king's titles, dominions, and glorious acts, with an appropriate panegyric on his courage, liberality, and extended power. When this was ended, all heads still bowing to the ground, and the air had ceased to vibrate with the sounds, there was a pause for about half a minute, and then his majesty spoke. The effect was even more startling than the sudden bursting forth of the mollahs; for this was like a voice from the tombs—so deep, so hollow, and, at the same time, so penetratingly loud."— Sir R. KER PORTER's *Travels*.

CHAPTER VI.

It has been mentioned in a previous chapter that Goorgeen, or George, who had succeeded his father Heraclius as Czar of Georgia, had written to Fetteh-Ali Shah making his submission to that monarch, and that Fetteh Ali had accepted this act of allegiance on the part of the Iberian prince. The war which had been waged between Russia and Persia in the cause of the Czar Heraclius seems not until long afterwards to have been concluded by a formal treaty of peace. At the death of Catherine and of Aga Mahomed, hostilities on both sides ceased. The caprice or policy of the Emperor Paul caused a check to be placed for a time on the aggressive movements of the great northern power, and Fetteh Ali Shah, as we have seen, was fully occupied in putting down the various pretenders to the Kayanian crown. The traditional policy, however, which had been inaugurated by Peter the Great, soon prevailed over that passing freak of the eccentric son of Catherine.   Russian agency was allowed to use its influence over the feeble mind of the last occupant of the throne of the Bagratides, and the result was that, by an instrument dated the 28th of September of the year 1800, the Czar George XIII. of Georgia, in his own name and in the names of his successors, renounced his crown in favour of the Emperor of Russia.   This act, we are told, drew down upon him the hatred and curses of the nobles of his country.* His queen was ashamed of the pusillanimity which had induced her timid husband to yield compliance to the insidious· demands of the agents of Russia, and when it was wished to arrest her person in order that she might be conveyed to Moscow, the indignant princess drew her dagger and wounded the Russian officer who had attempted to seize her.   Prince Alexander, the younger brother of George, was not disposed to see the crown thus pass from his father's family without making an effort to secure it for himself.   He used his utmost endeavours to raise a general revolution ; but the chiefs of the country saw the hopelessness of attempting to throw

---

* The following is an extract from the proclamation of the Emperor Alexander to the Georgian nation of the date of September 12, 1801 :—
" Ce n'est pas pour accroître nos forces, ce n'est pas dans des vues d'interêt, ou pour étendre les limites d'un empire déjà si vaste, que nous acceptons le fardeau du trône de Géorgie ; le sentiment de notre dignité, l'honneur, l'humanité, seuls nous ont imposé le devoir sacré de ne pas resister aux cris de souffrance partis de votre sein, de detourner de vos têtes les maux qui vous affligent, et d'introduire en Géorgie un gouvernement fort, capable d'administrer la justice avec équité, de protéger la vie et les biens de chacun, et d'étendre sur tous l'égide de la loi."

off the Russian yoke, unless they could obtain the armed support either of Persia or of Turkey. Alexander accordingly tried to enlist both of those powers in his favour; but the Turkish Government was occupied in watching the progress of Napoleon, and Fetteh Ali was not at that time disposed to draw down upon himself the antagonism of his powerful northern neighbour. Alexander was, however, hospitably received by the chief of the Avars and by the Khan of Karabagh, both of whom agreed to join him in an attempt to expel the Russians from Georgia. But these schemes became known at Tiflis in time to admit of measures being concerted to thwart them; and General Lazeroff, by the aid of his superior artillery, gained on the banks of the Lora a decisive victory over the hardy followers of the Georgian prince. The Russian commander of the troops in the Caucasus attacked the town of Genja, the modern Elisabetpol, and the severity with which he treated the inhabitants was meant to be a warning of what those had to expect who should presume to withstand the power of the Czar. From Genja, General Seeseeanoff advanced to Erivan, being led on by a promise of the governor of that fortress that he would yield it to the Russian commander.

The court of Persia was with reason alarmed at these proceedings, and the crown-prince was instructed to take the field and to march on Erivan, while the Shah himself, in order to be near to the scene of operations, encamped upon the plain of Oojan. The crown-prince sent one of his officers, Mehdi Kuli Khan, with six thousand horsemen, to the Turkish frontier for the purpose of bringing back some wandering tribes of the province of Erivan, whom the governor of that place had persuaded to cross the border.

As this officer was returning, after having successfully accomplished the object of his expedition, he suddenly found himself confronted by the troops of General Seeseeanoff. His forces were in no condition to withstand the artillery of the Russian army, and he therefore avoided an encounter. By rapidly retiring by alternate squadrons he covered the march of the tribes; thus defied the efforts of the enemy to overtake him; and was enabled to make good his junction with the forces of the crown-prince. General Seeseeanoff then advanced to the neighbourhood of the celebrated monastery of Etchmiadzeen, the residence of the Patriarch of the Armenian church, where he encountered the Persian army ready to oppose him. Abbass Meerza, the crown-prince, drew up his forces in three divisions, of the central one of which he took command in person, being attended in the battle which followed by the son of the deposed Czar of Georgia. The conflict lasted for three days, and the Persians assert that though they suffered much from the Russian guns, they were not defeated. General Seeseeanoff then marched to Erivan, the governor of which town now refused to fulfil the compact into which he had entered. This personage was consistent in wishing throughout to be on the side of the strongest, but when he saw that the Russian troops could not drive the Persians before them, his estimate of the strength of the invaders at once went down, and he sent his confidential agent to the prince's camp, offering to return to his duty to the Shah, provided he were assured of pardon. Having been satisfied on this point, he informed the Russian officer who had been sent to treat with him for the cession of Erivan, that he had nothing further to say to his master. General Seeseeanoff was exasperated at this breach of faith, and he determined to execute a sudden movement which might have the effect of establishing Russian prestige. The Persian army had followed him to the neighbourhood of Erivan, and on the morning of the sixth of Rebbi-es-Sani, 1219,* he surprised the Shah's forces in their camp. The Persians were unable to make head against the impetuous attack of the disciplined Russian infantry, and they fled in confusion, notwithstanding all the efforts of the prince to stop them. The Russian general then besieged Erivan and opened a fresh negotiation with Mahomed Khan, the governor. The Persian prince collected the remnants of his army at Derek, forty miles from the field of battle, where he resolved to await the instructions of the Shah. Reinforcements were at once sent to him, and the king prepared to follow in person. On reaching the river Araxes, the Shah, foremost of all, forced his horse into the current, and the brave example of their monarch inspired all ranks to follow his example. On reaching Nakhtchivan the king conceived it to be a good omen that he was met by an officer bearing the heads of several Russians, which, according to the barbarous custom of the Persians, had been severed from the bodies of some soldiers who had fallen in a night attack on the invader's camp. The Shah on joining the crown-prince became convinced that his irregular troops could not successfully encounter disciplined infantry in the open field, and he therefore gave orders for a night attack upon the Russians in their

* A.D. 1804.

entrenched position. According to the Persian accounts
this movement was executed by seven Persian divisions,
who inflicted considerable loss upon the enemy. The
same mode of attack was in turn adopted by General
Seeseeanoff, but an intimation of his intended movement
was conveyed to the Persian camp by the prince's spies.
The Shah upon this withdrew his forces to a neighbouring
hill, on which his guns were placed in such a position
as might enable them to pour a murderous fire on the
camp beneath, so soon as the enemy should have entered
it. But the Russians in this night march lost their way,
and only arrived at their destination in time to discover
by daylight the advantageous position in which the
Persians were posted. An engagement took place
between them which ended in both parties returning
to their former camps. General Seeseeanoff in the
meantime made but little progress in his operations
against Erivan, and he began to be severely pressed by
the want of stores and of ammunition. An expedition
which he sent out for the purpose of conducting into his
camp a convoy of provisions of war from Tiflis, was
opposed by the Shah and forced to return to before Erivan.
All the roads leading to that place were strictly watched
by the Persians, and the failure of an attempt to bring
a second convoy from Tiflis into his camp forced the
Russian commander to raise the siege and to depart by
night from before the city. His hurried retreat was
followed by the corresponding advance of the Persian
cavalry, who were able to inflict considerable annoyance
upon his shattered divisions. Thus the Shah was for a
time again master of the province of Erivan. Before
proceeding to recapitulate the subsequent events of this

war, it is necessary to glance for a moment at the state of things at other portions of the extensive Persian frontier.

The career of Nadir Shah had caused a general disturbance of landmarks throughout central Asia, and one of the events which followed his death was the occurrence of a change in the reigning dynasty of Bokhara. The son of the Ameer Daniel, the Ameer Massoom, commonly known by the name of Beg-i-Jan, not only consolidated his power over the Oozbegs, but was enabled by his powerful cavalry to overrun the province of Khorassan, and to possess himself of the town of Merve. This prince at his death left two sons, the elder of whom took up arms against his brother, who was thus forced to take refuge with the King of Persia. The Shah received him in the most cordial manner, adopted him as his stepson, and instructed the governor of Khorassan to endeavour to give effect to the views of the exiled prince with reference to his being able to obtain the mastery over his brother.

At the close of the reign of Ahmed Shah, the first king of Affghanistan, a chief of the tribe of Ghilzye who feared the supremacy of the Abdallis, had, by the permission of Kereem Khan, possessed himself of the district of Nermansheer in Beloochistan, in the government of which he had been succeeded by his son. Fetteh Ali Shah at a later period ordered the governor of Kerman to extend his authority over the neighbouring Affghans, whose chief on hearing of this proceeded to the Persian court and obtained from the king counter-orders to the governor of Kerman, and an investiture to the government of both Nermansheer and Seistan; this chief, however, whose name was Mahomed Khan, on returning to his home threw off his allegiance to the Shah, and accordingly a Persian army invaded the district of Nermansheer, and after having driven the Affghans from it, the governor of Kerman annexed it to the province over which he ruled.

In the year succeeding that which had been signalised by the Shah's campaign at the base of Mount Ararat, the royal camp was pitched upon the plain of Sultaneeah, and the crown-prince was ordered to pursue the war in the province of Karabagh. Ibraheem Khaleel Khan, the chief of Sheeshah, who has been mentioned in a previous chapter, had voluntarily given in his submission to Russia, and had sent his grandson to General Seeseeanoff as a hostage. Upon the approach of the crown-prince he besought Russian aid to enable him successfully to defend himself; three hundred soldiers were accordingly sent to assist irregular cavalry in the defence of the bridge of Khuda-Afereen on the Araxes, by which the prince would approach Karabagh. The Persians, however, made good their passage, and the forces of Ibraheem Khan were compelled to retire with loss. Upon this the crown-prince advanced towards the fortress of Sheeshah, and the governor of that place once more pressed upon General Seeseeanoff the urgent need in which he stood of assistance. Strong reinforcements were accordingly sent to him from Tiflis, but they were encountered by the troops of Prince Abbass Meerza ; these were forced to entrench themselves in a cemetery, and, according to the Persian account, after six days' incessant fighting the Russian troops retreated, and their camp and camp-equipage fell into the hands of the prince. At the same time the important city of Erivan was taken possession of in the name of the Shah. At the opening of the campaign Mehdi Kuli Khan, whose successful cavalry manœuvre before the forces of General Seeseeanoff has been already mentioned, had been sent on by the king to Erivan with instructions to ascertain the real intentions of the governor of that place, Mahomed Khan. It would seem that that chief had once more listened to the overtures of the agents of Russia, and Mehdi Khan accordingly determined that he should be superseded. He entered the fortress with some of his followers, and, under the pretext of preparing the place against a fresh siege by the Russians, he was enabled to introduce all his troops without having aroused the suspicions of the governor. Upon an appointed signal being given, his soldiers manned the walls and took possession of the gates, and Mahomed Khan, when it was too late, discovered that Erivan was no longer his to betray.

About this time the Russian commander-in-chief conceived the idea of making a descent upon the coast of Gilan, and from there threatening the Persian capital; but he had not fully taken into account all the difficulties that lay in the way of such an undertaking. The Russian ships landed at Enzelli, a small seaport which commands the entrance to the lake or lagoon of the same name. Of that place the soldiers possessed themselves, and from there their commander prepared to advance on Resht, the chief town of the province of Gilan. The lake of Enzelli is about twelve miles in breadth, and for a part of that distance it is so shallow that only small boats can pass over it, and these must be carefully steered in order to avoid being stopped by the mud which is continually being deposited by the river of Peer-Bazar. To cross the lagoon in the ships was thus impossible, and a sufficient number of boats could not be procured to convey the soldiers, the stores and the guns to the mainland. The Russian commander, therefore, determined to march his troops round the border of the lake; but the marshy ground which surrounds it was so heavy that it was with the greatest difficulty that guns could be dragged over it. A thick forest occupies the surface of the country between Enzelli and the chief city of Gilan, and in this forest the Gileks were concealed ready at the suitable moment to open a fire upon the invaders. It would be almost impossible to imagine a more difficult undertaking for a general than in the face of an enemy to transport an army with stores and artillery over the muddy and marshy thickets that lie before the town of Resht; and accordingly it is not to be wondered at that when the Gileks opened fire from their ambush the Russians should have been thrown into confusion from which they found they could not extricate themselves. The order was given to retreat on Enzelli, and the expedition there took ship, leaving behind, if we may rely on the Persian accounts, some guns and stores of war.

The Russian commander-in-chief in Georgia marched out of Genja and took up his position on the banks of the river Tatar. The Shah instructed the crown-prince to endeavour to make himself master of Genja, and, in order to occupy General Seeseeanoff, Ismaïl Khan was sent to make a diversion in front of the stream, on which that officer had taken up his position. He thence dislodged the Russian general, and the prince then obtained possession of Genja, the inhabitants of which city were

removed to Tabreez.   General Seeseeanoff subsequently
marched on Sheeshah, which fortress was made over to
him by Ibraheem Khaleel Khan.   From there he proceeded
to Genja.   The governors of Koobeh and Derbend, and
of Bakoo, and the chief of the Lesghis, having sent to
ask assistance from the Shah, a Persian force was sent to
their aid.   The Russian squadron had steered from
Enzelli to Bakoo, where it was attacked by the guns
of the governor, whereupon the Russians landed before
the fortress and inflicted severe damage by their artillery.
The governor, however, was reinforced by an army from
the Lesghi mountains and from Derbend, and the Russian
commander was compelled to re-embark and steer for the
coast of Taleesh.   General Seeseeanoff marched to attack
the chief of Sheervan, who professed to yield to his wishes.
The Russian commander-in-chief then proceeded to
Bakoo, to which place the squadron returned from
Taleesh.   The crown-prince in the meantime threatened
the Russian general with an attack on his rear, from the
direction of Ardabeel; and Seeseeanoff, fearing lest he
should be hemmed in, proceeded to open a negotiation
with the chief of Bakoo for the surrender of that fortress.
That chief resolved to meet the Governor-General of the
Caucasus with an act of treachery as flagrant as that to
the commission of which he was invited.   Pretending to
listen to his arguments, he sent to the Muscovite camp
to inform the General that he wished to have a personal
interview with his Excellency for the purpose of settling
the precise terms upon which Bakoo was to be given up.
Seeseeanoff fell into the snare which the unscrupulous
Persian had thus prepared, and whilst he was occupied in
conversing with the Khan beneath the walls of Bakoo,

he was beset by assassins who at once put an end to his existence. Whilst the confusion consequent upon the loss of its commander still reigned in the Russian camp, it was attacked and broken up by the Persian troops, and the squadron which lay in the harbour once more put out to sea.

We have thus seen the reöpening of friendly inter-course or hostile operations between Persia, under Fetteh Ali Shah, and England and Russia. We have next to record a further interchange of peaceful relations between that king and France. We are informed that in the year of the Hegira 1216,* an Armenian merchant, who came to Tehran from Baghdad, professed to be the bearer of cre-dentials from the Government of the Emperor Napoleon. But no one at Tehran could decipher the French charac-ters in which the letters were traced, and consequently the soi-disant envoy had to submit to the neglect from which his appearance and following were not sufficient to rescue him. No doubt, however, could be felt as to the authentic nature of the mission of the next French envoy, whose coming was announced to the court of Persia. But this envoy, who had been sent from Páris, in conse-quence of a wish expressed on the Shah's part to the French ambassador at Constantinople that he might receive the support of France,† was arrested near the Persian frontier, by the agents of the Pasha of Byazeed,‡ and was conducted to that town, where he was for eight months confined in a dry subterranean cistern. The Pasha of Byazeed died at the end of that time, and the news of the victory of Austerlitz, which penetrated into

* A.D. 1801.   † M. LANGLES' *Notes on Persia.*
‡ *Voyage en Arménie et en Perse, par* P. A. JAUBERT: chap. 6-9.

the heart of Turkey, was likely to give increased security
to the agents of France ; and when the crown-prince of
Persia demanded the release of M. Jaubert, he was permitted to continue his journey.   He arrived at Tehran in
the month of May, 1806, and after a short stay, returned
to Europe, in the company of a Persian ambassador
accredited to the Emperor Napoleon.   This ambassador
proceeded to Tilsit, where he concluded a treaty, which
was ratified by the Emperor at Finkenstein, in May,
1807.* †

It has been stated that the chief of Karabagh, the
same Ibraheem Khaleel Khan who had so long withstood
the power of Aga Mahomed, had voluntarily admitted
the Russians to the fortress of Sheeshah.   But on mature
reflection that aged chief came to the conclusion that it
was not the duty of a faithful Mussulman to assist in
establishing the power of an infidel government over a
population of true believers.   The reproaches of his con-
science were quickened by the messages he received from
his sister, who was the wife of Fetteh Ali Shah, and
from his son, who was in that monarch's camp.   The
result was, that he determined to destroy the Russian
garrison of Sheeshah, and to hand over that stronghold
to the Persian authorities.

On this resolution being communicated to the king,
the crown-prince was ordered to march to Karabagh, so
that he might be at hand to support Ibraheem Khaleel
Khan.   The prince accordingly set out for Karabagh,
and despatched in advance the son of the Khan of that
province ; but on reaching the bridge of Khuda Afereen

---

* BLACKWOOD'S *Edinburgh Magazine*, vol. xxi., 1827.
† *Progress of Russia in the East.*

on the Araxes, his Highness was met by the soldiers of
the son of Ibraheem, whose downcast eyes and mournful
bearing announced that a chief of the people had fallen.
Ibraheem Khan had, it appeared, quitted the fortress
with two thousand followers, and proceeded to a camp
four miles distant from it, with the intention of awaiting
the arrival of his son.   Amongst those to whom he had
communicated the plot which had been concerted, was
his grandson; and this youth, who hated his uncle,
betrayed the whole scheme to the Major in command of
the Russian garrison.   That officer was equal to the
critical situation in which he now found himself placed.
Taking with him the grandson of the Khan, he proceeded
in the dead of night with three hundred men to the
camp of Ibraheem, and in the confused affray which
followed, that chief and thirty-one of his family or servants were put to death.   The Russian commander then
appointed one of the sons of the deceased Khan to be
governor of Karabagh, and shut himself up in Sheeshah
in expectation of receiving reinforcements from Tiflis.
These were promptly sent into Karabagh, and they were
encountered by the forces of the crown-prince at a spot
called Khansheen, where, after an obstinate struggle,
success attended the arms of Persia; the Russian soldiers
being obliged to retreat in confusion.   The Persian irregular troops were then spread over different parts of the
country of Georgia, for the purpose of laying it waste, and
the Persian commander returned towards the Araxes.   A
force had been despatched to bring the tribes of Karabagh
over to Persia, and as one of these was averse to the
movement, it sent to ask Russian aid to enable it to
withstand the Persian troops.   A regiment was accord-

ingly sent to its aid, and the Persian detachment was defeated. Reinforcements were, however, despatched to his countrymen by the prince, and the result was, that the Russian commander, after having strengthened the garrison of Sheeshah, retreated to Tiflis. The prince then marched into the province of Sheervan, for the purpose of punishing the disaffected governor of that district, and having carried out this object he returned to Tabreez. The Khan of Derbend had in the meantime given in his adhesion to the Russian cause.

In the same year the Persian arms were employed in another quarter. Between Uroomeeah and Kermanshah lies the frontier district of Shehr-i-zoor, which was governed by a Pasha named Abdur Rahman. This Pasha, being oppressed by the governor-general of Baghdad, took refuge with the Shah of Persia, who at once agreed to afford him his protection. Through his influence he was restored to his government, and at the same time the Shah's eldest son, Mahomed Ali Meerza, was appointed viceroy along the Turkish frontier. After this the Pasha of Baghdad once more treated Abdur Rahman in such a manner as obliged him a second time to seek refuge in Persia. His quarrel was espoused by the prince, and Suleiman Pasha, the son-in-law of the governor-general of Baghdad, advanced to oppose him with thirty thousand men. In the action which ensued, the Turks were defeated, and they were followed by the Persians to the neighbourhood of Mosul. Their commander, who had been made prisoner, was sent to Tehran in chains, and on his being released the Shah appointed Abdur Rahman to be governor of Shehr-i-zoor.

It would, I fear, weary the reader, were I to state in

A HISTORY OF PERSIA.

detail the various operations which ended in the possession being secured to Russia of the provinces of Derbend, Bakoo, Sheervan, Sheki, Genja, Taleesh, and Moghan. The Northern Power, as her arms obtained a mastery in Europe, was enabled gradually to bring her vast resources to bear upon the field of operations in Asia. A want of vigour and consistent action was to be observed in the operations of the Persian Government, while, on the other hand, no means were spared by the agents of Russia to work upon the passions and the self-interest of the unprincipled Khans who governed the people of the country which was the scene of the war. According to the Persian statements, some of the Khans remained true to the Shah, but were obliged to quit their governments on account of their people having declared for the Czar. Others were won over by Russian gold, and Russian blandishments. One gave in his adhesion to the Emperor on condition that his local enemy should be put to death ; and the result in every case was the same. The hardy warriors of the North gradually established their authority over the outlying provinces of Persia.

In the year of the Hejira 1222,* a short but bloody war took place betwixt the Persians and the Affghans. It arose with reference to the frontier fortress of Ghorian in the territory of Herat. When the Affghan prince Feerooz Meerza had been a suppliant refugee in Persia, the Shah, as has been written, had instructed the governor of Khorassan to support his cause. Ghorian was taken, and it remained in the hands of the Persians. The deputy-governor, however, agreed to give it over to the Affghans, and Prince Feerooz, with an utter forget-

---

* A.D. 1805.

fulness of his obligations to the Shah, sent troops to attack Ghorian, where a battle was fought, which ended in the signal defeat of the Affghans, whose commander was slain in the golden howdah from which he viewed the battle. The governor of Khorassan now advanced to the gates of Herat, and Prince Feerooz was forced to pay a sum of money for tribute of the last two years, and to agree to pay such tribute in future with regularity. He further gave his son as a hostage for his faith, and delivered up to the Persians the deputy-governor of Ghorian.

About this time the Governor-General of the Caucasus who had been appointed to succeed the ill-fated Seeseeanoff, sent an envoy to the Persian court, to propose that peace should be concluded on the basis that Karabagh, Sheervan, and Sheki, should be made over to the Czar. He received a reply * to the effect that no peace could be concluded which should not provide for the restoration to the Shah of all the provinces that had formerly been the property of Persia.

The Shah of Persia had demanded the assistance of the British Government of India in the war which he was prosecuting with his Northern neighbour; but in the earlier stage of that war, England was in alliance with Russia, and therefore did not afford the aid which Persia required. In the meantime the geographical position of Persia made the alliance of the king of that country an object of importance to the enemies of England. From two very different Powers the Shah nearly at the same time received an ostentatious embassy. The first was from the Talpoors of Sindh, who already had become

---

* *Persian History.*

alarmed at the encroaching policy of the Britsh Government in the East, and who claimed the Shah's alliance
and protection against the English.   The other embassy
was from the Emperor Napoleon.   General Gardanne
arrived at Tehran, accompanied by seventy officers.   He
brought with him the treaty with Persia that had been
ratified by the Emperor, and the Shah saw no other
means of being able to recover his lost provinces than by
entering into an alliance offensive and defensive with
France.   The officers of General Gardanne were accordingly employed to drill the Persian soldiers upon the
model of European infantry and artillerymen.   It was
the hope of the Shah, in which he was encouraged by
the French ambassador, that in any treaty of peace
which   might   be   made   between   Napoleon   and   the
Emperor   of   Russia,   it   would   be   stipulated   that   the
latter should restore to Persia the provinces of Georgia
and Karabagh.   An envoy from the Governor-General
of the Caucasus was sent to Tehran with proposals
for peace, and the opinion of General Gardanne was
consulted as to the answer that should be sent to the
Russian Governor.   The Shah would not, by ceding his
provinces, forego the hope of recovering them by an
European treaty; but General Gardanne used his influence to prevent both sides from engaging in further
hostile operations in the meantime.   He assured the
Russian authorities, that should they abstain from advancing towards the Persian frontier, no move would be
made by the Shah; and on the other hand, he engaged
to the Persian monarch that he should suffer no loss
from his temporary inaction.   Such was the state of
things when the news reached Tehran that a treaty of

peace had been concluded between the Emperors at
Tilsit, in which no provision whatsoever was made for
the cession to the Shah of the provinces of Georgia and
Karabagh.

But though the most pressing demand of Persia was
thus set aside by France, the Emperor Napoleon had
still an object in securing the alliance of the Persian
Government. In case of his thinking fit to attempt the
invasion of India, it must be by way of Persia that such
invasion would have to be effected; and in sight of the
possibility of such an attempt being made, the Indian
Government determined to put forth all its influence to
dislodge the embassy of France from the Shah's court.
General Malcolm was despatched to the Persian Gulf in
the year 1808; but on being requested to address himself
to the prince-governor of Fars, and not to advance nearer
to the capital, he at once returned to India to receive
instructions from the Governor-General as to the measures
which it would be necessary to adopt for the purpose of
compelling the Persian Government to adhere to its
treaty engagements. At the same time that General
Malcolm had been sent to Persia from the Government
of India, an ambassador had been despatched to that
country direct from the court of St. James's; and whilst
preparations were in train for the occupation of the
island of Karrack, in the Persian Gulf, by an English
force from India, the ambassador of England proceeded
to Bushire, and thence to the Persian capital, where he
drew up a treaty with the Shah's Government, by which
Persia renounced her alliance with France. Indeed, Sir
Harford Jones stipulated that General Gardanne should
receive his passports as the condition upon which alone

he would consent to advance to Tehran. In the Anglo-Persian treaty it was agreed that Great Britain should pay an annual subsidy to the Shah for the expenses of the war he was waging with Russia, whilst England should be at war with that Power. This subsidy was to be furnished from the Indian treasury, and the Governor-General of India resolved to send an envoy under his own immediate orders, who might make the necessary disbursements to the Persian Government. At this time there existed a regrettable jealousy and want of common action between the embassy sent to Persia from England and the British authorities in India. Sir Harford Jones was accused of having used to the Persians language calculated to lower in their estimation the dignity of the Government of India; and, in return, that Government did its best to lower the estimation in which the King's ambassador was held at the Persian court, by dishonouring the bills which he drew on Calcutta.

General Malcolm, who had been disappointed at the setting aside of his scheme for seizing the island of Karrack, was equally ready to return to Persia in a more peaceful guise.* At the head of a mission which, we are told, the Governor-General of India readily agreed to render more imposing than the embassy that, under the conduct of Sir Harford Jones, represented the crown of England, General Malcolm landed once more at Bushire,† from which point he made a progress through the country such as was calculated to leave a permanent impression on the minds of the people of the wealth and liberality of the rulers of India. The exact relation in which the Anglo-Indian possessions stood with respect to the British

---

* *The Life of Sir John Malcolm,* by J. W. KAYE.   † A.D. 1810.

crown was not easily understood by the Persian Government. They saw the two envoys striving against each other for influence, as if, so far from belonging to the same country, they had been the representatives of two hostile Governments; but a solution of this puzzling enigma, which seemed eminently satisfactory, soon suggested itself to the Persian mind. General Malcolm was the more open-handed of the two envoys, and as he was known to be the representative of the Government of a commercial company, they inferred that he of course received a per-centage upon all the money which he spent during his mission, and that therefore it was for his own interest that he should disburse as much money as he might find the Persians willing to accept.

In addition to the direct objects of this mission from India, there were other ends which it was meant to secure. The want of accurate information relative to the countries beyond India on the North-west had long been severely felt by the Government of that country; and it was the more necessary to obtain this information at a time when the invasion of India by an European enemy was supposed to be a probable event. Several enterprising young officers were for this purpose attached to the staff of General Malcolm; and to the exertions of Pottinger, Christie, Macdonald-Kinneir, Monteith, and others of their number, Europe was indebted for the greater part of the reliable statistics regarding the countries situated between the Black Sea and the Indus which were known for the next quarter of a century.

In the meantime hostile operations between Persia and Russia had been resumed. The general commanding-in-chief the army of the Caucasus had advanced to

Erivan, to which city he laid siege, while he sent forward
a separate force to occupy the crown-prince of Persia in
the direction of Khoi. The prince, on his part, sent
reinforcements to Erivan, and prepared to advance to
the Araxes. He encountered a Russian force at Nakhtchivan, which, being unable to make any sufficient impression upon his battalions, retreated towards Mount
Ararat and pressed the siege of Erivan. The fidelity of
the governor of that place was tried by the agents of
Russia, but as he still held out, orders were given for a
night assault on the city. Of this intention the Persians
received timely warning, and their soldiers were instructed
to maintain a dead silence until the moment when the
Muscovite troops should attempt to scale the battlements
of the fortress. At that moment a simultaneous discharge from the muskets and matchlocks of the Persian
infantry threw the ranks of the assailants into confusion,
and, after having undergone a heavy loss, the Russian
general withdrew his forces to their camp. After this
he only remained before the city sufficiently long to
admit of preparations being made for his retreat; when
he marched upon Genja, being annoyed by the way
by the light troops of the Persians who followed in his
wake.

The Persian king and the crown-prince were most
anxious to obtain the aid of General Malcolm and of his
officers in the prosecution of this war. His advice to
them was to avoid attacking the Russians in line or in
their strong posts, but to keep their newly-raised infantry and ill-equipped artillery in reserve; and to limit
the employment of these to the defence of forts and
difficult passes, whilst they pushed forward every horse-

man the country could furnish to distress and harass the enemy. General Malcolm would not consent to accompany the Persian army into the field, unless he should be instructed to do so by the English ambassador : but this was a step which was not, under the circumstances, thought by his Excellency to be advisable. Two English officers were, however, placed at the crown-prince's disposal; and General Malcolm returned towards India, after having received the Order of the Lion and Sun, which was instituted in his honour.

In return for the embassy from King George III. the Shah sent Haji Meerza Abul Hassan Khan, the nephew of the late prime minister, on a mission to London, with the especial object of clearly ascertaining who was to pay the subsidy which he was entitled by treaty to receive from England.*

About this time the Wahabi Arabs attacked the island of Bahrein, on the Arabian coast of the Persian Gulf— an island to the sovereignty over which Persia advanced pretensions.† The Imam of Muscat informed the prince-governor of Fars of his inability to make head against the Wahabis; and Sadek Khan, who commanded in Fars, was instructed to undertake an expedition for the purpose of punishing them : a service which he accomplished in a manner which satisfied the Persian Government, but which does not seem to have been followed by any permanent results.

In the meantime the Georgian war continued to rage. The 'Shah's eldest son was instructed to take 20,000

* It is this Persian envoy whose mission has been so amusingly described in *Hajee Baba in England.*
† *See* PALGRAVE'S *Arabia.*

men with him, and to endeavour to penetrate to Tiflis. He had to content himself, however, with ravaging the country up to the Gokcheh Lake, whence he returned to Erivan. The crown-prince also advanced to the neighbourhood of Genja, which place the Armenians resident in it promised to deliver up to him. Of this plot the Russian commander obtained intelligence, and he put the Armenians in chains, on which the prince marched back in the direction of Tabreez. The Russian commander-in-chief afterwards advanced to a spot called Haji-Kara, where an engagement took place between his forces and those of the Persian prince. On another occasion a Russian battalion was, we are told, captured, and was sent with its colours to Tehran.

The year 1812 was marked in the annals of Persia by a signal disaster which occurred to the army of the crown-prince. Of the events of the short campaign waged in the autumn of this year, we possess a vivid account from the pen of one who took part in them.* Sir Gore Ouseley, who was now the English ambassador at the court of Pérsia, had joined the prince's camp near the Araxes, in the hope of being able to act as mediator between his Royal Highness and the Russian commissioner. A Russian general-officer was sent to the Persian camp to propose the appointment of deputies on both sides, who should meet on the banks of the Araxes. This arrangement was agreed to, but it failed to produce any satisfactory results. The Russian deputies would cede nothing, and the Persians would not accept an arrangement based on the actual state of possession of

* Dr. CORMICK. *See* Appendix to *Life of Sir John Malcolm*, by J. W. KAYE. Vol. ii.

territory. In the meanwhile a report had reached Tabreez to the effect that a peace had been brought about between England and Russia, and, as this report was in some degree confirmed by a letter from a Russian officer in the Caspian, Sir Gore Ouseley ordered the English officers with the Shah's army not to take any further part in the military operations against Russia. He further informed the Russian commissioner of his having issued this instruction. On the entreaty, however, of the crown-prince and his ministers, the English ambassador permitted two of the British officers, with thirteen sergeants, to remain in the Persian camp. These officers received no specific orders as to how they were to conduct themselves, but they thought that they were bound in honour not to refuse to fight for the prince under whom they were serving. The Persian army marched to the Araxes, to a place called Ooslandooz, where they encamped with their front to the river, having a small tributary stream on their right. There they remained for ten days in a state of undisturbed quietness, and of blind, incautious security. But from this dream they were rudely aroused on the forenoon of the 31st of October, by a sudden attack of the Russians.* No one in the Persian camp had in the slightest degree anticipated their approach, and before the troops could be drawn up to oppose them they had advanced through a clear, open plain to within a few hundred yards of the Persians, and were in possession of a little hill in their rear, which commanded every part of their camp. The prince had intended to go out hunting, and as the

---

* The Russian force consisted of 2,300 men, with six pieces of artillery. The Persians were very much more numerous.

English officer in command of the Persian artillery * had
been ordered to attend him, the guns narrowly escaped
from falling into the hands of the enemy. The other
English officer † had drawn up his infantry, as well as
hurry and confusion would admit of, between the Persian
camp and the hill of which the Russians had gained possession, being determined there to oppose their entrance
into the camp. They opened fire upon him from above
with one gun, and three hundred men advanced upon
him in skirmishing order. Then followed a scene
illustrative of the childishness of the Oriental character.
Whilst the English officer was preparing to charge the
enemy, an order reached him from the prince to retreat
across the small stream to the right of the camp; and
when Captain Christie sent a sergeant to represent the
impropriety of retiring, and the necessity of annihilating
the small number of men opposed to him, the prince completely lost his temper, abused the nation of the officer
who was exposing his life in his service, himself galloped
to the soldiers, and, seizing their colours, ordered them to
run away. Two companies remained with Captain Christie, and with these he followed the retreating troops, carrying with him some wounded officers. The artillery also
was conveyed across the stream, where it was rendered
ineffective from the want of ammunition. The Persian
camp, and everything it contained, fell a prey to the
Russians, and the crown-prince collected his scattered
troops, and took up a position within shot of the enemy,
and divided from him by the above-mentioned stream
and by six hundred yards of jungle. Lieutenant Lindsay, at the head of twenty of his men and one of the

---

* Lieutenant Lindsay.　　　　　† Captain Christie.

prince's gholams, made a gallant dash into the camp, and each man succeeded in carrying off six rounds of ammunition. In the new position the Persian right was under a hill, which it was intended to strengthen, a task which was the more easy as there already existed a ditch and several holes round it. Their front faced their former camp, and their left extended along the little stream. With two companies Captain Christie drove the Russians out of the intervening jungle, and Lieutenant Lindsay, with two guns, silenced an equal number of Russian field-pieces which were opposed to him. Such was the state of things when darkness came on. It was represented to the crown-prince by the English officers, that as the ammunition of the infantry was nearly exhausted, he had not the means of renewing the fight, and that, as the Russians would certainly attack him if he should remain where he was, it was absolutely necessary that he should retreat. His Royal Highness, however, would not act upon the suggestion thus proffered to him, and passed the night in asking the advice of every one about him. He consulted all within his reach, but he would be guided by no one, and as he himself, his minister, his meerzas, and his secretaries, all issued orders, his camp presented a picture of inconceivable confusion. Soldiers, gunners, horsemen, mules, horses, and camels, crowded the little hill within the ditch, round which there was only room for two hundred men, and which was unfortunately nearly full of houses with thatched roofs. The prince finally ordered that two guns should be taken to the top of this hillock, from which it was impossible that they could be used with any advantage. Even the ordinary precaution of posting

pickets in the direction of the enemy was neglected by
the infatuated Persian commander, and it was only at
half-past four o'clock on the morning of the 1st of
November, that Captain Christie received permission to
take his men to any position he might think proper,
whilst Lieutenant Lindsay was peremptorily ordered to
bring his guns to the base of the hill-fort, into the ditch
and the holes round which eleven of thirteen guns soon
fell.   At that very hour the Russian troops were in the
Persian camp, and, meeting with no resistance, they
carried all before them.   The Persians on the hill, in
their senseless confusion, fired upon their comrades
below, and the returning fire from the Russian artillery
kindled the thatched roofs of the fort.   The flames at once
spread, and three hundred men were consumed by fire.
Captain Christie was shot through the neck, and as he was
seated helpless on the ground, we are told, the Russian
commander * ordered two men to advance and put him to
death.   The prince's army was totally annihilated, all his
guns were lost, and he himself retreated to Tabreez.

After this defeat a year elapsed, and the opposing
forces still remained in arms, ready to resume hostile
operations.   We may well believe that at that memor-
able epoch Russia had too much to attend to in Europe
to admit of her following up adequately the advantage
she had gained in her struggle with Persia.   Nevertheless, tried as she was by the invasion of Napoleon, she
found means to prosecute her advance along the shore
of the Caspian.   Lankoran † was now the object of her

---

* Kotlareffsky.

† Lankoran is a flourishing town lying on the coast between Bakoo
and the frontier of Persia. *Lankoran* means in the Persian tongue *the
place of anchorage.*

attack, and of that town she gained possession after an obstinate struggle, in which the Persians state their own loss to have been five thousand men.* On the other hand, the Russian arms sustained a check on the Araxes, and the Shah advanced once more to Oojan, where he formed a camp for the purpose of attempting to drive the Russians backwards. But news of a rise of the Turkomans induced his majesty to adopt more peaceful counsels, and not to gratify the crown-prince in his wish to be allowed an opportunity of wiping off the disgrace of the preceding year. By the request of the Russian Governor-General of Georgia, Sir Gore Ouseley used his good offices with the Persian Government for bringing about a peace, and accordingly commissioners were sent for that purpose to a place called Gulistan, in the province of Karabagh. On the 12th of October, 1813, a treaty of peace was there concluded between General Rtischeff and Abbass Meerza, by which Persia ceded to Russia the provinces of Georgia, Derbend, Bakoo, Sheervan, Sheki, Genja, Karabagh, Moghan, and part of Taleesh,† and by which she agreed thenceforth to maintain no navy in the Caspian Sea, while Russia, on her part, became bound to aid the crown-prince at the proper time in securing his accession to the Persian throne.

---

* Lankoran was taken by assault by General Kotlareffsky, on January 1 (Russian) 1813.

† Persia further by this treaty ceded whatever rights she may have possessed over Mingrelia and other parts of the Caucasus.

It has been said that the Shah was led to conclude a
peace with Russia as news had reached him that his
dominions were threatened from another quarter.
Indeed, such was the condition of Central and Western
Asia at this time that the King of Persia was forced to
maintain an effective army ready to operate at an hour's
warning upon any point of his extensive frontiers. The
Shah had four grown-up and warlike sons upon whose
aid he chiefly relied for the guardianship of the different
provinces of his empire. Of these four the eldest was
Mahomed Ali Meerza, to whom was assigned the government of Kermanshah and the defence of the Southern
portion of the Turko-Persian frontier. This prince had
been set aside in favour of his next brother, Abbass
Meerza, who had been selected to be *Veli Ahed,* or heir-

apparent, to the Persian throne. The law of succession to the crown of Persia is not the same as that which regulates the inheritance of the royal and princely families of Turkey and Egypt. Of them the eldest male is chosen to be the reigning prince, but in Persia the selection of the heir-apparent depends upon the free-will of the sovereign on the throne. Mahomed Ali Meerza, however, by no means acquiesced in the choice which his father had made. On one occasion the Shah ordered that at the public reception which he was to hold on the following day no one of the princes excepting Abbass Meerza was to appear before him wearing a sword. The morrow came, and with it came the princes to attend upon their sovereign. All, save Mahomed Ali Meerza, appeared unarmed, but that Shahzadeh wore his sword as usual, and when he was asked by the Shah why he had not obeyed his command he replied that there was only one way of making him obey it, and that way was to take his sword from him by force. He further announced his readiness to fight with his brother Abbass then and there, and to abide by the event of the duel. After so open a display of discontent on the part of one who had a better right than Abbass Meerza to be selected to be the Shah's heir, it seems strange that Mahomed Ali Meerza should have been employed at the head of an armed force in the field; but while Abbass Meerza was being driven before the Russians his elder brother was once more overrunning the frontier province of Turkey; humbling the Pasha of Baghdad, and reëstablishing the governor of Shehr-i-zoor in his office.

The second of the Shah's four elder sons was, as has been said, Abbass Meerza, the crown-prince, who was entrusted with the government of Azerbaeejan, the richest province of Persia, and with the defence of the Russo-Persian, and of the northern part of the Turko-Persian, frontier.   Azerbaeejan is the most important province of Persia.   Bounded as it is on one side by Turkey and on another by Russia, its position admirably fits it for commercial intercourse with foreign nations, and hence Tabreez is the principal emporium of Persian trade.   The climate of Azerbaeejan is healthy and bracing, its soil is fertile, and its inhabitants are hardy, active, and industrious.   From this province the Persian army is supplied with the best recruits it receives.   It is not easy to state with accuracy what may be the numbers of the population of the province, as no census of the people has ever been taken ; but, according to the opinion of intelligent Persians, * Tabreez contains 200,000 souls, while Uroomeeah, Khoi, Maragha, Ahar, and Ardebeel, each claim from 20,000 inhabitants and upwards.   The principal productions of Azerbaeejan are wheat, barley, rice, fruits, butter, wax, tobacco, wool, cotton and gums.   Iron and copper abound in the hills of Karadagh, and coal is found in the vicinity of Tabreez.   Water is, however, so scarce that in summer the owner of a garden does not grudge to pay a sum equal to twelve pounds sterling for the use of a stream for twenty-four hours.   The suburbs of Tabreez are very extensive, occupying a space of about sixteen miles in circumference.   The city numbers thirty-two caravan-serais, occupied by merchants, containing more than a thousand counting-houses, and a proportionate number

---

* See Report on the trade of Azerbaeejan, by Mr. W. DICKSON, for 1859.

of store-rooms. Besides these there are thirty-seven caravanserais for the special accommodation of muleteers and their animals.

To the third of the Shah's elder sons, Hassan Ali Meerza, was assigned the third of the four most important provinces of Persia, Sheeraz; and to the fourth, Mahomed Veli Meerza, was given the almost equally important government of Khorassan. It was in that quarter that the next danger threatened the safety of the kingdom. The Turkomans of the neighbourhood of Astrabad were roused to war by a man called Haji Yoosuf, a native of Central Asia, who had been outlawed by the King of Bedekhshan. These marauders, however, in a fight which ensued with the Shah's forces, were discouraged by the loss of their leader; and as they could not restore him to life, they thought that the next best thing to do was to cut off his head, in order to secure to themselves the reward which had been offered for it by the King of Bedekhshan. A more serious rebellion, which occurred at the same time, was that of the chiefs of Khorassan, who took the opportunity of Abbass Meerza's defeat to rise against Prince Mahomed Veli. They possessed themselves of Meshed, and whilst they continued to act in concert the prince was unable to oppose any obstacle to their proceedings; but the son of the deceased Syed Mehdi opportunely espoused the cause of the Shah, and by adroitly sowing the seeds of jealousy in the minds of the chiefs, he caused the temporary breaking up of this formidable combination. The chiefs dispersed to their respective strongholds, and the prince resumed the government of Meshed.

In the meantime the ruler of Bokhara, who had been

invited by the insurgents to undertake the invasion of
Persia, advanced towards Khorassan, where he found the
Shah's authority to be already reëstablished. He had
committed himself very openly to hostilities against the
King of Persia, but Oriental potentates, judging of the
conduct of others by what, under similar circumstances,
they would do themselves, look with a lenient eye upon
any infringement of neighbourly duties which may be
likely to be attended with successful results ; and Fetteh
Ali listened with complacency to the explanations offered
by the envoy of the Ameer of Bokhara, who declared that
his master had been beguiled by the protestations of the
rebellious chiefs of Khorassan. The Shah then sent a
force to Meshed, which defeated the troops of the
rebellious chiefs, who were thus forced to return to
their duty. About the same time the Turkomans
again rose in arms against the Shah, being headed by
Mahomed Zeman Khan, one of the chiefs of the upper
branch of the Kajar tribe. This leader and his son were
made prisoners, and the Turkoman tribes, as is their
custom after a defeat, retired into the dreary recesses
of the deserts of the Attreck. The Khan of Khiva, or
Khorassan, had advanced towards the Persian frontier
at Astrabad to the support of the chiefs of Khorassan,
but he unexpectedly found himself opposed by a Persian
force superior in strength to his own. Of this superiority
its commander was fully aware ; and when the terrified
Oozbeg potentate sent an envoy to deprecate the vengeance of the Kajar chief, the latter compelled the Oozbeg
diplomatist to pass the night in the undignified occupation of playing on the harp for the delectation of the
Persian generals. This insult naturally fired with wrath

the mind of the Khan of Kharesm, but his forces were insufficient to enable him to avenge it, and he sustained a severe defeat from the troops of the Shah.

But the results of the rebellion of the chiefs of Khorassan did not end with the discomfiture of their ally. The most powerful of these chiefs was Isaak Khan, Karai, a man who had raised himself from the lowest rank of life to the position which he now occupied. In his youth he had held the office of mace-bearer to the chief of Kara Tartar, and had been entrusted by his master with a considerable sum of money, to be expended in building a caravanserai, which he converted into a fort,* where he afforded shelter to all the discontented individuals of the tribe to which he was attached. In the troubled condition to which the country was reduced he had, by the exercise of courage and prudence, contrived to consolidate his rising power, and had in time attained to the foremost place amongst the proud leaders of the mailed horsemen of Khorassan. His possessions extended on the north of the gates of Meshed for the distance of a hundred miles, whilst they stretched as far to the south in the direction of Khaf. His revenue was considerable. His force included six thousand men. Whilst this extraordinary man never failed in his efforts to conciliate the good opinion of his superiors, he was dreaded and hated by his equals, and greatly beloved by his subjects, who, under his watchful sway, lived free from all oppression. This chief added to the character of a petty ruler that of a merchant prince, and under his sagacious sway, Turbat, his place of residence, rose from the condition of a village to that of a considerable city, where his

---

* *History of Persia*, by Sir J. MALCOLM.

hospitality was daily extended to several hundred guests. Isaak Khan had given in his adhesion to the sovereignty of Aga Mahomed, and had been treated with great confidence and distinction by that politic monarch, whose example in this respect was followed by Fetteh Ali Shah. But Isaak Khan seems to have viewed with personal dislike the Kajar Prince Mahomed Veli Meerza, who had been appointed to rule over Khorassan, and again and again he attempted to obtain from the Shah the recall of his son. These intrigues were not unknown to the Veli of Khorassan ; but Isaak Khan continued as usual to attend the levées of the prince, and to obey his authority. The Shahzadeh, fearing lest at last he should lose his government owing to the hostile influence of the Karai chief, determined upon taking a step at which the boldest might have hesitated. No man in Persia possessed more influence than Isaak Khan, and no man was so likely to be missed as he whose unbounded hospitality had been experienced by hundreds of thousands of the subjects of the Shah. But fear for his own position drove the prince to desperation, and on a certain day when the chiefs were assembled at his levée Isaak Khan and his son were successively seized and strangled in his presence. Such an act, as might have been predicted, called down on the prince a storm of indignation, which it was difficult to appease. The other chiefs, each fearing for himself, fled each to his stronghold, and the king was compelled by the general clamour to recall the governor of Khorassan. But it was said that in this act Mahomed Veli was only carrying out the policy prescribed to him by his father, who, like Tarquin, was of opinion that his son's course would be more unrestrained in a garden from which the tallest poppies should have been removed. Mahomed Veli survived the threats of vengeance which his act called forth, and fifty years later he descended to his grave mourned as the honoured elder of the Kajar race.

The government of Meshed was next conferred by the Shah upon another of his sons, Hassan Ali Meerza, a prince of a warlike disposition, and well calculated to reduce to submission the turbulent nobles of Khorassan. As they declined to appear at his court, he marched against them at the head of his troops, and he brought them one after another to acknowledge his authority. But one Hezareh * chief still held out in his stronghold of Mahmoodabad, and the prince, who was preparing to march upon Herat, determined to reduce this fortress by the way. As his soldiers defiled before its walls, a rash matchlockman fired a shot on the Persian troops, and this unfortunate measure determined their commander to adopt the severest measures against the Hezareh hold. It was assaulted in due form; one hundred and twenty of its defenders fell in the assault, and three hundred and fifty of their comrades were made prisoners. Their commander, however, escaped on horseback, although for twenty miles he was pursued by the prince in person. Disappointed in the hope of taking him, the Persian Shahzadeh turned his vengeance upon his prisoners, some of whom he caused to be nailed to the ground. The prince, it has been said, was at

---

* The Hazarah, a tribe and descendants of Moguls, and of Tshingis Khan. Most of them are totally destitute of beards. They are partly Sunnees and partly Sheahs. . . . They are cruel, treacherous, inhospitable, and vile robbers and murderers.—*Missionary Labours*, by the Rev. JOSEPH WOLFF.

12

this time proceeding to Herat. The governor of that city had some time previously invaded the district of Ghorian, and to resist this measure the governor of Khorassan was now in arms against Feerooz-ed-Deen Meerza, the prince of Herat. The fate of Mahmoodabad struck terror into the heart of Feerooz-ed-Deen, and he sent an envoy to the Persian prince, offering to give up Ghorian, and praying him to spare Herat. The prince accepted the fort of Ghorian, but continued his march towards Herat.

Probably no city in the world has so frequently witnessed the horrors of a siege as has Herat within the last hundred years. It lies in a valley surrounded by lofty mountains, and contiguous to the northern ridge which separates the territory of Herat from the country of Bactria or Bokhara. The valley extends for at least thirty miles from the east to west, and is about fifteen miles in breadth, being watered by a river which rises in the mountains, and runs through the centre of the vale. The valley is highly cultivated, its whole extent being covered with villages and gardens.* The city spreads over an area of four square miles, and is fortified by a lofty mud wall with towers, and a wet ditch; having on the northern side the citadel elevated above the wall. This is a small square castle, with towers at the angles built of burnt bricks, and encompassed by a wet ditch, over which is a drawbridge. Beyond this there is an outer wall with a dry ditch, and the city has two gates on the northern side, and one in each of the three other directions. From each gate a bazaar extends to the market-place, the principal one being vaulted in its whole length. In

---

* Narrative of a journey by Captain Christie.

market days these bazaars are so crowded as almost to be impassable ; on either side of them are spacious serais, where the merchants have their places of business. The city is abundantly supplied with water, each serai having its own cistern independently of those on either side of the bazaars. In the early part of the nineteenth century the city of Herat was believed to contain a hundred thousand inhabitants : Affghans, Moghuls, Hindoos, and Jews. It is the chief emporium of the trade between Hindostan, Kashmeer, Cabul, Candahar, Bokhara, Merve, Khorassan, Yezd, and Kerman. In addition to the advantages which it derives from this active trade, and the transit dues arising therefrom, Herat gains much wealth from the manufactures which are carried on by its citizens ; but after all it is to its situation as the key to Affghanistan that it owes its chief importance. Prince Hassan Ali Meerza advanced from Ghorian to Herat, and began to besiege the city in due form.* The watching of each of its gates was assigned to his different leaders, and Ismaïl Khan, his best general, began to work his way up to the city ditch by regular approaches. These preparations terrified Feerooz-ed-Deen into absolute sub-mission, and on paying a fine of fifty thousand tomans he was permitted to continue to be governor of the city on condition that the khotbeh, or public prayers for the king, should be read in the mosques for the Shah, and that the coinage should thenceforth be in his name.

After concluding this successful arrangement, Hassan Ali Meerza next turned his attention to the pursuit of the fugitive governor of Ghorian, who, with two other Khorassan chiefs, had found a place of refuge in the

---

* A.H. 1232 : A.D. 1817.

country of the tribe of Feerooz Koh.   One of these chiefs
was the mortal enemy of Ibraheem Khan, the head of a
branch of the powerful tribe of Hezareh ; and accordingly
Ibraheem, without waiting for the arrival of the prince's
army, determined to attack the tribe of Feerooz Koh. He
did so, and being defeated had to take refuge in the
camp of Ismaïl Khan, who had advanced in command of
the leading corps of the Persian army. The country
through which that army had now to make its way, is
described as presenting the greatest difficulties to the
progress of troops, and especially to that of artillery. For
eleven days, day after day, the prince had to lead his
men over rocky mountain gorges, and, in order to encourage them to exertion by his example, he marched
on foot, and lent his personal aid in dragging the guns
over some of the most inaccessible passes.   The Sirdar
Ismaïl Khan had in the meantime apparently reduced
the fugitive chiefs to the necessity of submitting at discretion to the authority of the prince.   They agreed to
surrender themselves after the delay of two days, if,
during that time, they should be unable to effect something for their own deliverance.   The delay which
they wished was granted to them, but their only
object in asking it was to give time to their Feerooz
Kohi allies to come up to their assistance.   At the
end of the forty-eight hours no signs of the coming of
the chiefs were discernible, and Ismaïl Khan accordingly
ordered his brother to advance to the destruction of the
pent-up mountaineers.   This officer succeeded in mas-
tering the outlying troops opposed to him, and his soldiers
having effected this service, thought their work was over,
and committed the mistake which has so often proved

fatal to an Oriental army, that of prematurely plundering the camp of the enemy. Booneead Khan, one of the fugitive Khorassan chiefs, saw from his position on the mountain the mistake committed by the Persian troops, and without losing a moment, he led his remaining followers through a gorge into the camp where the plunderers were at work. The result was their complete overthrow, and Ismaïl Khan, who advanced to their support, was unable to resist the impetuosity of the triumphant troops from the mountain. His followers fell back in disorder, but their gallant chief would have preferred death to the dishonour of defeat. He threw his sheep-skin hat to the ground to show those around him that he was determined to die on the spot; but this sign of resolution was in-sufficient to turn the tide of victory, and Ismaïl was forced to mount a horse and to follow his men, in the hope of being able to rally them. The news of his defeat was as a thunderbolt to the prince, but the latter resolved to present a bold front to this crushing mis-fortune. He caused his artillery to fire a salute, for the purpose of inspiriting his men, and advanced to receive and protect the fugitive troops of the Sirdar. The general himself was that day nowhere to be found; but in the middle of the night, directed by the glare of the camp-fires, he found his way to the prince. It was then confessed between them that as they were so far from their base of operations, they did not possess the means of prosecuting the mountain war at that time, and accordingly their remaining troops retraced their steps to Meshed.

* * * * *

In the year 1814, Mr. Henry Ellis was sent from

England on a mission to Persia, for the purpose of
modifying the treaty then in force between those two
countries. Mr. Ellis accordingly, in conjunction with
Mr. Morier, then British Minister at the court of Persia,
agreed with the Shah's government as to the conclusion
of an amended treaty, by one of the articles of which it
was stipulated that the subsidy of 200,000*l.* a year that
England had engaged to furnish to Persia, in the event
of her being attacked by any European power which
might reject the mediatory offices of Great Britain, should
not be payable in the case of Persia beginning a war
upon either of her European neighbours, or invading the
territory of either of them in the first instance. But a
short period was destined to elapse ere the exact obligation of Great Britain in this matter was to form a subject
of prolonged and earnest discussion. In return for the
advantage conferred by this article, Persia, on her side,
engaged to obstruct the advance of the armies of any
European power seeking to pass through her territory for
the purpose of invading India. From this time forth the
Persian court was destined to become the place of residence of ministers plenipotentiary from the sovereigns of
England and of Russia ; and as Persia was thus assumed
to be a civilized power, she was obliged thenceforth to
conform herself in some respects to the practices of
civilized nations. The mere residence of foreign ministers at his capital of itself greatly tended to increase the
stability of the throne of the Shah, whilst it conferred a
greater dignity upon his court than it was in his power
to purchase with all his treasure. But a semi-barbarous
government was not all at once to be brought to observe
the customs that are the fruit of many centuries of civi-

lization; and on more than one occasion it has been found necessary to threaten the Ministers of the Shah with the withdrawal of all intercourse with them, in the event of the repetition of certain outbreaks of needless cruelty. On the whole, however, the intercourse between Persia and European nations has been highly beneficial to that country. From it she has learned some lessons as to the necessity of upright dealing and a faithful observance of treaty engagements. From it she has learned to respect the opinion of the civilized world, and to abstain from barbarous acts, for fear of calling down upon herself the ridicule and indignation of the European press; and from it has arisen and gradually extended a trade by which the subjects of the Shah are supplied to a greater extent each year with the produce of European enterprise and industry.

At the time of the conclusion of the treaty of Gulistan, the Persian Government had been led to indulge the hope that, through the good offices of England, the Czar might be induced to restore to the Shah some portion of the territory which was by that treaty ceded to Russia. The same ambassador who had previously visited England was accordingly sent to St. Petersburg with instructions to spare no effort to induce the Emperor's Government to accede to the wishes of the Shah. But in respect of winning back one square foot of territory from the iron grasp of Russia, the efforts of the Persian ambassador were utterly futile, and all the result they produced was an idle promise that General Alexander Yermeloff, the newly appointed Governor-General of Georgia and ambassador to Persia, would discuss the matter upon his arrival at Tehran. General Yermeloff in due time came

to Persia at the head of a splendid following, and being
the bearer of presents of a value calculated to impress
upon the mind of the Shah a just idea of the grandeur
of Russia.   At a court composed of persons at once
so vain and so venal as those who counselled the
Shah, there was every reason to suppose that General
Yermeloff would obtain a favourable answer to all his
demands.   Persia had felt the power of his master, and
she now saw his reflected magnificence.   She had lately
been opposed to him in arms; she was now invited to
become his ally.   The Czar's representative wished the
Shah to agree to join him in an offensive engagement
against the Sultan; but the King of Persia had already
felt what it was to have his interests overlooked by his
European allies at the time of concluding peace, and
he wisely declined to provoke the enmity of the Sublime
Porte.   General Yermeloff next demanded permission
for the passage of a Russian army through the provinces
of Astrabad and Khorassan, on its way to attack the
Khanate of Khiva; but he was told that as the treaty of
Gulistan contained no clause justifying such a demand,
the permission could not be granted.   The ambassador
then requested the sanction of the Shah for the residence
of a Russian commercial agent at Resht in Gilan; but
compliance with this request was categorically refused.
A similar answer was given to the Russian proposal to
supply officers for the purpose of disciplining the army of
the Shah.   On his side, General Yermeloff was equally
firm.   He would not consent to the restoration of a
single acre of the territory which had been won from
Persia by the force of his master's arms ; and thus the
business of his embassy was brought to a close equally

unsatisfactory to either party. But not the less hospitable
for this was the treatment which the Czar's representative experienced at the Persian court. The utmost
refinements of the ornate, complimentary style of Persian
composition were called into use for the purpose of
expressing the regard felt by his Kajar Majesty for his
Northern neighbour, and for the Lieutenant of the Caucasus ; and the presents made to the ambassador on his
departure were in keeping with those of which he had
been the bearer from the Czar.

Having granted an audience of leave to his powerful
visitor, the Shah was at liberty to turn his attention to
the punishment of those who had committed a serious
infringement of order which occurred in the province of
Yezd. That city stands in a plain, or broad valley,
which is continuous with that of Naeen, nearly equi-
distant from parallel ranges of mountains on the northern
and southern sides, and bounded by a sandy desert on
the western and eastern directions. On the southern
side the plain for some miles has been partially laid under
cultivation. The city is enclosed by a ditch and double
wall, with numerous detached towers around it,* all in
tolerable repair, and its circumference is about two and
a half miles, the area within being crowded with houses
and gardens. At the eastern side, within the walls,
stands the citadel, an irregular square of about four
hundred paces in diameter, possessing a ditch, a double
wall and towers, and devoted to the purpose of sheltering
the soldiers of the garrison. The city is surrounded by
numerous habitations and gardens, the circumference of
which may be about five miles. The bazaars of Yezd

* " *Notes on the Cities of Southern Persia,*" by K. E. ABBOTT.

contain about a thousand shops, and are arched over in
the usual Persian style. The town possesses thirty-four
caravanserais, in fourteen of which the merchants and
traders transact their affairs. The only public building
deserving of notice which this city contains is the Mesjid-
i-Juma, a mosque, the construction of which is attributed
to Ameer Chakmäk, an officer in the army of Timur.
Its lofty façade and minarets, though they are now in a
ruinous state, form an imposing object, and have been
highly ornamented. There are also in the city about
thirty other mosques and eleven medressehs, or colleges,
for students of divinity; Yezd is denominated in official
papers the *Dar-el Ibádeh,* or seat of devotion. The city
and the surrounding suburbs are divided into twenty-
four wards, and owing to the great depth at which the
water that supplies the town is found, the houses are
constructed very far below the level of the streets, sometimes being sunk as much as twenty or twenty-five feet.
The population has been estimated* as being about forty
thousand souls, forming for the most part an industrious
body; many persons being engaged in the manufacture
of silks, cotton, &c., whilst others devote their time to
various branches of trade. In addition to the Mahomedan population of Yezd, that city contains some Hindoo
merchants, some Jews, and a considerable number of
Guebres; but the people of the last-mentioned sect,
owing to the oppression from which they have suffered,
are year by year withdrawing themselves, as they find
opportunities, from the rule of the Shah, and hastening
to join their more prosperous co-religionists in India.
The climate of Yezd is considered to be very salubrious,

---

* By Mr. Abbott.

and is extremely dry; occasionally, however, an epidemic makes its appearance, and at one blow does the work which in other places is scattered over years. In 1846 the cholera was fatal to between seven and eight thousand of the inhabitants. This city surrendered to the Affghans, who, on entering it, set on foot a general massacre of the people; the bodies of the victims were interred in long lines of vaults on the margin of the ditch, and after the lapse of a hundred and twenty years, these vaults were opened, and it was observed by an English traveller* that the clothes in which the bodies had been buried still clung undecayed round the skeletons, affording a proof of the extreme dryness of the climate and the soil. The districts of Yezd are small and thinly populated, owing to the encroachments of the desert and the scarcity of water. The soil of the finest district of the province—that of Ardekan—is said to yield from thirty to sixtyfold of grain in return for high cultivation. Wheat and barley are the staple crops; and fruits of numerous descriptions, including nectarines, grapes and cherries, dates, melons and pomegranates of exquisite quality, are produced in the gardens. The plain of Bafk possesses large groves of palm-trees. Here, as in every part of Persia, the mineral productions of the country have excited little or no attention. The only mine now worked is one of lead at Zerekan, the daily produce of which is said to amount to between seven and thirteen hundred pounds' weight, the smallest of which measures is valued at Yezd at about ten tomans, or rather less than five pounds sterling. The deserts surrounding Yezd afford shelter and subsistence to wild

* Mr. K. E. ABBOTT.

boars, antelopes and hares, and to jackals, wolves and foxes, wild sheep, wild goats and wild asses; and in the hills are found the three kinds of partridge known in Persia—the royal partridge, the ordinary bird of that name, and the smaller kind, called teehoo. The hump-backed oxen of the country, which are small, hand-some, and high-bred, are used as beasts of burden, and are guided by a halter passed through their nostrils.

This province from its situation is particularly exposed to danger and annoyance from the inroads of plundering Belooches and Bakhtiaris. The former travel immense distances across the desert, being carried by small, swift camels, on each of which two riders sit, placed back to back on a double saddle. The camels move either at an easy but rapid amble or at a trot, which pace they keep up for a surprising length of time, and if they obtain a fair start, they are not easily over-taken by horsemen. When their riders are obliged to halt and fight, they draw up the camels in the form of a ring or of a square, and, making them lie down, endeavour to keep off their enemies from passing this living rampart. A prolonged defence under these circum-stances causes but little embarrassment to the Belooches, as they have all they require with them, and can, in case of necessity, provide themselves at once with food and water by slaughtering one of their camels. They are a hardy race, and so destitute in many instances of worldly substance that they do not hesitate to under-take, for the sake of plunder, a journey of thirty or forty days across the sandy desert. They are reputed to be more ferocious and more cruel than the Bakhtiari, being addicted to the custom of killing those whom they have plundered; whereas the Bakhtiari rarely add murder to robbery, unless in the case of resistance being offered. The Belooches assault their victims with match-locks and swords, and they defend themselves with shields of asses' skin. I have given this minute descrip-tion of Yezd, partly because it may tend to afford the reader some idea of the conditions of life in Persia, where the state of things in one province more or less resembles that of another province; and partly because Yezd claims notice as being the last spot in Persia where the descendants of the fire-worshippers* who so long ruled the empire have found a resting-place, on the condition of cultivating the earth for their alien masters.

The number of the Guebres in and around Yezd is reduced to about eight hundred families. They possess two fire temples in the town of Yezd, and one in each of the eight villages occupied by them in its vicinity. These consist of arched apartments open to the weather, and paved with small stones. These are the houses of prayer, and in a dark room adjoining each is preserved the sacred fire buried beneath a heap of ashes on a raised piece of brickwork or on a regularly-constructed altar of stone. The Guebre priests are of two degrees—the *Moobid*, or chief priest, and the *Destear*, or inferior clergy. The Moobid, before going to meals, recites a prayer, when he places before him fire, holy water, and the *Hom*, a knotted plant found in the desert. To his care is confided the Zendavesta and the Dessateer, or book of prophecies; whilst the sacred

---

* In several parts of this work, the Guebres, or Parsis, are called fire-worshippers, because they are generally known to English readers by that name.

fire is watched over by attendants called Heerhed.
Four fasts in each month are ordained to be observed
by the Guebres, but at all other times they are at
liberty to eat flesh.   The flesh of all birds is lawful
food for them, excepting that of the cock.   That bird,
and the dog, are regarded by them as preventatives
against the approach of evil spirits, and on this account
the presence of a dog is generally secured at a Guebre
death-bed.   Like the Mahomedan, the Guebre is enjoined
to pray five times each day—at dawn, at sunrise, at noon,
near sunset, and after it; at which periods two orisons are
recited—the one a short, the other a lengthy prayer.
The Guebres of Persia turn to the sun during their
devotions, but they do not regard that luminary as a
deity.   They look upon it as an emblem of the Creator,
calling it the light of God.   They consider the four
elements as sacred and not to be defiled unnecessarily.
The Guebres of Yezd wear a sacred girdle, a thick
narrow ribbon, composed of seventy-two threads of the
wool of sheep or goat, which is bound on at the age of
fourteen, a ceremony which is celebrated with rejoicing.
The lower orders of this people, of the male sex, are
distinguished by their costume of dull yellow, a short
vest or petticoat, and a striped turban.   The Guebres
have two places of pilgrimage in the vicinity of Yezd—
Anarck, in Peeshkoh, and Zerjo, near Ayhda.   They
believe that at these places two daughters of Yezdigird,
the last of the Kayanian kings, were miraculously translated when pursued by their enemies—the rocks having
opened to receive them.   Sheep * and oxen are there
offered up in sacrifice.   It is touching to witness the

* *Notes* by Mr. K. E. ABBOTT.

reverence paid by the fire-worshippers, so-called, of Yezd to the memory of the last monarch of their ancient faith, and to that of his immediate descendants. They have adopted the date of the death of Yezdigird as an epoch from which to count their periods of time. They now, as did their ancestors of old, date the commencement of their solar year from the 21st of March, when the sun enters the sign of Aries. Their months are of thirty days, and the five extra days of each year are distinguished by each day having its distinct name. They have no division of time corresponding to a week. Five days of each month are sacred, and the months are for the most part called after the names of angels. The Guebres of our day do not bury their dead, but it has been observed that this custom would seem to have been departed from in ancient times in the case of their sovereigns, whose tombs, hewn in the rocks, are found at Nakhsh-i-Rustem and at Persepolis. The places at which the bodies of the dead are laid out to be decomposed by the action of the atmosphere are simply walled enclosures, without roof or covering, on the summit of mountains or rocks. The Guebres no longer make use amongst each other of the language handed down to them by their ancestors. Their children learn the Persian tongue alone, and a knowledge of the Zend is confined to the priesthood.

*　　*　　*　　*　　*

In the city of Yezd there dwelt, in the earlier part of the reign of Fetteh Ali Shah, the chief of a sect of Mahomedans who hold that the lawful succession to the Imam Jaffer belonged to his son Ismaïl, and who are therefore denominated Ismaïlites. These sectaries were

devoted to their chief, who was on this account a man of
great influence throughout Persia.   Some of his servants
having quarrelled with some shopkeepers of the city, the
latter pursued them to their master's house.   The affray
soon increased in dimensions, and the shopkeepers, being
headed by one Moolla Hassan, succeeded in overpower-
ing the Ismaïlites, whose chief they put to death.   The
news of this event was received with the greatest concern
by the Shah, who dreaded lest he should be held responsible by the dangerous sect of Ismaïlites for the death of
their sacred chief.   Accordingly the ringleader of the
disturbance was sent for to Tehran, and was flogged and
otherwise severely punished in the Shah's presence.
The actual perpetrators of the assassination of Shah
Halilullah, who boasted descent from him from whom
the assassins are named, had met their death by the
hands of his followers, and Fetteh Ali adopted his son
Aga Khan, Mahalati, and added a considerable property
to the estates which the boy had inherited from his
father.

In the same year* the port of Mahooya on the coast
of the Persian Gulf was added to the dominions of the
Shah, having been taken by Mahomed Zeki Khan.

In the earlier portion of the following year the attention of the Shah's government was again engrossed by
the appearance of a most formidable combination of
the powers of Herat, Central Asia, and Khorassan.
Feerooz-ed-Deen Meerza, the Prince of Herat, had no
sooner agreed to hold his principality under the King
of Persia than he began to shrink from the consequences of having offended his brother, the Shah of

* A.H. 1232.

Cabul. He accordingly sent to demand from him the assistance of a military force, for the purpose of enabling him to withstand the pretensions of the governor of Khorassan. This demand on his part was met at Cabul, with instant acquiescence. That kingdom was then nominally ruled over by Mahmood Shah, but virtually by his able Vizeer, Fetteh Khan, Barukzye, who subsequently became more widely known from his having paved the way to the rise to power of his celebrated brother, Dost Mahomed Khan. Fetteh Khan had placed most of his numerous brothers at the head of the different provinces of Affghanistan, and he was glad of an opportunity of displacing the Sedozye ruler of Herat. Accordingly he marched to that stronghold with a military force, with which he encamped before the walls of the city, but he carefully declined to enter Herat until he had made himself sure of the coöperation of its leading men in the scheme which he desired to carry out. Having prepared his way, he entered the city for the ostensible purpose of bidding adieu to Feerooz-ed-Deen Meerza before setting out for Ghorian ; and he made prisoners of the prince and his family, sent them under an escort to Cabul, and put the Vizeer of Herat to death. He then despatched his brother Keendil, commonly called Kohendil, Khan, with orders to possess himself of the fortress of Ghorian, and he wrote to each of the chiefs of Khorassan, inviting him to join in a combination for throwing off the supremacy of the Shah of Persia in Herat, Ghorian, and the dependencies of Meshed. He further engaged in his interests the Khan of Khiva, and the chiefs of the two powerful tribes of Feerooz Kohi and Hezareh, the last of whom, Ibraheem

Khan, had lately been the ally of the governor of
Meshed. Amongst the Khorassan chiefs who joined his
standard was the surviving son of Isaak Khan, Karai.

The governor of Meshed lost no time in making
the Shah's ministers aware of the extent of the danger
which threatened the Persian power in the East, and
in their turn the Shah's ministers lost no time in carrying into effect such measures as seemed to them to be
best fitted for meeting the emergency. Meerza Abdul
Wahab Khan, the Moëtemed-ed-Dowleh, was in the first
place sent to Khorassan with instructions to spare no
effort to win back to the interests of the Shah some
amongst the warlike chieftains of that country. In the
next place, such troops as were at hand and could be
spared were pushed forward to Meshed, and the Shah
prepared to follow them in person after the celebration of
the annual festival of the Nowrooz. At the same time the
king endeavoured to add security to the foreign relations
of his country by sending an ambassador to the Sublime
Porte, from whence the same envoy was to proceed to
the courts of Vienna and Paris, on his way to England,
which was his final destination. On the arrival at
Meshed of the reinforcements from Tehran, Prince
Hassan Ali Meerza found himself in a condition to take
the field at the head of a body of 10,000 men. He was,
however, at a loss as to the direction to which he ought
to turn his arms. The Khan of Khiva had advanced with
a powerful force to Serekhs, and the prince could not
but be certain that if he should lead his troops against
him, Fetteh Khan, who, with 40,000 men, was on the
border of Khorassan, would advance to the city of
Meshed. Under these circumstances, he determined to

attack the nearest enemy, and accordingly he marched towards Ghorian, and soon found himself in the presence of the army of Fetteh Khan, which was encamped at a place called Kohseveeah, a short distance on the Herat side of the Persian frontier. The resolution displayed by the prince seems to have produced some effect on Fetteh Khan, who probably was not aware of the inferior number of the army of his adversary. He sent to inform his Highness that he had no wish to fight with him, and that upon the condition that Ghorian should be left in the possession of the Shah of Cabul, and that his two allies, Mahomed Khan Karai, and Ibraheem Khan, should be secured in their respective rights over Turbat and Bakhers, he would engage not to undertake any hostilities against the King of Persia. To this overture the governor of Meshed returned a taunting reply, and both sides thereupon prepared for battle. The advantage in point of numbers was greatly in favour of the Affghans, but the Persian troops were more accustomed to unity of action than were the motley elements of which the army of Fetteh Khan was composed. Nevertheless, the Persian soldiers could scarcely bear up against the weight of numbers, and the Semnan regiment was already taking to flight, when its colonel, Zulfikhar Khan, dismounted from his charger, which he deliberately hamstrung, declaring to his clansmen that if they should abandon the field of battle they would leave their chief in the hands of the enemy. Fetteh Khan's immediate followers seem to have fought bravely; but he was unable to exercise authority over some of his allies, who stood aloof during the battle, in order that they might be the better able to plunder the Persian

13—2

camp so soon as the fighting should be over. A bullet, which struck Fetteh Khan in the mouth, decided the event of the day, and the field was left in the hands of the Persians.

One of the Khorassan chiefs, who had espoused the cause of the Affghans, was mistaken for the prince-governor of Khorassan by the Moëtemed-ed-Dowleh, one of the ministers of the Shah, who thus fell into his power. Such an event might seem at first sight to be a success for Fetteh Khan; in reality it proved to be the reverse. Under no circumstances need one despair of being able to corrupt the fidelity of a Persian; and the Moëtemed-ed-Dowleh, who was aware of the character of those he had to deal with, took advantage of the opportunity of suggesting to his captor that he should go over to the side of the prince. His words were not wasted on the rebellious chief, who authorized him to make terms for his return to duty. The governor of Khorassan accordingly agreed to name the chief to a subordinate government under himself, and the Shah's minister was sent with all honour to the Persian camp, while his late captor made haste to join in the spoiling of the now fugitive Affghans. The King of Persia received the news of this decisive battle when he was on his way from Tehran to Meshed, and he followed up his advantage by besieging and taking the fort of Bem, whose governor had rebelled. Here an ambassador met him from Mahmood Shah of Cabul, disavowing the proceedings of his Vizeer, Fetteh Khan, and deprecating the anger of Fetteh Ali Shah. The king, in reply, required that Fetteh Khan should be made over to him in chains, or that he should be blinded by Mahmood, failing which concession he threatened to invade Affghanistan. In the meantime a force was sent to encounter the Khan of Khiva. That potentate did not wait to receive it, but retreated to the regions whence he had come. The condition imposed by the King of Persia was at once accepted by the Shah of Cabul, and the unfortunate Fetteh Khan was blinded and afterwards barbarously murdered. But his death was speedily avenged by his brother, Dost Mahomed ; and the next envoy from Affghanistan to Persia was sent by Kamran Meerza to implore the protection of the king, and to announce that, save the fortresses of Herat and Candahar, nothing of Affghanistan remained to him or to his father, Mahmood Shah.

In the year of the Hegira 1236,* hostilities broke out at the extremity of Persia most distant from the scene of the military operations in which the Shah's army had last taken part. A dispute arose between the frontier Persian and Turkish authorities—between the Prince-Governor of Azerbaeejan and the Seraskier of Erzeroum— on account of two wandering tribes claimed by the former as Persian subjects, and to which the latter afforded his protection. The Seraskier was recalled, but his successor showed himself to be even more unfriendly towards the Persians, imprisoning an agent sent by the governor of Tabreez to remonstrate on the subject of some grievances. After this insult the Shah's Government became convinced that friendly relations were no longer possible between the frontier authorities, and Abbass Meerza was accordingly instructed to invade the Turkish dominions. His troops crossed the border, and possessed themselves

* A.D. 1821.

of the fortified places of Toprak-Killeh and Ak Serai. They were opposed by a force sent from Erzeroum; but this was insufficient to withstand them, and they overran the border districts, and took possession of Abshekr, Diadeen, Moollasgird, Bitlees, Moosh, Ikhlot, Adelace-jawas, and Khandoosh.

On the other hand the Turkish Government prepared to counterbalance these advantages by invading, from Baghdad, the frontier government of Shehr-i-zoor. The force sent by the Pasha for this purpose was opposed by the prince-governor of Kermanshah, who defeated the Ottoman army, and followed up his victory by advancing to the outskirts of Baghdad. The Pasha possessed no further means of stopping his progress, and when he had almost arrived at the gates of the City of the Caliphs, he was implored to spare the place which now lay at his mercy. This appeal to the moderation of a Persian general would probably have been of little avail, had not the prince found himself to be stricken with a mortal disease which would have prevented him from exercising a control over his army. He accordingly spared Baghdad, and prepared to return by the shortest route to Kermanshah. He had crossed the vast plain which lies between the Tigris and the mountains of Kurdistan; but when he had reached the middle of the imposing pass by which the upper country of Persia in that direction is approached, his ailments increased to such a degree as to prevent his further progress. A messenger was despatched to Baghdad, to summon to his assistance an European physician; but he was already beyond the aid of medical science, and as he felt himself to be dying, he was careful to send to their native mountains the Looristan and Bakhtiari chiefs in his camp, knowing that they would in all probability raise disturbances after his decease. At a lonely spot in the pass of Kerrind, marked by the remnant of an ancient arch, died the eldest son of Fetteh Ali Shah, at the early age of thirty-seven, and his removal from the scene probably saved his country, at a later period, from a renewal of the horrors of civil war, to which, in the preceding century, she had for so long a time been given over. When the news of this occurrence reached Tehran, it was, according to Persian custom, at first concealed from the king. Gradually his ministers and nobles assumed the garments of mourning, and it was not until after the lapse of a week that the news of his son's demise was revealed to the Shah from the lips of his youngest child.

In the meantime, the war continued to rage upon the frontier of Azerbaeejan. The Porte appointed a new Seraskier to Erzeroum, and under him were three Pashas, each of whom took the field at the head of a separate force. Of these, one undertook the siege of Toprak-Killeh, while the other two marched towards the Persian frontier, with the intention of invading Azerbaeejan. A Persian officer starting from Erivan encountered a Turkish force, which he defeated, taking its commander, and a thousand men, prisoners. These were sent to the Crown-Prince of Persia at Khoi, and as he was anxious for a termination of the hostilities that were being carried on, he despatched them all free from ransom to the Pasha of Erzeroum, with an expression of his desire to see peace re-established. But the Seraskier, in Persian phrase, imagined that he could discern the image of victory in the mirror of his consciousness, and he turned a deaf ear to the suggestion of the Prince. During this time, Toprak-Killeh held out, and Abbass Meerza marched from Khoi with the hope of being able to relieve that fort. In passing through the Armenian district of Kara-Keesia, he was met by a procession of the priests of that persuasion, headed by their archbishop, who implored his Highness's protection, and consecrated his sword. Orders had been given to the commanders of the Persian detachments on the frontier to hasten to join the Prince's standard. No troops in the world, it may safely be asserted, are capable of so much continued endurance of fatigue as are the veteran soldiers of Persia. On this occasion several regiments marched towards their destination for many days together at the rate of thirty miles a day.* Very few men, however, had joined the Persian commander ere he found himself within sight of Toprak-Killeh, and of the Turkish army.

On the Pashas' becoming aware of his inferiority in point of numbers, they resolved at once to attack him, but he was able to stand his ground until seven thousand of his troops, of whose approach he was aware, had joined him. Still his forces were much inferior to those to whom he was opposed, but the system of divided command which had been adopted by the Osmanlis, now served to neutralize their superiority in numbers. The

---

* The reader may compare the distance—here stated to have been accomplished in such a time by Persian soldiers—with the account given by Xenophon of the marches of the army of Cyrus. *See* XENOPHON's *Expedition of Cyrus*, book i., chapter ii., 22 parasangs in 3 days; and chapter v., 90 parasangs in 13 days. 1 parasang equals 3 miles 787½ yards, or 3¼ miles all but 92½ yards.

struggle which ensued was long and bloody, but we can scarcely give our credit to the Persian historian,* who asserts that fifty thousand Turks were left dead upon the field of battle. The corps of one of the Pashas suffered severely, and its commander's flight decided the day in favour of the Persians. The siege of Toprak-Killeh was immediately raised, and the three Ottoman camps, with all that they contained, fell into the hands of the crown-prince. So little prepared were the Turks for the flight to which they had betaken themselves, that many jewelled coffee-cups were found in their tents, which had only been half-emptied. After this victory the crown-prince once more offered terms of peace to the Seraskier of Erzeroum, but that Pasha nobly replied that, so long as the Persian general should maintain a threatening attitude upon Turkish soil, to talk of peace was impossible. Abbass Meerza accordingly withdrew his army to within the Persian frontier, and the Seraskier was empowered by the Porte to conclude a treaty with the plenipotentiaries nominated by the Shah. But during the time that the war still raged, great confusion prevailed along the length of the Turko-Persian frontier. In the direction of Baghdad the disputed province of Shehr-i-zoor became once again the theatre of military operations, and with a view, at the same time, to put down his opponents in this quarter, and to secure for himself a sufficient escort during a pilgrimage which he wished to make to the shrines of Hussein and of Ali, the Shah gathered around his standard a military force, at the head of which he marched to Hamadan. On the one hand, however, the Turks were defeated near the border by the

---

* Riza Kuli Khan.

son of the late governor of Kermanshah ; and on the other, the king's troops had to be dispersed on account of the ravages which the cholera was making amongst them. That disease appeared this year for the first time in Persia, and is said to have carried away one hundred thousand victims, but this number must be set down as a mere guess, since no mortuary statistics are kept in the Shah's dominions.

At another part the frontier was disturbed by an inroad made by the Kurds of the mountains upon the peaceful Christians of the district of Salmas, six thousand of whom are said to have been on this occasion put to death.   In this portion of the kingdom of Persia, there is a Nestorian population of about thirty thousand persons, five thousand of whom dwell in the mountains, and twenty-five thousand in the plain of Uroomeeah, gaining their livelihood almost exclusively by the cultivation of the soil.   Their landlords supply them with grain seeds, and when the harvest is reaped two-thirds of it are retained by the owner, while the remaining third is made over to the ryot.   But under various pretexts a considerable portion of the cultivator's substance is extorted from him by the rapacious landowner, who is sufficiently powerful in the support of his mountain border clansmen, and sufficiently far removed from the seat of government at Tehran, to treat with indifference the orders which are sent from time to time by the Shah for the just and equitable treatment of his Christian subjects.   It must be added that the arbitrary exactions levied on the Nestorians are not dictated by prejudice against their religion, but are in a great measure the same as those practised upon Mahomedan cultivators at a, distance from the capital, and where the landowner can fall back upon his tribesmen for support in case of resistance. Two bodies of foreign missionaries, American and French respectively, have for many years past devoted their painstaking endeavours to the improvement of this portion of the Christian population of Persia. The system followed by the American missionaries is to afford the best secular education which they have it in their power to bestow upon the pupils who attend their schools, and to instruct the Nestorians in the tenets of that sect of Christianity to which they profess to belong. No proselytism of any kind is attempted by these missionaries. The French priests at Salmas direct their labours towards the extension amongst the sectaries of Persia of the faith of Rome. The education which many children of both sexes are year after year receiving in these charitable establishments would be much more highly appreciated if there were more means open to Christian ryots of honesty and capacity for securing to themselves advancement in the different walks of life; but in a country where fair-dealing between man and man is scarcely believed in, and where Christianity is a despised religion, the earnest labours of many devoted men during long years have not as yet produced any appreciable effect upon the general material condition of the Christians of Persia.

The attack on Salmas which I have mentioned was repulsed after a time by an armed force sent from Tabreez, and tranquillity was for the time re-established along the Turko-Persian frontier. The Pasha of Baghdad soon again gave trouble, but was obliged to pay a fine to the Shah, and to engage not to levy any toll upon

the Persian pilgrims who might pass through the limits
of the territory subject to his jurisdiction, on their way
to Kerbela and Nejjef. One of the articles of the treaty
brought to Tehran by the Turkish envoy for ratification
was disapproved of by the Shah, and this caused a delay
in the ultimate conclusion of peace, but both parties
finally agreed to the terms upon which the hostilities
between them should be brought to a close, and each
power retained the territorial possessions which had
belonged to it at the commencement of the war.*

Shortly after this event the Khan of Khiva died, and
his son signalized his accession to the musnud by
invading Khorassan. But the prince-governor collected
several squadrons of the famous horsemen of that province,—clad in mail wrought by the descendants of the
sword-makers of Damascus, who were carried into captivity by Timur,—proceeded to attack the formidable
host of Oozbegs and Turkomans advancing against him,
and after a severe struggle drove the young Khan of
Khiva back into the deserts whence he had issued. As
a warning against such attempts for the future, the
prince then caused a pyramid to be erected of two
thousand skulls of the Turkomans that had been slain
in the action.

---

* Treaty of Erzeroum, between Persia and Turkey—A.D. July 28,
1823 : A.H. Zilkadeh 19, 1238.

CHAPTER VIII.

FROM the perusal of the preceding chapter it will have
been seen that so unsettled was the condition of Persia
in the reign of Fetteh Ali Shah, that scarcely a single
year elapsed without the occurrence, in one direction or
another, of some outbreak in the kingdom or on the
frontiers, which called for the armed interference of the
king's representatives. Such was the normal state of
things, but as these outbreaks for the most part soon
subsided, and left Persia in the same condition in which
they had found her, they were not looked upon by the
Shah's government as being very serious calamities.
If they had their darker aspect, they had also a brighter
side on which they might be viewed. If they excited
discontent amongst the people of the districts ravaged
by the insurgents or invaders, they in turn afforded to
an unpaid army the opportunity of enriching itself by

plunder.   There had been but one war in which Persia,
since the accession of the Kajars, had been obliged to
cede any territory, and the Shah was therefore only
careful to avoid giving occasion for another struggle with
the powerful neighbour whose might he had so sorely
felt.   But notwithstanding this sincere desire on the
part of Fetteh Ali, perverse circumstances once more led
to a serious and threatening misunderstanding between
his Government and that of Russia.   The treaty of
Gulistan was not worded with sufficient accuracy as
regarded some portions of the line of frontier which was
thenceforth to separate the respective possessions of
Russia and of Persia ; and although many years had
elapsed since its ratification, no definite arrangement had
been concluded for the settlement of the points in dispute.
When at length commissioners were nominated, and
when they met on the ground under dispute, matters did
not seem to have advanced at all towards a satisfactory
settlement, for fresh discussions were created as the
commissioners became personally acquainted with the
localities they visited.   The Russian agents, conscious of
the power by which they were backed, determined to
adhere to that view of the treaty of Gulistan which
appeared to them to be most in accordance with the
interests of their master, while the Persian commissioners, who perhaps knew more of the real meaning
of the disputed article of the treaty, refused to give up
any portion of the territory, which, according to their
view, belonged to the Shah.   There were three small
portions of land which formed the chief subject of
discussion, the principal one of which was the district of
Gokcheh, which of right belonged to the Shah, and

which lies to the left of the beautiful lake of the same name, and between it and Erivan. The other two districts in dispute were those of Guni and Balakloo. The lands of Kapan were also made a subject of contention.

Agents were sent from the Governor-General of the Caucasus to Tabreez, and from the Crown-Prince to Tiflis, and on two occasions the points in dispute seemed to be in the way of being satisfactorily settled. On the first, however, the provisional agreement entered into by the Russian *chargé d'affaires* at Tabreez was not ratified by General Yermeloff at Tiflis, and on the second, the engagement drawn up by the Persian agent at the latter city was not ratified by the Shah. With a view to obtain the royal consent to this treaty, the Russian *chargé d'affaires*, who by the King's wish resided at the Court of the Crown-Prince, visited the Shah's camp in the summer of 1825, and on his efforts for the abovementioned end proving unsuccessful, the Government of Georgia occupied with a military force the district of Gokcheh.

This step is said * to have convinced the court of Persia that Russia was determined to make use, in the settlement of the frontier question, of the convincing argument that might makes right, and the remonstrances which the Shah at once addressed at Tiflis against this seizure, were met by the reply that Gokcheh would be given up, provided that, on the other hand, the lands of Kapan, to which Russia advanced a claim, were given up by Persia.† In the meantime, a very strong feeling against Russia had been arising throughout the Shah's dominions, which owed its origin to more than

---

* Rauzat-es-Sefa.   † *Blackwood's Magazine*, vol. xxi.

one cause. The people had had time to breathe since the last war between the two nations, and anger at the loss of so many rich provinces could not but rankle in the minds of the vain inhabitants of Iran. But what chiefly excited their hatred against their Northern neighbours, was the story that reached them of the contemptuous manner in which the Muscovites treated the Mahomedans who were subject to their sway. Indeed many of the inhabitants of the Moslem districts of Transcaucasia, and many also from amongst the Christians of that country, had made secret overtures of assistance to the Shah, in the event of his one day seeking to re-conquer the provinces which had been reft from his empire. The occupation of Gokcheh by Russia at once blew into a flame the embers of religious frenzy which were already alive throughout Persia. The priests, taking the lead in the movement, proclaimed aloud, from the pulpits of the mosques, the necessity of chastising the infidels who had dared to lower their religion; and so great was the pressure brought to bear upon the Shah, that he found himself under the necessity of engaging to go to war with Russia, unless she should agree to the evacuation of Gokcheh. The crown-prince, untaught by past experience, was anxious to measure himself once more in the field against the Russian commanders; and there were only two men, it seemed, in the whole kingdom, who supported the Shah in his wish to avoid a war, if a war might yet be avoided. These were his Minister for Foreign Affairs, who, having filled the post of ambassador to Russia, was acquainted with the vast resources of that power, and the Moëtemed-ed-Dowleh, of whose capacity the Shah had had abundant proof. The chief religious authority in Persia, too, the high priest of Ispahan, seems to have retained some slight remnant of prudence, after that quality was no longer discernible in the conduct and language of his professional brethren. He sent a confidential messenger to the king, to inquire whether or not it were the royal wish that the people should be excited to war, and following closely after his agent to Tehran, he there had an interview with the Shah. But the religious excitement had now attained to such a pitch, that it was useless to try to arrest its development, and Fetteh Ali had to allow himself to be carried along by the current. He started for his summer camp at Sultaneea.

At this time news reached Persia of the death of the Czar Alexander and the accession to empire of his brother Nicholas; this intelligence was quickly followed by the announcement that Prince Menchikoff was on his way to the court of Tehran. The Russian envoy was received with distinction, the Shah entertaining the hope that through his means the points in dispute between Persia and Russia, as to their frontier, might be satisfactorily arranged. But scarcely had the negotiations opened, when a long train of priests from the capital, headed by the Imam-i-Juma of Ispahan, arrived at the royal camp. Prince Menchikoff had no power to consent to the evacuation of the district of Gokcheh, and the Shah was therefore forced to break up the conferences and to give the prince his passports. He was, however, up the last, treated with the utmost distinction, and the king strove by the richness of the presents which he bestowed on this occasion, to lessen the chagrin which the Russian envoy might be expected to

14

feel on receiving his dismissal from the Kajar court.* The whole people of Persia seemed to be united in the determination to enter upon a religious war, and the king's last scruples were removed on his receiving intimation of the threat that if he should still decline to lead his people to battle, his subjects would find another leader for themselves. The nation was indeed roused to action as it never had been roused since the period when its energies had been directed by Nadir. From the Bakhtiari mountains and from the hills of Looristan; from the vales of Khorassan and the plains of Irak; troops in thousands came to join the standard of the crown-prince, to whom was assigned the task of conducting the war, which was now begun without recourse being had to the preliminary ceremony of a formal declaration.

The first blow struck in this war was given by the hereditary chief of Taleesh, who, with the object of rescuing his wife from the hands of the Russian authorities, attacked a detachment on its march to Lankoran.

* It is interesting to compare the manner in which European ambassadors in modern times are received at the Persian court with the treatment they met with in the time of the Sefavean Shahs. The following extract from Chardin's *Travels* describes the reception of a Russian envoy at Ispahan (vol. iii. p. 177).

"Celui de Moscovie parut un quart-d'heure après. Il entra du même côté, amené sur les chevaux du roi par l'introducteur des ambassadeurs : ... L'introducteur mit pied à terre à cent cinquante pas du palais, et dit à l'ambassadeur de descendre aussi de cheval. Je ne sais si le Moscovite avait été informé que l'ambassadeur Lesqui n'avait descendu de cheval que beaucoup plus proche de l'entrée, ou que par grandeur et pour l'honneur de son maître il voulut passer et aller plus avant, tant y a qu'il fit resistance, et donnant ses talons à son cheval il le fit avancer trois ou quatre pas malgré l'opposition des valets de pied de l'introducteur, qui avait mit la main à la bride de son cheval pour le retenir. On l'arrête alors tout à fait. ... Le roi ne leur dit [aux ambassadeurs] point une parole, et ne les regarda pas seulement."

Being thus committed so seriously with the Muscovite government, the Khan lost no time in rousing the people of the province to take up arms against the infidels, and at the same time he sent to ask the support of the Shah in an undertaking, the sole object of which, he declared, was to restore Taleesh to the Persian crown. A corps of ten thousand men was accordingly sent to his aid, with which body he was enabled to lay siege to the Russian station of Lankoran. That place was abandoned, and the garrison took refuge in the adjacent island of Sari, thus leaving the whole of the mainland of Taleesh in the hands of the Persians.* A division of the Shah's troops, commanded by one of his sons, hastened in the meantime to cross the Araxes, and the crown-prince lost no time in bringing up the reinforcements under his orders. The Russians were found to be altogether unprepared for so sudden a beginning of war, and at first the impetuous Persians carried all before them. The disputed districts of Gokcheh, Balaklu, and Guni were taken possession of in the name of the Shah, and Abbass Meerza made ready to advance on the important fortress of Sheeshah in Karabagh. He did not, however, march upon this place so rapidly as not to allow the Russian officer who commanded there to have sufficient time to call in some detachments from the neighbourhood, and to put himself in a posture of defence.

It may here be remarked as strange that the Governor-General of the Caucasus should have taken no more effectual measures to guard against being surprised by the Persians at a time when the envoy of Russia was refusing to accede to the Shah's peremptory

* A.D. 1826.

demand for the evacuation of the territory of Gokcheh. The language used by the representative of Russia should have been based upon a firmer state of preparation to resist the force of Persia. Taken as they were by surprise, the Russian officers, with the exception of the colonel commanding at Sheeshah,* had no choice but to quit their posts and fall back upon places of safety. A Persian division marching into Karabagh under the command of the Shah's son, Ismaïl Meerza, encountered at Khunzerukh a Russian detachment which was making its way towards Sheeshah. The weather was extremely hot, and the Russians were parched with thirst, and to these circumstances their colonel afterwards attributed the fact of his regiment surrendering to the Persians. Four hundred soldiers were killed or wounded, and the rest of the battalion, as well as two guns, fell into the power of the prince, who sent his prisoners to the Shah's camp. There half of the private soldiers thus taken soon enlisted themselves in the Persian service. After this, the Russian general who commanded the district bordering on Erivan, retired to Lori, a strong position on the Tabeda river, from which Hassan Khan, the brother of the hereditary Sirdar of Erivan, found it impossible to dislodge him. The Persian troops, however, were for the present unopposed in the open field, and they carried terror and destruction up to the Russian outposts—the Sirdar penetrating in one raid to the immediate vicinity of Tiflis. The Russian officer in command at Genja, having marched across country to the assistance of the general commanding at Lori, the Mahomedans of Genja rose upon,

* Colonel Réut.

and massacred, the garrison that had been left in the place, and at the same time exterminated the Armenian inhabitants of the town. They then sent to entreat Abbass Meerza to advance to their support, and the prince responded to this appeal by despatching his eldest son, together with Ameer Khan, chief of the upper branch of the Kajar tribe, to the assistance of the men of Genja. His Highness at the same time sent forward the hereditary chief of the place, but he himself remained before the fortress of Sheeshah. The rising throughout the whole of the provinces inhabited by Mahomedans continued to spread. The hereditary chiefs of Sheerwan, of Sheki, and of Bakoo returned to their respective governments from their places of exile, and were soon employed actively in coöperating with the officer in command of the Shah's troops in Taleesh; whilst at the same time the wild mountaineers of Daghestan did not lose the opportunity of adding to the confusion prevailing by descending to the plains, and plundering Russians and Persians with utter impartiality. In the course of three weeks, Russia had lost for the time nearly all the territory that had been ceded to her by the treaty of Gulistan. Sheerwan, Sheki, Taleesh, and Genja were evacuated, and the few remaining Russians to the east of Tiflis were forced to seek shelter in the forts of Bakoo, Derbend, and Kooba. The only advanced post which the troops of the Governor-General now held was the fortress of Sheeshah, which continued to defy the power of Abbass Meerza.* The prince remained before that place for six weeks, the effect which his guns produced upon the walls being concealed from him by canvas stretched behind them.

---

* September, 1826.

In the meantime a large force was being concentrated at Tiflis ; and the foremost Russian division, consisting of 9,000 men of all arms, was pushed forward to Shamkar, a village in the vicinity of Genja. The young prince, Mahomed Meerza,* who now commanded in that place, moved out at the head of about 10,000 men to engage the advancing Russians. A battle was fought on the banks of the Zezam, a small stream of which the contending armies occupied the opposite sides. The Russian force, about a third of which was cavalry, was drawn up in one line, its left resting on the stream, and the whole of the cavalry being placed on the right, and separated by the guns from the infantry. Half of the Persian force consisted of cavalry, which was placed behind the line in which the infantry was drawn up. The Persian horse moved to the flank, with the intention of attacking the Russian cavalry ; but it was kept in check, and soon forced to retire, by the well-directed fire of the Russian artillery. Upon this the cavalry advanced and pursued the Persians along the whole line of their infantry and to the rear of that body. General Madadoff, the Russian commander, upon this ordered his infantry to advance, which had the effect of enclosing the Persians between two fires. They thereupon broke and retired in confusion, leaving their field-pieces in the hands of the enemy. Of the two Persian commanders, Ameer Khan was shot by a Cossack when in the act of endeavouring to rally his troops ; and Mahomed Meerza, the future king of Persia, had actually fallen into the hands of the Cossacks, when he was rescued by a Shahsevend chief, who carried him off behind him on his horse. This was the turning-point

---

* He was afterwards Shah of Persia.

of the war.   From that day the Russians began to roll back the tide of victory upon their foes.   General Madadoff now recovered Genja without a struggle, and connected the town and citadel with a strong line of communication.   Fresh reinforcements were ordered up from Tiflis, and the command of the army in the field was conferred upon General Paskievitch, who advanced to a position some miles to the south of Genja, where he determined to await the approach of Abbass Meerza.

The crown-prince hastened to repair the disaster which had happened to his son, and on the 26th of September the hostile armies met each other.   The force commanded by the prince now numbered about 30,000 men, and the siege of Sheeshah was carried on by another division.   It cannot be doubted that it was a mistake on the part of the Persian commander-in-chief to risk a general engagement with the Russian troops. The latter would have been far more readily overcome had the Persians contented themselves with laying waste the country over which extended the route of the enemy. As it was, every advantage was voluntarily given by the prince to the Russian commander, who was allowed to choose his own fighting ground; and when the Persian troops came within a short distance of the enemy they were kept under arms during the succeeding night, in order to avoid the risk of a surprise.   On the following morning the prince left his camp at an early hour, and, after a march of about ten miles, found the enemy drawn up in squares on the level plain to the east of the fort and suburb of Genja, which covered their rear.   The Russian army consisted of about 10,000 or 12,000 infantry, a regiment of dragoons, about 2,000 Cossacks, 3,000 irregular troops of the Caucasus, and twenty pieces of cannon. The cavalry were placed on the flanks and the artillery in the centre. To oppose this force the Persian commander had under his orders about 30,000 men, of which 16,000 were infantry, and the remainder irregular cavalry, with some artillerymen. He had also twenty-two light field-pieces, directed by an Englishman in his service. The infantry regiments were drawn up in one long line, having fourteen guns to their right and eight to their left, while the cavalry covered the flanks and rear. The battle commenced by a cannonade from both sides; the Russian artillery being so ill-served that the shot for the most part went over the heads of the Persians, doing little or no execution; while the fire of some of the Persian guns was so well directed as to compel one of the Russian divisions to retire and abandon its cannon. Two battalions, composed of the men of Karadagh, charged the retiring square, and had the remaining Persian infantry made a corresponding move-ment in advance at that critical moment, it is probable that victory would have crowned their effort. The great body of the troops, however, remained stationary; and the two Karadagh battalions, being unable to maintain their position without support, fell back in confusion.

It is said that at this juncture Prince Abbass Meerza was so ill-advised as to send a message to his sons to withdraw themselves from the thick of the fight. The messenger either misunderstood the order which he was to convey, or he was himself misunderstood in the midst of the noise and confusion of the battle. The result was that the young princes conceived the notion that their father wished them to withdraw the troops under their command, and accordingly the line gave way and a general rout ensued. The regiments of infantry, composed of men from Irak, broke without having fired a shot, and retired in the utmost confusion. The loss of the Persians upon this occasion would have been greater had not their retreat been covered by some artillery, which, assisted by the prince's guards, kept the pursuers in check. One battalion of Russian light infantry, together with the dragoons and the irregular horse, followed the Persians for about eight miles ; but the pursuers were not able to effect much injury. Abbass Meerza endeavoured in vain to rally his broken army, and remained with his guns till the last shot had been fired. He then withdrew towards Ooslandooz, accompanied by a small body of infantry and nearly 5,000 horsemen. The remainder of the army dispersed in various directions, and made for the banks of the Araxes. At the beginning of the action the Russian cavalry had been charged by the Persian horse, and driven back amongst the trees and ruined suburbs of Genja ; but this partial success was rendered unavailing by the defeat of the infantry, and the horsemen followed their retreating comrades. The actual loss of the Persians on this day did not exceed 1,500 men, but the survivors were dispirited, and all organization was for the time being gone. Only one piece of artillery was captured by the Russians, and its loss was owing to three of the horses attached to it having been killed.

But disastrous as was this day to Persia, it might have proved an useful one to that country, had her rulers been possessed of sufficient wisdom and energy to profit by the lessons it taught. The Persian army had at one time been on the point of· driving the

enemy from the field, and the temporary success was
to be attributed to the disciplined courage of two regiments from Karadagh, and to the fire of the prince's
artillery. These battalions, as well as the artillerymen,
had been trained by competent and zealous foreign
instructors, and had the whole army been equally well
drilled, there can be no doubt that the fate which befell
the Persians would that day have befallen their enemies.
Could the Shah have convinced himself of the fact that
in his hardy and obedient subjects he possessed the
material for an army capable at any time of defending
his dominions against invaders, provided that his troops
should be properly drilled, the lesson would have been
cheaply paid for by the disaster of Genja; but the
rulers of Persia have not grown wiser by the experience
of the past, and to this day the Shah's army is only
half-drilled, and is in reality less effective, either for the
purposes of defence or of offence, than if it were not
drilled after the fashion of European armies at all.

At Genja the command of the Persian troops was
shared by the crown-prince with the Asef-ed-Dowleh—a
proud nobleman who occupied the post of prime minister
to the Shah. The Asef-ed-Dowleh quitted the field at
the first alarm of danger, and, accompanied by a slender
retinue of well-mounted horsemen, pressed his flight
with such unwearied diligence that he reached the
Araxes, a distance of a hundred and fifty miles from
Genja, on the night of the day after the action. On the
following evening the crown-prince rejoined him, when
mutual recriminations took place between them. Each
accused the other of being the author of the catastrophe
which had occurred, and they parted in hostility, each

taking the route towards the camp of the Shah. The roads were now covered with fugitives proceeding to their homes, and many of those who were intercepted and brought into the royal camp, were found not to have tasted food for several days. After the battle of Genja, the Russian general lost no time in sending on reinforcements to the garrison of Sheeshah, the siege of which place was now discontinued. The Shah on his part proceeded to Tabreez, and took immediate steps for the assembling of a fresh army, the command of which was to be entrusted to the luckless crown-prince. Abbass Meerza was not deficient in courage, but he had not the qualities required by the leader of an army, and his self-possession invariably deserted him in the hour of battle. The prince, too, was on such bad terms with more than one of his brothers, that, even at the present critical juncture, they refused to serve under him. It was found necessary to give to Ismaïl Meerza a separate command; and Abdullah Meerza, the governor of Zinjan, in bringing up his contingent, stipulated with the Shah that he should not be called upon to act under the orders of his brother, the crown-prince. The Zinjan troops were accordingly sent to the Erivan frontier, to coöperate with those of the Sirdar of that city.

It had been the Shah's policy throughout his reign to humble the hereditary nobles of the country, and now at each chief city of the kingdom one of the numerous members of the royal family presided. With the exception of some of the princes and the Sirdar of Erivan and his brother, the Shah now possessed no general capable of handling troops in the field. The ablest soldier in Persia was undoubtedly Hassan Ali

Meerza, the governor-general of Khorassan. That
prince offered his services in the prosecution of the
war against Russia; but it was considered by the
government that at such a crisis it would be unsafe to
remove the check which his presence in Khorassan
imposed upon the turbulent chiefs of that province.
Some of the Khorassan squadrons of cavalry were, however, directed to march to Azerbaeejan; and the prince
of Kermanshah received orders to bring up the whole
disposable force of his province and a body of horsemen
from Looristan, making together a corps of twelve
thousand men. The ruling weakness of Fetteh Ali
Shah was an extreme unwillingness to part with money.
This avariciousness increased with his years, and it was
peculiarly disagreeable to him to be forced now by circumstances to disburse to his army one year's pay in
advance, besides having to expend the sum of fifty thousand tomans in refurnishing the arsenal at Tabreez.

On the Russian side, General Sewadzamidzoff quitted
his position at Lori, and marched by the route of Gumri
upon the fortress of Erivan; but he was so much harassed
by the troops of Hassan Khan, that, after having approached to within a short distance of the city, he was
forced to retire with the loss of four hundred men and
a portion of his baggage. The Russian force thus
discomfited was composed of about five thousand men,
and was scarcely inferior in point of numbers to that
under the Sirdar of Erivan. But an occasional display
of activity and bravery on the part of some of the Shah's
troops was not sufficient to counteract the influence of
the disciplined organization of the Russian army.
Through the most shameful malversation on the part

of some Persian officials at Tabreez, the arsenal at
that place was quite unfit to supply the troops with
the most necessary articles for carrying on a campaign.
Not more than two thousand shot were to be found, and
of these the half were either too large or too small for
the calibres of the guns for which they had been cast ;
and the whole city of Tabreez could not supply lead
for musket bullets, nor even paper for the construction
of cartridges.   The Shah declared that he was tired of
drill, and he threatened to gather a body of a hundred
thousand horsemen, and to overrun and lay waste the
Caucasian provinces of Russia.   But at the same time
that he uttered this threat he was inwardly pining for
the return of peace, and his ministers were instructed
to discuss with each other, and with the representative
of the Government of India, the terms upon which an
end might honourably be put to the war.

The council of the king was divided into two factions,
one of which was in favour of a continuance of war, while
the other voted for concessions and peace.   To the first
party belonged the Asef-ed-Dowleh, who was the most
powerful nobleman in the kingdom, and allied to the
Shah by marriage, and he was seconded in his policy
by the Kaim-Makam, a vizeer of great capacity.   To
the opposite party belonged the minister for foreign
affairs, and the Moëtemed-ed-Dowleh, who were backed
by the personal influence of the Shah, and by that of
his confidential Georgian eunuch.   It was at length
determined to send an envoy to Tiflis with instructions
to endeavour to pave the way for the restoration of
peace, and he was the bearer of letters from the Shah's
minister to Count Nesselrode, expressive of the regret

with which they would view a continuance of the war. This envoy, however, could not at first proceed further than Tabreez, in consequence of the vicinity of a Russian force to that city. The Governor-General of the Caucasus had been reinforced by the arrival of ten thousand men at Tiflis, while the division of Astrakan came up to Kooba and Derbend, and compelled the Shah's troops in that direction to retire. It seems then to have occurred to General Yermeloff to make immediate use of the additional force of which he was now master, and accordingly two Russian divisions moved into the enemy's country in the heart of winter. One of these bodies of men, consisting of infantry, cavalry, and artillery, crossed the Araxes at a point from which it might have marched either on Ardabeel or on Tabreez. Both of these cities were undefended, the Persian troops having been dismissed to their homes for the winter.

Notwithstanding this circumstance, it would have been an act of rashness on the part of the Russian officer who commanded the invaders to have attacked Tabreez with so slender a force as that which he had under his orders, but it was open to him to march upon the city of Ardabeel. Indeed it is difficult to conceive what object other than the hope of capturing this city could have induced the Russian military authorities to expose their troops to the dangers and privations of a winter campaign in a country so trying as that bordering on the river Araxes. The possession of Ardabeel by the Russians would have been a standing threat both to Tabreez and to Tehran, whilst from that commanding position the Russian leaders would have exercised a paramount influence over the warlike tribes of the vast plains of Moghan. But these considerations seem to have exercised no influence on the conduct of the Russian commander of the force which now invaded Persia; for, after having exposed his men to all the trials of a winter march through a hilly country destitute of roads and covered with snow, he retired as he had come, and allowed the Persians to recover from the consternation into which his approach had plunged them. The only fruit of his expedition was the seizure of some stores of wheat and rice, the property of Abbass Meerza. After the retreat of this predatory expedition, the Persian envoy found his opportunity of proceeding to Tiflis, and as a peace-offering, he took with him some hundred of Russian prisoners whom the Shah released without ransom. But at Tiflis he learned little which it would give satisfaction to the Shah to hear. The Russian authorities gave it to be understood that in order to secure peace, Persia must be prepared to relinquish the possession of the provinces of Erivan and Nakhtchivan, which lay between her former frontier and the Araxes, and further to defray the charges of the war. The envoy was then permitted to return to Tabreez with the assurance that the reply of Count Nesselrode to the letters from the Persian ministers, would be forwarded to Tehran. That reply, when received, was found to be couched in haughty terms, which showed that Russia did not as yet share the wishes of the Shah for the restoration of peace.

The Persian monarch at this juncture,* which was one of the greatest importance as regarded the future destiny of his kingdom, did not act in such a manner

* A.D. 1827.

as to show his subjects that he was worthy of being the absolute director of the policy of Persia. He wished for peace, but so great was his pride, that it had required all the efforts of the representative of the Indian Government to induce him to consent to the mission of an envoy to Tiflis; while, on the other hand, he could not be persuaded to devote a sufficient portion of his ample treasure for the purpose of equipping an army in such a manner as to enable his son to carry on the war with effect. His parsimonious disposition made it harder for him to part with his gold than to see his armies vanquished, and his territory invaded by the enemy. The following anecdote gives proof of the extent to which the unprincely vice of avarice had by this time gained possession of the mind of the Shah. Some boxes containing mirrors and lamps had been left in the royal camp by Prince Menchikoff, and Fetteh Ali caused them to be seized on the flimsy pretence that the Russian envoy had intimated that they were intended to be given as a present to the Persian monarch. It was feared by the peace party of his court, that if this act of spoliation should be repeated to the Russian authorities it would be likely to raise a personal feeling against the Shah, and so to retard the conclusion of peace. But the king fiercely refused to relinquish his prey, and at length Abbass Meerza had to purchase the mirrors and lamps from his father in order that they might be restored to Prince Menchikoff. In the same spirit the Shah insisted on throwing the expense and burden of the war upon the single province of Azerbaeejan, the revenues of which belonged to the crown-prince.

With the spring of the year 1827, both sides prepared to resume hostilities, and the regularly-drilled regiments of Abbass Meerza were employed in garrisoning the forts, and protecting the passes along the line of the Araxes,—a duty which might have been equally well performed by irregular Persian troops, had the Shah placed such at the disposal of the prince.   So short-sighted a line of conduct is altogether inexcusable on the part of the Persian king, who was at that moment master of an available force of eighty thousand men, exclusive of the contingents of Fars, Kerman, and Azerbaeejan.   On the 25th of April, the Russian division, commanded by Prince Sewadzemizoff, broke up from its camp at Lori, and marched to the Armenian convent of Etchmiadzeen, twelve miles distant from Erivan, and from there reconnoitred the fortress of Sirdarabad; in performing which service it encountered opposition from the Persians, and met with some loss.   In Karadagh, the Russian division under General Madadoff approached the Araxes near the bridge of Khoda-Afereen.   On the morning of the 4th of May, the engineers endeavoured to construct a floating bridge of rafts, but they were prevented from doing so by the Persians, who kept up a very heavy fire of musketry from behind the rocks that at that point stretch almost to the water's edge.   Many of the Muscovite soldiers engaged in the work were killed, and some were forced to seek safety in the river, in the rapid currents of which, however, they only found a watery grave.   Two Persian field-pieces, which had been brought up during the preceding night, now opened fire on the Russian camp near the stream, and the whole corps then retired with precipitation, leaving some tents on the ground, as well

15

as the timber with which they had intended to construct
the raft and repair the bridge. The troops who thus
retreated, are said to have numbered ten thousand men,
while the Persians were less numerous. The result of
this action was to be attributed to the nature of the
ground where it took place, in which the Russian artillery was of no service whatever. The position of
Etchmiadzeen was well calculated as a base for further
operations. From Tiflis the Russian general had brought
with him Archbishop Narses, to act as patriarch of the
Armenian church, and under such auspices it was easy
to obtain the good wishes and active coöperation of the
Christian inhabitants of that portion of Armenia. To
the strongly-walled village of Etchmiadzeen the Russian
commander brought up from Lori stores of all kinds,
which were deposited in the ample rooms of the monastery. At this juncture General Yermaloff, who had
arranged the plan of a summer campaign, was suddenly
recalled from his government, in which he was succeeded by General Paskiewitch. The latter officer now
took the field in person, to command a disposable force
of about twenty thousand men. The object of the Russian Governor-General was to obtain possession of the
important city and fortress of Erivan. It was attempted
on the part of a Russian agent, to win over the Sirdar
Hassan Khan; but that chief and his aged brother
remained true to the interests of the Shah.

On the 6th of May the siege of Erivan was commenced, and two days later the investment of that place
was complete. Hassan Khan attempted to annoy the
besiegers from without, but his horsemen were driven off,
and the city continued for several weeks to be beleaguered.

On the morning of the 8th of June, a Russian column, consisting of two thousand infantry, and an equal number of cavalry, with six pieces of artillery, crossed the Araxes, near which stream the guns and infantry were posted, whilst the cavalry advanced to attack Hassan Khan, who, with a similar number of irregular horseman, and two regiments of infantry, had taken up his position on the slope of a hill, called Koh-i-zoor. Some Polish lancers charged the Persians, and broke through their ranks; but Hassan Khan, taking the supporting Cossacks in flank, drove them before him, and forced them to make the circuit of the plain in order to rejoin their reserve. An officer of the Affshar horse, fancying that he recognized in the colonel of one of the regiments of Cossacks the same person who in a previous affair had slain his brother, was fired with an ungovernable desire to perform what to a Persian is the sacred duty of avenging a relative's blood. Singling out his adversary, he followed him throughout the circuitous pursuit, and having cut him down between two Russian guns, succeeded in effecting his own escape. In the meantime the siege of Erivan was still prosecuted. On the arrival before that place of General Paskiewitch on or about the 25th of June, the garrison was called upon to surrender, with the offer of being allowed to retire with the honours of war. But Hassan Khan replied that it would ill become him to close his long life by an act of treachery to his king, and the Russian approaches were thereupon pushed onwards near to the city. New batteries poured for four or five successive days a heavy but fruitless fire into the place, and not a single man suffered from its effects. At length, on the 1st of July, after the investment of the fortress had lasted for eight weeks, the Imperial army broke up from before Erivan, and General Paskiewitch, leaving that stronghold behind him, marched on Nakhtchivan, after having sent his sick and wounded men to the Monastery of Etchmiadzeen. Thus for the third time the troops of the Czar failed in their efforts to take the fortress of Erivan.

On the 12th of July the Russian moveable force, consisting of 18,000 men and thirty pieces of ordnance, marched from Nakhtchivan to Abbassabad, a fortress on the northern bank of the Araxes, a little lower on the stream. This place was held by 3,000 men and was well supplied with provisions. Abbassabad had been fortified by a French engineer and was capable of presenting considerable obstacles to the besieging army. But treachery lurked within its battlements, over which the Russian eagles were destined soon to wave their wings. The chief of the tribe of Kangerloo had been won over to the cause of the Russians, and he only awaited a fitting opportunity for delivering up the place into their hands. On the night of the 14th of July an attempt was made to carry Abbassabad by escalade, but the assailants were repulsed with heavy loss. The fort was then closely invested by the Russians, who were in turn watched by the troops of Abbass Meerza; by those of Hassan Khan; and by those of the Asef-ed-Dowleh; the last-mentioned person being put to flight in an affair which took place on the 16th of July. On that occasion Hassan Khan crossed the Araxes with his cavalry and attacked the Russian outposts, but he was driven back by the infantry and pursued by the cavalry and by a number of foot-soldiers who were conveyed over the stream at the backs of their mounted comrades, each horse carrying two men. The Persian guns opened on this body so soon as it had formed on the right bank of the Araxes. The Russians thereupon, finding the ford impassable, threw ropes from one bank to the other higher up the stream, in order to prevent their men from being swept away by the current, and by these means they transported three thousand infantry to the right bank. Hassan Khan was unable to interrupt this movement, and as his men and their horses were exhausted with fatigue, he sent a message to Abbass Meerza requesting that the Asef-ed-Dowleh might be ordered to attack with his cavalry the half-formed battalions of the enemy. This suggestion was not complied with, but on the other hand the Russians turned their guns upon the Persian horse, as they stood crowded together in a ravine, and drove them in confusion from the field. The troops under the immediate command of the crown-prince were withdrawn in good order, and those of Hassan Khan held their ground, whilst the Russians recrossed to the left bank of the Araxes. But the flight of the troops of the Asef-ed-Dowleh afforded to the base chief of the tribe of Kangerloo the opportunity which he waited for, of delivering up Abbassabad to the foe. The garrison for the most part made terms with General Paskiewitch, with the exception of a regiment of Bakhtiari that crossed to the right of the stream before the fall of the fort. But no sufficient attempt was made to follow up this success, and the Russian commander-in-chief, after having left a suitable force in Abbassabad, retired by Nakhtchivan to the frontier with the intention of allowing to his troops some time for repose. It may have been necessary for General Paskiewitch to spare his

army, but by so doing he lost a precious opportunity
of following up the advantage he had gained at Abbassabad. Had he crossed the river and marched towards
Khoi, where the Shah was then encamped, he would
have thrown his majesty into the utmost state of consternation, and might have wrung from his fears an advantageous peace.

The Prince Abbass Meerza was now most desirous
that a term should be put to the war, and he accordingly sent a confidential agent to Tiflis who was charged
with a letter from the representative of the Indian
Government to the Russian commander-in-chief on the
subject of a negotiation for peace. In consequence
of this step, M. Grebaïodoff, a gentleman whose subsequent melancholy fate made his name to be remembered,
was deputed by General Paskiewitch to the Persian
camp for the purpose of offering the following conditions
of accommodation : namely, that there should be an
armistice for five weeks ; that Persia should cede to the
Emperor in perpetuity all the countries now belonging
to her to the south of the Araxes ; and that the Shah
should pay the sum of 700,000 tomans in compensation
for the expenses of the war and the ravages committed
by the Persian troops. The prince would not accede to
these terms, and, as General Paskiewitch would not
grant an armistice on any other basis, the negotiations
were broken off, and Abbass Meerza, with the Sirdar
Hassan Khan, marched towards Aberan, whilst the other
Persian commanders were so placed as best to protect the
extensive frontier from Karabagh to Taleesh. The prince
and the sirdar now determined to attack the monastery
of Etchmiadzeen ; but in the neighbourhood of that place

they encountered a Russian force which had been brought
up from Aberan by General Karkoffski on his hearing a
cannonade in the direction of the three churches. The
Persians here numbered about five thousand infantry,
and as many cavalry, with twenty-eight guns, while the
Russians had the same number of infantry, but only one
thousand cavalry and twelve guns. At evening, General
Karkoffski arrived at Asterick, a village about six miles
distant from Etchmiadzeen, and having rested there for
the night, he resumed his march on the following morning. At a short distance from the village he passed a
division of the Persian army, which was posted on some
heights near the road, and a little further on he came
abreast of a second column, under the command of the
Sirdar of Erivan. Here the action commenced with a
fire from the Persian artillery, so destructive that the
Russians could not proceed, but were forced to endeavour
to fall back upon Asterick. Their retreat was intercepted by the advance of a division led by Prince Abbass
Meerza, and from that moment the battle became general
throughout the line. The repeated charges of the
Persian infantry, who, anxious to wipe off the disgrace of
Genja, advanced in excellent order and with great intre-
pidity on the Russian squares, succeeded in throwing the
latter into disorder. The fire of the prince's guns had
the effect of preventing the Russian soldiers from re-
forming, and changed the well-organized battalions into
a tumultuous throng. The Muscovite general was borne
away from the field wounded; his brother, a lieutenant-
colonel, was killed; and most of the officers of the
division received wounds or death, after having made
brave but fruitless efforts to rally their men. Some of

them fell alive into the hands of the Persians, and these gentlemen, while estimating the loss on their side at nearly three thousand men, affirmed that, had their opponents evinced more moderation and less barbarity in the moment of victory, not one of the Russians would have escaped. The eagerness of the Persians to cut off the heads of their slain or wounded enemies gave time for many hard-pressed men to effect their escape; and many who had thrown aside their arms with the intention of surrendering, took courage on viewing the fate of their comrades, and fought with desperation their way towards the friendly walls of Etchmiadzeen. It is but just to the memory of Abbass Meerza to state that he did his best to discourage amongst his soldiers the practice of decapitating their slain enemies : he gave no reward for the heads which were brought to him after the battle of Asterick, but the sum of eleven tomans for each living prisoner. About one thousand of the Persians were killed or wounded in this action, in which it was fairly proved that the battalions of Azerbaeejan, which had been disciplined by a Major Hart and other English officers, were a match in the open field for nearly a similar number of Russian infantry.

Abbass Meerza, however, sensible that unless he should be supported by the whole power of Persia, he would not be able long to cope with the resources of Russia, addressed to his father a note setting forth the unvarnished truth, on the receipt of which the Shah fell into so ungovernable a fit of rage, that he sentenced the Vizeer who delivered the note, to pay a fine of six hundred tomans, and could not be approached for hours afterwards. On coming to his senses, after having consigned his son a hundred times to perdition, the king determined to send his Vizeer of Foreign Affairs to London, to press the British ministers to use their influence with Russia for the reëstablishment of an honourable peace ; but the mission of the Vizeer was postponed, pending the reply to some communications which had been already addressed to his Britannic Majesty's Ministers.   General Paskiewitch, in the meantime, relieved the garrison of Etchmiadzeen, and the Persian commander retired to the south of the Araxes.

Towards the close of the September, the fort of Sirdarabad, near Mount Ararat, was deserted by its garrison, and fell into the hands of the Russians, and as General Paskiewitch was strengthened by the arrival of five thousand fresh troops, as well as by that of a siege-train, he now once more undertook the siege of Erivan.   By the fall of Abbassabad and Sirdarabad, Erivan was now isolated, and it was the only post wanting to secure to the Russians the possession of the portion of Persia which lay to the south of the river Araxes.   Up to this point of he campaign, the Russian commanders had owed their successes more to the supineness of the Shah and to the discontent of some of his subjects, than to any military talent or any remarkable energy displayed by themselves.   But for the treachery of the garrisons of the above-mentioned two fortresses, it is probable that the campaign of 1827 would have left the belligerents in the same position relatively to each other in which it had found them at its opening.   But fortune favoured General Paskiewitch, and the utterly infatuated conduct of the Shah rendered it only needful for the Imperial officers to come and see and conquer.   When the heats of summer had subsided, Fetteh Ali Shah retired to Tehran, having positively refused to dole out any more money for the purpose of enabling his son to carry on the war. The resources of Tabreez were now exhausted, and the prince, therefore, with much reluctance dismissed the greater part of his troops to their homes for the winter, thus leaving the capital of Azerbaeejan undefended. Of this state of things General Paskiewitch was early made aware through the Armenians who corresponded with Archbishop Narses, and a corps of his army was accordingly pushed forward to Marend on the south of the Araxes, a town forty miles distant from Tabreez. The gloomy aspect of affairs seems at length to have broken the firmness of Hassan Khan, for we read that only eight days after the opening of the trenches before his city for the last time by the Russians, the hero of a hundred fights surrendered himself, and his brother's fortress, to General Paskiewitch, who thus earned the title of Count of Erivan.

A greater calamity was in reserve to punish the avarice and supineness of the Shah. Sensible when too late of the terrible consequences that were likely to follow the dismissal of his forces for the winter, the crown-prince made many fruitless attempts to reässemble his soldiers, and was on his way from Khoi to Tabreez with the few troops remaining to him, when, at the distance of one day's march from the place, he learned to his horror that its gates had been thrown open to Prince Aristoff, who with a force of 5,000 men had advanced from Marend. The dismay of the prince on receiving. this intelligence may be more easily conceived than described. His wives and children had been left in Tabreez, and that city contained his palace, his artillery, and his military stores. He dismounted from his horse, and at once entreated Sir John Macdonald, the British envoy, to send one of his officers to arrange for an interview between his Royal Highness and General Paskiewitch. At the same time, as he was seated disconsolate under the shade of a willow-tree, he implored the envoy to lend him 3,000 tomans, to defray his current expenses. The British officer forthwith ordered that the sum specified should be handed over to the prince. But the Russian commander was not so courteous towards the royal personage in distress. Probably possessed by a feeling of secret satisfaction at being able to humble so exalted a personage, General Paskiewitch declined for the present the interview proffered by his Royal Highness. The prince had no resource but to brook this insult, and he retreated with the Sirdar Hussein Khan to Salmas, to await the pleasure of the conqueror.

The immediate cause of the fall of Tabreez may be stated to have been the disaffection of the chiefs of Marend, whose father had been put to death by Abbass Meerza, for having in the previous year deserted his post at the fortress of Genja. These young men, intent on revenge, were made aware of the discontent with which the people of the city endured the rule of the Asef-ed-Dowleh; and they accordingly assured Prince Aristoff that he would meet with no opposition in marching on the capital of Azerbaeejan. Nevertheless, the Asef-ed-Dowleh discharged with his own hand some shots pointed on the advancing Russian columns, and thus caused Prince Aristoff to suspect the truthfulness of the chiefs

of Marend.   But at the close of that day the high-priest
of Tabreez, backed by many of the chief citizens, took
the keys of the city from the gate-keepers, whom the
party threw down from the top of the city wall.   They
then proceeded to the Russian camp, and invited the
general to take possession of the place.   On the receipt
of this intelligence, General Paskiewitch brought up the
bulk of his army, and on his arrival he omitted no means
of soothing the inhabitants of Tabreez.

The standard of revolt was now raised by several of
the discontented chiefs of Azerbaeejan, who, deprived by
the policy of the Shah of much of their hereditary influence, thought to regain it under the sway of the Czar.
Amongst these were the lords of Maragha, who liberated
the Russian prisoners confided to their care, and proffered
their own allegiance to the Emperor.   Another insurgent
was Jehangeer Khan, chief of the great tribe of Shekaki,
and the son of the celebrated Sadek Khan, who had disputed the possession of the Persian throne with Fetteh Ali
Shah, and who had perished so miserably at Tehran.   This
chieftain was now appointed to be governor of Ardabeel,
in the name and on the behalf of the Emperor of Russia.
Two of the best regiments in the Shah's service belonged
to the tribe of Shekaki, and at the word of their chief
they at once dispersed, and carried to their homes their
arms and accoutrements.   In short, the parsimonious-
ness and neglect of the Shah had brought about a state
of things when his empire was fast crumbling to pieces;
and, to crown all, the Russian commander-in-chief declared
his intention of marching on Tehran, unless his demands
should be instantly complied with.   There existed indeed
but one obstacle, namely, the pass of the Kaflankoh, to

the advance of a force from Tabreez to Tehran ; but to
have pushed forward the small body of troops at his
disposal * 400 miles further from his base of operations,
would have been a proceeding of so hazardous a nature,
that nothing but the assurance of his being unopposed
by the Persians could have justified it in the eyes of
European tacticians. But in the same way the advance
by Prince Aristoff on Tabreez—a city of 200,000 warlike
inhabitants—with only 4,000 men, may be characterized
as rash. Rashness is sometimes the most prudent
course in war with irresolute Oriental enemies ; and it
is probable that had General Paskiewitch carried into
execution his threat of marching on into the interior of
the country, he would have obtained possession of the
Persian capital.

The demands of the Russian plenipotentiaries at the
conferences which now took place between them and
Abbass Meerza at Dehraghan were that, in addition
to Erivan and Nakhtchivan, the district of Makoo, on
the south of the Araxes, and the province of Taleesh,
should be given up to the Czar, together with the
enormous sum of fifteen crores of tomans, or nearly
4,000,000l. sterling. The negotiations were protracted
from the middle of November, 1827, until the end of
the month of February of the following year, owing to
the almost insuperable reluctance of the Shah to part
with a portion of the treasure which it had been the
task of a long reign to amass. Judging of European
faith by his experience of the absence of truthfulness in
the Persian character, Fetteh Ali Shah did not scruple

* The Russian force at this time in Tabreez amounted to 15,000
infantry and cavalry with fifty guns.

to express his apprehensions lest General Paskiewitch should accept the Persian gold and then expend it in the prosecution of the war. It was fortunate that there yet remained one person to whose word the Shah expressed himself willing to trust. This was Sir John Macdonald, the British envoy; and Fetteh Ali positively refused to pay any portion of the sum asked by Russia unless the English representative would guarantee that General Paskiewitch would fulfil the conditions of the contract. This pledge, at the request of the Russian general, was readily given by Sir John Macdonald, and the negotiations were accordingly proceeded with. But it required the utmost pressure to induce the aged Shah to agree to the sum to which the Russian plenipotentiaries consented to reduce their demand, and it was to the personal influence exerted over his majesty by Mr. McNeill, of the British Mission, that the conclusion of peace was in a great measure to be ascribed. A treaty was at length agreed to on the 21st of February, 1828, by the plenipotentiaries assembled at Turkomanchai, a village a few miles to the west of the pass of Kaflankoh. The Shah's consent had not been given too soon, for the rebellious chiefs of Azerbaeejan had offered to the Russian general the assistance of 15,000 horsemen in the march to Tehran; and his Excellency, tired of delay and mistrustful of the honesty of the Shah, was preparing to move on the capital.

CHAPTER IX.

Provisions of the Treaty of Turkomanchai—Alteration of the Treaty between England and Persia—General Confusion in Persia—Supineness of the Shah's Government—M. Grebaïodoff—Murder of the Members of his Mission—Terror of the Shah—Embassy to Petersburg of Prince Kosroo—Severe Earthquakes in Persia—Campaign of the Crown-Prince in Khorassan—Fall of Ameerabad and of Khabooshan—Assault on Serrekhs—Origin of the Affghan War—Death of Abbass Meerza—The Kaim-Makam—Last Days of Fetteh Ali Shah—His Character—Burial-place of the Persian Kings.

As the provisions contained in the treaty of peace concluded between the plenipotentiaries of Russia and Persia respectively, at Turkomanchai, now form the basis of the intercourse between Persia and the nations of Europe, it is desirable to examine this treaty with some care. By the fourth article the following line of frontier is laid down as that which was thenceforward to separate the territories of Russia and of Persia. From the frontier of the Ottoman dominions nearest in a straight line to the summit of the lesser Ararat a line was to be drawn from that mountain to the source of the lower Karasou, which runs from the southern slope of the lesser Ararat, and it was to follow its course as far as to its junction with the Araxes opposite to Cheeroor. Having reached that point, the line was to follow the bed of the Araxes to the fortress of Abbassabad, round the outer works of which a line of three versts was to be traced, and all the ground enclosed in this line was to belong to Russia.

From the place where the eastern extremity of this line should have rejoined the Araxes the frontier was to continue to follow the bed of that river as far as to the ford of Yediboulak, from which the Persian territory was to extend along the Araxes for the distance of twenty-one versts. From there the frontier was to lie on the right of the plain of Moghan to the river Bolgarou, to twenty one versts below the confluence of the Adina-bazar, and the Lava Kamysche. From there the line was to follow the left bank to the junction of these two streams, and to stretch along the right bank of the eastern Adina-bazar to its source, and thence to the summit of the heights of Jikoir, so that all the waters that flowed towards the Caspian should belong to Russia, whilst those that flowed in the other direction should belong to Persia. As the watershed of the mountains marked the limit of the dominions of the two states, it was agreed that all the northern slope should belong to Russia, whilst all the southern slope should belong to Persia. From the crest of the heights of Jikoir, the line of frontier was to extend to the summit of Karakonia, the mountain which separates Taleesh from the district of Archa. Here also the crest of the mountain was to mark the division as far as to the source of the river of Astera, which was to complete the line of demarcation. By the sixth article of the treaty the Shah of Persia engaged to pay to Russia as an indemnity a sum of twenty millions of roubles, or five millions of tomans. By the seventh article Abbass Meerza was designated as the heir to the Persian monarchy, and Russia agreed to recognize him as Shah from the date of his accession to the throne. By the eighth article the Russians were secured in the right of freely navigating the Caspian sea and landing on its coasts. As to vessels of war, as those of Russia had from of yore enjoyed the exclusive privilege of traversing the waters of the Caspian, the same privilege was to be continued to them. By the tenth article it was stipulated that Russia should possess the right to name consuls or commercial agents wherever the demands of commerce should require them, and that each of these consuls was not to have a suite of more than ten persons. By the thirteenth article of the treaty it was agreed that all the prisoners of war made on either side, as well as the subjects of either power in captivity, should be liberated within the term of four months. The two governments reserved to themselves the right of at any time claiming prisoners of war or subjects of either power respectively, who might, from some accidental reason, not be restored within the specified time. By the fifteenth article the Shah granted an amnesty to the chiefs of Azerbaeejan, who were given the term of one year to remove to the Russian dominions, without any hindrance, should they decide upon doing so. By the second article of a protocol to the same treaty, it was regulated that three crores, or a million and a half, of tomans should be paid by Persia in the course of the first eight days succeeding the conclusion of the treaty, and that two crores of tomans should be paid fifteen days later; three crores by the 13th of April of that year, and that the two crores which should remain still due to Russia, should be liquidated by the 13th of January of the year 1830. By the third article of the same protocol it was determined that in the case in which the sums due by Persia should not be paid to Russia on or before the 15th of August of 1828, the whole province of Azerbaeejan

16

should for ever be separated from the kingdom of Persia, and either added to the Russian dominions, or erected into a separate Khanate. Khoi was to remain in the possession of the Russians after they should have quitted the rest of Azerbaeejan, as a material guarantee for the payment of the portion still to be paid of the indemnity.

By another protocol it was agreed between the contracting parties that so soon as the Persian Minister should receive notice of the arrival at Tiflis of a Russian ambassador, he should make choice of an individual of a rank corresponding to that of the ambassador, and send him to meet the envoy at the frontier, and act as his *Mehmandar*, becoming responsible for his safety in his journey to the court, and also being responsible for the rendering of all the honours due to his rank. By the same protocol it was arranged that the ambassador was to be received at each station by an *istikball*, or deputation, composed of the chief man of the place ; of the dignitaries, and a suitable suite. In the case of the ambassador passing through a city of which one of the Shah's sons should be governor, his vizeer was to be sent to meet the envoy. On the day following that of his arrival at the capital, the Shah's Ministers were to call on the ambassador, who on the next day was to have an audience of the Shah. In the case of the arrival of a minister plenipotentiary, or of a chargé d'affaires, the same ceremonial was to be observed, with the exception that the Shah's chief Minister was not to pay the first visit.

By the commercial treaty of Turkomanchai, concluded on the same date, it was fixed that Russian traders should enjoy in Persia all the privileges accorded to the subjects of the most favoured nation. Goods passing from one country to the other were to be subjected to one sole duty of five per cent.,* levied at the frontier. Russian subjects were to have the right to acquire *en toute propriété* habitable houses and magazines into which the employés of the Persian government should not have the right of penetrating by force, except by the sanction of the Russian Minister or Consul. The representatives of Russia, with the gentlemen attached to them, and the consuls of the same nation, were to have the privilege of being allowed to import, free from duty, all kinds of articles which should be intended solely for their own use, and Persians employed by the Russian officials were to enjoy Russian protection in the same manner as Russian subjects. The settlement of all disputes between Russian subjects in Persia was to be entirely confided to the Minister or Consul of his Imperial Majesty; the treatment of them to be according to the laws of Russia. Disputes between subjects of the two governments were to be settled by the two courts of religious law and of equity, but a Russian employé was to be present during the hearing of each case.

Such were the provisions of the Treaty of Turko-manchai, concluded between General Paskiewitch and Monsieur Obrescoff on the part of Russia, and Prince Abbass Meerza on that of Persia, and signed in the presence of the Asef-ed-Dowleh and the Persian Minister for Foreign Affairs. The chief difficulty in carrying the provisions of this treaty into effect lay in the extreme unwillingness of the Shah to part with his treasure. His Majesty consented to give six crores of tomans,

---

* Cinq pour cent.

and the British envoy on the part of his Government consented to give 200,000 tomans, with the provision that on the one hand the Persian territory should
be at once abandoned, and that on the other the
third and fourth articles of the then.existing definitive
treaty with England should be expunged from that
document, and the stipulations therein contained be
thenceforward deemed null and void.   The Russian
general at length agreed to evacuate the province of
Azerbaeejan, with the exception of Khoi, on the receipt
of six and a half crores of tomans, or 3,250,000*l*., and
the 50,000 tomans wanted to complete this sum were
supplied by Prince Abbass Meerza.

The Persian Government held that the original occupation by Russia of the district of Gokcheh constituted an
act of aggression, and that, therefore, Persia was entitled
to receive from Great Britain a subsidy for the whole
period of the war. This claim, however, was not admitted
by the English Government, who held that Persia by
invading Russia had been the real aggressor in the war.
It is beyond question that Russia, in occupying the district of Gokcheh, had no thoughts of making war upon
Persia, and there can be no doubt also that no war
would have occurred but for the religious outcry which
was raised in the Shah's dominions.   The decision,
therefore, of the British Government was in conformity
with justice; but at the same time they saw the delicacy
of the situation in which they would have been placed
had Russia in reality commenced the war, as in such
a case, they would have been in the position of supplying
Persia with a subsidy for the purpose of carrying on war
with a Power in friendly alliance with England.   It was

a signal service on the part of Sir John Macdonald to extricate his Government from such an obligation, and the necessities of Persia made the receipt of 200,000 tomans of peculiar value to her at that crisis. But for the payment of that sum, General Paskiewitch would have continued to hold Azerbaeejan.

In the meantime troubles arose in several parts of Persia. The Turkomans, as might have been anticipated, rose in rebellion. The people of Yezd drove the Shah's son, their governor, from that city, and took possession of his effects. The inhabitants of Ispahan refused the payment of the revenue due by them, and the great province of Kerman presented a scene of open revolt; to crush which the Prince Hassan Ali Meerza was now sent at the head of an army. The crown-prince at this time intended to proceed in the autumn of the same year upon an embassy to Russia; and in the month of May he visited Tehran, to consult personally with the Shah, over whom he regained all that influence which had been dormant for a time in consequence of the events of the late war. The king now conferred upon him the governments of Kermanshah and Hamadan, in addition to that of Azerbaeejan, which he had up to this time held, and he triumphed over his late colleague Allah-yar Khan, the Asef-ed-Dowleh, who was dismissed from the post of prime minister and publicly degraded by receiving the punishment of the bastinado. It was the Shah's command that the prince should superintend the infliction of this chastisement, and it is illustrative of the anger with which the recollection of the ex-Vizeer's pusillanimity filled him, that the prince inflicted with his own hand several blows on the feet of the prostrate man.

The court of Persia was now occupied in speculating on the probable results of the war between Russia and Turkey. The Shah was besought by both sides to take a part in the contest. There was little fear of his again provoking the anger of Russia, but his son desired that in the event of the downfall of the Ottoman empire, the frontier of Persia might be extended to Erzeroum and to the Tigris. It was determined to remain neutral for the present, but to be prepared to take advantage of any events that might occur. In the meantime the Shah, whose thoughts dwelt on the advantages he might gain by the downfall of the Sultan, was on the point of forfeiting the most valuable of his own provinces. By the treaty of Turkomanchai it was stipulated that in the event of the third instalment of the pecuniary indemnity due by Persia not being paid to the Russian agents by the 27th of August of the year 1828, the whole of Azerbaeejan should for ever be separated from Persia. Notwithstanding this clause, the Shah's government, with a recklessness entirely characteristic of Persians, took no thought up to the last moment as to the manner in which the required money was to be raised; indeed, the Vizeer of Azerbaeejan was unaware of the obligation into which the Shah had entered, until the specified passage of the treaty was brought to his notice by Sir John Macdonald. At the eleventh hour the required sum was gathered together—the British envoy becoming security for the payment of 100,000 tomans—and the district of Khoi was evacuated by the Russian troops.

In another direction the aspect of affairs was such as to lead the Shah to the reflection that it became him to

attend to the conservation of the dominions he already
possessed, rather than to seek to extend them on the
ruins of the empire of the Sultan.   The sons of Hassan
Ali Meerza, who were left in charge of Khorassan,
appeared in arms against each other, and this was the
signal for several of the turbulent chiefs,—amongst them
those of Boojnoord, Koochan, Kelat, and Turbat,—all
inveterate enemies of the Kajars,—to raise the standard
of revolt.   One of these entered the city of Meshed in
August 1828, and got possession of the citadel and of
the person of the governor.   The venerable Sirdar,
formerly of Erivan, a warrior of ninety years of age,
was despatched to Khorassan; but his military talents
had not the effect of reducing the unruly chiefs to
order.

Persia was still in a troubled and disordered condition
when an event occurred which might have furnished a
pretext for the forcible dismemberment of the monarchy
and the overthrow of the Kajar dynasty.   Monsieur
Grebaïodoff, a Russian gentleman related by marriage to
the count of Erivan, had been selected as envoy extraordinary and minister plenipotentiary from the Czar to
the court of Persia.   He arrived at Tabreez in the
month of October, 1828, and there leaving Madame
Grebaïodoff and a part of his splendid suite, he proceeded
to Tehran, with the purpose of presenting his letters of
credence to the Shah, and of shortly returning to Azerbaeejan.   The imperial mission was received with the
utmost distinction by the king, who commanded his
nobles to do their best in order to render the stay of
the strangers at the Persian capital as agreeable as it
might be made.   The Order of the Lion and Sun was

conferred on the gentlemen of the embassy; and the limited resources of Tehran were employed to the utmost extent in order to increase the good-humour of the representative of the Czar.

That representative was a gentleman of an honourable and upright disposition, and he was fully determined to uphold the dignity of, and to exact the rights due to, his imperial master. He was, perhaps, of too unbending a character to have qualified him for being a suitable representative to such a court as that of Persia; but if this were a fault with which he might have been charged, he paid a heavy penalty for his firmness. It is said that the fact of his Cossacks being often seen in a state of intoxication in the streets of Tehran, raised a feeling of disgust against the Russians in the minds of the people of the Persian capital, and that this was increased by the refusal of the Minister to grant redress in the case of some complaints against the conduct of his followers which were brought to his notice. But any discontent which may have existed was not permitted to display itself openly; and the Minister had obtained from the Shah his audience of leave, and was on the point of setting out on his return to Tabreez, when Yakoob Khan, the second chief eunuch of the royal harem, came to the house of the Imperial Mission, and claimed protection, on the plea of his being a native of Erivan. By the treaty of Turkomanchai, he had the right to return to his native place within a specified period, which had not then expired; but M. Grebaïodoff used all the arguments that occurred to him for the purpose of persuading him to relinquish his intention of returning to his native place, pointing out that he had been long estranged from the habits in which he had been brought up, and that he would find himself in an altered position should he return. But the eunuch, fired with spite against his recent masters, insisted on the enjoyment of the privilege to which the treaty entitled him, and he at length obtained shelter in the Russian Mission. This most unfortunate occurrence placed the Imperial Legation in direct opposition to the household of the Shah, and caused much ill-feeling; but it was of small importance compared to another event to which it led.

The shelter afforded to Yakoob Khan induced the Shah's Ministers to press certain claims on the Russian representative, and the annoyances to which he was subjected roused his haughty spirit to desire to enforce the claims which he, on the part of his own Government, was legally entitled to advance. Two days after the flight of the eunuch from the Shah's harem apartments, M. Grebaïodoff advanced a demand that two Armenian women from the ceded provinces, and who were now Mahomedans and inmates of the house of the Asef-ed-Dowleh, should be delivered up to the Russian Mission. An attempt was at first made by the Persian Government to evade this requisition; but on its being pressed, Allah-yar Khan was ordered to give up the women, who were accordingly taken to the house occupied by M. Grebaïodoff, and committed to the care of the eunuch Yakoob Khan. The Asef-ed-Dowleh had all along been the inveterate foe of the Russians, and it is probable that he did his utmost to fan the flame which now burst forth. It is probable also that the knowledge possessed by M. Grebaïodoff of the sentiments of Allah-yar Khan had led him to press a request so humbling to the pride of that nobleman as the demand for the delivery of two of the ladies of his harem. The case was referred by the roused populace to the decision of the priests; and the chief mujtehed gave a *fetwah*, or statement of his opinion, that it was lawful to rescue from the hands of infidels two women professing the faith of Mahomed, and who belonged to the household of a true believer.

On being informed of the rising tumult, the Shah directed the Minister for Foreign Affairs to entreat the envoy to enter into some arrangement which might have the effect of calming the excited populace. M. Grebaïodoff agreed to do so on the following day; but this delay proved fatal to himself, and was the cause of an indelible disgrace befalling the people of the capital of Persia. Between eight and nine o'clock on the morning of the 11th of February, 1829, the bazaars of Tehran were closed, and the inhabitants flocked in wild confusion toward the residence of the Russian envoy, with the intention of taking the law into their own hands, releasing the disputed women, and seizing the eunuch Yakoob. No sooner had the crowd succeeded in forcing its way into the court of the house of the Russian Legation than the envoy's stern resolution at length gave way, and he ordered that the ladies should be restored to their lord. But a contest ensuing between some of his followers and the foremost of the crowd, who were dragging the eunuch towards them, a fatal shot was fired, by which a citizen of Tehran was killed. His body was forthwith conveyed to the neighbouring mosque, and there the bigoted priests proclaimed the disgrace that would follow the omission of exacting blood for the blood that had been spilt. The envoy made every effort to appease the infuriated mob, so long as peaceful measures seemed likely to be attended with success: he even caused his treasure to be thrown amongst the crowd; but this only quickened the desire for plunder, and when the eunuch Yakoob was torn to pieces, the Cossacks of the envoy's guard were ordered to fire upon the murderous rabble. The resistance offered by M. Grebaïodoff and the members of his mission prevented the Persians from entering the room they occupied; but with ill-timed ingenuity it occurred to the assailants to remove a portion of the roof of the apartment, and by throwing down sticks and stones and clods of earth from above, they forced the Russian gentlemen to seek safety in the court-yard, where they were soon overpowered, and despatched by the daggers of the infuriated throng. All that the house contained was then carried off, and on one of the populace crying out that the horses of the Russian Mission were in the stable of the British Legation, a simultaneous rush was directed towards the English palace. The gates withstood the efforts that were made to burst them open; but the cupidity of the mob was not thus to be thwarted, and an entrance to the stable-yard was effected from the adjoining house, the wall of which was scaled. It is remarkable that any traces of moderation should at that moment have been discernible in the conduct of the Persian rioters; but they drew a fine distinction between what in their opinion was, and what was not, their lawful prey. Whilst they possessed themselves of all the horses and all the horse-clothing belonging to the Russian Mission, they inflicted not the slightest injury upon a single article of British property.

Having put to death a Georgian groom and two Cossacks, they led out the horses, and, departing to their homes, the tumult suddenly subsided.

On the first news of this outbreak reaching him, the Shah instantly ordered the governor of Tehran and the commander of the forces to do their utmost to quell it; but it appeared that the authority of these princes was utterly set at defiance, since, after having received personal insults, they retired to the citadel, the gates of which were shut under the apprehension lest the rising should extend itself even to the precincts of the abode of the Shah. The king overwhelmed with shame and dismay upon learning what had taken place, hastened to protect the person of M. Malzoff, the first secretary to the Russian Mission, and the only survivor of the party.

That gentleman had been lodged with the Persian in charge of the Mission, in a house, or rather a suite of rooms, adjoining the scene where the catastrophe occurred. From his windows, according to his own statement, he saw the crowd pour into the court of the Minister's house, and the gathering at once became so dense as to deprive him of the means of proceeding to join his comrades. Seeing the extremities to which the multitude resorted, he retired with his servants to an upper room, where he might more easily defend himself if attacked, and there he distributed the sum of two hundred ducats amongst the Mahomedan guards attached to him. These men and his servants now ranged themselves in front of the room where he had taken refuge, and told some inquiring Persians that the apartment was occupied only by Mahomedans. The number of Russian subjects massacred is stated to have been thirty-five, including M. Grebaïodoff, M. Adelung his second secretary, the physician of the mission, the Persian secretary, a Georgian prince attached to the mission, an officer in the Russian service, eleven Cossacks, an European servant, and several Armenians and Georgians. The body of the murdered envoy was handed over to the care of the Armenian clergy, and it was subsequently transported to Tiflis. The fate of this talented gentleman was the more melancholy from the reflection that but a few months before he had wedded a Georgian princess of remarkable beauty, who was thus early doomed to bemoan his untimely death. M. Grebaïodoff was a poet of considerable celebrity, and his works are still perused widely throughout the Czar's dominions. It may have been to this circumstance that he owed, as he is said to have done, the dislike of his Imperial master, who looked upon the pursuit of literature as being a mere waste of time, and unworthy of a soldier or a statesman.

Nothing could exceed the dismay into which the intelligence of this deplorable occurrence threw the crown-prince, Abbass Meerza, who was at the time at Tabreez. In the middle of the night a servant of the harem was despatched for the British envoy, to whom the prince, after many exclamations expressive of despair, declared that a deed had been done at Tehran, the stain of which all the waters of the Euphrates could not efface. The prince could find a grain of consolation only in the fact that the Mehmandar attached to the late Russian Minister had been severely wounded in his defence, whilst several of his Persian guards had been killed in the act of attempting to resist the rabble. The Shah and his government spared no effort to convince the Czar of their entire innocence of the slightest participation in the recent occurrences which had terminated so fatally at Tehran. M. Malzoff was able to testify to the same purport, and the British envoy was entreated to request the Minister of his Government at the court of Russia to add his assurances to those of the persons mentioned. In addition to this, it was determined to send an ambassador charged with full powers to offer any reparation that might be demanded by the Czar. But this embassy was looked upon as a service of the greatest danger. The Persians believed that the Czar would very probably exact life for life, and none of them at first cared to act the part of Curtius on the occasion. At length Kosroo Meerza, a son of the crown-prince, was selected for filling the post of the Shah's representative, and he accordingly proceeded to Petersburg. The demands of the Czar were regulated by the exigencies of the situation in which Russia was then placed, rather than by the enormity of the crime which had been committed at Tehran. The imperial armies had sustained reverses on the Danube, and it was feared that Persia,* if pushed too

---

* M. Fonton states, at page 404 of *La Russie dans l'Asie Mineure:* "Les embarras du moment s'aggravèrent encore par une démarche précipitée du consul de Russie à Tebriz: cédant aux insinuations des Anglais, il avait quitté son poste sans en avoir reçu l'ordre." It would be more in accordance with facts if he had said that, " yielding to his own fears, M. Ambourger had quitted his post." The same author goes on to state that, on the receipt of the news by Abbass Meerza of the defeat of the Turks by the Russians at Akhaltsikh, the Persian prince assumed a more humble tone towards General Paskiewitch. " Il fit répandre le bruit qu'au cas où les intrigues de ses frères amèneraient une collision, il chercherait avec les siens refuge et protection auprès du général-en-chef Russe. Tout sa cour prit en même temps le deuil à l'occasion de l'assassinat de Téhéran. Cette demonstration fut bientôt suivie d'une démarche plus significative encore. Ali Yusbachi, l'un des confidens d'Abbass Mirza, vint à Tiflis ; il exprima, au nom de son

far, might unite her force to that of Turkey, for the purpose of driving back the troops of the North from the
plains of Armenia and the borders of the Euxine. The
Emperor, therefore, was prepared to accept the assurance
of the Shah's representative that the Persian government
had been neither actively nor passively in any way concerned in the late lamentable occurrence at Tehran,
which, his Royal Highness said, they looked upon with
the utmost regret and horror.

The Shah's ambassador had been well chosen. At

---

maître, les regrets que lui avaient fait éprouver les mésintelligences sur-
venues entre les deux pays, protesta du dévoûment de l'héritier présomptif
du trône, et se dit chargé de recueillir de la bouche du Comte Paskévitch
les conseils de son expérience dans la situation difficile où il se trouvait."
The following is the reply of the Count of Erivan:—"Votre Altesse me
demande, comment elle doit agir dans les circonstances difficiles qu'à
amenées pour elle la rupture des relations amicales avec la Perse? . . .
Le très puissant Schakh, votre père, veut commencer la guerre. Supposons
qu'obéissant à ses ordres, et cédant aux intrigues de vos frères, vous com-
menciez les opérations ; vous ne rassemblerez dans le royaume que soixante
mille combattans au plus. Nos provinces limitrophes n'ont pour défense,
il est vrai, que les troupes qui occupent les forteresses. Vous pourrez, donc,
pénétrer dans le pays ouvert ; vous pourrez le ravager, mais vous ne
prendrez pas les places fortes.
"De mon côté. . . . je me porte par Baïazeth et Khoï sur Tebriz. . .
Je fais la conquête de ce pays, pour ne plus jamais vous le rendre. Tout
espoir de monter un jour sur le trône de votre père sera dès-lors perdu pour
vous. Il ne se passera pas un an que la dynastie des Kadjares aura cessé
de régner. Ce qui a eu lieu dans la dernière guerre aura lieu encore à
présent. Ne comptez ni sur les promesses des Anglais, ni sur les assertions
des Turcs. . . . Les Anglais ne vous défendront pas ; leur politique n'a eu
vue que les intérêts de leurs possessions dans les Indes. Nous pouvons,
en Asie, conquérir un royaume, et personne ne s'en inquiétera. En Europe
chaque pouce de terrain peut donner lieu à des guerres sanglantes : la
Turquie est nécessaire à l'équilibre Européen ; mais les puissances de
l'Europe ne regardent pas qui gouverne la Perse. Votre indépendance
politique est entre nos mains. . . . Il n'est qu'un moyen d'effacer le
souvenir de l'attentat qu'elle déplore, c'est de solliciter le pardon de notre
grand monarque, pour la perfide trahison de la populace de Téhéran.
Vous pouvez atteindre ce but en m'adressant un de vos frères, ou un de vos
fils, à Tiflis, d'où je l'expédierai en ambassade a St. Pétersbourg. Je prends
sur moi de faire agréer cette démarche à notre souverain.

the audience which Kosroo Meerza obtained of Nicholas, the Persian presented the handle of his scimitar to the Czar, and declared himself willing to give his life for the life which had been taken from the Czar's representative in Persia. The Emperor was contented with a more moderate reparation ; namely, that the persons mainly concerned in the murder of the members of the Mission should be punished ; that the priest who had given the *fetwah*, or order for taking the Armenian women from the house of M. Grebaïodoff, should be exiled; and that the plundered property should be restored. Compliance with these demands was readily promised, and Kosroo Meerza returned to his country after having obtained from the Czar the relinquishment of his claim for one of the two crores of tomans, which, under the terms of the treaty of Turkomanchai, were still due by Persia to Russia. By this act the Emperor wiped away a stain which till then had adhered to the good faith of a Russian officer. At the time of the conferences which preceded the signing of the treaty of Turkomanchai, General Paskiewitch had requested the British envoy to tell the king that in the event of the due and regular payment by Persia of the amount of the indemnity owing to Russia, he would take it upon himself to make the Shah a present of 100,000 tomans. But so great had been the need of ready money on account of the Turkish war, that the performance of this promise was evaded by the Russian agents. However, the Czar now made ample amends for any shortcomings on the part of the Governor-General of Georgia, since he relinquished his claim for 500,000 tomans.* At the

---

* About 250,000*l.* sterling.

same time, it must be borne in mind that Russia had already received from Persia about two millions of pounds sterling—a sum which exceeded the losses and expenses that her subjects and her government had incurred during the Persian war. Prince Dolgorouki was now sent as Minister to Persia, and on his declaring himself in the name of the Emperor to be satisfied with what had been done by the Shah in atonement for the massacre of the members of the Imperial Mission, the troops in garrison at Tabreez were paraded in the presence of the Minister and of the Crown-Prince, when a royal salute of twenty-one guns from the artillery, and a *feu de joie* from the infantry, announced the reconciliation of the two governments.

The year 1830 was marked in Persia by the occurrence of a series of shocks of earthquake. In the month of April the town of Demavend suffered severely; not less than five hundred persons are said to have been buried under the ruins of the houses which were overthrown. The towns of Semnan and Damghan, and the villages in their neighbourhood, likewise sustained great injury; and in all seventy towns and villages are said to have been partially destroyed. The Shah at this time undertook a journey to Ispahan and the south of Persia, and the crown-prince was entrusted with the government of Khorassan, in addition to those he already held. He was summoned from Azerbaeejan to Tehran with a view to his being sent thence to the eastwards for the purpose of arranging the affairs of his new province. On his arrival at the capital, however, it was deemed expedient that he should proceed in the first instance to Yezd, at which place the habitual energy of Hassan Ali Meerza

17

had not been attended with the result of a restoration of
public tranquillity. Abbass Meerza proceeded thither, and
the chief people of the town came out to meet him, and
tendered the declaration of their submission to his will.
His brother upon this proceeded with his troops to
Kerman, to which place he was followed by the crown-
prince. The latter had received instructions to send
Hassan Ali to the presence of the Shah, and a regiment
of infantry was ordered to accompany his Highness,
nominally as an escort, but in reality to prevent his
evading the orders of his sovereign—so jealous is despotism, and so forgetful of past services, provided that
at the present time one's evil star be in the ascendant!
The crown-prince was welcomed by the citizens of Kerman, and after having established some sort of government and public confidence in that place, he returned to
Ispahan, to which city the Shah had again repaired, and
where his Majesty issued orders to the prince to proceed
forthwith to Khorassan, and to do his best to reduce the
refractory chiefs of that province to obedience. On his
way to Meshed, the prince succeeded in taking two forts
which were held by rebel chiefs.

The young Kosroo Meerza had led his father's army
from Kerman across the desert to Toon and Tubbaz—an
undertaking which was attended with great difficulty, and
the successful accomplishment of which bears testimony
to the patient endurance of the troops, and to the capacity of their youthful general. The Persian army on this
occasion had to carry with it for long distances even a
supply of water. The instructions given to Abbass
Meerza were to reëstablish the Shah's authority up to
the river Oxus, which had been fixed by Nadir as the

boundary of Persia. With this view his Highness wrote to the Khan of Khiva, or Kharesm, demanding that he should renounce all pretension to that portion of territory which was claimed by the Shah. The envoy, however, who was the bearer of this note, could proceed no further than Kelat, where he was detained by illness. In the meantime prince Kosroo Meerza undertook the siege of the fortress of Tursheez, by the reduction of which an effective blow was struck at the powerful combination of the Khorassan leaders, who now sought to make terms with the representative of the Shah.

The most powerful of the chiefs of Khorassan was the Eelkhani of the Kurdish tribes of that province. Seeing that the prince had been able to win over some of the more considerable of the other chieftains, this Khan entered upon a negotiation for becoming reconciled to the governor; but failing to come to terms the latter marched to the fortress of Ameerabad, which belonged to the former, and took it by assault. On this occasion the commandant of the prince's artillery was killed, and this occurrence served to add to the fury with which the Persian soldiers were inspired. Launching themselves upon the unhappy inhabitants of the fort, they slew all whom they encountered, notwithstanding the orders of the prince to cease from slaughtering. The carnage was only at length put a stop to by Abbass Meerza entering the place and purchasing from his infuriated soldiers the lives of the surviving inhabitants for the sum of twenty thousand tomans. The Khan of Khiva had advanced by this time to Serrekhs, and Mahomed Meerza was detached with a force to encounter him—but the news of the fall of Ameerabad had the effect of frightening the

Khivan ruler, and he retreated without having risked the result of an action with the Persians. But the Eelkhani still held out, and Abbass Meerza advanced to besiege his last stronghold, the fort of Khabooshan. The forces of the Eelkhani and of the prince were nearly equal, each army consisting of twelve thousand men; but Abbass Meerza had the superiority in artillery, and the Eelkhani was discouraged by the retreat of his ally, the Khan of Khiva. The ruler of Herat, too, who had promised to assist him, had, on seeing the turn that affairs had taken, sent his Vizeer to the prince's camp to announce his sympathy with the cause of the Shah. For all this, the Eelkhani would not surrender his fort, and the Persians accordingly prepared to assault the place. A mine was laid under the outer ditch, which, on being sprung, opened the way for the advance of the assailants up to the foot of the wall; and their courage was animated by the arrival, at that juncture, of the son of the Asef-ed-Dowleh, —the afterwards well-known Salar,—who had been sent by the Shah as the bearer of a number of royal *khilats*, or robes of honour, conferred by his Majesty on those who had distinguished themselves at the taking of Ameerabad.

It is the custom in Persia for those who are honoured by being made the recipients of royal *khilats* to show respect to the Shah by making an *istikball*, or formal reception, to the robe of honour. Notwithstanding the critical position in which the Salar, on his arrival at Khabooshan, found the besiegers of that place, the custom of going to meet the Shah's *khilats* could not be departed from, and accordingly Abbass Meerza caused the assault to be postponed in order that he and his

officers might take part in the *istikball*. But this ceremony was not regarded with equal reverence by the
Eelkhani, who, to the intense mortification of the prince,
rudely disturbed the slowly-winding procession by the
discharge of a gun on the rampart of the fort. Even
after this affront terms of accommodation were still
offered to the Eelkhani, and on their being declined, the
order was given to assault Khabooshan simultaneously on
each of its four sides. But now the Eelkhani came to
the conclusion that he had done enough for honour, and
he accordingly sent a messenger to the prince to intimate
his willingness to agree to terms of arrangement. In
reply he was told that he must surrender at discretion, or
take the consequences of not doing so. He came to the
Persian camp and was received with distinction by the
prince. His Royal Highness entered Khabooshan, and
permitted to himself the relaxation of going to the Eelkhani's bath, on coming out of which he was received by
the son of that chieftain, who, in the name of his mother,
presented him with an offering of ten cashmere shawls,
and as many of the finest horses that were to be found in
the tents of the tribe. The prince embraced the opportunity of exercising the power which success in arms had
given him, without calling upon the tribesmen to change
the allegiance which they had till now owned to the
family of their chief. The Eelkhani was deposed; but
his son, Sām Khan, who was the bearer of the offering,
was then named Eelkhani in place of his sire. The
fortifications of Khabooshan were destroyed, and the
Persian army received orders to march to Ak-derbend,
to which place the prince proceeded after having visited
Meshed.

The object to which he now turned his attention was the reduction of the city of Serrekhs.* That place is considered by the Persians to be one of the four chief cities of Khorassan. From its situation in the desert between Meshed and Merve, its possession is a matter of necessity to an invader approaching from either side with the purpose of possessing himself of one or other of the above-mentioned cities, and Prince Abbass Meerza could not have reasserted the power of Persia to regain the line of the Oxus as her frontier without having first possessed himself of Serrekhs. That city is said to have derived its name from Serrekhs, the son of Gooderz, a chief of Turan. It was held by the Saloor tribe of Turkomans, and its possession had been successively disputed by the Khan of Khiva and by the Ameer of Bokhara, respectively. The Saloors are called after the title of Tuli Khan,† the son of Genghis, and they form one of the most powerful divisions of the Turkomans. They are not addicted to the practice of making excursions into Persia for the purpose of plundering, but they were accused by Abbass Meerza of being in the habit of supplying arms to other tribes, to be used against the peaceful subjects of the Shah. In return for those arms, or for other commodities, they received many Persian prisoners, whom they detained as slaves, or sold to the inhabitants of Khiva and Bokhara. At this juncture

---

* A.D. 1832.

† " The Harem of Zingis was composed of five hundred wives and concubines; and of his numerous progeny, four sons, illustrious by their birth and merit, exercised under their father the principal offices of peace and war. Toushi was his great huntsman, Zagatai his judge, Octai his minister, and *Tuli* his general."—*The Decline and Fall of the Roman Empire*, c. lxiv.

there were three thousand captive Sheeahs within the city of Serrekhs.

Abbass Meerza appeared before that fortified place, and summoned it to surrender. In reply, Adina Khan, one of the chief of the Saloor tribe, proceeded to the camp of the prince, taking with him the wives and children of a number of Turkomans who had previously been sent as hostages to Persia. The chief of the Saloors agreed to liberate the Persian captives on receiving back the hostages, and his proposals were emphasized by the tears and entreaties of the women and children. But these failed to make any impression on the prince, who informed the chief that the hostages were not in his camp, and who went so far as to detain Adina Khan and those he had brought with him; the Persian commander being of opinion that men-stealers, such as the Turkomans, were not entitled to the benefit of the usages established for war between civilized nations. The Persian artillery opened fire on the city, and the Turkomans thereupon had recourse to the expedient of placing their Sheeah captives—men, women and children—in such a position as that they should be exposed to the full effects of the fire of the besiegers. This device caused the prince to suspend for a time the cannonade from his artillery. But he was roused to fresh measures against the Turkomans by the perusal of a petition which he received from his father's captive subjects, imploring him to rescue them from a captivity in which they were constantly exposed to hear the Sheeah faith blasphemed, and to see their wives violated. Adina Khan was sent into the city as the bearer of the prince's ultimatum; which was, that the place should be surrendered to him, unconditionally, within one hour, or that it should feel the effects of his power. The hour elapsed, and the prince gave his troops the order to assault Serrekhs, and to execute a *Katl-i-am*, or general massacre upon its stubborn inhabitants. The onset did not terrify the brave tribesmen of Saloor, who met the assailants with the Suni war-cry, " *La Allah-il-Allah* ; " but the Turkomans were overcome, their chief was slain, and no quarter was asked by the vanquished, or offered by the victors. For the space of one hour the carnage raged, but at the end of that time the hunger after plunder prevailed over the thirst for blood, and the soldiers left off slaughtering in order that they might secure the spoil with as little delay as might be possible. The riches found in Serrekhs are said to have exceeded all computation, and the troops were permitted to retain for themselves whatever fell into their hands. Four hundred and fifty slave-dealers were given over to the liberated slaves, by whom they were torn in pieces, and after the walls of Serrekhs had been levelled with the ground, the prince turned back towards Meshed. His successes had inspired such terror throughout Central Asia, that it is said Turanian mothers could hush their children by pronouncing the dreaded name of Abbass.

The last recusant chieftain of Khorassan—the ruler of the Kara tribe—now submitted to the representative of the Shah. He was deprived of his government, and detained in custody along with the former Eelkhani. The declared intention with which the crown-prince had set out from Ispahan, of reasserting by force the right of the Shah to all the country lying between Khorassan and the

Oxus, had not been carried into execution : not even
as far as to Merve had the arms of Abbass penetrated ;
but yet he was now in some sort enabled to carry out
the instructions he had received from the Shah.   Five
thousand prisoners of the tribe of Saloor still remained
in his camp, and for their ransom the Khan of Khiva
offered to pay the sum of fifty thousand tomans.   Abbass
Meerza consented to liberate them only upon the
condition that he should receive, besides the ransom-
money, a paper wherein it was stipulated that Persian
merchants proceeding to Central Asia should be conducted as far as to the Oxus by guards of the Saloor
tribe, who should be responsible for their safety ; that
that tribe should undertake to prevent the Turkomans
of the tribes of Tekeh and Saroock from making incursions into Khorassan ; that if they could not in all instances effectually prevent these incursions, they should
at any rate give timely notice to the nearest Persian
authorities to take measures for their own defence ; that
they should agree never to receive or have any dealings
with slave-dealers of any country ; and finally, that they
should consent to furnish tribute and horsemen to the
Shah at stated intervals. These conditions were accepted
by the Turkomans, who probably had no intention at all
of adhering to them ; but the document in which they
were embodied remained in the hands of the prince,
and the honour of the Persian government was vindi-
cated.

    After this, Prince Abbass Meerza, elated by the
success which had attended his arms in Khorassan,
turned his attention to the scheme of conquering a
portion of Affghanistan.   Yar Mahomed Khan, the

Vizeer of Prince Kamran of Herat, was then in the
Persian camp, and Abbass Meerza desired him to inform
his master that the Shah, being now not engaged in
Russian wars, was at leisure to assert by force of arms
the claims of the Kings of Persia to dominion over
Affghanistan. This declaration on the part of the
Persian crown-prince was the beginning of a series of
events which greatly contributed to bring about the
subsequent Affghan war. Prince Kamran was required
to acknowledge the authority of the Shah, and to pay
tribute to him as a vassal, or else to be prepared to feel
the effects of his power. The ruler of Herat endeavoured by means of a soft answer to turn away the
prince's wrath, but this did not have the effect of inducing his Highness to forego the resolution he had
taken of marching upon Herat. His son, Mahomed
Meerza, was at his request appointed Vali of Khorassan,
so that the crown-prince might be at liberty to devote
his exclusive attention to the great scheme of conquering
Affghanistan. He wrote to the Shah, requesting large
reinforcements for the realization of his brilliant plans;
but the king, while approving of the resolution to add
Herat to his dominions, and while sending the required
forces to Khorassan, directed that they should be led by
Mahomed Meerza, and that the crown-prince should
return to Tehran. He doubtless felt that his own days
were numbered, and was therefore unwilling to risk the
occurrence of the confusion which he knew would ensue
in Persia in the event of his dying while the heir-
apparent should be far away in Affghanistan.

The crown-prince returned to Tehran, bringing with
him the fallen chiefs of Khorassan. He also brought

with him Abdul Rezak Khan of Yezd, who had risen in rebellion against the Shah during the occupation of Azerbaeejan by the Russians, and who had forced the governor of Yezd, Mahomed Veli Meerza, to make his escape from that place. This Khan had also insulted and ill-used the family of the prince, and had expelled the members of his harem from Yezd. Abbass Meerza had promised to intercede with the Shah for the pardon of these prisoners of rank; but Abdul Rezak Khan so much dreaded the effects of the revenge of Mahomed Veli Meerza, that, ere reaching Tehran, he twice attempted to commit suicide,—in the first instance by taking a large quantity of opium, and afterwards by inflicting upon himself a wound with his dagger. In this state he was brought before the Shah, and having been, along with the other two captives, severely reprimanded, he was made over to the custody of Mahomed Veli Meerza, with the distinct understanding that, though he was to be disgraced, his life would not be taken, and that he was to receive no bodily injury. What follows is illustrative of the barbarism which still lingers in the Persian character. The prince was beset by the women of his family who had been ill-treated by Abdul Rezak, and, no longer able to restrain his desire for the blood of his foe, he entered the apartment where the Khan was being attended by doctors, who were endeavouring to bandage the wound which his own hand had inflicted on his person. These were ordered to retire, and Mahomed Veli nearly severed the Khan's head from his body with one blow of his sabre. Upon this the women of his family rushed into the apartment, and after having mangled the body, caused it to be thrown out into the street. I nowhere read that this shocking act drew down upon the perpetrator any censure from the Shah.

Abbass Meerza was now bent upon returning to Khorassan, but the state of his health was such as to alarm the king, and the prince was earnestly entreated by his friends to act upon the advice of his medical advisers, and to repair to some place where he might hope to enjoy the repose which he so much required. He replied that the necessities of his position were such as to put it out of his power to retire from affairs for a time, as the report would in that case get abroad that he was dangerously ill, and would have a prejudicial effect on his interests. He accordingly, much against the wish of the Shah, set out once again for Khorassan, and he saw his father's face no more. Efforts were at this time made on the part of the Russian Government to bring the crown-prince to throw himself into the hands of that power. His Highness's fickle and wavering mind was swayed to and fro between the schemes of ruling by the favour of the Czar, or of owing his crown to his own efforts, and to the aid of some English officers who were now sent from India for the purpose of drilling and commanding his troops. He chose the nobler part, and declined to become the slave of the power whose legions he had so often faced in battle.

His Highness proceeded towards Meshed, and on the way he had the misfortune to hear of the death of his English physician, Dr. Cormick, who had attended him during a period of twenty-three years, and who, by his professional skill and his intimate acquaintance with the prince's constitution, might perhaps have been the means

of saving his life. After his arrival at Meshed his illness rapidly increased, and he became aware that his end
was approaching. He now devoted his few remaining
hours to the services of religion. Twice each day he
proceeded on foot to the shrine of Imam Reza, and when
his last hour was come he turned his face to Mecca, and,
worn out by war and woes, calmly yielded up the ghost.
He had, amongst one hundred and fifty-nine children,
been ever the favourite of his father, and though he was
fickle and easily worked upon and passionate, he was,
notwithstanding, the noblest of the Kajar race. Abbass
Meerza had attained the age of forty-six years, when his
ashes were consigned to the sacred earth beneath the
shrine of Imam Reza.*

The difficult task had now to be performed of
announcing to the Shah the intelligence of his son's
demise. At all times to be the bearer of ill news is a
duty most repugnant to the feelings of a Persian, but
on this occasion the news to be conveyed were of so
peculiarly mournful a nature, that it was feared the Shah
in the first outburst of his grief would order the bearer
of the evil tidings to be put to death. During two whole
days no one could be persuaded to undertake the task,
and at the end of that time the king's two youngest
sons were together sent to lisp to their aged father the
tale of the demise of the heir to his throne.

The outrageous grief of the Shah was not occasioned
solely by the loss for ever of his beloved son's society.
Some time before this the king, it is said, had commanded the royal astrologer to cast his horoscope, so
that he might gain some knowledge of the fate that

* A.D. 1833.

awaited him. The astrologer, in the performance of this delicate duty, was, perhaps, guided by his common sense more than by any conjunction of the stars. In all probability the crown-prince would survive his father, and therefore he would not be put to shame before the latter by the answer which he delivered. It was that the prince's death would precede by about a year that of the king. He could have little calculated on the literal fulfilment of his prophecy.

Before the death of the heir-apparent, his son Mahomed Meerza had advanced upon Ghorian, in the territory of Herat, and having found that place obstinately defended, had left it in his rear and proceeded to attack the capital of Prince Kamran. The inhabitants of Herat defended themselves with the courage and steadiness which they have manifested during each of the numerous sieges of that fortress. On one occasion they sallied out from the place and defeated one of the divisions of the Persian army; but Mahomed Meerza was assisted by the talent and experience of Monsieur Beroffsky, a Polish officer who had come to Persia with the design of inducing that power to league with Turkey against Russia at the time of the Polish insurrection. The siege of Herat would probably ere long have been conducted to a termination favourable to the Persians, but it was brought to a sudden close in consequence of the death of the crown-prince. The ruler of Herat agreed to pay tribute to the Shah, and Mahomed Meerza returned to Meshed, and proceeded to Tehran, where he was pronounced the heir-apparent to the throne, and appointed to be governor of Tabreez. The removal of the crown-prince from the scene gave fresh hope to those who had intended to dispute with him the accession to the regal dignity, and, from the feeble health of the king, men were prepared soon to witness the miseries of civil war.

Prince Mahomed Meerza, now the acknowledged heir to the Persian throne, returned to Tabreez to undertake the government so long held by his father. This prince was at this time twenty-eight years of age, but, young as he was, he was already enfeebled in constitution, and he paid the penalty of his devotion to the pleasures of the table by having to submit to frequently-recurring attacks of gout. The province of Azerbaeejan had suffered greatly from the excessive peculation of his brothers, two of whom, Jehangeer and Kosroo, were now sent to well-merited confinement in the fortress of Ardabeel. Of these two young men their own mother is said to have declared that it was impossible to tell which was the worst; and we are therefore not surprised to read that Kosroo Meerza, who had been ambassador to the court of Russia, was afterwards condemned to be deprived of sight. But though Mahomed Meerza was the nominal governor of Azerbaeejan, the real authority over that province lay at this time in the hands of Meerza Abdul Kassim, the Kaim-Makam, who had long filled the important office of vizeer to Abbass Meerza, and who was subsequently called to the still higher post of Grand Vizeer of Persia. This nobleman stood unrivalled for talent in the estimation of his countrymen. He was an able financier, and was well acquainted with the condition of every province in the kingdom, and was moreover versed in the relations between Persia and the foreign States; but the quality in the possession of which he was chiefly pre-eminent, was the power of deceiving others—a power which it would seem was in no way lessened by the circumstance that his falseness was widely known. He made it a principle never to refuse a request made of him, and by these easy means he contrived to send away petitioners contented, for the time being. The Kaim-Makam estimated others by what he knew of his own character. He would trust no one, and as he insisted on himself transacting all affairs of importance, the business confided to him remained always in arrears, and the people of Azerbaeejan were left to vent in grumbling the discontent engendered by the miserable system of government under which they were condemned to live.

The aged Shah had for some time past been in indifferent health, and his demise was thought to be not far distant. Under these circumstances his son, Hassan Ali Meerza, the Firman-Firma, or governor-general, of the province of Fars, who had made up his mind to be king after his father should die, thought it would be wasting money to pay in the arrears which he owed to the royal treasury. In order to compel him to do so, Fetteh Ali, whose ruling passion of avarice was as predominant as ever, determined upon undertaking another journey to the south of Persia. His march would also, he hoped, have the effect of putting down the rumours of his death which had been circulated for some time past, and which were the cause of much lawless disorder in the provinces at a distance from the capital. The Bakhtiari mountaineers had even gone to the length of inflicting a poignant blow on the Shah by seizing on a portion of the royal treasure which was being conveyed to Tehran from Ispahan. A large force, said to have amounted to thirty thousand horse and foot, was assembled for the purpose of accompanying the Shah. In the autumn his Majesty quitted Tehran, and at Koom went to inspect the gorgeous sepulchre which he was destined soon to fill. At Kashan he remained for eight days in the delightful palace of Feen, and thence proceeded to Ispahan. The monarch, whose life had been spent in travelling from place to place, had now made his last journey. He was met near the city by the whole population of Ispahan, and a gorgeous carpeting of cashmere shawls was spread on the ground to be pressed by the feet of the king as he entered the palace of Sadetabad. Six days later the Firman-Firma arrived from Sheeraz, but in place of the 600,000 tomans * which were due from the revenue of Fars, the prince brought with him only 13,000 tomans. This was too trying for the Shah's patience, and after having vented his anger in abuse of his son, he ordered him to be confined until the remaining arrears should be collected by the commissioners whom he appointed to that duty. The Grand Vizeer was ordered to proceed to Fars with ten thousand men, and there to employ the severest measures for coercing the inhabitants into a settlement of the claims against them. The Firman-Firma, having been thus temporarily superseded, was permitted to return to the south.

After this the Shah held a public salam, or levée, at which he desired the governors and vizeers present to dismiss from their minds the vain idea that he was too old to be able to enforce the payment of what was due to him. Three days later, his Majesty suffered from a slight attack of fever, which increased to an

---

* About 300,000l. sterling.

18

alarming extent in the course of the two following days, but up to the last hour of his life the Shah continued to transact the business of the state. On the day before his death he held the usual levée, and gave his prime minister his audience of leave. On the next day—the third of his illness,—he sent his eunuchs with messages to the different officers of the government whom he could not see personally; as his fever obliged him to remain in his harem apartments, where he was nursed by his favourite wife, the Taj-ed-Dowleh, a lady whom his will had raised from the condition of a dancing-girl to that of the ruling sultana of the royal family. When on this day, the 23rd of October, 1834,* the hour of evening prayer arrived, the king endeavoured to perform his accustomed devotions; but his strength was exhausted, and all that remained for him was to ask that his feet might be placed in the direction of Mecca. As the sultana hastened to perform the dying request of her lord, the Shah fell lifeless at her side, having expired without a groan or a sigh.

Fetteh Ali had attained to the age of sixty-eight, and he had ruled over Persia for thirty-seven years. His character may be described in a few words. Where money was not in question he was pronounced by competent authority to be the most sensible man in his dominions; but his violent lust after gold obscured his common sense, and caused him to sacrifice some of the most important provinces of his kingdom, rather than supply the means necessary for their defence. Throughout his whole reign this passion was predominant, and for its more complete gratification he was ready to put

* The 19th of Jemadi-es-Sani, A.H. 1250.

aside the suggestions of dignity and the promptings of gratitude. Thus we read that when his Britannic Majesty's Government decided upon handing over to the authorities in India the management of the relations between Great Britain and the Persian court, the Shah consented to the change under the belief that the envoy from India would lay before him an offering upon the same costly scale as that which Sir John Malcolm had brought from the shores of Hindostan. But the Government of Fort William no longer felt the necessity of paying a very heavy price for the good-will of the Shah and his ministers, and accordingly their envoy was instructed to limit his offering to the sum of fifty thousand rupees. The anxiety of Fetteh Ali on this point was so great that he directed those who had access to the envoy on his way towards Tehran, to endeavour to extract from him some information regarding the amount of the present which he intended to lay before the king. These endeavours were not attended with success, and the envoy arrived at the court without having given any hint as to his intentions. Upon this the Shah sent two of his ministers to wait upon the envoy with the express purpose of asking him how much money he intended to offer to the king; and when these vizeers had ascertained that the offering was to be fifty thousand rupees, they did not scruple to affirm in the name of their master that the Shah, by being offered so small a sum, would consider himself to have been almost deceived, since in accepting the proposal made to him to receive an envoy from the subordinate Government of India, he had of course taken it for granted that the offering to be made to him would be on the same scale as that of the former envoy from

Calcutta.   The result of this barefaced proceeding was exactly what the Shah wished—since the envoy was bullied into exceeding the amount which his government had assigned as that which might be offered to the Shah.

With the exception of the one glaring vice of avarice, Fetteh Ali's character did not exhibit many very objectionable traits, and on the whole it will bear a favourable comparison with that of the generality of Oriental monarchs.   That he was not without the qualities requisite for a Persian King, is proved by the fact of his having been able to put down the numerous competitors who disputed with him the possession of the throne, and by his having been able to maintain himself upon that throne for thirty-seven years; but he was indebted for his successes more to the precautions taken by his uncle than to any merits of his own.   His talents were rather of a kind suited to an Oriental statesman than to a soldier.   There is no reason to doubt that he possessed in his youth a sufficient share of courage, but after he had firmly secured possession of the throne, he did not care to expose his person too much to the chances of battle; and in his later years, by deserting the army opposed to the Russians, near the Araxes, he laid himself open to the charge either of inexcusable apathy towards the national cause, or of an unworthy desire to place himself beyond the reach of the inconveniences attending a residence in a camp before the enemy.   But if Fetteh Ali was not without faults, he was also gifted with several good qualities.   His affection for his children was excessive, and there is something touching in the constancy with which he clung to Abbass Meerza, even at a time when that prince was the cause, or the victim, of great national disasters. Fetteh Ali was attached to the Mahomedan religion, but he was by no means a fanatic, nor did he evince any dislike to the society of those who were not of Islam. He was unremitting in his attention to the discharge of the business of the state, and if in reading the history of his reign we find some acts of barbarity recorded, we must make due allowance for him on account of the character and customs of his subjects; the unsettled nature of the times on which he was cast, and the necessity of making himself feared by those who would have wished to ascend his throne. The Shah's body was conveyed from Ispahan to the tomb which he had caused to be prepared at Koom.

Koom is a city which was built in the year of the Hejira 203,* and which lies about eighty miles to the south of Tehran, on the road from that place to Ispahan. It at one time † possessed a considerable population, but it owes, in modern times, its celebrity to the mosque of Fatima, which makes it a favourite place of burial. In one of the finest of the gardens adjacent to the city was the mausoleum of Rustem Khan, a prince of the royal house of Georgia, who had embraced the tenets of the Mahomedan religion in order to obtain the viceroyalty of his native country. In the time of the Sefaveeans, Koom boasted of handsome quays along either side of its river, a well-built bridge across it, and large bazaars for the transaction of commerce, both wholesale and retail; also of commodious caravanserais and beautiful mosques. It was, however, subsequently almost completely destroyed

---

* MACDONALD-KINNEIR'S *Geographical Memoir of the Persian Empire.*
† *See* CHARDIN'S *Travels,* vol. ii.

by the Affghans in 1722, and only a portion of it has been since rebuilt.

It owes, as has been said, its celebrity to the possession of the mosque and sanctuary erected to the memory of Fatima, the daughter of Imam Reza, and which for centuries past has been the burial-place of the Kings of Persia. Attached to this sacred edifice are four courts, and the dome of the building, which is of gold, bears witness to the piety of Fetteh Ali Shah. The tomb of the Holy Virgin of Koom is protected from the defilement of the vulgar by a railing of massive silver, crowned at the corners by balls of gold. In adjoining chapels lie the ashes of several of the Persian monarchs : amongst them those of two of the Sefaveeans ; Sefi the first, and Abbass the second. Nothing can exceed the beauty of these places of burial. The flooring is of tablets of porphyry painted in gold and in blue, and the vaulted roofs are equally rich and picturesque. The tomb of Sefi is composed of ivory, ebony, camphor-wood, aloes and other sweet-smelling timber worked together in mosaic, and fastened by ligatures of fine gold. The chapels of the more recent royal personages whose ashes repose at Koom are attended by a service of priests, who by day and night read from the Koran and pray for the souls of those whose tombs they guard. To one of these chapels, and to the reverend care of the priests of Koom, were consigned the mortal remains of Fetteh Ali Shah, in the full hope and confidence that when the last trump should sound and the dead should rise to life, the monarch would be found to be under the all-availing protection of the Holy Virgin Fatima.

CHAPTER X.

THE death of the aged Shah was the signal for which two pretenders to the throne had long waited. These were Hassan Ali Meerza, the Firman-Firma, or governor-general of Fars, and the Zil-es-Sultan,* the governor of Tehran. Both of these princes had to a certain extent the advantage over Mahomed Meerza, the rightful heir to the Persian throne. The Firman-Firma at the time of the death of Fetteh Ali, was sufficiently near to Ispahan to be able to reach that city, and take possession of the jewels and treasure which the late king had brought with him, before the royal stores had been to any considerable degree diminished ; while the Zil-es-Sultan, on his part, from his position at the capital, had the opportunity of acquiring even a larger quantity of money and valuables than that which fell to the lot

---

* The *Zil-es-Sultan*, or Shadow of the Sultan, was so called from his remarkable resemblance to his father, Fetteh Ali Shah.

of his brother. Each prince lost no time in proclaiming himself king, and in organizing a military force sufficient to give effect to his pretensions. But in the meantime, others were taking effective measures for carrying into execution the will of the dead Shah, who had designated his grandson Mahomed Meerza to be his successor. The representative of Russia offered to seat him on the throne by a Russian military force; but the effective measures adopted by Sir John Campbell, the British envoy, who was at that time at Tabreez, rendered it unnecessary for the young Shah to have recourse to the aid thus proffered by his powerful neighbour.

Mahomed Meerza was at this time completely under the surveillance of his minister, the Kaim-Makam, and that Vizeer was so jealous of any one gaining influence over his master, that he took every precaution to prevent all but his own creatures from approaching the person of the youthful Shah. Yet the Kaim-Makam did not exhibit at this critical juncture the qualities that mark a vigilant and able statesman. Instead of using every possible effort to hasten the preparations for the king's march to the capital, he urged puerile objections to the plans suggested by the British envoy for facilitating the royal advance to Tehran. He alleged the want of military stores as a reason for delaying his master's departure, and when the English representative had himself furnished money for their purchase, the Vizeer declared that he had not the means of procuring horses to drag the artillery with which the Shah must be accompanied. But all the apathy of the Kaim-Makam was insufficient to damp the energy of Sir John Campbell, who advanced more money on account of the Shah, and himself visited the arsenal several times each day in order to encourage and stimulate the workmen. Fetteh Ali Shah had expired on the 23rd of October at Ispahan. News of the event was officially communicated to the British representative at Tabreez on the 7th of November, and on the 10th of that month, by means of unremitted exertion, Sir Henry Lindsay Bethune was enabled to march from Tabreez on Meeaneh in command of the troops, upon whose aid the Shah relied for overcoming the formidable competitors for sovereign power. On the 16th of November, 1834, the Shah and his court left Tabreez, without having previously made any arrangement for the despatch to Tehran of either men or stores. The Kaim-Makam knew that these matters were being looked to by the English representative, and he had not sufficient respect either for himself, or for the government of his master, to feel at all troubled by the incongruity of throwing upon a foreign minister the burden of providing for the successful progress of the king. On the 24th of November, the Persian troops under the command of the English officers who had been lent to the Shah, arrived at the place of rendezvous.

Colonel Bethune was now at the head of a considerable force which possessed twenty-four guns, and when he had taken up a position at Zenjan, half-way between Tabreez and Tehran, he was made aware of the approach of some of the adherents of the Zil-es-Sultan. But the Shadow of the Sultan was already fast declining. His followers no sooner were informed of the strength of the king's army, and of the fact that his Majesty was accompanied by the representatives of Russia and of England, than they hastened, one after another, to secure their own pardon by deserting from their colours and coming to the royal camp. At Kasveen the last semblance of opposition on the part of the Zil-es-Sultan disappeared, by the submission of his general, Imamverdi Meerza, and his whole army. On the 21st of December the Shah reached Tehran, and the troops of Sir H. Bethune took possession, in his Majesty's name, of the city, the palace and treasury. The astrologers fixed upon the 2nd of January, 1835, as being the first day which had a fortunate hour for the entrance of the Shah into his capital. On that day he quitted the palace outside the walls where he had taken up his temporary abode, and entered the ark, or citadel. On the 31st of the same month, it being the feast of Bairam, Mahomed Shah was crowned King of Persia, and amongst those who assisted at the ceremony was his uncle, the Zil-es-Sultan.

But a more dangerous competitor was still at large, and the British envoy pressed upon the Shah's Minister the necessity of losing no time in despatching an army to encounter that of the Firman-Firma. Such, however, was the listlessness of the Kaim-Makam, and so great was his reluctance to furnish money for the purpose of making an advance to the soldiers, that it was not until the 3rd of February that Sir H. Bethune was enabled to march towards Ispahan. His force consisted of three battalions of regular infantry, with a small number of horse and sixteen guns. He was to receive an addition to his strength on the way, and reinforcements were sent after him under the command of the Moëtemed-ed-Dowleh. In the meantime the reins of government were held tightly in the hands of the Kaim-Makam, who exercised over his master an imperious authority, similar to that

which Cardinal Mazarin wielded over the mind of Louis
the Fourteenth.   The Shah at this time, it was averred,
scarcely ventured to give an order to his personal
attendants without having previously obtained the consent of his Grand Vizeer.   Sir Henry Bethune marched
to within eighty miles of Ispahan, when he learned that
the troops of the Firman-Firma were approaching from
the other direction with the intention of taking possession of the city.   He determined upon this to be beforehand with the pretender, and he accordingly executed a
forced march which only Persian troops could accomplish ; traversing the eighty miles that lay between him
and Ispahan in the space of little more than thirty
hours.*   Ispahan had been the scene of the greatest
disorder, the *lootis*, or vagabonds, of the place having
been encouraged in their lawlessness by the Sheikh-el-
Islam, and by the Vizeer of the deceased king, who had
espoused the cause of the Firman-Firma.   The arrival
of Sir Henry Bethune was the signal for the restoration
of order.   He had not been a week at Ispahan when
intelligence reached him of the approach of the governor-
general of Fars, whose army was commanded by his
brother, Hassan Ali Meerza, the Shuja-es-Sultaneh.
On receiving this information, Colonel Bethune put a
portion of his army again in motion.   He took with
him only two regiments of infantry, some troops of
cavalry, and twenty guns.   In all, his force did not
amount to four thousand men, and he was to be opposed
to the ablest leader in Persia.   The Shuja-es-Sultaneh
endeavoured to turn his opponent's flank by taking a less-
frequented road through the hills, by which Ispahan

* FRASER's *Travels in Kurdistan.*

could have been reached ; but information of this manœuvre was speedily conveyed to the English officer,
who thereupon made a flank march, which brought him
face to face with the enemy at a place near Kumeesha.

The Shuja-es-Sultaneh arranged his army in six
divisions, of which two were to guard the baggage,
while the remaining four were to engage the troops of the
Shah. He posted his infantry behind the ruined walls
of a deserted village, from which position they might aim
at their opponents without being themselves exposed.
But the advantage which Sir Henry Bethune possessed
in artillery was sufficient to counteract the favourable
disposition of the troops of Fars, and a discharge of
round shot brought the mud walls down over the heads
of those behind them, and killed forty or fifty men.
The remaining soldiers who had been posted in this
position attempted to make their escape, but were all
overtaken and made prisoners. This decided the event
of the contest. The horsemen of the prince did not
even attempt to make a stand, and the Shuja-es-Sultaneh
fled, taking with him ten thousand tomans, but leaving
his camp, guns and baggage in the hands of the victors.
After this engagement, Sir Henry Bethune pushed on at
once to Sheeraz, the affairs of which city he found to be
in the greatest confusion. The Eelkhani of the nomad
tribes of Fars having been affronted and pillaged by
the Firman-Firma, determined to seize the hour of his
Highness's misfortune for avenging his wrongs, and at
the same time performing a marked service to Mahomed Shah. He accordingly, on the approach of the
king's army, possessed himself of the avenues leading to
and from the city of Sheeraz, and thus prevented the

escape of the Firman-Firma, and his brother, the Shuja-es-Sultaneh. These princes were forthwith sent under an escort to Tehran, from which place, after the Shuja-es-Sultaneh had been deprived of sight, they were despatched as state prisoners to the fortress of Ardabeel.

Ardabeel, the state prison of Persia, stands on a well-watered plain on the Northern extremity of the high table-land of Iran. The population of the city was formerly considerable, but the plague and cholera have reduced it so much that it now contains but three thousand families. On the southern side of the place is situated the fortress—a small work, about two hundred yards square, erected by Abbass Meerza. The inhabitants of Ardabeel reckon their city to be, save three, the most ancient town in Persia; and the truth that the table-land of Iran was once covered with water has given rise here to the fable that King Solomon, by the aid of the two *deevs*, Ard and Beel, opened a passage through the mountains, by which the waters that covered the earth were drained off into the Caspian Sea. The town of Ard and Beel is famous as being the place of sepulture of Sheikh Sefi, the renowned progenitor of the Sefaveean kings. Here also was buried Shah Ismaïl, the first monarch of that dynasty. Their tombs, and the buildings in which they are enclosed, are ornamented with gold, silver and inlaid-work, and the chapel of the Sheikh has its walls lined with velvet, which now hangs in tatters. In the apartment devoted to prayer there is a carpet bearing the date 946 of the Hejira, woven into the pattern. The library is said to contain a considerable number of old volumes; but the value of the collection is believed to have been somewhat

lessened by the visit of the Russians to Ardabeel in the
reign of Fetteh Ali Shah.   In another part of the same
structure there is a magnificent hall ornamented with
lacquered work of azure, where is kept a large collection
of china vases that were made use of for holding the
daily supply of rice—said to have been 3,600 pounds—
granted for the sustenance of those who came to pay
their devotions at the tomb of Shah Ismaïl.   The value
of the religious endowments of this shrine is said to
have formerly amounted to the large sum of two crores
of tomans,* but of all this wealth nothing now remains
to the few attendants of the tomb further than a yearly
allowance of some hundreds of maunds of grain.   The
government long ago confiscated the landed property,
and under the Kajar kings contributions are no longer
made towards the support of the shrine of the ancestor
of the Sefaveean Shahs.†

The Firman-Firma died while on the way to his
prison; but many of Fetteh Ali Shah's descendants—
amongst them the Zil-es-Sultan and the son of the late
Mahomed Ali Meerza of Kermanshah—were doomed to
pass their remaining days at Ardabeel, and there to
reflect on the disadvantages of having been born in the
purple.   No more blood was spilt on this occasion; nor,
with the exception of the Shuja-es-Sultaneh, was any one
deprived of eyesight.   Order was now reëstablished over
the greater portion of Persia, but, as might have been
expected, the province of Khorassan was agitated throughout its length and breadth.   Save Meshed, Nishapoor
and Subsewar, not a place remained to the Shah.   The

---

* A century ago such a sum represented about one million sterling.
† *Narrative of a Journey*, by K. E. ABBOTT, Esq.

people of the other towns expelled the troops in garrison in them, and refused to pay any further taxes. The Khans of Boojnoord and Deregez, and other Khorassan chiefs, set up the standard of rebellion, and the governor had no sooner proceeded in one direction to put down revolt, than news reached him of fresh revolt in another quarter. Prince Karaman was the full and the favourite brother of Mahomed Shah, and he exerted himself to the utmost to secure the safety of Khorassan. His labours were at length followed by the return of the turbulent chiefs to their duty.

The confusion and vexation caused by the obstinate persistence of the Kaim-Makam to trust to no one, but to carry on every branch of the administration himself, were tolerated for a short time. The spring of the year 1835 wore away without any serious occurrence. In the south of Persia a disturbance was put down; and Prince Bahram, the governor of Kermanshah, succeeded in pacifying the troubled districts of Looristan and Arabistan, being aided by a young English officer, then as afterwards remarkable for energy and talent—Lieutenant Henry Rawlinson. But the murmurs of the people at length forced themselves on the notice of the Shah, and determined that monarch to take some step for securing the safety of his throne and the well-being of his people. In Persia there is but one step from splendour to disgrace. A minister, when his services are no longer wanted, may not fall back upon a dignified repose. He must at all hazards retain his post, or make up his mind to be ruined. The Shah, when he was reluctantly forced into action, followed the custom of the country by ordering that his prime minister, the Kaim-Makam, should be seized: an act which was quickly followed by the arrest of his sons. No tumult succeeded this step, but, on the contrary, it produced universal satisfaction. The king himself attended to the administration of justice and the chief direction of public affairs. In the course of the few days which immediately followed the disgrace of the Kaim-Makam, numerous accusations were, as might have been expected, advanced against the fallen man, and the Shah could not fail to be convinced of the corruptness of his former minister, and the deficiencies of his administration. The result was that orders were given that the ex-minister should be strangled in his prison—a sentence which was carried into execution on the night of the 26th of June, 1835.

But the Shah now found that it was not so easy to construct a government as it had been to break one down. At this time the plague and the cholera were raging in the capital, and amongst those who fell victims to one or other pestilence were many of the members of the court. The Asef-ed-Dowleh, the maternal uncle of the king, had been appointed to the government of Khorassan ; but he was anxious to recover his old post of prime minister, and, on hearing of the fall of the Kaim-Makam, he came without permission, and in the greatest haste, from Meshed to Tehran. The choice of the king, however, fell upon Haji Meerza Aghassi, a native of Erivan, who had in the course of his early travels in Arabia acquired so much knowledge that on his return to Tabreez he had been appointed tutor to two of the sons of Abbass Meerza. Amongst other accomplishments he boasted of possessing the art of predicting future events, and in the lifetime of Fetteh Ali Shah he confidently assured Mahomed Meerza that he should one day be king of Persia.   Our opinion of his discernment is, however, somewhat lowered by our being told* that he privately made the same promise to others of the sons of Abbass, so that the chances might be multiplied of his being able in after years to claim the credit of having predicted so important a fact.   Haji Meerza Aghassi, however learned he may have been in Arabian lore, was not a minister calculated to lead Persia in a path of progress.   He was suspicious of the designs of foreign governments, and was entirely ignorant of the principles which at that time were recognized by Europe as those which should be regarded as axioms in political economy.

By the Treaty of·Turkomanchai it was stipulated that Russia should have the right of placing consuls in Persia wherever the demands of trade might require their presence.   It was not stated who were to be judges of the requirements of trade, and Fetteh Ali Shah had to the last persisted that no consuls were required.   On the other hand, the successive representatives of Russia at the Persian court had demanded the royal permission for the establishment and recognition of a consul at Resht, the chief city of Gilan.   This permission was withheld, but a compromise was effected by one of the members of the Russian Legation being annually deputed to Resht to reside there during the four months when the silk-trade demanded the presence of a government agent.

Towards the close of the reign of Fetteh Ali Shah, the attention of the British Government was directed to the subject of the foreign trade of Persia.   A British

---

* HOLMES's *Shores of the Caspian.*

consul* had pointed out that, provided the Persian monarch should throw no unnecessary obstacles in the way of the new scheme, a commercial intercourse between England and Persia, most profitable for both countries, might be easily established. The project was that English goods should be introduced into Persia by way of Turkey; but before attempting to carry it into execution it was necessary to be secure of some guarantee from the Persian government, against the future imposition of arbitrary exactions or preventive restrictions. When the government of Azerbaeejan had been held by Abbass Meerza, that enlightened man had readily issued the necessary orders for the security of British trade; but orders not depending on the rights of treaty were liable at any time to be recalled, and after the death of Abbass it became more than ever desirable that a commercial treaty should be entered into between Great Britain and Persia. But the Shah's government could not see that a trade which at that time annually drained their country of a considerable amount of gold, could possibly be profitable to Persia, and it consequently turned a deaf ear to the proposals of Sir John Campbell for the conclusion of a treaty. That envoy was of opinion that an agent deriving his power directly from the Crown, would have more influence at the Court of the Shah than he himself possessed as the representative of the East India Company. Advantage was accordingly taken of the accession to the throne of Mahomed to change the direction of the British Mission at Tehran. Mr. Ellis was sent to Persia as his Britannic Majesty's ambassador charged to congratulate the Shah

---

* Mr. BRANT.

on his accession, and authorized to reöpen negotiations for the conclusion of a commercial treaty. But still the prime minister of Persia objected to the establishment of English consuls in the Shah's dominions, and urged the British ambassador not to press the matter until such time as the Shah might feel himself sufficiently powerful to defy the anger with which the Russian Government would be filled, by a concession which could not fail to be to a certain extent injurious to the interests of Russian traders. The period during which the matter was to rest unsettled was, as Mr. Ellis observed, indeed indefinite.*

At the period when the first mission had been sent from India to the Persian court, the British authorities in the East were under considerable apprehension lest the sovereign of the Affghans should invade Hindostan; and the British envoy was accordingly instructed to endeavour to induce the Shah to march upon Affghanistan. But a change had in the course of time taken place in the policy of Great Britain with reference to the dealings of the Persians towards the Affghans, and the English Minister at the Persian court was instructed to use all his influence for the purpose of restraining the Shah from the prosecution of any scheme for the conquest of Affghanistan. The successes of Abbass Meerza in his last campaigns had filled the Persians with an exalted idea of their own superiority in arms over other Oriental nations, and the Shah, who was himself an experienced soldier, had no sooner put into order the internal affairs of his kingdom, than he prepared to march towards Khorassan, at the head of a numerous army destined for the reduc-

---

* Published despatches of Sir H. Ellis.

tion of Herat, and the conquest of a considerable portion of Affghanistan. The pretensions of the Persian government to sovereignty in that direction were at this time, somewhat arbitrarily, stated by the Shah's prime minister to extend over that portion of the country which lay between the Iranian frontier and the fortress of Ghizni. The successes of the late Prince Abbass Meerza had alone been the cause of these antiquated pretensions being now advanced. The claim to dominion over Affghanistan had been renounced by Persia in the first treaty with the Government of India, inasmuch as the Affghans were acknowledged to be an independent power; and as the whole of Affghanistan had belonged to the dominions of the Sefaveean princes, it was evident that the Kajar Shahs, as the successors of those princes, could only in reason claim the whole of the country in question if they laid claim to any portion of it. According to the opinion of those who have made the principles of international law their peculiar study, so long a time had elapsed since the country of the Affghans had passed from the power of the Persian kings, that Mahomed Shah had no sufficient claim, based upon the law of nations, to any portion of Affghanistan, in as far as such claim was founded on the extent of the dominions of former Persian kings. If such a pretension had been admitted to be a just one, the Shah might with equal fairness have claimed his right to establish by force of arms his dominion over the territory lying between the Kurdish mountains and the Tigris; or, if there were to be no fixed period of limitation, he might have laid claim to what Persia had once possessed in Asia Minor.

But the Shah had now other and more valid grounds

for undertaking a war against the Prince of Herat, besides those founded upon the conquests of a bygone dynasty. Of the three engagements which Prince Kamran had contracted during the last years of the lifetime of Fetteh Ali Shah, he had fulfilled not one. He had not razed the fort of Ghorian, neither had he despatched to their homes certain Persian families who were to be released from captivity ; nor had he paid to the king of Persia the sum stipulated for as the amount of tribute. The Shah was therefore fully justified in determining to compel him by force of arms to fulfil his engagements. There was also another reason for the advance of the King of Persia upon Herat.   On the borders of Affghanistan, and lying between that country and Persia, extends the province of Seistan.   Seistan had been added to the Affghan kingdom by Ahmed Shah, the founder of the Sedozye dynasty.   During the lifetime of that monarch it continued to appertain to Cabul, but in the troubled times which followed his death, when his successors had difficulty in consolidating their power, the chiefs of Seistan succeeded in establishing the independence of their province.   The Persian government during the reign of the first Kajar Shah, and the early years of his successor, had enough to occupy its attention without going into the question of its right to dominion over Seistan.   But as the dynasty became established, its ambition gradually became enlarged, and by the time of the accession of Mahomed Meerza to the throne, Seistan had come to be considered at Tehran as an integral portion of the dominions of the Shah ; although up to that time, the Persian monarch could boast no more immediate control over the Seistanis than was implied by a rival claimant to the chieftainship invoking the king's assistance, on the condition of his promising to acknowledge the king's right to sovereignty over the province. But in the course of the year in which Mahomed Shah was crowned, Yar Mahomed Khan, the Vizeer of Kamran, succeeded in establishing either his own or his master's authority in Seistan, and he thereby furnished another pretext for the hostilities which the Persian monarch now determined to undertake against the Prince of Herat.

At this time the British government was, by the treaty then in existence with Persia, not entitled to interfere in the international affairs of the two countries with each other: it was, in fact, bound not to interfere between them. It was the interest of Russia at this juncture to encourage the designs entertained by the Shah against the tranquillity of Affghanistan, inasmuch as if Herat, or any portion of that country, should become a portion of the dominions of the King of Persia, the Czar would, by the treaty of Turkomanchai, become entitled to place consuls there for the protection of Russian trade. Outward symbols, and the conscientiously-rendered services of a few well-chosen agents, can effect much on peoples so impressible as those of the countries of the East; and in view of this fact, the Government of his Britannic Majesty did wisely in opposing itself to the expedition which the Shah announced; the evident or avowed purpose of which was the conquest of Herat or the subjugation of Affghanistan. While the question was still under discussion, and while the Shah had not yet set out from Tehran, Prince Kamran thought proper to add fuel to the flame which had been already kindled, by putting some Persians in his dominions to death, and by driving others

of the same race out of his city; but, in justice to the
character of the prince, it must not be omitted to be
stated that these measures were in all probability undertaken for the sake of self-preservation. A conspiracy
against Prince Kamran was known to exist in Herat,
which had originated with the Persian inhabitants of
that place, many of whom had agreed to rebel against
him whenever the army of Mahomed Shah should appear
before the city. With reference to his declaration of
war, the Shah observed at a public levée, that since the
English Government thought itself justified in following
up the interests of each individual merchant, he was
surely within the limits of his rights in taking measures
to prevent his subjects from being carried into captivity
or driven from their homes by the Turkomans.

At this time Dost Mahomed Khan of Cabul was
endeavouring to establish his uncertain power by making
suitable foreign alliances. His dethroned rival, Shah
Shuja-ul-Mulk, was a pensioner in the British dominions
in India, and he was endeavouring to enlist the Indian
Government in a scheme for the recovery of his kingdom.
His proposals were not accepted, but he at length contrived to obtain an advance of the pension which he was
receiving. If this indulgence be considered together
with the fact that the Indian Government was well aware
of the purpose to which the money so advanced would
be applied, and that it took no steps to prevent its
pensioner from preparing a warlike expedition against
Dost Mahomed; the latter chief will not be judged
to have been without grounds for believing that the
British Government of India was hostile to his interests.
He consequently determined to seek the alliance of

Persia, with the double view of putting a limit to the Shah's plans of conquest in Affghanistan, and of securing his aid in future struggles with Shuja-ul-Mulk. Haji Hussein Ali Khan was empowered by the Barukzye Sirdar to negotiate a treaty of offensive and defensive alliance between him and Mahomed Shah, on the conditions that a joint attack should be made on the territories of Prince Kamran, and that in the event of success, a partition of conquests should take place, by which Herat, and the districts lying to the west of the river of Ferrah, should belong to Persia, and the country on the eastern side of that river, with Sebzewar, to Dost Mahomed. The Affghan nobleman found reason to doubt whether the conclusion of such a treaty would really be of advantage to his master, and he seems to have been superseded in his capacity of Affghan pleni-potentiary, by the arrival at Tehran of Azeez Khan; who had been sent thither by the chiefs of Kandahar, brothers of Dost Mahomed, and who agreed with the Persian Government on the terms of a league against Prince Kamran,—the Shah acknowledging the independence of the Barukzye Sirdars.

In the summer of the year 1836, Mahomed Shah put his army in motion towards the east. His Majesty's operations were in the first instance directed against the Turkomans, and they were not distinguished by any remarkable result. Prince Feridoon was detached with a division of the army to attack the fortified town of Karakillah, which place he found on his arrival to have been evacuated by the tribes in whose possession it had been. They had retired to the mountain fastness of Sooknak, from which the Persian general now endeavoured in vain to dislodge them. The Oozbegs of Khiva collected their forces, and opened communication with the Affghans of Herat, for the' purpose of arranging measures in concert with the Turkomans for their mutual defence. The Shah lingered for many weeks in the vicinity of Astrabad, and the dearth of food in his camp became so great that the soldiers plundered even the provisions destined for the use of the king. The Turkomans were in the meantime ever on the watch to cut off Persian stragglers, and their light horsemen kept alive a perpetual alarm in the Persian camp from dusk till daylight. The want of success which attended the operations of the Shah on the banks of the Goorgan, could not fail to raise the spirits of the Affghans of Herat; whose final reply to his Persian Majesty was that they were ready to make him a present, but that they would give no hostages for their future good behaviour, and that if the king were not contented with this answer, he was at liberty to advance to the attack of Herat. But insuperable obstacles presented themselves to the fulfilment at this time of the intentions which the Shah had so often avowed, and towards the end of the year he was forced to return discontented to Tehran.

In the following year the Shah once more set out to the eastward. He mustered his army at Bostan, where it was found to consist of about 8,000 effective infantry and 1,500 cavalry. Four battalions and thirty guns had been sent on in advance to Sebzewar. The government of Herat, on hearing of the king's approach, left no means unused for preparing for the defence of that city. The whole of the provisions to be found in the country were removed into the fortresses, and the forage which could not be carried away was burnt. Even the grass on the plains was set fire to, and all the villages within twelve miles of Herat were destroyed; the inhabitants being removed to the fortresses, or to places at a distance. Ten thousand chosen horsemen were ordered to keep the field, and the remaining troops were directed to garrison the city and the neighbouring strong places. The season of the year, it being the early part of winter, was most unfavourable for military operations in a region where the winter is so rigorous as it is in northern Affghanistan. The troops of the Shah suffered greatly in their progress through Khorassan, and the king himself was unable to walk even from his tent to his carriage. Still he did not depart from the intention with which he had set out, and he himself proceeded with the main body of his army to Herat, while one of the divisions was told off for the duty of besieging Ghorian, and another was sent against the Turkomans and Hezarehs.

The preparations for the defence of Herat were superintended by Yar Mahomed Khan, the Vizeer; Prince Kamran being too much given over to intoxication to be able to direct the business of his government. The ambitious Vizeer was at this time paving the way for his own advancement to the supreme power on one pretext or another, and he disposed of the greater number of chiefs who were likely to oppose his pretensions. By such measures, and his tyrannous conduct towards the people, a spirit of discontent was raised within the city, the Sheeah portion of the inhabitants of which were fully disposed to welcome the Persian king. The condition of the fortifications of Herat was not such, at this time, as to have prevented European troops from taking

the place by assault; but the energetic Vizeer contrived
to put Herat in such a state as to enable it to present
considerable obstacles to a Persian force. The rampart
was patched up and the ditch deepened; and as on the
occasion of the previous siege of the place by the son of
Abbass Meerza, the officer in command of the Persian
artillery had been bribed not to fire shot or shell into the
citadel, it was hoped that the same exemption might be
once more purchased. At this time there arrived at the
city of Herat a young English officer of artillery, and
Yar Mahomed Khan had sufficient sagacity to perceive
at once the immense benefit which might be derived by
his master from the services of Lieutenant Eldred
Pottinger. That officer had travelled through Affghanistan in the disguise of an Oriental costume; and when he
made it known to the Vizeer that he was an Englishman,
the latter from that moment sought to engage him in
the task of defending the city. It would weary the
reader were I to follow minutely the events of the tedious
siege which now ensued. It was carried on, on the side
of the Persians, with a disregard to the usages of civilized
warfare; for which they may have imagined they were to
be held excusable, inasmuch as the men of Herat had
formerly professed obedience to the Shah, and were now
in arms against him. But most of the atrocities now
committed were traceable, in the first instance, to the
ungovernable promptings of hunger. When men came
to report to the Persian authorities that the provisions
which they had brought to the Shah's camp for sale had
been seized and retained by the soldiers, all the compensation that awaited them was to be rudely abused, and
afterwards turned out of the camp.

On the 23rd of November, 1837, Mahomed Shah arrived within a mile of Herat, and a skirmish ensued between the irregular horsemen of both sides. One prisoner was brought before the Shah, who, in order to show the spirit in which he intended to carry on the war, ordered him to be bayoneted before the royal tent. On the following day a trench was commenced to be dug round the Persian camp. The Shah in person superintended the opening operations of the siege, and continued during the subsequent days to watch the progress of events from a small tent on a hillock. Sixteen miles distant from Herat was a village inhabited by Sheeah Syeds, who of all men might have been expected to have least to fear from the soldiers of a Sheeah monarch. A party of Persians arrived at this village in quest of provisions, and the chief man of the place came out and informed the Persian officer who was in command, that all that the village contained of provisions was at his disposal, and would be brought to his camp, provided he would agree to restrain his men from entering the place. The commander assented to the arrangement, but the soldiers were not to be baulked of the opportunity of plundering, and they paid no attention to the restriction which was put upon their entering the village. Their commander upon this requested the Syeds to terrify his troops by firing upon them from the village wall. They did so, and eight Persians fell; whereupon the survivors assaulted the place, and, having stormed it, revenged the death of their comrades by that of thirty of the holy men: they also committed every kind of atrocity.

In the journal of one who was at this period in the

royal camp before Herat,* I read, under date of the 7th of December : " The Shah sent for three Turkoman prisoners, and also for an Affghan, Mahomed Azeez Khan, who had been taken, and ordered them to be put to death, as an act pleasing to God. This order was executed in his presence. The Shah goes daily to his place of observation, and employs himself in reading the Koran." The passage I have quoted affords a melancholy picture of sectarian fanaticism, and of the barbarities to which an Oriental monarch must be accustomed. In an entry of the same journal for the 9th of December, I read that the Persian soldiers were reduced to such extremities that they went about offering the locks of their muskets for sale. For the previous twenty-five days no provisions had been issued. On the night of the 12th of December, a note was thrown over the walls by a Sheeah, stating that those of that sect within the city were powerless to effect a diversion in favour of those without, and begging that the Shah would lose no time in ordering an assault, as there was nothing to be feared from the Affghans. On the following day a Persian officer held a parley with some men on the city walls, and having been invited to enter the town and see Yar Mahomed Khan, he obtained the king's permission to do so. He was ordered to remind the Vizeer of Herat that his brother, who had yielded the fortress of Ghorian, had experienced no ill-treatment in the Persian camp, and he was told to work upon the Vizeer's fears by dwelling on the insecurity of his position under a drunkard like Prince Kamran, who might at any moment, in a fit of senseless fury, issue orders for his execution. The

* MEERZA AGHA.

officer accordingly entered Herat, and delivered his
message to the Vizeer; but his Highness stated in reply
that he had once, in the time of Abbass Meerza, proceeded to a Persian camp, and had been seized and
imprisoned, and that therefore he would not trust again
to Persian good faith, nor place himself in the power of
the Shah; but he desired the Persian to inform his
master that should he withdraw his troops to Meshed,
a present, as large as the men of Herat could afford to
make it, would be sent to him to that place, and that he
might satisfy himself as to the capabilities of the Heratis
in this respect by sending accountants into the city to
examine the lists of revenue. The Vizeer of Herat took
advantage of the same opportunity to offer to supply
provisions to General Samson, the commander of the
Russian regiment in the Shah's service, who had afforded
him kindness when he had been a prisoner in the camp
of Abbass Meerza.

During this dreary winter the Shah's army was only
kept alive by means of continually sending out large
parties of soldiers to plunder the surrounding country far
and wide. The atrocities which were then committed
were such as to excite the commiseration even of many
of the hardened Persians who had accompanied the king
to Herat. The fate of the men of the villages who
remained to watch over their wives and property was
usually to be ruthlessly slain, while that of the women
of all ages was to be violated. Even little children were
not secure from death and blows. I read that they were
generally sent out with copies of the Koran in their little
hands, as being the messengers best fitted to awaken
feelings of humanity in the breasts of the approaching

soldiers. But these men were then beyond being influenced by an appeal to motives of religion or of humanity. They used to strike the children or to kill them, and the women whom they left in possession of life were stripped of all their clothes, even of articles so insignificant that a Jew would not have purchased them for the smallest copper coin. The Persian who is my authority* for this statement exclaims : " If I were about to die of hunger, I would not again accompany one of those plundering parties, to witness such enormities." He adds, in a burst of honest indignation : " May the fathers of these Serbaz burn in hell!" On the 28th of December two hundred naked and starving wretches, all of them claiming descent from the lawgiver of Mecca, came to the Shah's camp from the villages of Ghorat, to implore help from the king; but his religious Majesty passed them without having deigned to acknowledge their presence by the slightest notice. On the 29th of the same month one of the bastions of Herat fell into the hands of the Persians, the troops who won it having been conducted by a deserter from Prince Kamran; but the Affghans were roused to suitable measures of defence, and retook the bastion from the Persians.

The siege lingered on month after month, the pride of the Shah preventing him from giving up the enterprise he had undertaken, and the besieged being animated by the perseverance of the energetic Vizeer, and by the skilful efforts of Lieutenant Eldred Pottinger. In the spring of the year 1838, Mr. McNeill, the English Minister at the Persian court, arrived in the camp of the besiegers, and endeavoured to persuade the king to

---

* ARAB ALI KHAN.

renounce the plans which he had formed of taking
Herat. He was listened to by his Persian Majesty with
attention, and during the succeeding few days those of
the Persians who were anxious to return to their homes
indulged the hope that their king would act according to
the arguments put before him by the English representative. But a few days later came General Count Simonich, the envoy extraordinary of Russia, who gave the
Shah advice in a sense entirely opposite to that of
Mr. McNeill. Count Simonich succeeded in inducing
the Shah to continue the siege, and went so far as to
advance money to his Majesty, and to place at his
disposal the services of his aide-de-camp, Captain
Blaranberg, who now undertook the direction of the
operatious against Herat.

Just before the arrival of Count Simonich, Mr.
McNeill had, by the wish of the contending parties,
entered the town of Herat, to endeavour, if possible,
to conclude a negotiation. The Shah had consider-
ably modified the terms he had hitherto insisted on,
for he no longer demanded that a Persian garrison
should occupy Herat, or that he should appropriate
the revenues of that state ; but he required that
Kamran should renounce the title of Shah, and that
Yar Mahomed Khan should come to wait upon him
in his camp. On the night on which Mr. McNeill
entered Herat, preparations had been made by the
Persian army for a general assault ; but a truce of some
hours' duration was agreed to by both sides, for the purpose of giving time to the British diplomatist to bring
the negotiation to a close. The Persian prime minister
assured Mr. McNeill, as he was about to leave the camp,

that he was at liberty to act for the Shah's government with as full powers of discretion as he would be invested with in a matter directly concerning the British Crown. The night was already far advanced, and everything was in readiness for the assault, as the Minister crossed the trenches. He found the Affghans full of courage and confidence, and his astonishment was excited by contemplating the strength and extent of the fortifications of the city, which had been constructed since the commencement of the siege, and which seemed to Mr. McNeill to be capable of being defended successfully against better troops than those of Persia. The English diplomatist passed the remainder of the night in conversation with Yar Mahomed Khan, whom he pronounced to be one of the most remarkable men of his age and country, and with whom he arranged the terms of a treaty by which all the Shah's demands were conceded, excepting that for the independence of Herat. On the following morning, that of the 20th of April, 1838, Mr. McNeill returned to the camp; Count Simonich also arrived before Herat, and the treaty was therefore rejected by the Persian king.

The Shah, for some days after the arrival of Count Simonich, was elated with the hope of a speedy conquest; but the besieged still opposed a successful resistance to all the efforts of the besiegers, and after the lapse of about a fortnight the spirits of the Shah and his minister had so far sunk that the latter once more called upon Mr. McNeill to mediate between the contending princes. The draft of the treaty which had been formerly rejected was now accepted, with the stipulation that Mr. McNeill, on the part of the British Government, should guarantee its

20

observance by Prince Kamran. There now seemed to be nothing left that could retard the conclusion of peace, further than that the English Minister should again enter Hérat and obtain the ratification of the treaty by Prince Kamran. But this step the Persian Government on various pretences evaded sanctioning.

The fickle and tortuous character of Persian policy was never more fully exemplified than on this occasion. A reverse in the operations of the siege threw the Shah and his Minister into despair, and induced them to have recourse to the assistance of Mr. McNeill; a slight gleam of success renewed their confidence in Count Simonich. The Persian government required the British Minister to engage that, in the event of Prince Kamran refusing to ratify the treaty, he would no longer consent to conduct negotiations for Herat; and the Persian Minister at the same time promised that on Mr. McNeill's writing a note to this effect, a man would immediately be sent to conduct him to the city. To this proposal Mr. McNeill assented, on the condition that the Shah should pledge himself not to remain before Herat for more than five days after the conclusion of the treaty, and to quit the territories of Prince Kamran within ten days thereafter. No answer was at first returned to this note, and no man was sent to conduct Mr. McNeill to Herat. On his pressing for a reply to his note, he was informed by the Persian Minister that it was necessary that some of the other civil and military officers of the Shah should first be consulted; though the promise was at the same time renewed by his Excellency of sending a man to conduct her Majesty's Minister to Herat. This guide was to make his appearance at the tents of the

English mission on the evening of the succeeding day; but the promise made by Haji Meerza Aghassi was not fulfilled, and when Mr. McNeill asked for an explanation, he was informed that the Shah required to be indemnified for the losses he had sustained, or at least that he should receive a sum of money to distribute amongst his troops, who had suffered great privations. Mr. McNeill remonstrated against this attempt to annex new conditions to a treaty which had been already agreed to, not only by the Persian prime minister but by the Shah himself, and the formal conclusion of which had been prevented only by the impediments opposed to it by the Persian government, in violation of the written promises of the prime minister. On the following morning Mr. McNeill received a note from Haji Meerza Aghassi, which stated, in reply to his remonstrance, that the treaty could not be considered as binding on Persia, because the Affghans still continued to fire and to make sorties; declaring that the losses of Persia in this campaign had amounted to five or six crores of tomans;* expressing his conviction that the British Government could not desire to see Persia exposed to so great a loss; and concluding by what he said was mentioned merely in jest, viz. that as Mr. McNeill was reported to have given a large sum of money to the Vizeer of Herat when he had visited that place, it was hard that he should have given nothing to the writer. It was evidently hopeless to continue negotiations between two princes, the minister of one of whom could so easily repudiate his own written agreements. The cause of the sudden change in the views of the Shah was the arrival of a

* One and a quarter or one and a half million of pounds sterling.

messenger from Kandahar, with letters from Kohendil Khan, the brother of Dost Mahomed, containing the promise of aid from that quarter. The bearer of the letters assured the Shah, too, that he had nothing to fear from the direction of Cabul.

A few days later Mr. McNeill sought a private audience of the king, and represented the imprudence of the line of conduct he was adopting, inasmuch as it tended to alienate from him the sympathy and friendship of Great Britain. Several causes of complaint against the Persian Government had arisen out of the difference of opinion between it and the British Government respecting the advisability of the siege of Herat. The numerous embassies which had successively been sent from England or from India to the Persian court ; the costly presents which had been lavished upon Fetteh Ali Shah and his Ministers ; and the stipulations which had been agreed to with respect to furnishing Persia with money and arms in the event of the occurrence of certain contingencies : all these had combined to establish in the mind of Mahomed Shah, and in that of his Minister, the idea that Great Britain placed a very high value on the friendship of Persia ; and that rather than break the alliance between the two States, and so drive Persia into the arms of Russia, England would suffer almost any amount of neglect and indignity. The Shah and his Minister soon found that they had been mistaken in their estimate of the long-suffering of England. As subsidies were at this time no longer paid to Persia by the representative of the Governments of England and of India, there was a disposition on the part of the Shah's Government to make that representative feel his loss of influence, and, by means of petty annoyances and vexatious delays, to try whether it could not extort from him the price of more honourable treatment. It was prepared to push this system to the utmost point short of a rupture, and it was convinced that if it should go too far, a mission to England and a few words of explanation and apology would satisfy the Government of her Majesty, which could not afford to dispense with the alliance of Persia. In addition to these promptings of avarice, it must be remembered, in explanation of the line of conduct adopted at this time by the Persian government, that the Shah's ruling passion was a desire for military renown, and, connected with this wish, a determination to extend his territories, especially in the direction of Affghanistan. These views were encouraged by Russia and opposed by England, and this circumstance could not fail to raise in the Shah's mind the hope of deriving greater advantage from the cordial coöperation of Russia, than from intimate relations with England. Such being the spirit which at this time animated the Persian court, we are not surprised to read that it showed itself in several acts which it was impossible for the British Minister to pass over without obtaining redress. The safety of the officiating British resident at Bushire was insolently threatened by the governor of that place ; and a courier of the English mission was stopped, seized and ill-treated in the neighbourhood of Meshed, and then forced to return to the camp of the Shah. In addition to these things, the conclusion of a commercial treaty with England, to which the Shah's Government was pledged, was evaded on frivolous pretences. Mr. McNeill obtained from the Shah the admission that even if he were to succeed in taking Herat, he would be unable to hold it, and that in that case it was his intention to give it to Kohendil Khan of Kandahar. The conversation terminated by the Shah's agreeing to fulfil the terms of the treaty drawn up by Mr. McNeill, provided that he could find a suitable pretext for raising the siege of Herat. He accordingly requested Mr. McNeill to address to him a letter threatening him with the anger of the British Government in case he should persist in his operations against the beleaguered city.

In the formal representation which Mr. McNeill then addressed to the king, he embodied a statement of the other grounds on account of which his Government had to complain of Persia, in addition to the investment of the city of Prince Kamran. But in the course of two or three days, and after Mr. McNeill had been granted another private audience of his Persian Majesty, that Minister received a letter from the Persian foreign office, from which it appeared that the Shah had no longer any intention of availing himself of the pretext which he had sought from Mr. McNeill for raising the siege of Herat. It was also sufficiently apparent from this letter that the object of the Persian government was to obtain a large sum of money as the price of abandoning the enterprise against the city, or rather, that the Shah had been diverted from his previous intention to accommodate atters with Herat and to agree to Mr. McNeill's demands, by the hopes held out to him by his advisers of their being able to extort from the English Minister a large pecuniary recompence for complying with those demands. Mr. McNeill, however, distinctly assured the Persian Ministers that the hope of extorting money from him by such means was futile. Ten days elapsed, and no further communication took place between the British legation and the Persian court; but on the 30th of May, Mr. McNeill had again a private audience of the Shah, and pointed out to his Majesty the discrepancy between the language held by his Ministers and that held by himself. Two days later the British envoy received from the Persian Government a despatch, with the contents of which he may well have been surprised, since, while it made some show of concession on other points, it treated as an invasion of the Shah's independent sovereign rights the terms Mr. McNeill had employed, in accordance with the king's own request, with regard to the offensive light in which the siege of Herat was looked upon by her Majesty's Government.

The treatment to which the British Minister had been subjected had now brought to an end the amount of patience which the calmest of men could be expected to display, and Mr. McNeill accordingly reluctantly arrived at the determination of quitting the court of the Persian king. The Shah had failed to redeem one of the many promises he had made to comply with all or a part of the demands which had been submitted to him, and had evaded every attempt which Mr. McNeill had made to procure adequate redress for the detention and ill-treatment of his messengers. The conduct of the Persian government with regard to the proposed treaty with Prince Kamran, which it had at first accepted, and which it afterwards declined to conclude, and the use which had been made of Mr. McNeill's compliance with the Shah's request that he would furnish him with a suitable pretext for quitting the enterprise in which he was engaged—these considerations, coupled with the perseverance of the Persian government in its resolution to prevent any of its servants, excepting the prime minister and the deputy minister for foreign affairs, from holding any intercourse with the British Mission, determined Mr. McNeill to demand leave to depart from the camp, and to proceed to the frontier of Turkey.

The Shah still persevered in his policy of vacillation. He was unwilling to see the English Minister depart from his court, and he therefore made a pretence of disbelieving a fact so notorious as was the ill-treatment to which Mr. McNeill's messenger had been subjected. Mr. McNeill was asked to prove the correctness of the statements he had advanced; but this he could only do by Persian evidence, which it was of course vain to expect to obtain in a case where the Shah and his prime minister were amongst the delinquents. Mr. McNeill left the royal camp on the 7th of June for Meshed and Tehran. At Shahrood he received despatches from England instructing him to place before the Shah the expression of the strongest disapproval of her Majesty's Government of the line of conduct his Majesty was pursuing towards Herat; and he accordingly sent Colonel Stoddart back to the royal camp with instructions to deliver to the Shah a verbal message to the effect, that the enterprise in which his Majesty was engaged was looked upon by the Queen's Ministers as being undertaken in a spirit of hostility towards British India, and as being totally incompatible with the spirit and intention of the alliance which had been established between Great Britain and Persia. Colonel Stoddart was further directed to say that the Queen's Government

would look upon the occupation by Persia of Herat, or
any portion of Affghanistan, in the light of a hostile
demonstration against England ; and he was to refer to
the fact that the Shah must be already aware that a
British naval armament of five ships-of-war had arrived
in the Persian Gulf and taken possession of the island
of Karrack.

Soon after the departure of the British Minister from
the royal camp the troops of the Shah, after- six days'
incessant battering, were led to the assault of Herat,*
and repulsed with considerable loss ; the number of killed
and wounded being said to have amounted to about
eighteen hundred men. The loss of the higher officers
was great in proportion to the total number of men
killed ; but the person whose death was most severely felt
was the Shah's Polish officer, Monsieur Peroffski, who
held the rank of major-general. Amongst the wounded
was General Samson, the colonel of the Russian battalion
in the service of the Shah. The Persian troops are said
to have assaulted with gallantry, and to have planted
their standards three successive times on the breach ;
but they were unable to maintain their position.
The Affghans attacked them sword in hand with irre-
sistible energy, and drove them with great slaughter
across the ditch. It is said that of the killed and
wounded in the Persian ranks three-fourths received
sabre-wounds. This assault was the great event of the
siege of Herat. It had been planned by Count
Simonich, and that circumstance is said to have afforded
to the Shah and his Minister some consolation for the
want of success which had attended it : so fickle and so

---

* On the 23rd of June.

jealous was the Persian court! The Russian envoy-extraordinary had, throughout the campaign in Affghanistan, taken upon himself to act in accordance rather with what he believed or knew to be the wishes of the Imperial Cabinet, than in accordance with the written instructions which he had received from Count Nesselrode. In reply to the remonstrances which the representative of the British Government was instructed to address at St. Petersburg, he was offered permission to peruse the original drafts of all the despatches which had been addressed to Count Simonich for his guidance as to his conduct with reference to the Shah's expedition against Herat; and, out of deference to Great Britain, Count Simonich was recalled, on the plea that he had exceeded his instructions.

On the 11th of August Colonel Stoddart arrived at the royal camp before Herat, and on the following day he found his Persian Majesty at length disposed to listen to reasonable proposals for a cessation of hostilities. When Colonel Stoddart had come to a pause in his address, the king interrupted him with the words—"The fact is, if I don't leave Herat there will be war. Is not that it?" The English officer replied—"It is war. All depends on your Majesty's answer; and may God preserve your Majesty!" Whereupon the Shah stated that this declaration was all he wanted; that he had asked Mr. McNeill for it, who had declined to make such a declaration. Two days later Colonel Stoddart was summoned to the royal presence, when the king said—"We consent to the whole of the demands of the British Government. We will not go to war. Were it not for the sake of its friendship we should not return from before Herat.   Had we known that our coming here might risk the loss of its friendship, we certainly would not have come at all." The Shah's words were this time followed by corresponding deeds. A letter was addressed from the Persian foreign office to Mr. McNeill, couched in terms similar to those which had been used by the Shah to Colonel Stoddart, and his Majesty ordered preparations to be made for the breaking up of the camp and the return to Persia.   Colonel Stoddart offered his own services on the part of the British Minister as mediator between the Shah and Prince Kamran, but he firmly declared that the British Government would not consent to admit of any other foreign mediation between the contending parties.   The counsels of Count Simonich had now in turn lost their weight with the Persian king; and it is said that Monsieur Goutte, the interpreter of the Russian Mission, who had been sent into Herat for the purpose of inducing the Vizeer to permit the departure from that place of a Prussian subject, was uncourteously desired to depart from the city forthwith.   The Prussian subject was, however, sent over, after a few days, to the Persian camp.

The Shah seems from this time to the conclusion of the siege to have acted with good faith, though still with some vacillation of purpose.   He at first agreed to accept Colonel Stoddart's mediation for the conclusion of a treaty with the Affghan prince, and he desired his under-secretary for foreign affairs to acquaint that gentleman that he would not permit the interference of Russia in the conclusion of an arrangement with Herat.   The preparations for the departure of the king were continued; but it was necessary to wait for some time before a sufficient number of mules could be collected. Count Simonich took advantage of this delay to send a letter into the city offering to interfere between the Shah and Prince Kamran; but the prudent Vizeer of Herat returned no answer to the proposal of the Russian Minister. By this time rumours had reached the place of the preparations on the part of the Government of India for a military expedition, undertaken with the view of restoring the Sedozye Shah Shuja to power. The news greatly depressed the Barukzye allies of the Shah, who had come to his camp from Kandahar; and, as might have been anticipated, the same intelligence caused a corresponding rise in the spirits of the Sedozye defenders of Herat. Seeing an approaching termination to the siege which they had so gallantly sustained, the Affghan rulers were no longer willing to accede to the terms of the treaty which had been rejected by the Persian king; and this information was communicated by his Majesty to Colonel Stoddart on the 19th of August. His Majesty wished Colonel Stoddart to state whether the British Government desired him to depart from before Herat without having made any arrangement with Prince Kamran. The English officer volunteered, if authorized to do so by the Shah, to enter the city and endeavour to bring the ruler of that place to conclude the treaty which had been drafted by Mr. McNeill; but the Shah finally determined to break up his camp and to retire from before Herat, without having concluded any arrangement with Prince Kamran. The latter ruler was now reaping the fruits of the long course of dissoluteness and debauchery in which he had indulged while he had entrusted the management of his state to Yar Mahomed

Khan. That sagacious Vizeer had gained great glory from the successful defence of Herat, and his master was tortured by the fear lest after the raising of the siege the Vizeer should dethrone him. He accordingly resolved not to lose the only opportunity which was open to him of getting rid of so dangerous a subject; and with this view he addressed a secret note to his brother-in-law, in which he expressed his wish that Mahomed Shah would relieve him of the presence of his Vizeer. The note was seen by Colonel Stoddart: it bore the private seal of Prince Kamran, and with reference to it Mahomed Shah observed to the English officer—"Without Yar Mahomed Khan, Kamran would be nothing: he is mad to be afraid of him."

On the 25th of August a letter was addressed to Mr. McNeill on the part of the Shah, requesting that he would come back to the Persian court; and at the same time his Majesty forwarded a royal rescript to that gentleman, assuring him of the favourable reception with which he would be met on his return to the royal presence.

The Shah's army was detained before Herat by want of baggage animals until the 8th of September, and at the last moment one more attempt was made to extort from the royal family of the Sedozye prince some mark of homage to the Persian king. At midnight, or shortly after, on the 6th of September, Colonel Stoddart was roused from his sleep by the noise of some footsteps approaching his tent. A man entered in disguise, and in that still hour he communicated to the English officer that he was Sheer Mahomed Khan, the Affghan Sirdar, and that he had been sent by the Persian prime minister

expressly for the purpose of endeavouring to induce
Colonel Stoddart to persuade the mother and the son of
Kamran to come and make their obeisance to the Shah,
after which they might return to the city. A conversation which lasted for two hours, failed to persuade
Colonel Stoddart to accede to the proposal of the prime
minister of Persia. So that Vizeer and his master had at
length—after a siege which had lasted for upwards of
nine months—to make up their minds to turn towards
Tehran, with the bitter reflection that all the Shah's power
had been unable to carry into effect a single one of the
objects to secure which that siege had been undertaken.
The fortress of Herat was much stronger than it had
ever been before, and its inhabitants had now a character
for bravery and endurance to support, which might be
expected to make the reduction of their city at any
future time by a Persian army a still more difficult
undertaking than it had hitherto been. Prince Kamran
had not furnished a single shahi of tribute ; neither had
he returned any captive subjects of the Kajar king; nor
had he engaged to restrain in any way the Turkomans,
who were thus at liberty to carry on their marauding
expeditions into Khorassan, and for the sale of whose
Sheeah slaves the marts of Herat were open. The Shah,
with further mortification, had to reflect that the peoples
of Central Asia had witnessed how little good he had
derived from the friendship he had sought to establish
with the Autocrat of the North. They had seen the
fortress of Prince Kamran baffle all the efforts of a
Russian engineer (so called) to take it, and they had been
the witnesses of the utter failure of an assault which had
been planned by a Russian major-general.

The Persian army marched from the camp before Herat on the 9th of September of the year 1838, and on the morning of that day Colonel Stoddart, before setting out on his ill-fated journey to Bokhara, had the satisfaction to be able to report to Mr. McNeill: "The Shah has mounted his horse 'Ameerij,' and is gone."

CHAPTER XI.

Demands of her Britannic Majesty's Government from the King of Persia—
    Evasive Answers of Haji Meerza Aghassi—Suspension of Diplomatic
    Relations between England and Persia—Advance of Russia in the
    East—British Expedition to the Persian Gulf—Hussein Khan—
    Firmness of Lord Palmerston—The Shah yields—Rising of the Chief
    of the Assassins—His Success and subsequent Failure—Bunpoor—
    The Belooches put their Families to Death—Affairs of Kurdistan—
    Unsettled State of Turks—Persian Frontier—Commission appointed
    for its Delimitation—Persians' Sufferings at the Hands of Turkomans—
    Massacre at Kerbela—Banishment of the Asef-ed-Dowleh—War in
    Khorassan—The Bâb—Death of Mahomed Shah.

The Shah had promised, unconditionally, to Colonel
Stoddart at Herat, as has been stated in the preceding
chapter, to fulfil the whole of the demands of the British
Government.   These demands were, that the Persian
monarch should cease to occupy any portion of Affghanistan, and that he should, further, afford reparation for
the violence which had been offered to the courier of the
British Legation.

With regard to the first point, the siege of Herat had
been indeed abandoned in consequence of the threatened
hostility of the English Government ; but, on the other
hand, the Shah still retained possession of the fortress of
Ghorian, which he had taken from Prince Kamran, and
his troops still continued to occupy Ferrah, Sebzewar,
and Khurukh; all of which places formed part of Affghanistan.   With regard to the second point—reparation,

namely, for an insult offered to a courier—the measures adopted by the Persian king did not satisfy the demands of the British Government. The outrage for which redress was now required had been of a nature so gross, that, had it been passed over without reparation having been exacted, the safety and efficiency of those employed by the English Mission in Persia would thereafter have been seriously compromised, and a stain would have remained on the honour of the Government which should have permitted one of its servants to be so maltreated.

The circumstances under which the outrage had been committed were these :—A courier had been sent by Mr. McNeill to Meshed, in 1837, to be in readiness to bring back a letter in which the British Minister was to be authorized by the government of Herat to conclude an amicable adjustment of its differences with Persia, and of which permission he was to avail himself in case the difficulties encountered by the Shah in the prosecution of the enterprise on which he was at that time bent should be such as to induce him to accept of foreign mediation. The courier was to await at Meshed a communication from Fetteh Mahomed Khan, an envoy from Herat, who was returning from Persia. But for some reason—probably because he feared lest the road from Herat to Meshed would be unsafe for an Affghan messenger—Fetteh Mahomed Khan induced the courier to proceed with him to Herat, where he was detained for some weeks. He finally left the place as the bearer of letters from Yar Mahomed Khan and Lieutenant Eldred Pottinger to the address of Mr. McNeill. When within about three stages of Meshed, and after he had already passed the Persian army then marching towards Herat,

21

the courier, Ali Mahomed Beg, was recognized by M. Beroffski; who, on learning that he was returning from Herat, reported the circumstance on his arrival in the Shah's camp. Horsemen were then despatched in pursuit of the English courier, and they were instructed to bring him back forcibly to the camp of the Shah. He was stripped of a portion of his clothes, the horses which he was bringing with him were seized, and he himself was dragged to the camp and there placed in custody. He succeeded, however, in making his way to the tent of Colonel Stoddart, and was by that officer conducted to the prime minister, who, after he had been informed that the courier was in the service of the British Mission, ordered him to be again placed in custody; while Haji Khan, an officer holding the rank of brigadier in the service of the Shah, not only used very offensive language towards Colonel Stoddart, in the presence of the Persian prime minister, but, after the courier had been released by direction of his Excellency, seized him once more in the midst of the camp; stripped him in order that he might search for any letter there might be about his person; took from him what letters he found; and used towards him violent threats and opprobrious language. In a country where many of the usages of the feudal system are still in force, a pointed insult offered to a dependant is looked upon in the same light as if it had been offered to his master. Therefore, in addition to being an infraction of the law of nations, the treatment to which Mr. McNeill's courier had been subjected, was an open and public affront given in the face of the Shah and his whole camp to the English Minister and to the Government of which he was the representative. When

Mr. McNeill demanded apology and reparation for the treatment received by his messenger, the Shah and his Minister, as has been already stated, had endeavoured to excuse themselves from affording it by denying the accuracy of Mr. McNeill's statements, and calling upon him to prove them. They finally sought to compromise matters by dismissing Haji Khan for other conduct, while denying that the British Government had any just cause of complaint against him. The written apology which Mr. McNeill demanded from the prime minister for his share in the transaction was categorically refused.

Under these circumstances it was clearly impossible for Mr. McNeill to resume diplomatic relations with the Persian court until such time as the promise made by the Shah to Colonel Stoddart at Herat, of granting all the demands of the British Government, should be carried into execution. Mr. McNeill did not return to Tehran, but he awaited in the direction of the frontier the result of a remonstrance which he directed his Secretary of Legation to make to the Shah's Ministers against the non-fulfilment of the royal promise. Colonel Sheil joined the Shah's camp on the way from Meshed to Tehran, and he continued with it until its arrival at the capital, on the 9th of November. He, however, found the Shah in no humour to make further concessions to the British Government. His Majesty indulged ill-will against that Government for having thwarted his scheme of adding Herat to his dominions, and he determined to withhold the satisfaction demanded by Mr. McNeill, and yet not wholly to break with that Minister until he should have learnt the result of a complaint against the conduct of the British Government, which he had caused to be laid before the cabinet of the Sublime Porte. Mr. McNeill, however, on the expiry of the time he gave the Persian government for coming to a decision, broke off diplomatic relations with that government ; and, having ordered the English officers who had been lent to the Shah to proceed towards Baghdad on their way to India, he retired to Erzeroom with the members of his Mission.

Previously to this, Hussein Khan had been sent by the Shah on a mission to England, with the view of inducing her Majesty's Ministers to recall Mr. McNeill from Persia. In the memorandum with which he was furnished for presentation to the English Ministers, and copies of which were sent to France, Russia and Turkey, the Shah entered into an exposition of the wrongs which, he conceived, had been inflicted on him by Mr. McNeill and by the Government he represented. It commenced by stating, what was without doubt true, that the King of Persia had received great provocation from the people of Herat, and had been perfectly justified in going to war against them. Mr. McNeill had never questioned the Shah's right to punish the people of Herat, and to obtain security from them for their future good behaviour ; but he had drawn a distinction between obtaining just satisfaction from Prince Kamran and annexing Herat to Persia. The king protested in the memorandum, that if by his conduct he had opened to Russia the road to Cabul, it was with no such intention that he had undertaken the expedition to Affghanistan ; the object of which was to rescue Persian subjects from slavery. Mr. McNeill was accused of having incited the people of Herat to continue their defence, and of having bestowed on them eight thousand tomans,—a statement which was at variance with truth.   He was further accused of having sent couriers to Kandahar, Cabul, Seistan, the Hezarehs, and Meimaneh, inviting the rulers of those places or tribes to come to attack and plunder the camp of the Shah.   This statement, too, was utterly groundless.   He was further accused of having done his best to produce a scarcity in the Persian camp, and of having persuaded the conductors of caravans whom he met on his way to Meshed not to advance towards Herat, as they would infallibly be plundered, and have to submit to see their cattle seized. This assertion was so entirely the reverse of correct that Mr. McNeill had, contrary to the wish of the commandant of the Persian escort which had accompanied him, insisted that that escort should be employed in conducting a caravan back to the camp.   The memorandum concluded with a solemn declaration that the expedition against Herat had been undertaken without any hostile intention towards England.   The king felt sure that the English nation would not sanction the oppression to which he had been subjected.   If otherwise, he must seek shelter under the shadow of a great mountain.

The threat contained in the last words of the preceding sentence was followed by a corresponding act.   A few weeks later the Shah caused a letter to be addressed to Count Nesselrode, in which he piteously complained of the restraint put upon him by the British Government. " I beg your Excellency," the letter said, " to examine impartially if ever in this world greater tyranny and oppression than this were practised ; that a powerful monarch, who never broke a treaty, should be prevented from obtaining his objects when on the point of success, after having encountered so much toil and expense in subduing a refractory province of his own dominions, the people of which have been incessant in slaughtering, plundering and carrying into slavery the inhabitants of Khorassan and Seistan; who never observed a treaty, and who have been in the habit of selling the people of these two provinces in Khiva and Bokhara." The Persian Minister went on to say that his government had full hope and expectation that Russia would relieve her neighbour from the burden of so obvious a tyranny, which had been exercised towards her on the plea of her friendship for Russia. In conclusion, the Persian government expressed its willingness to act in the matter according to the arbitration of Count Nesselrode.

The Russian Minister being thus satisfied of the submission of the Persian government, and being unwilling to see Karrack in the hands of the English, instructed the representative of the Czar in London to endeavour to induce her Majesty's Government to resume its amicable relations with Persia. On the whole, indeed, the Emperor had cause to be contented with the aspect of affairs in Central Asia. Great Britain had gained for the present her point of preventing Persia from taking possession of Herat; but, on the other hand, she had lost all her influence in Persia. She had shown herself in the light so odious to the Persian Sheeahs—that of the well-wisher of Affghan Sunis. If Russia or her ally had not done all she wished to have seen accomplished, she had yet the satisfaction of being able to reflect that immense strides had, in the course of a few years, been made by the Czar towards the realization of the projects of Peter the Great, and which have been kept in view by his suc-

cessors with such undeviating constancy. In less than
forty years the Russian eagles had advanced from the
gates of the Caucasus to the banks of the Araxes, and
from the embouchure of the Terek to that of the Astëra.
This was to the west of the Caspian ; but to the eastward of that sea their progress, though less prominent,
had been no less constant and successful. The line of
Orenburg and of the Lake of Aral afforded to the Russian
generals an admirable base of operations, from which
they could advance with equal facility by the Oxus or
the Jaxartes in their operations against the Oozbeg States.
Those States, instead of drawing together in a league
against the gigantic and insidious Northern Power which
was gradually advancing to devour them, were wasting
their strength in fighting with each other. Russia had,
indeed, in the preceding year sustained a considerable
check ; but her Government, far from being discouraged
by the disaster, only endeavoured to turn to account the
experience so dearly purchased in the deserts of Khiva.

A talented Russian agent was now at work in Central
Asia: one from whose past successes his countrymen were
justified in expecting much. M. Witkewitsch was a native
of Lithuania, who, on account of a college squabble, had
been sent into banishment to a military colony in the
. Ural, where he remained many years, and acquired a high
character among the Cossacks for gallantry, enterprise
and intelligence. While residing in the government of
Orenburg he gained a thorough knowledge of the Persian
and Turkish languages, and otherwise prepared himself
for travelling in disguise amongst Mahomedans, he having
from an early period been destined by the government
for service in Central Asia. He was first directed to

make the journey to Bokhara in company with a caravan of merchants, and when an officer was wanted to proceed to Cabul, Captain Witkewitsch was selected for the duty. There he out-manœuvred the British envoy, Alexander Burnes, at the court of Dost Mahomed Khan, and, having rejoined Count Simonich at Herat, was despatched by his Excellency to Kandahar, from which place he was to proceed once more to Central Asia.

During the absence of the British Mission from Tehran, the spirit evinced by the Shah towards the English nation was reflected by several additional insults committed by his subjects; for which, as a matter of course, the Minister at the head of the Foreign Office demanded apology and redress. The British Residency at Bushire was removed to the Island of Karrack, which was protected by a squadron under the command of Sir Frederick Maitland.

In the meantime Hussein Khan proceeded on his way to London to urge his complaints against Mr. McNeill; being in nowise deterred by the warnings he received at Constantinople and at Vienna, that he would not be recognized at the Court of St. James's as a diplomatic agent. With regard to the main object of his mission, he received at Vienna, by order of Lord Palmerston, the discouraging assurance that in the demand for the recall of Mr. McNeill, her Majesty's Government only saw an additional proof, if any were wanted, that that Minister had faithfully and ably performed his duty towards his sovereign and country.*. Nor were the efforts of the Shah's ambassador to establish communication with England by means of a neutral power

---

* Published correspondence relating to Persia, 1841.

attended with any more success. Prince Metternich transmitted to London a memorandum from Hussein Khan, together with the offer of his Highness's services as a channel of communication. The offer was so far taken advantage of by Lord Palmerston, that the Prince was requested to be so good as to return the memorandum to Hussein Khan.

From Vienna Hussein Khan proceeded to Paris, where he applied to Marshal Soult for a passport to enable him to visit England as a private individual. He at length succeeded in being admitted to an interview with the English Minister for Foreign Affairs. The conference broke up with the understanding that Lord Palmerston should embody in a memorandum the principal points required of Persia, which memorandum Hussein Khan was to transmit to his government. The demands of the British Government were nine in number. A written apology was required for what had happened with regard to the British messenger. A firman must be published in Persia assuring protection to all persons employed in the British Mission. Ghorian, and the other places in Affghanistan still held by the Shah, must be restored to the Affghans. A written apology must be given for the illegal seizure at Tehran of the house of a British officer. All persons who had been concerned in the outrage on the broker of the British Residency at Bushire must be punished. The governor of that port, who had affronted Sir F. Maitland, must be removed from his office, and the reason of his removal stated publicly by the Persian Government. The claims of a British subject on account of some iron-works at Karadagh must be liquidated. The sums due to the officers of the British detachment lately serving in Persia must be paid; and, lastly, the signature of a commercial treaty between Great Britain and Persia must accompany the reëstablishment of diplomatic relations between the two States.

These demands were made in London on the 11th of July, 1839; but it was long before the Persian Government could be persuaded to comply with them all. Little by little that government yielded to the demands of Lord Palmerston, and it pertinaciously contested almost every point in question. But at length the desire to see Persian soil free from English occupation, and to own once more the island of Karrack, overcame the reluctance of the Shah and his Minister to do what was required of them. The point to which they were most loth to consent was that Ghorian should be evacuated; but at length the order was given that it should be delivered over to the officers of Prince Kamran, or, as he called himself, Shah Kamran. A further pretext for delay in this matter was furnished by the retirement at this time of the British mission under Major D'Arcy Todd from the court of Herat. But again the order was issued at Tehran to the governor of Khorassan to make over the fortress of Ghorian, and this command was carried into execution on the 31st of March, 1841.* This event was very contrary to the views and interests of Yar Mahomed Khan, who was now in opposition to the British Government; since it afforded to his adherents and to the wild tribes whose horsemen were his chief hope, an unequivocal proof that England and Persia had

---

* The evacuation of Ghorian was witnessed by the late Doctor Riach, the estimable physician to the British Mission in Persia, who was deputed for this service by Sir John McNeill.

arranged their differences, and that, therefore, he had nothing to expect from Persia.

The Persian Government had now performed the essential conditions upon which the Government of her Majesty had consented to reëstablish diplomatic intercourse between the two States; a mission was accordingly despatched from London under the direction of Sir John McNeill, which arrived at Tehran on the 11th of October, 1841, and which was most cordially received by Mahomed Shah. Not so flattering was the reception of Hussein Khan, who, on his return from Europe, had to expiate his want of success in Western diplomacy by submitting to a severe application of the bastinado.

Shortly after the return of Mahomed Shah to Tehran from his Affghanistan campaign, he found his right to sovereignty disputed by a rival of a different order from that of those with whom he had had ere this to contend for the peaceful possession of his throne. The sect of the Ismaïlites has been already mentioned in a previous chapter. Agha Khan,* the son of Shah Khalilullah, who had been put to death at Yezd, and who had himself been taken under the protection of Fetteh Ali Shah, thought that the time had now come when he might assert with advantage the religious character of which he was the inheritor. There is no reason for believing

---

* This personage based his claim to being considered a spiritual ruler upon the fact of his being descended from the last chief of the Assassins of Persia, who is popularly known by the designation of "the Old Man of the Mountain." His castle is still to be seen in its ruined condition in the Elburz mountains near Casveen.—For an account of the Ismaïlites, see MARCO POLO's *Travels* and GIBBON's *Decline and Fall of the Roman Empire*.

that he especially selected the moment of the Shah's
return from an unsuccessful campaign for attempting to
set up his own dominion in opposition to that of the king;
for his pretensions were to spiritual authority more than
to temporal, and in the East, religious enthusiasts have
generally been guided in their appeals to men more by
the fancied promptings of some invisible power than by
the suggestions of common sense. Agha Khan had for
some time dwelt in the region of Mahalat, near Hamadan; and, fearful lest the movement of a portion of the
Shah's troops which marched to that quarter should be
directed against him, he recommended his followers
to disperse, and took the opportunity of sending his
family to perform the pilgrimage to Kerbela. Being
then unincumbered, he crossed by bypaths the country
lying between the plain of Hamadan and the remote
cities of Yezd and Kerman. At Kerman he produced
forged letters by which he was appointed governor of
that place: a position which he was soon called upon
to maintain by force of arms, for the real governor
returned from Ispahan, and hastened to meet the usurper
in the field. Numbers of the sect of Ismaïl had by
this time flocked round their leader; who, nevertheless,
declined to abide the issue of a contest with the troops
of the Shah, and decamped during the night preceding the day on which the battle was to have been
fought. Agha Khan betook himself to the fortress of
Lar, and, on being chased thence by the troops sent in
pursuit of him, he found a refuge during the heats of the
coming summer in the mountains of that district.

In the spring of the next year the chief of the
Ismaïlites once more appeared in the field. He had con-

trived not only to raise a numerous force, but also to procure some artillery. On hearing of his movement, the governor of Kerman lost no time in despatching troops to confront him; but while doing so he committed the error which has so frequently proved fatal in operations of greater magnitude than that of which I now write— the oft-repeated error of the Aulic Council. He divided his force into three parts, and thus gave to the rebel the opportunity of defeating each detachment in detail. The first was under the command of the governor's brother, who had under his orders the troops of Bem and Nermansheer. Amongst these there were many who secretly held the tenets of Ismaïl; the result was, that in the action which ensued, they went over in a body to Agha Khan, and their leader, Isfendiar, was killed. After this success, the Ismaïlite chief advanced to meet the second detachment, which he defeated without difficulty. On his way to Kerman he encountered the third body of troops that had been sent against him, whom he easily dispersed, taking their commander prisoner. Elated with his success, he then wrote to the nobles of Kerman, ordering them to seize their governor; but the high tone which he now adopted was not any further supported by corresponding acts. The governor of Kerman, taking with him a chosen body of troops, marched in person to encounter the rebel; Agha Khan, reflecting that in case of defeat he could expect no mercy from the man whose brother his followers had slain, did not choose to risk an action, but sought safety in flight, leaving his followers and his camp at the mercy of his adversary. He fled to Nermansheer and was hotly pursued; but he succeeded in making his way to Beloochistan, from whence he passed to the south. He did not again attempt, by means of his spiritual authority, to win for himself an earthly crown, but turned his attention to the safer employment of horse-racing in Western India.

The chief of Bunpoor in Beloochistan had taken advantage of the rising of Agha Khan to make hostile incursions into the province of Kerman. Over all the ancient country of Gedrosia the modern Shahs lay claim to possess a vague right of dominion. The whole of the vast tract comprehended between the latitudes 24° 50′ and 30° 40′ north, and longitudes 58° 55′ and 67° 30′ east, in addition to two provinces stretching far to the east and west, was bestowed by Nadir Shah, in the year 1739, on Nasser Khan, who at the same time received the title of Begler-Beg of Beloochistan.* Founding its pretensions on the conquests of Nadir, the Persian Government considers itself to have a seigneurial right over this country, in spite of the circumstance that for a hundred years that right has been in no way recognized by the chiefs of the tribes of Beloochistan. In the first years of the reign of Mahomed Shah, this country included the region of Kohistan, in which lies the town of Bunpoor. Habeebullah Khan, the commandant of the Shah's artillery, who had been sent to the assistance of the governor of Kerman in his struggle with Agha Khan, was now directed to undertake the task of punishing the chief of Bunpoor. He accordingly marched against that place, which was yielded up to him. But on one of his soldiers attempting to carry off a Belooch woman, the

---

* *Travels in Beloochistan*, by Lieut. HENRY POTTINGER.

fury of the excitable tribesmen was aroused, and after
having put their wives and daughters to that death
which, like Virginius, they thought was better than
dishonour, they fell upon the troops of Habeebullah
Khan, to whom they had formerly surrendered.   A
sanguinary conflict now ensued ; the Belooches having
nothing left for which they cared to live, and the Persians being encouraged by their chief to kill and not
to spare.   After a time the carnage ceased, and so great
was the effect which the account of it produced upon the
Shah, that he sent orders for the immediate liberation of
the surviving captives of Bunpoor.

About the beginning of the month of June of the
year 1842, an occurrence took place on the western
frontier of Persia, which was nearly being the cause of a
war between that Power and Turkey.   In the preceding
year Mahmoud Pasha, the governor of Suleimanieh, had
been obliged to take refuge in Persia.   He had repaired
to Tehran, and there succeeded in obtaining a recom-
mendation from the Shah's government to the Porte that
his successor, Ahmed, should be dismissed, and that he
should be reinstated in his former post.   Ahmed was
accordingly removed, but Mahmoud was not restored to
power.   A second request was, however, made in his
favour, and he proceeded to the frontier government of
Senna, there to await its result.   He was not restored to
his former position, in which a relative of Ahmed Pasha
was placed.   Upon this the Vali and the Vizeer of Ardelan
advanced with Mahmoud towards the Turkish frontier at
the head of a considerable force, and Abdullah, the
brother of Ahmed Pasha, assembled a force to oppose
them.   An officer of the Vali's army was detached by a

circuitous route to take possession of a defile in the rear of Abdullah's camp, and at the same time Mahmoud marched towards Suleimanieh. Information respecting the latter move was conveyed to Abdullah Pasha, in the expectation that, on hearing of it, he would at once return to Suleimanieh, and so be surprised in the defile by the troops detached by the Vali. Abdullah, however, rendered this calculation futile by advancing to attack the Vali's own camp. By so doing he was obliged to invade the Persian territory; but he was forced to take this step by the seizure of the pass within the Turkish territory by the troops of Ardelan. He was successful in his attack on the Vali, and the Vizeer of Kurdistan hastened to misrepresent the matter to the Persian government, in the hope that it might be committed to hostilities against the Porte before his own share of culpability in the affair should be ascertained. The Shah, on reading the reports sent to him from Ardelan, was so highly incensed that he at once gave orders for the assembling of a number of troops at Hamadan, with which it was his intention to march to the Ottoman frontier. He also ordered that all Persian merchants should forthwith quit the dominions of the Sultan.

There was, indeed, at this time a long list of grievances, on account of which Turkey and Persia complained each of the other State. A brother of the Shah had made a wanton incursion into the district of Byazeed and plundered several villages. In that same district a large and valuable Persian caravan had been despoiled by the Kurds. At the close of the year 1835, Khan Mahmoud, a Kurdish chief, dwelling near the Lake of Van, had ravaged the districts of Kutoor and Khoi. About the same time the Meer of Ravandooz had attacked and plundered the district of Mergaver in the mountains of Uroomeeah. During the absence of the Shah at Herat, the thriving commercial town of Mohamera, situated near Bussora in the district of Chab in Khuzistan, had been attacked by the Turkish troops and completely destroyed. It is asserted that this aggression took place at the instigation of the Pasha of Baghdad, who was anxious to get rid of a commercial rival to Bussora, it having been discovered that the trade of the latter port was rapidly passing over to Mohamera. Persia had also to complain that some of her Kurdish tribes had been unfairly abstracted from her territory by the Pasha of Byazeed. She also claimed pecuniary compensation for the permission she had some years since granted to the Turkish tribes of Suleimanieh to pasture their flocks on Persian soil during the months of summer. Turkey, on the other hand, complained of the retention by Persia of the district of the bridge of Zohāb on the frontier of the province of Kermanshah. To determine the frontier line between the two countries, a mixed commission was appointed, and the commissioners were to be guided in the adjustment of their differences by the opinion of a Russian officer who was to accompany them over the line of frontier. To this commission a British member was afterwards added; but so complicated were the questions to be solved, or so great the labour of surveying and mapping, that more than twenty years have been insufficient to bring the work to an end. The representatives of England and of Russia at the Sublime Porte and at Tehran used all their influence to prevent a war at this time between the two great Moslem powers;

and through their exertions the troops which had been assembled near either frontier, and which for some time were held back like greyhounds in the leash, were at length withdrawn into the interior, leaving the commissioners to do their work.

At this time the usual state of petty hostilities between the Persians of the province of Astrabad and the Yemoot Turkomans of the Goorgan desert was varied by the despatch of a large force sent by the Shah to compel payment of tribute by the tribes, and to obtain the restoration of slaves. The result of the expedition was that of all similar ones. The Turkomans gave way, and were pursued, and consented to pay tribute and to restore slaves ; but when the Persian battalions had begun their retrograde movement, the tribesmen once more issued from their deserts, and recommenced their system of marauding. So incensed was the Shah at the injury done to him in carrying off his subjects into captivity, that he determined upon undertaking a military expedition against the Khan of Khiva, whose capital was one of the chief markets for Persian captives. In order, if possible, to avert renewed war in Central Asia, the English chargé-d'affaires at Tehran had offered to send a member of the mission to Khiva, at the same time that an envoy proceeded thither on the part of the Shah. This mission * had not been attended with success, the Khan of Khiva refusing to promise anything further than that he would exchange some of the Persian captives for an equal number of such Turkoman captives as might be in the hands of the Persians. A Khivan envoy was, however, subsequently sent to Tehran,

---

* Mr. WILLIAM T. THOMSON proceeded to Khiva on this occasion.

and the threatened hostilities were averted. The Khan of Khiva soon afterwards died, and his successor declared his intention of signalizing his accession to the post of cup-bearer to the Sultan * by the liberation of fifteen hundred Persian captives. But I do not find that these captives were actually set free. Indeed, except in the case of such as were the immediate property of the Khan, it was not easy to give effect to any measure such as the Shah wished to be carried out; for the Persian slaves had been purchased by persons who would by no means consent to give up their property unless upon receiving their value in money. Many of these Sheeah slaves were permitted to work out their own redemption, but upon obtaining it they were not at liberty to quit the territory of Khiva.† This cruel

---

* That this title is given to, or assumed by, the Khan of Khiva, I learn from M. VAMBERY's recently published *Travels in Central Asia.*

† What Persian slavery amongst the Turkomans is, may be best learnt from one who has himself witnessed it. "I was astonished to find how many of my fellow-travellers—the poorest of the poor—in spite of the noble hospitality of which they had been partakers, were already weary of the Turkomans; for it would, they said, be impossible for men having the least sentiment of humanity to be eye-witnesses any longer of the cruel treatment to which the wretched Persian slaves had to submit. . . . . The compassion evinced by my fellow-travellers, and the imprecations they used against the Karaktchi for their inhumanity, convey the least impression of the sufferings to which the poor captives are exposed. Let us only picture to ourselves the feelings of a Persian who is surprised by a night attack, hurried away from his family, and brought hither a prisoner, and often wounded. He has to exchange his dress for old Turkoman rags, that only scantily cover parts of his body, and is heavily laden with chains that gall his ankles, and occasion him great and unceasing pain every step he takes. He is forced upon the poorest diet to linger the first days —often weeks—of his captivity. That he may make no attempt at flight, he has also at night a kara-bagra (iron ring) attached to his neck and fastened to a peg, so that the rattle betrays even the slightest movements. No other termination to his sufferings than the payment of a ransom by his friends. . . . . To the rattle of the chains I could never habituate my ears. It is heard in the tent of every Turkoman who has any pretension to respectability or position."—*Travels in Central Asia:* VAMBERY.

22—2

restriction, however, was, after a time, removed, and I read of a body of several thousand Persians preparing to return to their native land.

The beginning of the year 1843 was signalized by an occurrence, which was, of all things that could have happened, the most likely to bring to an abrupt termination the negotiations that were being carried on between Persia and Turkey, and to rouse to instant action the warlike tendencies of the Shah. The Pasha of Baghdad thought proper to march with a military force against the holy city of Kerbela in Arabia. A breach of forty yards' length was made in the walls, and the place was carried by storm. The fighting went on in the streets for some hours, until the tomb of Abbass was taken, and eight hundred persons, who had sought refuge within it, massacred. All resistance then ceased, and the Turkish soldiers, furious at the opposition they had encountered, lost for the time all regard to discipline, and massacred every one they met, without distinction of sex or age. The loss of life was estimated by the survivors at from fifteen to eighteen thousand souls ; but this calculation was probably very greatly in exaggeration of the truth. The motive for this attack was the fact that for many years Kerbela had, for practical purposes, almost entirely rejected the authority of the Pasha of Baghdad. A large number of outlaws had sought safety in the neighbourhood of the Shrines, and had usurped authority over the district; the Pasha of Baghdad was therefore justified in enforcing his power over the unruly city. It is asserted that he gave warning to the Persians within it to retire before the assault ; if this were so, and they neglected his advice, they exposed themselves to the horrors which their abodes now witnessed.   One princess was severely wounded, and hundreds of the Shah's subjects shared the fate that befell so many thousands of the inhabitants of the town.

The news of this event travelled to Tehran without the explanation of the causes that had brought it about ; and the messenger arrived at that city at the time when the people were engaged in the celebration by a religious ceremony of the martyrdom of Hussein.   Had the contents of the despatches which reached the Government been at once divulged, there is little doubt that the people, already in a state of high excitement, would have been goaded to frenzy by the eloquence of their priests.   But the Shah's Minister wisely kept the news that had reached him secret, until the expiration of the ten days of mourning.   When at length the inhabitants of Tehran learned that the city containing the tomb of their favourite saint was in the hands of those whose swords had been stained with the blood of so many of their fellow-countrymen, they demanded vengeance from the Shah and his Minister. The latter knew that to argue with men under the influence of fury would be a waste of time, and he accordingly at once acceded to their demand.   Troops were ordered to prepare for marching, and immense stores were called for.   Couriers were sent about in every direction, and one would have imagined that the Shah's government really intended to avenge on the inhabitants of Baghdad the wrongs of the citizens of Kerbela. But all this time Haji Meerza Aghassi had no thoughts whatever of commencing hostilities.   He was naturally a humane man, and he had seen enough of campaigning during the siege of Herat to make him resolve to study war no more. The result of his conduct on this occasion was exactly what he had foreseen. The people not being irritated by contradiction, and witnessing the seeming zeal of the minister, had gradually subsided into calmness, and the affair passed over on the Turkish Government expressing regret and giving assurances of its readiness to make suitable atonement for what the Persians had suffered in the massacre at Kerbela.

The power of Haji Meerza Aghassi was now thoroughly established : the king looked upon him with a feeling little short of veneration ; and it was well that there was at hand so merciful a minister to temper the stern decrees of so cruel a prince. Haji Meerza Aghassi feared the influence of no rival, and as long as Mahomed Shah continued to reign, his former preceptor continued to administer justice in his name. The Haji even went so far in his conduct towards his master as freely to show his anger when he felt displeased with the Shah. On one occasion the king resisted the minister's demand for the dismissal of four persons of the royal household who were obnoxious to him. Fourteen days were allowed to pass by the latter without his going to pay his usual daily duty to his sovereign ; and at the end of that time it was not the Haji who yielded, but the Shah. The Vizeer had retired to one of his country-seats, and thither the Shah repaired ; but the Haji had disregarded alike the duties of hospitality and the respect due to royalty, and the king found no one to welcome him at the house which he honoured by his presence. The minister, on hearing of the royal approach, had retired to another residence which he possessed, and the Shah remained his guest for an entire week without having been waited upon by his host. During all this time, while the Haji's ill-temper lasted, there was a total cessation of the business of the central government of the country.

It has been mentioned that the Shah's maternal uncle, the Asef-ed-Dowleh, had been appointed at the beginning of the king's reign to be governor of Khorassan. He had retained this important post ever since, but he had never ceased to hanker after the higher office which he had held in the time of Fetteh Ali Shah. His jealousy of Haji Meerza Aghassi sometimes broke out in words and acts, and was sometimes smothered until a more fitting occasion should occur for its display. But the influence of the Minister over his former pupil was paramount, and all the efforts of the Asef-ed-Dowleh to shake it were attended with as little result as the beating of waves against a rock : the Asef-ed-Dowleh could not shake the Minister, but by his efforts to do so he broke himself. There are two great offices in the Shah's gift which must be held by two persons residing in the city of Meshed. Of these two persons one acts as a check on the other. The governor of Khorassan is kept within bounds by the vicinity of an individual of character and influence who is in no way under his orders, and the custodian of the shrine of Imam Reza is bound to regard the opinion of so powerful a personage as the Vali of Khorassan. The Asef-ed-Dowleh succeeded in uniting in his family these two important posts. He represented to the Shah that he was old, and that he wished to consult his interests beyond the grave by devoting his few remaining days to the task of guarding the holy places at Meshed. He was accordingly made custodian of the mosque, and his son, the celebrated Salar, was appointed to be the governor of Khorassan. But the Asef-ed-Dowleh had no sooner got rid of a troublesome spy in the person of the former custodian than another thorn in his flesh appeared to vex him. This was one Mahomed Hassan Khan, a chief of Nardeen, who by means of making presents at Tehran contrived, without the Asef-ed-Dowleh's knowledge, to be named governor of his native district. Nardeen lies between Meshed and Astrabad, and is subject to the government of Khorassan. It lies along the Turkoman frontier, and its new ruler showed his gratitude to his patrons at Tehran by making himself a scourge to the hereditary enemies of the Persians. This was too much for the patience of the Asef-ed-Dowleh, and a body of horsemen was, by his instigation, sent against the chief of Nardeen with orders to put him to death. These orders were faithfully executed; but Allah-yar Khan was called upon to account for the deed that had been done. As a matter of course he protested that he had not been accessary to the death of Mahomed Hassan Khan; but he was nevertheless ordered to repair to Tehran. This he declined to do, on the ground that he could not leave the shrine of Imam Reza without a custodian: a pretext of which he was deprived by the immediate appointment of another person to fill that holy office. He then slowly and reluctantly approached the capital of the Shah, having previously written to his Majesty to point out how utterly unfitted the prime minister had shown himself for the task of ruling Persia. At Tehran the sentence of exile awaited him. He was ordered to make the pilgrimage to Mecca, and to reside for his remaining days at Kerbela, in case the journey through the sands of Arabia should not be enough to quench the spark of life which animated his aged body. Thus passed from the scene the former prime minister of Iran, and who was by birth and position the most noble of the nobles of the land.

It was not intended to take away the government of Khorassan from the family of the Asef-ed-Dowleh; but as his son, the Salar, was suspected of entertaining the design of making himself independent, his elder brother was sent down from Tehran to supersede him in the government. The Salar, however, was of a more commanding spirit than his brother, and instead of being put down by him he brought him over to his own views. The son of Allah-yar Khan was now sufficiently powerful to be an object of serious alarm to the Persian court. In addition to the wealth and weighty influence of his own house, his cause derived support from a formidable combination of the chiefs of the Turkomans and of Khorassan. Prince Hamza Meerza, one of the brothers of the Shah, was invested with the chief power in the eastern province of Persia, and was enjoined to proceed with an army to put down the audacious rebel. The Salar was at this time encamped on the plain of Maiyanmai with a force of twenty-five thousand cavalry. Prince Hamza Meerza might well hesitate to encounter him; but, as is not unusual with Persians, he attempted to conceal his weakness under a boastful pretence of clemency. He sent a messenger to his opponent, advising him to reflect well while there was still a choice open to him. "You are the first of your race," the message went on, "who have aspired to sovereignty.

We have ruled and you have obeyed. What new thing
is this, that the servant should rise against his master
and the slave against his lord?" The mention of the
word "slave" stung to the quick the proud Salar, who,
replied to the prince's communication by a defiance
to mortal combat; adding a Persian verse to this
effect : *

> " What use my life to me,
> Since though I be Salar
> I still a *slave* must be?"

On receiving this reply the prince advanced towards
the camp of the rebels; but as he did so, the forces
opposed to him began to disperse, and their leader found
himself compelled to consult his safety by retreating to
Boojnoord. Thither he was followed by Hamza Meerza,
and the Salar and the chief of Boojnoord were forced to
fall back upon the Turkomans. It was the intention of
Prince Hamza to pursue them, but he was recalled to
Meshed by the news of a rising at that place. The
governor whom he had left at Boojnoord contrived to
make himself so disagreeable to the people that they
opened communication with their former chief, Jafer
Kuli Khan, who, with the Salar, returned from the
Turkoman desert, and once more took possession of
Boojnoord. Twelve thousand men flocked to their
standards, and the prince had to hasten from Meshed
to oppose them. They retired on his approach and
fell back on their Turkoman allies; but this time they
were pursued to the deserts bordering the Attrek river.
The chief of Boojnoord, after a number of adventures,
succeeded in making his way to Herat, where he was

---

* "Maran ar ayed az zendagee, ke salar basham kunam bendagee."

detained for some time in captivity by Yar Mahomed Khan. The Salar found his way to Serrekhs, and, falling in with a body of several thousand Turkoman horse, he doubled upon the prince, who was pursuing him, and attempted by means of a forced march to gain the city of Meshed. By the 'orders of Hamza Meerza a body of cavalry was sent to oppose him; but the Salar was victorious in the fight which ensued, and he continued his way to Meshed. He was not, however, in a condition to face the artillery which the prince now brought up against him, and he was once more driven to seek safety in flight, and shelter amongst the Turkomans of the desert.

At this time there occurs the first mention in the Persian records of· a man whose name is destined to hold an enduring place in Persian history.* The East, so prolific in originators of creeds, had produced a fanatic who was able to obtain spiritual authority over the minds of hundreds of thousands of his countrymen. Syed Ali Mahomed, though boasting descent from the lawgiver of Mecca, was the son of a grocer of Sheeraz. Being of a religious disposition, he was sent in his youth to Kerbela, where he sat at the feet of a celebrated doctor of the Mahomedan law. From Kerbela he proceeded to Bushire, and at the latter place he endeavoured by

---

* Bábism, though at present a proscribed religion in Persia, is far from being extinct, or even declining, and the Báb may yet contest with Mahomed the privilege of being regarded as the real prophet of the faithful. Bábism in its infancy was the cause of a greater sensation than that even which was produced by the teaching of Jesus, if we may judge from the account of Josephus of the first days of Christianity. Far from foreseeing the future spread of that religion, the Jewish historian contents himself with observing—" And the tribe of Christians, so named from him (Christ), are not extinct at this day."

the practice of certain austerities to acquire the reputation of peculiar piety. One of his singular proceedings at this period was to expose himself bareheaded to the rays of the burning summer sun, in order that men might see that his power extended even over the orb that had been the object of the veneration of the Persians of old. It is said, however—and any one who has visited Bushire in summer will readily believe the statement— that the sun's influence had the effect of rendering his brain disordered. He now gave out that as Ali had been the gate by which men had entered the city· of the prophets' knowledge, even so he was the gate through which men might attain to the knowledge of the twelfth Imam. It was in accordance with this doctrine that he received the distinguishing appellation of Bāb, or gate; from which his followers were styled Bābis. His pretensions rose in proportion to the credulity of those who placed faith in his mission from above. We are not informed in what manner he reconciled his new statements with preceding declarations, with which they were not consistent; but we may infer that after each new revelation he told his disciples that it had been necessary to prepare them for it by the preceding one. Not contented with the character of the forerunner of the twelfth Imam, he presently gave out that he was no other than the long-looked-for Mehdi himself; and finding that the higher his pretensions rose the more his followers increased in numbers and in zeal, he next gave out that the holy prophet of Medina had revisited the earth, and appeared in his person. His impiety lastly reached the blasphemous height of his declaring that he was an incarnation of the eternal God.

The success which had attended the preaching of the
Bāb at Bushire induced that personage to attempt the
dangerous experiment of endeavouring to bring over to
his doctrines the inhabitants of his native place. He
assumed the pretension of being able to work miracles;
but the only two said to have been performed by him of
which I can obtain any record were certainly of the most
simple description. One was his foolhardy attempt to
brave the power of the rays of the sun on the shore of
the Persian Gulf; the other was the assertion of being
able to write faster than merely mortal fingers could ply
the pen. But if his actual performances would scarcely
have entitled him to whatever credit may be due to
a clever deceiver of men's senses, his deficiencies were
fully made up for by the power of imagination and
of belief possessed by his followers. These spread his
fame far and wide throughout Persia, and his naïb, or
vicegerent, was sent to Sheeraz to pave the way for the
approach of the Bāb himself. But the naïb was unfortunate enough to have to deal with a hardened unbeliever
in Hussein Khan, who after his return from England
had been appointed governor-general of the province
of Fars. By his orders the naïb was seized and bastinadoed, and, in order to prevent him from going from
house to house, the governor ordered that the tendons
of his legs should be severed. But this ungracious reception of his forerunner did not deter the Bāb from
carrying into execution his project of visiting Sheeraz.
On his arrival there he was sent for by the governor,
with whom he had a private interview. In order that he
might the better prove the secret thoughts of the Bāb,
the governor pretended to be half disposed to believe in

his mission. He declared that a few days before, the
Bāb had appeared to him in a dream, and while
reproaching him with his treatment of the naïb had
declared that he considered it beneath his dignity to
punish him for the same. The Bāb, it appears, had
unlimited belief in the powers of credulity of those
whom he encountered ; it never occurred to him to
suppose that Hussein Khan was not sincere in what
he said, and he therefore determined to complete his
conversion by affording him a proof of his superhuman
power. " You have correctly stated what I said to you,"
he replied ; " but it was not in a dream that I appeared :
I was present to you in the body." Upon this Hussein
Khan declared himself to be convinced of the heavenly
mission of the Bāb. This was a great accession to the
ranks of the faithful, and the powerful neophyte was forthwith promised that he should one day sit on the throne
of Stamboul. It was a satisfactory prospect for the
future; but in the meantime Hussein Khan suggested
that the Bāb should come with him and confront the
assembled moollahs and ulemah of Sheeraz. It would
not have accorded with the Bāb's pretensions had he
declined to accede to this proposal; and he faced the
priests and doctors of the Mahomedan law with all the
more confidence that he believed himself to be secure of
the support of the strong arm of the governor of Fars.
He boldly declared to the astonished assembly that the
mission of Mahomed, which had served its purpose, was
now at an end, and that he had come down from heaven
to dwell amongst men for the purpose of inaugurating a
new order of things. The doctors gave him an attentive
hearing, and as some parts of his discourse were con-

fused, they requested, not unreasonably, that he would furnish them with a written statement of that which they were required to believe. The Bāb made no objection to this request ; but when the statement came to be read it was found to be written in some other language than the Arabic or Persian. Upon this the assembled priests declared that the fanatic was mad, and in conformity with this opinion, they decreed that, instead of the sentence of death which the Bāb deserved to have passed upon him for having declared that he was God, he should receive the punishment of the bastinado, and be confined for life. The execution òf the first part of this sentence is said to have had the effect of causing the Bāb to acknowledge that he had been guilty of egregious folly; but it produced little or no effect on the spread of his fame and of his doctrine.

Many of the principal priests of Persia became secret converts to Bābism, and, while the Bāb languished in prison at Sheeraz, and afterwards at Ispahan and at Chereck in Azerbaeejan, his naïb, who had contrived to escape, was successfully engaged in preaching his religion at Yezd. So numerous in a short time were the followers of the Bāb that a decree was issued by the chief religious authorities in Persia, making it a capital crime for any one to profess the tenets of the false prophet of Sheeraz. Some of the followers of the Bāb, full of new-born zeal, thought that they were doing a service acceptable to the Almighty by assassinating some of the chief priests who had issued decrees condemnatory of Bābism ; and, on the other hand, the priesthood authorized a persecution of the followers of the Bāb. In this way the feelings and interests of a large body of men were entirely engaged in this religious question, and the blood of those who were martyrs for the faith contributed greatly to the spread of the tenets of Bābism; since the fact that men were found willing to lay down life for the cause, convinced waverers that it must rest on the everlasting foundation of truth.

The reader of this volume will probably before reaching this page have made to himself the observation that the history of modern Persia is for the most part a mere record of deeds of violence and blood. Such deeds, it may be observed, occupy a large space in the annals of every nation, but it is painful for a writer to find so little else worthy of being recorded in the history of the modern occupants of a country which so early and for so long a period filled a conspicuous place in the world. But though fully aware of the monotonous nature of the task I have undertaken, I can find little or nothing in the pages of the Persian chronicler, or in the volumes and documents upon which I have drawn, that would either interest or instruct the European reader. I have therefore confined myself to the relation of such facts as seemed to me to show the spirit of the times of which I have written, and to have had more or less influence in shaping the destinies of the nation ruled over by the princes of the Kajar dynasty. I am now drawing near to the end of the reign of the third Kajar king, and having recounted the wars and massacres of that reign, it remains to me to describe the more peaceful events which marked it. The greatest of these would be considered by philanthropists to be a decree of the Shah strictly forbidding the application of torture to any of his subjects. It is not to be supposed, however, that this decree was sufficient to put a stop, once for all, to a practice so congenial to the habits of petty governors placed in positions where they were independent in a great measure of the central authorities. Some governors still continued to torture at their pleasure, but one of these having been brought to justice through the representations of the British Minister, the practice came gradually to be looked upon as unsafe, and thus a greater regard to the laws of humanity came to be observed.

Another step in the path of civilization was the prohibition of importing into Persia African slaves along the seaboard of the Persian Gulf and by the harbour of Mohamera. This measure was the result of the continuous efforts of her Britannic Majesty's Government. A third event of this reign which it is a pleasure to record, is the conclusion of a treaty of commerce between Persia and England. Negotiations were long in progress for making a similar treaty between Persia and France. Following the example of her Majesty's Government, that of King Louis Philippe had sent out to Persia a congratulatory embassy upon the Shah's accession to the throne; the ambassador being permitted to enter into arrangements for the conclusion of a commercial treaty. No results followed this measure, and the embassy obtained permission to return to France; its chief, and the Marquis de Lavalette, his secretary, being made Khans of Persia. A few years later the Count de Sartiges renewed the negotiations which had been begun by his predecessor. But these were not attended by the wished-for result, and his Excellency had to content himself with confining the practical work of his mission to the protection of his co-religionists in Persia.

23

During the administration of Haji Meerza Aghassi some attention was paid to the development of the internal resources of the dominions of the Shah. The cultivation of the mulberry-tree, to supply food for the silkworm, was anxiously watched over in the province of Kerman ; and, amongst other projects, the prime minister entertained, and endeavoured to carry into execution, that of diverting into the plain of Tehran the broad river of Kerij, with a view to procure an abundant supply of water for the wants of the city. On the whole, the minister of Mahomed Shah showed himself, during the thirteen years of his administration, to be a man not altogether unqualified for the duty of ruling over an Oriental nation. He was not deaf to the claims of expediency, of justice and of mercy, and if his merits scarcely deserved the high opinion which he entertained of his own performances and his own capacity, he is at least entitled to the credit of having meant well to his country and his sovereign. That sovereign was now about to close a career the years of which had been evil as they had been few. In the autumn of 1848 he was overtaken by a combination of maladies which it was feared would speedily bring him to the grave. Gout and erysipelas had together effected the ruin of his constitution, and on the evening of the 4th of September, 1848, his Majesty, being then in his fortieth year, expired at the palace of Mahomediah in Shimran, without having at the last suffered pain. That palace, as well as the once splendid abode of the Vizeer hard by, has long since been stripped of its treasures ; in accordance with the Persian prejudice, which makes a son object to dwelling in the house in which his father has died. The marble baths and halls that were built for the use of Sultanas are now the refuge of the jackal and the owl. But at the epoch of the death of Mahomed Shah the palace of Mahomediah contained two ladies of princely rank, in the relative condition of whom a wonderful alteration was effected by the demise of the king. During the lifetime of his Majesty his affections had been centred, and his confidence bestowed, on one alone of the many fair women who formed the royal household. But that princess was not the mother of the heir-apparent, and she had now the mortification of being forced to yield the place of dignity and influence to her rival, the new queen-mother.

Nasser-ed-deen Meerza, the heir-apparent of Persia, was absent at the seat of his government in Azerbaeejan at the time of the death of his father. It was of the utmost importance, for the establishment of a feeling of public security, that the young Shah should be brought to the capital without any unnecessary delay. The Russian Minister, in conjunction with the English chargé d'affaires, had determined to send members of their respective Missions to Tabreez so soon as they should receive intelligence of the demise of the king. But certain persons, whose interest it was to prolong the state of lawlessness which commonly prevails immediately after the death of a Persian monarch, had, before the demise of the Shah, begun to assemble in threatening bands on the roads between the palace and the city, with the view of stopping the messengers who should be sent to announce to the hundred and thirty provinces or governments of Persia that the monarch of the land was no more. Under these circumstances, Colonel Farrant, who was then in charge of the English Mission, determined to act upon the medical information he had received to the effect that the king could not possibly survive for many hours; and by thus anticipating the event he enabled his messenger to arrive at Tabreez long before any other courier could reach that town. The crown-prince was thus enabled to make timely preparations for his march to the capital, and the mischievous designs of these intriguers were frustrated.

The character of the deceased Shah must have been apparent to those who have perused the preceding pages. He was just in his intentions and pure in his private life : no indulgence in any vice is laid to his charge. On the other hand, he was bigoted and cruel; but for his bigotry he was indebted to his early education, and for his cruelty, the bodily pain under which for so many years he suffered, and which soured his temper, may be admitted as some palliation. The custom prevalent in Persia during his reign, by which the monarch was not only the judge of criminals but the witness of the execution of capital punishments, could not but deaden the royal heart to sentiments of compassion. On the whole, Mahomed Shah's memory is entitled to the respect accorded to that of a man who, in the face of obstacles and infirmities, has consistently persevered in what he believed to be the path of duty. His obsequies were performed with the pomp and splendour usually observed at the burial of a Persian king, and his body was placed by the side of that of Fetteh Ali Shah in the mosque of Koom.

CHAPTER XII.

Flight of Haji Meerza Aghassi—Rival Parties at Tehran—The Queen-
Mother President of the Council—Serious Risings in the Provinces—
The Salar—The Ameer-i-Nizam—Measures of Reform adopted by him
—Combination against him—Mutiny of the Garrison of Tehran—
Seizure of Kotoor by the Turks—Ascendancy of the Belooches in
Seistan—Persian Claims to that Province—Protracted Siege of Meshed
—Bahman Meerza—Prince Sultan Murad presses the Siege of Meshed
—Foreign Interference offered for the Pacification of Khorassan—
Ravages of the Turkomans—Surrender of Meshed—Death of the
Salar.

SOMETHING of that feeling of satisfaction with which one
listens in a warm room to the roar of thunder and the
pelting of rain without, ought to be experienced by the
reader dwelling in a settled country while perusing an
account of the condition of affairs in an unsettled country
after the death of its ruler.

Mahomed Shah had scarcely breathed his last when
a large body of his most influential courtiers hastened
at night through the lanes and gardens of Tajreesh to
the encampment of the British Legation. To them it
was as the shadow of a great rock in a weary land, under
which they sought refuge till the calamities which they
dreaded should be past. These courtiers had formed
themselves into a council, with the purpose of carrying
on the administration until the arrival of the Shah.
Whilst they made the strongest professions of allegiance
to their new sovereign, they one and all declared that

they would no longer submit to the authority of Haji Meerza Aghassi, whom they were prepared to resist by force. They were informed by the English chargé d'affaires that he would act, in the emergency which had arisen, in concert with the Russian representative; and on the following day, they took part with him in a consultation with Prince Dolgorouky. A paper was sealed by most of the influential persons of the court, by which they gave in their allegiance to the young Shah; but in it they stipulated that Haji Meerza Aghassi should withdraw himself from public affairs until the commands of his sovereign should be received with reference to the formation of the new government: they also required that the Haji should disperse the armed force with which he had surrounded his person. In order to prevent loss of life, Prince Dolgorouky and Colonel Farrant agreed to request the minister of the late Shah to remain quietly at his village, and to abstain from interfering in public affairs. To the latter proposal he at once agreed; but on the morning of the day after the council had been held, he suddenly made his appearance in the citadel of Tehran, where he surrounded himself with twelve hundred followers, and shutting the gates, he cut off all communication with the city. He did not, however, remain there long, but, after wandering for a time about the plain of Tehran, took sanctuary in the shrine of Shah Abdul Azeem; to which he was pursued by some Shahzevend horsemen.

In the meantime much disorder ensued in the capital; the popular fury being vented on the retainers and clients of the Minister. The roads in the vicinity of Tehran became impassable; but the chief priest exerted himself to restore order, and after a time his efforts were attended with success. The government in the meantime assumed the form of an oligarchy. Every member of the council issued orders as he thought proper, and each aspired to fill the post of prime minister so soon as the Shah should arrive at the capital. But the president of the council was the queen-mother, who, under very difficult circumstances, showed herself to be possessed of judgment and of ability— qualities not often to be met with in Oriental ladies. There were two principal parties at this time in Persia : one of these was called the Azerbaeejan party, the other was that of the Asef-ed-Dowleh. The queen-mother was readily persuaded that it would be impolitic to ex- clude the members of the latter from all participation in power, and her Highness accordingly invited its chiefs to attend the council, and to take part in the delibera- tions on public affairs. Her Highness received visits from the foreign missions, and while she thanked them in the name of her son for the support they had given to his cause, she expressed her readiness to be guided by their friendly advice. To the party of the Asef-ed- Dowleh belonged one of the most influential noblemen of Persia, Meerza Agha Khan. He had formerly filled the post of Minister of War, but at the instigation of Haji Meerza Aghassi he had been banished from Tehran, after having been beaten and fined. He now made his appear- ance at one of the gates of the city, and requested the English chargé d'affaires to procure him permission to enter it. The queen-mother was glad to welcome back the banished man, and his reception by the people as he passed through the bazars on his way to the palace, showed either how popular he was, or how much the Azerbaeejan party, of which he was the opponent, was disliked by the populace.

It was not at Tehran alone that the announcement of the Shah's death had been the signal for disorder. The roads in all directions became infested with robbers, who effectually prevented all communication with the capital. The inhabitants of several towns availed themselves of this favourable opportunity for putting to death their tyrannical governors. Ispahan, in common with Kerman, Sheeraz and other cities, became the scene of lawless outrage. An affray took place between the garrison and some of the citizens, which ended in the murder of one of the principal assistants of the governor of Ispahan. The perpetrators of this act, which was committed in the most public manner in the mosque, and under the eyes of the chief priest, continued at large, in defiance of the civil authorities. The Imam-i-Juma * made at first no effort to appease the tumult, but when his aid was called in, he lent his assistance to the governor; who, having been reinforced by the arrival of some troops, attacked the rebels, and, after having met with much resistance, drove them from the town.

The city of Yezd was also thrown into a state of rebellion and confusion by the announcement of the death of Mahomed Shah. The governor, who possessed great firmness, but who was very unpopular, found himself besieged by a portion of the inhabitants headed by some notorious disturbers of the peace. After having attempted in vain to defend his place of residence, he was forced to retire to the citadel, where he and his few

* The chief priest.

attendants found themselves to be almost destitute of provisions. By the aid of four pieces of ordnance, however, they contrived not only to hold out for some days, but also seriously to annoy the townspeople. At length hunger compelled them to negotiate, and it was agreed that they should receive provisions and beasts of burden to enable them to quit the place. But these had no sooner been produced and admitted into the citadel, than the governor closed the gate, and refused to abide by the conditions to which he had agreed. The camels and asses were slaughtered to serve the garrison for food, and the followers of the governor began to congratulate themselves on the superior ability they had shown in outwitting the townsmen. It appeared, however, that both parties were suitably matched in point of bad faith, and the defenders of the citadel found that they were premature in thinking that all the advantage had been theirs in the late transaction ; it was ascertained that the bread they had received had been poisoned. They endeavoured to punish this attempt on their lives by renewing the fire upon the town, which the citizens, being without artillery, were unable to return. After these mutual discoveries of each other's treachery, it seems strange that they should have again had recourse to negotiation ; but no amount of experience of the bad faith of his countrymen has the effect of inducing a Persian to resolve not to trust to Persians for the future. The explanation of this singular, but incontestable, fact is to be found in the circumstance that vanity is even more strongly developed in the Persian character than is deceitfulness. Each Persian thinks that he of all men is sufficiently clever to be able to

decipher the character, and to divine the secret intentions, of those with whom he has to deal; and accordingly he is ever ready, in spite of his previous
experience, to believe in the promises, protestations
and oaths of his countrymen.   The governor of Yezd
renewed his overtures to the townspeople, and as his
arguments continued to be seconded by the fire of his
artillery, he found a ready disposition on the part of the
citizens to yield to his wish of being allowed to retire
unmolested.   But at this point of the negotiation some
troops arrived to his succour, and enabled him to leave
the citadel and appear openly in the town.   A few of the
rebels were then secured, but it was not until after the
lapse of some time that their leader was captured and
put to death.

The condition of the highways in the province of
Yezd was now such as to cause the greatest embarrassment to the trading community.   In the space of about
two months no less than fifteen hundred beasts of
burden, with their loads, were carried off, or detained
on their way to or from the provincial capital.   It was
no wonder that the merchants began to lose courage, and
to talk loudly of deserting a country where their property
was so slightly protected.

The city of Kasveen had been for fourteen years the
prison of Syf-el-Mulk Meerza, a son of that Zil-es-Sultan
who had disputed the throne with Mahomed Shah.   The
Ameerzadeh now suddenly appeared at the distance of
thirty-six miles from Tehran, at the head of a body of
horsemen.   He addressed a circular to the chiefs of the
wandering tribes in that vicinity, requesting them to
join his standard, and to aid him in preventing the ac-

cession to power of Nasser-ed-deen Shah. But the sole exploit of this paltry pretender to regal power was to rob a courier of the Russian Mission of the sum of three thousand five hundred ducats. His forces were soon afterwards routed, and he himself made prisoner by some horsemen of the Affshar tribe, who brought him, tied with cords, to Tehran.

But the most formidable opponent whom the young Shah had to put down was, as might have been expected, the gallant son of Allah-yar Khan. Some of his followers having taken sanctuary in the great mosque of Meshed, the servants of the governor of Khorassan, actuated by imprudent zeal, desired to drag them out from the holy precincts, or to slay them over the tomb of the saint. Such sacrilegious talking shocked the feelings of the priests and pilgrims, and they called on the people to assist in saving from insult the shrine of the blessed Imam. The appeal was not without effect, and the people of Meshed drove the impious soldiers from the mosque, and were from that hour devoted to the cause of the Salar. On the receipt of the news of the Shah's death, that chief lost no time in taking possession of the city of Meshed, and he forced the governor to take refuge in the citadel.

During the interval which elapsed between the death of Mahomed Shah and his son's arrival at the capital, the city of Tehran was a scene of intrigues and counter-intrigues which were planned in quick succession. No effort was spared by the ambitious and the unworthy to undermine those in whom it seemed likely that the Shah would place confidence. A priest named Nasrullah was now the chief of the Azerbaeejan party, and as he also

possessed to a certain extent the confidence of the followers of the Asef-ed-Dowleh, it was thought by many
that he was the person best fitted to fill the post of
premier, or Sedr-Azem.   But the Shah had already made
choice of a Grand Vizeer.   On the 20th of October, 1848,
his Majesty made his public entry into his capital, and at
midnight of the same day he was crowned King of Persia.
Nasser-ed-deen, the eldest son of the late Mahomed
Shah, and of Mahd-Aulia, the daughter of Cassim Khan,
Kajar, was at this time sixteen years of age.   He was not
remarkable for any premature development of mental gifts,
but he was possessed of sagacity sufficient to enable him
to discern in a man who accompanied him from Tabreez,
the qualities that were wanted in a Persian Minister.

Meerza Teki Khan, who was at this time appointed
to be the Ameer-i-Nizam, or commander-in-chief of
the Persian army, owed his elevation entirely to his
talents and his services.   He was a man altogether
of a different nature from that of his countrymen in
general.   Belisarius did not tower over the degenerate
Romans of his day more than did the Ameer-i-Nizam
over his contemporaries, the successors of the adversaries
of "the last of the Roman generals."   The race of
modern Persians cannot be said to be altogether effete,
since so recently it has been able to produce a man such
as was the Ameer-i-Nizam.   Feraghan, near Sultanatabad
in Irak, had the honour to give birth to him who perhaps
alone of all the Oriental statesmen and governors whose
names appear in the history of modern Persia, would have
satisfied the scrutiny of a Diogenes, and was fully entitled
to be considered that " noblest work of God," an honest
man.   The father of Meerza Teki occupied a humble

station in life, and from the post of cook was promoted
to that of steward in the household of the Kaim-Makam,
the first minister of Mahomed Shah. The son at an
early age entered the service of the Persian commander-
in-chief, and accompanied that officer to St. Petersburg
with the Mission on which Prince Kosroo was sent after
the murder of M. Grebaïodoff. On his return to Persia
after this his sole visit to Europe, the servant of the
commander-in-chief was promoted in the social scale,
and from being a menial retainer he became a Meerza,
or writer. · He was subsequently named to the rank of
Khan, and on the death of his patron he became Vizeer
of the army of Azerbaeejan. In consequence of the
illness of the Musheer-ed-Dowleh, who had been named
Persian plenipotentiary at the conferences of Erzeroum
for the settlement of the points in dispute between Persia
and Turkey, Meerza Teki Khan was sent to represent his
government; and we are told that he was beyond all
comparison the most interesting personage amongst the
commissioners of Turkey, Persia, Russia and Great
Britain, who were then assembled at Erzeroum.* During
his residence in that city Meerza Teki Khan had an
opportunity of witnessing the results of the introduction
of the Tanzimat in the dominions of the Sultan. On
his return to Tehran he was directed to accompany the
crown-prince to Tabreez when his Royal Highness was
named governor-general of Azerbaeejan, and thus a
considerable share in the actual government of the chief
province of Persia fell into his hands. From Tabreez
he proceeded to Tehran in the train of the new Shah,
and on the way he was offered by his Majesty the post

---

* *Armenia and Erzeroum*, by the Hon. ROBERT CURZON.

of Prime Minister of Persia. It is said—I know not whether correctly or otherwise—that Meerza Teki had from his youthful years confidently asserted that if he should live to middle age, he felt sure he would rise to be the prime minister of his native land; but he was somewhat disturbed by the recollection that each of the two preceding Kajar Shahs had put to death his first chief Vizeer, and, therefore, when the post was offered to him, he sought to reconcile ambition with prudence by declining the title of Sedr-Azem, which is usually conferred on a prime minister, and by taking in its stead the humbler designation of Ameer-i-Nizam.

On assuming charge of the administration of the government of Persia, the new minister found every department in the utmost confusion. But he was not a man to be daunted by difficulties, and he courageously set himself to reform every branch of the public service, and to abolish many abuses, such as the putting up of governments for sale. He took measures for at once improving the condition of the army; for relieving the peasantry from the oppressions under which they laboured; and for changing the whole financial system of the country. It was remarked at the commencement of the Ameer's ministry that too much reliance was not to be placed on his promises, since, after all, he was a Persian. But the Vizeer in every thing acted up to his expressed intentions, and if all his measures were not followed by success, their failure must be attributed to the little assistance and coöperation he received from others, rather than to any want of sagacity or energy on the part of the minister. His word was not readily pledged, but when it had once been given, implicit reliance might be placed upon it. It was no easy task that now lay before the Ameer. The province of Khorassan was in arms against the Shah, and had the measures adopted by the new government been unsuccessful, anarchy and confusion would have followed. It was openly predicted at this time that the days of the Kajar dynasty would very soon be over, and that Persia would be broken up into a number of petty states. Fórtunately these sinister anticipations were not fulfilled; men's minds were greatly calmed by the removal to Kerbela of Haji Meerza Aghassi, owing to whose avarice, nepotism and misgovernment, it was alleged, the general disorder had arisen.

The insurrection in Khorassan was not easily put down. Prince Hamza, having with him in the citadel only three thousand infantry of Azerbaeejan, could not take any active measures against the Salar, who was at the head of fifteen thousand men, and whose force was daily increased by the arrival of detachments from all parts of Khorassan. All the chiefs of that province, with one or two exceptions, espoused the cause of the insurgents, and the feeling of the people towards the brave and courteous Salar is described as having amounted almost to worship. On the other hand, Yar Mahomed Khan of Herat came at this time to Meshed to the relief of the prince-governor, with two thousand Affghan horsemen and a large supply of provisions. The motive—if any motive need be ascribed to him save the innate Oriental desire to take part in a disturbance— the alleged motive for this movement on the part of the ruler of Herat, was the promise held out to him by the governor of Khorassan of twenty pieces of artillery and a large number of muskets, which were to be given to him, together with two places on the frontier of Khorassan, on the condition that he should afford assistance towards putting down the insurrection at Meshed. After some fighting, the joint forces of Herat and of Prince Hamza found that they were able to make but little progress, and negotiations were therefore set on foot with a view to the cessation of hostilities. Jafer Kuli Khan of Boojnoord, who till now had been detained in custody by the ruler of Herat, was sent to the Salar on the part of the leaders opposed to him. But that chief was the worst envoy that could have been selected, for he was now burning to avenge, on the person and troops of Yar Mahomed Khan, the long imprisonment to which he had so inhospitably been subjected, and having joined his friend the Salar, he refused to return to the hostile camp. The attention of the Affghan chief was now directed to the movements of a cavalry force which was sent to devastate the border of the territory of Herat. The prince-governor of Khorassan was then obliged to evacuate the citadel of Meshed, and to retire towards the Affghan frontier.

The Ameer-i-Nizam had in the meantime sent a body of about six thousand infantry from Tehran to the assistance of the governor of Khorassan. Prince Sultan Murad, who was in command of this force, laid siege to the town of Sebzewar, which place was defended by the youthful son of the Salar; but Sebzewar held out, and the siege was soon raised. Prince Sultan Murad, careless of leaving a fortified place behind him, then went on towards Kuchan, plundering by the way several villages, in which he found an ample supply of provisions for his troops. Some chiefs of consideration joined his standard,

and through their friends he endeavoured to enter into
an arrangement with the people of Meshed. His brother,
Prince Hamza, was in the meantime encamped within
twenty-four miles of Herat. The Salar's party had lost
the assistance of some allies whose aid might have turned
the scale of victory. The chiefs of Mazenderan had
been driven into opposition, and almost into rebellion,
against the Shah's government by the vexatious policy
of Haji Meerza Aghassi; but on the guarantee of the
English representative at the Persian court that their
personal safety should be granted to them, at their own
request and by the desire of the Shah, they at once
repaired to court, where they received a flattering
welcome.

While Khorassan still continued in rebellion, the
process of amelioration in other parts of Persia was
found to be attended at every stage by difficulties that
were almost insurmountable. The Ameer-i-Nizam was
so thoroughly aware of the duplicity and venality of
almost all the Persian courtiers, that he for a time
could not fix upon a man who might with safety be
employed in the task of coöperating with him in re-
medying abuses, and establishing a system of equitable
government. But the Ameer himself was as laborious
as he was conscientious: he worked day after day
and week after week, late and early, at the noblest
task that can fall to the lot of man; nor was he discouraged or disheartened by the difficulties which he
had to surmount, and the intrigues he had to thwart.
He enjoyed the unbounded confidence of the Shah,
without which he could not have effected anything; but ✳
he had not been fortunate enough to be able to secure

24

the coöperation of the person who, next to himself,
possessed the greatest influence over the mind of the
youthful king. In a country where every one, from the
Shah downwards, looks on his neighbour with suspicion,
there is but one person in whom the sovereign feels that
he is sure, under all circumstances, to find a true adviser
and a sincere friend. The position and influence of the
Queen-mother so entirely depend on the life and prosperity of the Shah, that her counsels are ever listened
to by him without suspicion or impatience. One can
only speculate as to the motives which induced the
Queen-mother to withhold her confidence from the
Ameer-i-Nizam. She may have dreaded the effect upon
the selfish chiefs of Persia of the measures of reform
which the Minister had made up his mind to introduce.
She may have been brought to believe that the hereditary nobles of the land would never be induced to receive the law from a man of humble extraction, and that
her son's throne would in consequence be endangered
Or, her Highness's conduct may have originated in
some less worthy motive : such as jealousy of the influence which had been acquired by the Ameer over the
mind of the king. But for whatever reason, the Queen-
mother threw the weight of her influence into the scale
of the opposition, and afforded her countenance to the
host of influential and discontented persons whose
unlawful gains were curtailed in consequence of the
measures of the new Minister. At first, however, these
intrigues produced no impression upon the mind of the
Shah ; and had his Majesty been allowed to follow the
dictates of his own will, the Ameer would probably ere
now have, for a time, converted Persia from the condition

in which Hercules found the Augean stables into that in which he left them.

But it is not to be supposed that the Ameer alone could have permanently changed the characteristics of a whole nation, or could have overcome the combined influences of climate, of custom, and of religion. He might have effected much during his own lifetime; but it is highly improbable that another man could have been found to carry on the Shah's government on the enlightened principles adopted by the Ameer; and, therefore, Persia would in any case have sunk into the apathetic condition of all the surviving Mahomedan States which are not influenced from without.

The Ameer's system of government was that which experience has proved to be the most beneficial for an Oriental nation—an enlightened despotism. He made no pretence of wishing to educate the people, or of consulting their inclinations. He professed to endeavour to secure their material well-being, and to restrain their evil propensities. But the Minister aimed at far more than this; and had his measures been permanently effected, their adoption would have indicated nothing less than a radical change in Persian morality and Persian manners. The first idea which the word Persia suggests in the mind of a scholar is the flowery and overloaded style which for two thousand years has characterized the compositions of the poets and historians of the land of the fire-worshippers. The Ameer-i-Nizam resolved to suppress the meaningless and disgusting phraseology which is suited only to slaves and parasites, and he published a decree forbidding the use in petitions and official documents addressed to himself of more than

24—2

one specified title—that of "Jenab" or "Excellency."
A person of less rank was in like manner to be addressed
by one lesser title. People were astonished to hear of a
Vizeer who rejected the incense of flattery; but they
obeyed his commands, and probably few regretted the
high-sounding but meaningless expressions to which
their ears had been so long accustomed.

Persian immorality and dishonesty are unhappily
proverbial, and the Ameer-i-Nizam did not hesitate to
grapple with these most deeply-ingrained vices of his
fellow-countrymen. The public baths of Tehran had been
allowed to become the scenes of open debauchery; and
the Minister lost no time in punishing those who made
their profit by these practices, which he now put down.

Of all the traits which go to make up the Persian
character, that which, next to excessive vanity, is most
strongly developed, is a constant desire to acquire unlawful gains. The word "mudahil," for which there is no
exact English term, has, for Persian ears, a charm which
few Europeans can comprehend. "Mudahil" signifies
all that one can acquire by receiving bribes, by swindling
and extortion, and by all other irregular means. It is
"mudahil" and not salary which every Persian official is
anxious to secure. A salary regularly paid affords no
scope for the display of the talents in which Persians most excel—for dissimulating and overreaching,
oppressing and cringing—and, therefore, a post which
has only a good salary attached to it, and which affords
no good opportunities of making "mudahil," is looked
upon by Persians as being but a poor possession. The
Ameer-i-Nizam, himself altogether above being bribed,
resolved to suppress the wide-spread system of whole-

sale bribery which he saw around him. By degrees he effected much in the way of putting a stop to corruption; but his next task proved to be too much even for his energy and unlimited power. The sectarian spirit in Persia is kept alive mainly by the annual exhibition on the stage of the sufferings and the martyrdom of the Imam Hussein; and during the month of Moherrem the whole populations of the cities of Northern Persia are worked up into a state bordering upon frenzy; notwithstanding that the chief Moslem authorities hold that these exhibitions are contrary to the duty of the followers of Mahomed. The Ameer-i-Nizam endeavoured to take advantage of the weight of religious authority to do away with a custom so productive of fanaticism as is the Persian Tazeeah. The Sheeahs of Irak and Azerbaeejan were, however, too much attached to the yearly-recurring exhibition to submit to its suppression, and the Ameer was forced unwillingly to permit its continuance.

Soon after the arrival of the Shah at his capital, a royal commission was appointed to examine into the state of the finances of the kingdom, and to draw up for the king's information a statement of the revenues and of the expenditure of the country. At this time the latter far exceeded the former. It appears that one mode of courting popularity practised by the minister Haji Meerza Aghassi had been, seldom or never directly to refuse compliance with a petition for the grant of a donation or a pension. He had not made direct payments, excepting to his own tribesmen, as a general rule; but he had been in the habit of issuing government orders on the different provincial authorities.

It is said that he had never meant that these orders should be attended to, and that he had given the provincial governors to understand so. The result was that they seldom or never had been attended to; but the odium of the non-payment had fallen on the governors, while the credit of liberality had remained with the Haji. The consequence of this truly Oriental system of canvassing for popularity was, that the Ameer-i-Nizam now found upon his hands an enormous amount of government liabilities. He had the alternative of meeting them or of damaging the credit of the Shah by rejecting bonds issued by a minister of state. Most Persians would have attempted to evade choosing between these alternatives by having recourse to some ingenious subterfuge; and it is to the credit of the Ameer that he preferred boldly to face the difficulty. Probably no financier ever found himself to be placed in a more embarrassed position than that of Meerza Teki Khan in the beginning of the year 1849. Since the accession of the Shah no money had been paid into the royal treasury, and on the other hand the expenditure was necessarily heavy. The army in the field in Khorassan depended for its existence entirely upon the central government, and that government was in the unfortunate position of lacking the credit which could only result from confidence in its stability. But in addition to the financial difficulties to be overcome, there was the embarrassment to be dreaded from affronting and impoverishing so many powerful and unprincipled men. Colonels there were who had been drawing pay and receiving clothing for regiments which actually did not exist. The royal body-guard, during the reign of Fetteh Ali Shah, had consisted of an efficient

regiment of six hundred horsemen. During the reign of
that monarch's grandson it had been increased, upon
paper, to four thousand men, but reduced, at muster,
to three hundred. Nor was the state of things in the
civil department at all out of keeping with that of the
military department. Many persons were in the receipt
of large pensions which had been granted by Haji Meerza
Aghassi without the slightest reference to any service
rendered by them; and as many of these stipendiaries
were priests and men of influence, the task of compelling
them to relinquish their prey was all the more difficult of
accomplishment. Nevertheless, the Ameer had the firmness to cut down the expenditure of the government, and
to reduce or discontinue the pensions that had been
granted to so many idle princes and priests. The most
extraordinary, and even unaccountable, part of his conduct in the eyes of the Persians, was that he was utterly
inaccessible to bribery. This being the case, the money
which he refused to accept was employed for the purpose
of upsetting him. The Shah had shown himself to be
possessed of sufficient firmness to resist the attempts
that had been made to induce him to dismiss from office
the Ameer-i-Nizam; and his Majesty had even insisted
on giving to his Minister, in opposition to the wishes of
his mother and all his relations, the hand of his only
sister. The discontented noblemen, therefore, despair-
ing of being able to move the Shah, resorted to other
means for obtaining the dismissal of the Ameer.

There were at that time in the citadel of Tehran
about two thousand five hundred soldiers of regiments
belonging to Azerbaeejan, and these men were bribed to
mutiny, and to demand the life of the prime minister.

On the 11th of March, 1849, the regiments of the garrison of the citadel of Tehran refused to listen to the commands of their officers, and proceeded to the house of the Ameer-i-Nizam, in front of which they began to vociferate loudly, and to demand their arrears of pay. They were, however, persuaded to return to their quarters, on the promise that their alleged grievances would be inquired into on the following morning, and redressed if proved to be real. On the next day the troops again made their appearance unarmed; but they were confronted by the personal attendants of the Minister, who fired upon the clamorous mob. Upon this the exasperated troops returned to their barracks for their arms, and again came forth in a body, vowing vengeance against the Ameer. The Persian Minister had now recourse to the friendly interference of the English chargé d'affaires at Tehran. That officer had formerly been employed in the command of Persian troops, and he was listened to by the mutineers; but his efforts were insufficient to quell the tumult. The furious soldiers were unanimous in their demand that the Ameer should be dismissed or put to death; and not a word was now said as to their arrears of pay. The Shah had not the means of putting down this mutiny, at the outset, by force, and it seemed likely that he would be compelled to submit to the dangerous course of allowing himself to be dictated to by an armed throng. The Minister in this dilemma volunteered to retire from office; he left the citadel forthwith, and took up his abode in the house of Meerza Agha Khan, whose services to the government on this occasion won for him the entire confidence of the Shah and of the Ameer-i-Nizam.

The countenance of one of the principal hereditary noblemen of Persia was, at this conjuncture, of the greatest value to the plebeian brother-in-law of the Shah ; but the government was laid under still greater obligations to the Imam-i-Juma, the high priest of Tehran. That functionary possessed the greatest influence over the citizens, who, at his command, shut the shops in the bazaars, closed the caravanserais, and armed themselves for the purpose of resisting the mutinous soldiery. The excited townsmen, backed as they were by the approval of the Shah and his Minister, by the exhortations and blessings of the Imam-i-Juma, and by the full moral support of the foreign legations, were more than a match for the tumultuous crowd of soldiers without their officers. The victory was rendered no longer doubtful by the return of one of the regiments to its duty ; an appeal having been made to the men not to disgrace the English officers by whom they had been drilled. The danger to the government thus passed over, and the Ameer-i-Nizam quietly returned to the discharge of the duties of his office.

About this time the cause of the rebels in Khorassan received a severe blow by the desertion of Jafer Kuli Khan, the lord of Boojnoord. That chief quarrelled with the Salar, and he thereupon took advantage of the offer of the Shah's pardon, which had been guaranteed to him by the Ameer on the condition that he should return to his duty. On his arrival at Tehran his reception was in accordance with the assurances which had been held out to him.

The fort of Sebzewar was now surrendered to the troops of the Shah, but the atrocities which they com-

mitted in that town went far towards checking any inclination which the people of Meshed may have entertained
to imitate the example of those of Sebzewar.

It was at this time that the Turkish government took
advantage of the confusion that reigned throughout
Persia to seize the frontier district of Kotoor, in direct
contravention of the engagements which had been concluded between Persia and the Sublime Porte at Erzeroum. In spite of all remonstrances, Turkey has persisted in retaining Kotoor.

While the fate of Khorassan was still doubtful, neither
the authority of the Shah nor the position of his Minister
could be said to be secure. It was long before the governor of Ispahan could put down the insurrection that had
been raised in that city; and at the same time the chief
of Bunpoor, in Beloochistan, took advantage of the opportunity of revolting. A military force was assembled at
Roodbar for the purpose of being sent against him; but
it was determined to try, in the first instance, the effect
of negotiation with the insurgent chief. This mode of
settling the difference having failed, the troops took possession of Bunpoor. The town of Bunpoor is distant
from Roodbar about two hundred and forty miles, nearly
two-thirds of the road between them being an uninhabited tract of desert. It was at this time proposed to
the Shah's government, by the Prince of Kerman, to
invade the province of Seistan, on the plea of putting a
stop to the raids of the Belooches within the territory of
Yezd and Kerman. Some of the chiefs of Seistan had
lately sent to ask the assistance of the prince in support of
their claims to supremacy in their native province. The
Belooches in Seistan were gradually acquiring the ascen-

dancy over the races who had been longer settled in that country, and who were much divided amongst themselves. The Kayanian tribe of Seistanis, who boasted of being descended from the oldest dynasty of Persian kings, was long the ruling race in that province ; but this tribe was driven from Jelalabad by some others who united themselves together against it. The chief of one of these tribes (not a Belooch one), called Sirbendi, now exercised most influence in Seistan ; but on his death his son was unable to preserve his high position, and, in order to be able to put down his uncles, he reluctantly had recourse to asking the aid of the Persian governor of Kerman. One of his uncles also applied to the same person for aid ; and the Prince of Kerman thought that the conjuncture was a favourable one for practically asserting the vague claims of his master to the possession of the province of Seistan. The route by which a Persian army from Kerman could reach Seistan would be that by Tehrood, Bem, Koorook and Terij, and thence by places not marked in the maps of that region, along a distance of about four hundred and fifty miles in all ; the greater part of which is a desert tract having wells at intervals. A march over such a region, and in the face of active Belooches who would seize the passes, would not be likely to be attended with success, while it would certainly entail unusual hardships and difficulties. It may have been the dread of these, or it may have been the fact that the Ameer-i-Nizam had already more than sufficient to occupy the resources of the government, that induced the Shah's Ministers to reject the proposal of the Prince of Kerman to invade the province of Seistan.

The siege of Meshed continued, during a period of

eighteen months, to keep alive in the minds of the people of Persia a feeling of disquietude or of hope, according as they were well or ill-disposed towards the government established at Tehran. There were at this time absent from the kingdom, in banishment, two men who had been the most powerful, as well as perhaps the ablest, statesmen of Persia. One of the two was the Shah's uncle, Bahman Meerza, who had been implicated in the proceedings of the Asef-ed-Dowleh at Meshed. It was believed that the latter had offered to him the crown of Persia, and the discovery of this conspiracy had led to Prince Bahman being deprived of his government of Azerbaeejan, and to his being forced to retire to Georgia, where he remained under Russian protection. The other exiled Persian statesman was the Asef-ed-Dowleh, the uncle of the late Mahomed Shah. The Ameer-i-Nizam was urged to recall both of these illustrious exiles; but with regard to the case of Bahman Meerza, he observed that, should the prince be permitted to return to his country, his wealth, influence and popularity would quickly secure for him his former government of Azerbaeejan, which he would be likely to constitute an independent province. With regard to the case of the Asef-ed-Dowleh, the Minister observed that to grant permission for his return to Persia whilst his son continued in open rebellion, would be to make it appear that the Shah was unable to put down insurrection by force of arms, and that he was constrained to make terms with the insurgents. Prince Sultan Murad was instructed to strain every nerve, in order to bring to a conclusion the siege of Meshed. A messenger sent by the Ameer to that city with conciliatory letters and messages to the chief men of the place, totally failed in securing the object of his mission. The propositions which he had been instructed to name were at once rejected, and the priests of Meshed even urged the advisability of putting him to death. The Salar, however, not only protected him from violence, but treated him in the kindest manner, and sent him back to Tehran as the bearer of a proposal that a son of Fetteh. Ali Shah should be named governor of Khorassan, and that the Salar should be his vizeer ; the Azerbaeejan troops being withdrawn. These terms were rejected by the Ameer-i-Nizam.

Before this period it had been customary in Persia to concede an unusual degree of deference to the opinions and wishes of the foreign representatives accredited to the Persian court ; the influence of either the English or the Russian Mission being in the ascendant for the time, according as the inclinations of the Shah or of his minister of the day leaned towards England or towards Russia. To such an extent was this interference in the internal affairs of Persia allowed to be carried, that foreign representatives were sometimes requested to take under their protection individual subjects of the Shah. Thus at the time of the departure of the young king from Tabreez for Tehran, the English consul was asked to protect the Armenians resident in that place. The Ameer-i-Nizam did not fail to perceive that it was unbecoming that a government should not regulate the affairs of its own subjects, and he accordingly determined for the future to set himself against foreign interference in matters that only concerned Persia. Every impartial person must admit that the right of granting protection to subjects of the Shah, which was assumed by foreign ministers, though it had been sanctioned to a certain extent by the consent of the Persian government, was contrary to the principles of international law.*　But when the Ameer-i-Nizam showed symptoms of an intention to put a stop to the abuse which had arisen in this respect, the foreign ministers at the Persian court would by no means consent to relinquish a custom, the observance of which gave them so much influence over the Vizeers and subjects of the Shah.　The foreign ministers then resident at Tehran were too intent on establishing the influence of their respective governments in Persia, to be able to sympathize fully with the Ameer-i-Nizam in his endeavours to erect his country into a powerful and firmly-established monarchy upon the basis of law and justice. It was proposed to employ the good offices of the Russian and English representatives at Tehran for the purpose of bringing about a satisfactory compromise between the government and the rebels of Khorassan.　But the

---

* " The house of an ambassador ought to be safe from all outrage, being under the particular protection of the law of nations. . . . But the immunity and freedom of the ambassador's house is established only in favour of the minister and his household, as is evident from the very reasons upon which it is grounded.　Can he take advantage of the privilege in order to convert his house into an asylum to afford shelter and protection to the enemies of the prince ? . . . Such proceedings would be contrary to all the duties of an ambassador, to the spirit by which he ought to be animated, and to the lawful purposes for which he has been admitted into the country. This is what nobody will presume to deny.　But I will proceed farther, and lay it down as a certain truth, that a sovereign is not obliged to tolerate an abuse so pernicious to his state and so detrimental to society. . . . Thus. it belongs to the sovereign to decide, on occasion, how far the right of asylum, which an ambassador claims as belonging to his house, is to be respected ; and if the question relates to an offender whose arrest or punishment is of great importance to the State, the prince is not to be withheld by the consideration of a privilege which was never granted for the detriment or ruin of States.—*The Law of Nations*, by M. de VATTEL.　Edition of 1834, pp. 494-5.

Ameer, whilst acknowledging how much the Shah had owed to foreign assistance, was of opinion that foreign intervention in the affairs of Persia had been stretched to the utmost limits which were compatible with the dignity of the government, and he therefore would not avail himself of this mode of bringing the rebellion to an end. He is even reported to have said that it would be better for Persia that the inhabitants of Meshed should be brought back to their duty through the loss of twenty thousand men, than that that city should be won for the Shah through foreign interference.

The siege of Meshed went on with variable fortune : at one time the army met with a severe check in attempting to carry one of the gates of the place ; at another time the besiegers had the advantage in a combat with the troops of the besieged, whose sortie they repulsed. In the meantime the Turkomans, being left unopposed, gathered a rich harvest of spoil throughout Khorassan ; not a caravan could pass to or from Herat in safety, and the Khorassan villages far and near were plundered by these ruthless marauders. At the close of the year 1849 a fresh detachment of troops from Tehran arrived before Meshed ; but its commander, instead of joining the force of Prince Sultan Murad, thought proper to pitch his tents at a distance from those of the rest of the besieging army. This mistake was at once perceived and taken advantage of by the Salar, who sallied in force from the city and inflicted great loss on the newly-arrived detach-ment ; and then returned to within the walls. In con-sequence of the retreat of the Salar, the leader of the detachment, with the vanity never absent from a Persian, claimed to have gained a victory. Up to this time the

city had not been completely invested, one gate having
remained open through which provisions were introduced
under the safe conduct of the Turkomans. The besieged
further derived some encouragement from the arrival of a
brother of the Salar, who passed along the whole length
of Persia in the disguise of a pilgrim, carrying with him
a considerable sum of money. But at length the Shah's
troops obtained possession of some redoubts, which gave
them so commanding a position, that the citizens of
Meshed, fearing the result of a general assault for which
the preparations were in progress, entered into negotiations with Prince Sultan Murad. These negotiations
terminated in the surrender, first of the citadel, and later
of the entire city. The Salar took refuge in the mosque
of Imam Reza; from which, however, he was forcibly
expelled. He was then seized by the soldiers of the
Shekaki regiment, and the inhabitants of Meshed were
permitted to ransom their city from plunder by the
promise to pay a fine of one hundred thousand tomans.
The forbearance and discipline displayed on this occasion
by the Persian troops reflect the highest credit on their
commander, Prince Sultan Murad; but the glory he
acquired by the capture of Meshed is somewhat stained
by the suspicion which attaches to him of having put the
Salar to torture, for the purpose of compelling that chief
to reveal the amount and the locality of his treasure.
The Salar was then justly condemned to expiate the
crime of having rebelled against his sovereign by being
deprived of life; the instrument by which death was
inflicted upon him being the bowstring of Eastern story,
and a similar sentence was pronounced upon one of his
brothers, who had been his companion in arms.

CHAPTER XIII.

Rising of the Followers of the Bāb—Mode of carrying out Capital Punishments in Persia—Seizure of Zinjan—The Bāb put to Death—Tenets of his Followers—Hopeless Contest at Zinjan—Reckless Bravery of the Bābis—Courage of the Women—Terrible Cruelties—Exhibition of Fanaticism at Tabreez—Results of Administration of the Ameer-i-Nizam—Occupation of Ashoradeh by Russia—The Caspian Provinces—Fall of the Ameer-i-Nizam—Interference on his Behalf—Meerza Agha Khan, Sedr-Azem—Influences brought to bear on the Shah against the Ameer-i-Nizam—Conduct of the Wife of the ex-Minister— The Ameer's Death—Remembrance of his Administration.

It was hoped that the capture of Meshed would usher in a period of calmness and security, during which the Ameer-i-Nizam might have leisure to perfect the system of general reform which he had introduced into Persia. But no sooner had order been established in one direction than revolt and disorder appeared in another quarter. At Yezd, the followers of the Bāb assembled in such numbers in the spring of the year 1850, as to compel the governor of that city to take refuge in the citadel; to which they then laid siege. But the priests of Yezd, conscious that the spread of Bābism would be the signal for the downfall of their own power, lent to the governor all the weight of their influence. In the name of Mahomed, the messenger of God, they summoned the townspeople to attack the infidels, and they collected a force by which the Bābis were overthrown.

25

The zealots of the new religion then betook themselves to the adjoining province of Kerman.

The followers of the Bāb looked upon the Ameer-i-Nizam, by whose orders their chief was kept in prison, as an enemy to the faith, whom it was lawful, and even proper, to slay. A conspiracy was accordingly organized for the purpose of taking the life of the Minister; but the plot was discovered ere it was ripe for execution, and the conspirators were seized. Seven of them were condemned to suffer death, and the occasion of their execution was taken advantage of for introducing the custom of conducting capital punishments openly at Tehran. Previously to this time it had been usual to cause condemned criminals to be strangled before the Shah. On one occasion, when the representative of Russia at the Persian court was waiting to be summoned to the presence of the king, he was alarmed by hearing loud cries in his immediate neighbourhood in the palace garden, and as he was proceeding to the audience chamber, he encountered a number of executioners dragging along the still-palpitating bodies of some men who had been strangled. The prince was shocked beyond measure, and he was, with reason, offended at the indignity which had been offered to him in his being summoned to the royal presence at such a moment; he, therefore, expressed in strong terms to the Shah and to his Minister, his opinion as to the barbarousness of the usage by which executions were conducted before the eyes of the sovereign. The Ameer-i-Nizam fully concurred in the opinion of the Russian Minister on this subject, and he accordingly at once determined to put a stop to the practice complained of. It was feared, however, that a commotion might be excited by the unusual spectacle of men being publicly executed at Tehran ; but on the occasion of putting the Bābi conspirators to death, no such commotion took place. Some doubts existed in the minds of the people as to whether the alleged intentions of the conspirators had been fully proved against them, or whether it was right to punish for a mere intention as if for a crime that had actually been committed ; but it could not be denied that the sentence of death upon these Bābi backsliders from the Moslem faith was in accordance with Mahomedan law. Each of them was offered his life upon the simple condition of reciting the formula of the Moslem creed, but none of them consented to purchase pardon on such terms.

Another example was now added to those with which the history of the world abounds, of the utter inefficacy of persecution for the suppression of religious doctrines. The chief priest of Zinjan had embraced the tenets of the Bāb, and under his guidance the Bābis of that place took possession of a portion of the town. On the news of this revolt reaching Tehran, measures were at once adopted by the government for suppressing the insurrection ; and it is illustrative of the success which was already beginning to attend the Ameer's system for the amelioration of the army, that within five hours from the receipt at · the capital of intelligence of the revolt, troops were already marching from Tehran upon Zinjan. The Persian soldiers, much, no doubt, to their own surprise, saw themselves for the first time properly clothed and cared for, and received with regularity their pay and their rations. Persian soldiers are beyond comparison the most hardy, enduring and patient troops in the world, and had the administration of the Ameer-i-Nizam been prolonged, the King of Persia would have been the master of an army of one hundred thousand men, regularly drilled and accoutred. The Minister had announced his intention of maintaining such a force; and he was not likely to change his mind, or to neglect any precaution to ensure the efficiency of the army upon which depended the stability of the Kajar throne.

The insurrection at Zinjan took place in the month of May, 1850, and the Bābis long continued to defend themselves in that city against the troops of the king, with all the fiery zeal which is characteristic of the proselytes to a new religion. Zinjan is the capital of the district of Khamseh, and it lies on the direct road from Tabreez to Tehran. Whilst the siege was in progress, the founder of the new creed was taken from his prison in Azerbaeejan, and, after having been examined as to his religious belief, was condemned to death by the authorities of Tabreez for having renounced the faith of Islam. A circumstance that arose out of this sentence had nearly been the cause of setting the Bāb high above the temporal powers of Iran. A company of soldiers was drawn up in the great square of Tabreez, and before it was a hapless man whose arms were tied together: that man was the Bāb, and he was to be shot to death. On their captain giving the word to fire, the soldiers discharged a volley, the smoke from which threw a veil over the scene. When the smoke had been dispelled, great was the astonishment of the soldiers and of the lookers-on to find that the person of the Bāb had altogether disappeared. There could now be no doubt, they thought, of his having ascended to the heaven, which, when he was on earth, he had said was his home.

Nothing was wanted but this apparent miracle to establish Bābism on a sure foundation. But it happened, most unfortunately for the prospects of the creed of the Bāb, that its originator (who had been unscathed by the bullets which had cut the ropes around him) had taken the wrong direction while endeavouring to effect his escape when concealed by the smoke of the volley of musketry. Had he gained the bazar he would have been safe ; but he chanced to rush into the guard-room, from which place he was taken back to the square and shot. His death did not diminish the faith of his followers in his mission ; for, according to the doctrines which they had learned from him, he could not really die : the form which his spirit animated might be altered, but his soul must still exist. It was, as he taught, undoubtedly true that his mortal body could not be annihilated but must be resolved into other forms of life ; yet not the less were his followers shocked to see that body thrown into the ditch of Tabreez, by the orders of the brutal governor, to be a prey to the dogs and the jackals.

The main tenet of Bābism is utter indifference to, and disbelief in the existence of, good and evil. But nothing could be less in accordance with this theory than was the practice of the followers of the Bāb. Far from looking on the course of events, and the changes and chances of this mortal life, with the calm eyes of uncon-cerned spectators, they attempted to impose their opinions upon others by force. The earth, they said, had been given to them for a possession, and it was, therefore, lawful for them to appropriate to themselves the goods of unbelievers. They asserted that the time had come when Mahomedanism must fall, and that to them had been assigned the task of bringing about the decree of fate. In their opinion the restrictions imposed upon men by the Koran were too heavy to be borne. According to their creed all men were alike ; none were impure, since all human beings, with all other created objects, whether animate or inanimate, formed so many portions of one all-pervading and everlasting God. It was probably when in possession of this idea, that the Bāb had startled his disciples by the sudden announcement that he was God. The followers of the Bāb were to have all their possessions, including their women, in common : marriage being one of the puerile observances of the Mahomedan code which it was now time to abolish. The Bābis admitted of no hereditary claims to high rank ; nor did they see the necessity of any formal election of rulers or teachers : they admitted only such superiority as was conferred by the force of intellect, and that force, they held, would make itself felt without the adventitious aid of human laws. Hell was no longer a source of terror to men who had been enlightened by the teaching of the Bāb. Their master had explained to them that there was to be no hereafter beyond this enduring world ; he had laughed to scorn alike the Moslem prophet's description of the terror-striking bridge of Al-Sirath and of the black-eyed virgins who repose on green cushions and beautiful carpets, hidden from public view in the pavilions of paradise. This terrestrial globe was to be everlasting, and men need not fear what people falsely term death, since in truth they could not die.

These opinions explain the reckless bravery with

which the Bābis of Zinjan continued to maintain a hopeless contest against the troops of the Shah. They were driven into the south-eastern corner of the town, where they erected barricades, loop-holed the walls, and defended themselves with much skill. Their numbers were by degrees reduced by casualties, but their spirit could not be quenched : their women are as deserving of being praised for their bravery as are the maids of Saragossa. To the existence of heroines at Zinjan, at least, no doubt attaches : at Zinjan the maidens shed no " ill-timed tears " for the fall of their lovers, but they took their share in the fearful task of defending their desperate position, and they were not backward in hurling the missile which was to be their love's avenger. Three hundred fanatics continued to defy the artillery and the troops of the Shah. By night and day the loop-holes were watched by sharp-shooters, who hastened on every occasion to take advantage of the slightest indiscretion on the part of the besiegers. Two guns were constructed from bars of iron to reply to the fire of those without, and the fact that these were damaged by every discharge in no way damped the energy of the defenders. The invitations to surrender which were held out by the Persian commander were treated by the Bābis with derision, and they put to death on the spot a well-meaning but rash individual who proposed to act as mediator between the contending adversaries. Terrible was the lot of the Persians who fell into the hands of the Bābis : we are told that they were shod as horses, suspended from beams by one arm, or burnt to death. The priest who headed the defence seemed to expect a successful termination to the conflict, since he assigned to one of his people, as a reward for bravery, no less a prize than the government of the land of Egypt, and to others the possession of such and such villages and towns. The siege continued to be prosecuted throughout the summer of the year 1850. The scene of operations was visited in the month of October by Sir Henry Bethune, who had come to die in the country where he had acquired his glory, and he expressed his opinion that the reduction of the defended portion of Zinjan ought not to occupy ordinary troops for a longer period than three hours. But it was not until the last days of the year that the siege was brought to a conclusion. Moollah Mahomed Ali, the leader of the defenders, received a wound from the effects of which he died, and this event so dispirited the survivors that they had no longer any care to resist the attacks of the assailants. The position occupied by the Bābis was at length carried, and all who survived of the defenders—men, women, and children—were ruthlessly butchered by the Persian troops, who now displayed as much ferocity as they had shown pusillanimity during the siege.

Whilst the disciples and followers of the Bāb were endeavouring to undermine the faith of Islam, the priests of that religion were not blind to the expediency of doing something towards maintaining their hold over the minds of the Persian people. But the Ameer-i-Nizam was equally averse to tolerating the spread of Bābism and to encourage the Mahomedan priests in their ambitious views. He was the more anxious to weaken the influence of the Moslem doctors, inasmuch as he saw that no thorough reform could be carried out in Persia so long as the people retained their superstitious dread of incurring the displeasure of a band of selfish and narrow-minded moollahs. He found much difficulty in bending to his will the privileged and rapacious Mahomedan doctors; but he did not recoil from the labour of subduing them. The priests of Tabreez, about this time, resolved to show the world who believed in miracles that such manifestations of a direct interference with the ordinary course of nature were not exhibited solely through the medium of the person of the Bāb. They determined to try the effect of one in connection with a Moslem place of worship. A cow on the way to the slaughter-house twice took sanctuary in a mosque and was twice expelled; a third attempt to deprive the animal of the privilege of taking sanctuary was punished by the patron saint of the mosque, for the driver of the cow fell down dead. Such was the story that was noised abroad, and as it was received with credit, other miracles were attributed to the influence of the spirit who guarded the same holy place; blind men were said to have had their sight restored, and sick men to have been healed of their maladies. Much religious enthusiasm was accordingly excited, and, in honour of the distinction which had thus been conferred upon Tabreez, the city was illuminated. The mosque where the cowherd had fallen dead was pronounced to be a sanctuary, which must thenceforward be on no account violated, and it was publicly announced that it was lawful to slay any persons who might be discovered gambling or intoxicated in its neighbourhood. But the priests of Tabreez found that, although the people of that city were as credulous and fanatical as could be wished, there was a ruler in Persia who was possessed both of common sense and of firmness, and who would not permit the establishment of priestly domination over the populace of the most considerable city in the kingdom. The Ameer-i-Nizam sent to that city an Affshar chief, who had the courage and the adroitness to seize and carry off the Sheikh-el-Islam.

This blow at priestly influence having been delivered, the Minister next abolished the privilege which had up to this time been accorded to the Imam-i-Juma of Tehran, of affording sanctuary in his mosque to all who sought it. It was the consistent policy of the Ameer-i-Nizam to uphold the supreme authority of the Shah, and to check all encroachments upon it, from what quarter soever they might be directed. From his endeavour to carry out this policy he never swerved, notwithstanding all the ill-will which, by so doing, he excited against himself. The measures of the enlightened Minister were now beginning to be followed by some satisfactory and visible results. The system of taxation throughout the country was remodelled on a more equitable basis than had formerly existed. The various provincial treasuries were pronounced to be at length in a satisfactory condition. Trade between the different chief cities and provinces of the kingdom, as well as between Persia and her Russian, Turkish, Arab, Affghan, Indian, Oozbeg, and Turkoman neighbours, was being carried on with confidence, under the protection of a just and energetic government; and the Ameer-i-Nizam gratified the inhabitants of Tehran, and more especially the mercantile classes at the capital, by erecting a handsomer range of bazars than any other city in the world can boast of possessing. The caravanserai which bears his name vies in beauty and in commodiousness with the finest structures of Asia, and it was the intention of the Minister to undertake several other works for the embellishment and convenience of the city and neighbourhood of Tehran.

It is illustrative of the soundness of the Ameer's judgment that, although no man could have been more anxious than he was to maintain the dignity and independence of his master, he preferred to give way, even when he felt that he was in the right, rather than risk the effects of a quarrel with his powerful northern neighbour. By the treaty of Gulistan, Persia had renounced the right of maintaining ships of war on the Caspian ; and about the year 1836 the Shah's government had applied to the Czar for naval assistance against the refractory Turkomans who infest the south-eastern shores of that sea. Following this application there had been made, when too late, a request that the Russian naval commander might be placed under the orders of the governor of Astrabad, or that, failing this, the naval aid might be withheld. The Shah had subsequently intimated to the Russian envoy that as he had without assistance been enabled to capture the island of Cherken, the presence of the Russian vessels was no longer necessary. But the idea of the advantage of maintaining the police of the sea on the southern and eastern shores of the Caspian had not been relinquished at St. Petersburg, and in 1842 a Russian squadron appeared off Astrabad, and commenced the salutary operation of putting a stop to the predatory expeditions of the Turkoman pirates. To the eastward of a tongue of land which juts out from the Persian coast of the bay of Astrabad there is a small island called Ashoradeh, and of this island the Russian officer had taken possession, for the purpose of making it a naval station. This measure had alarmed the Persian Government, who anticipated greater danger from the establishment of the Russians on an island so near to the Persian mainland, than they did from any amount of Turkoman depredation. Every species of remonstrance had been had recourse to in order to induce the self-invited and unwelcome guests of Persia to take their departure ; but these protests and remonstrances had not been followed by any indication on the part of the Russian authorities to comply with the demand now made of them. The Persian ministers had at one time been told in reply that the occupation of the island had been a necessary consequence of the Shah's request for Russian naval aid ; at another time, they had been reproached with ingratitude and folly in not appreciating the value of the assistance gratuitously given by Russia in putting a stop to Turkoman piracy and devastation. That the presence of Russian ships in the southern waters of the Caspian sea is highly beneficial to the interests of humanity, cannot be questioned ; but, on the other hand, the tenure by which Russia holds the island of Ashoradeh is as illegal as are the proceedings of the pirates which she came there to check. Regardless of public opinion, and of Persian appeals to right and to international law, the Russians now look upon Ashoradeh as being as much a portion of the Czar's dominions as Bakoo or Derbend, and on this island all the buildings which are necessary for the permanent accommodation of a considerable force have been erected. The possession of Ashoradeh is most beneficial to Russian interests, for other reasons than that it affords a suitable station for the ships employed in maintaining the police of the sea. From

Ashoradeh steam-vessels ply along the Persian coast, conveying the produce of the three fertile provinces of Astrabad, Mazenderan, and Gilan, to the markets of Georgia, and in return bringing Russian wares to supply the requirements of the merchants of Persia. The fact, too, of a Russian force being always present at the south-eastern corner of the Caspian sea, gives to that power great political influence throughout the neighbouring provinces of the states of Central Asia.

In the year 1851 the island of Ashoradeh was protected by five Russian vessels of war, each carrying from four to eight guns ; but notwithstanding the presence of this force, the island was surprised by the Turkomans, who killed or carried off all the Russians they found upon it. The officers in the ships escaped the fate that overtook the men on shore, but it is said that one or two ladies were carried off to the desert of the Attreck. The time that had been chosen for delivering this humiliating blow was Easter-eve, when the Turkomans believed they should find the Russian sailors in a state of intoxication. It was thought necessary for the re-establishment of Russian prestige on the shores of the Caspian, to give out that the Turkomans alone had not been able to over-run Ashoradeh, but that they had been abetted by the Persians ; and on this account the Russian representative at Tehran demanded the dismissal from office of the Shah's brother, the governor of Mazenderan. The Ameer-i-Nizam at first refused to agree to the disgrace of a man whom he knew to have had nothing whatever to do with the affair at Ashoradeh ; but rather than risk the consequences of a rupture of peaceful relations with Russia, he bowed his pride, and yielded to the demand.

It was in consequence[*] of his having had to make a concession to one foreign mission, that the Ameer-i-Nizam now thought proper to make another concession, which up to this time he had refused to grant, to the request of another mission. An engagement was entered into, by which the right of searching for slaves in native vessels in the Persian Gulf was granted to British vessels of war, and the permission was accorded of removing any slaves who might be so found, to the British ships. This blow to the slave-traffic was one of the last notable measures of the Ameer's administration.

The enemies of the Ameer had never abandoned their efforts to shake the Shah's confidence in his Minister, and it is matter of surprise that a boy should have for so long a time been able to resist the oft-repeated solicitations of his mother and others for the dismissal of a plebeian Vizeer. Warnings against the clever and ambitious Minister were constantly poured into the royal ear ; the Ameer's virtues and successes were represented as crimes, and it was insinuated that it was the Minister's intention to grasp the sceptre. The Ameer-i-Nizam had greatly improved the condition of the Persian army, and the Shah was told that the soldiers were so devoted to their commander, that they would readily second him in carrying out the ambitious designs imputed to him. The king's fears were at length aroused, and as there were no means of checking the Ameer's power save by dismissing him from office, his dismissal was determined on. So persuaded had the Shah become of the evil intentions of the Minister, that he did not venture to

---

[*] *Glimpses of Life and Manners in Persia*, by Lady SHEIL.

depose him until he found himself in a position to defend
his person against any treasonable attack.   On the night
of the 13th of November, 1851, the king summoned
four hundred of the royal body-guard to the palace, and
thus fortified, he sent to inform the Ameer that he was
to be no longer prime minister of Persia, and that his
functions were thenceforward to be limited to the
command of the army.   But no accusation could have
less foundation in truth than that which imputed dis-
loyalty to the Ameer-i-Nizam ; he bowed in silence to
the decree of his sovereign, and awaited in his palace the
coming of the events which time would bring forth.

Meerza Agha Khan,* the Itimad-ed-Dowleh, who has
been before mentioned in these pages, was now raised to
the dignity of Sedr-Azem, or prime minister.   The idea,
not unnaturally, occurred to him that he could never
be secure in that post so long as his predecessor should
be alive ; as, sooner or later, the Shah and all his subjects
would see the immense difference between the Ameer and
his rival.   Indeed the king was already aware that the
commander of his troops was his loyal subject, since he
had not attempted to avail himself of the affection of the
soldiers for his person, for the purpose of creating any
disturbance of the new administration.   The new
minister was in close league with her Highness the
Queen-mother, and it was determined by them that the
Ameer-i-Nizam should forthwith be removed from the
capital ; for so long as he should remain there, there was
no chance of the king being persuaded to consent to the

---

* Agha Khan was not originally this minister's name, but was rather
the appellation by which he was known, first in his family circle, and afterwards by the public.

death of a man who had so faithfully served him, and to whom he was so much attached. At this time the king addressed two letters to the Ameer, in one of which he stated that although it had been thought advisable to dismiss him from office, yet he might be sure that the royal heart bled for him. But it was hoped by the Sedr-Azem that separation might have the effect of cooling the Shah's affection for his brother-in-law ; accordingly the Ameer was offered the choice of the government of Fars, of that of Ispahan, or that of Koom. It is to be regretted that he did not accept the offer now made to him. Had he retired for a short time from the capital, he might have lived to return to it as minister; but he knew too well the character of his fellow-countrymen not to fear that his life would be in danger so soon as he should be separated from the Shah. Under the working of this apprehension, the Ameer declined the offers made to him ; but, through the influence of the British Minister, it was at length arranged that he should be appointed governor of Kashan.

Such was the condition of affairs when the unfortunate interference of Prince Dolgorouky produced a sudden change in the temper of the Shah. That Minister, although he had found the Ameer to be the uncompromising opponent of Russian aggressive movements, had yet found him ever truthful, just and reasonable. He was therefore sorry to see him replaced by Meerza Agha Khan, who had enjoyed English protection ; and who, it was to be presumed, would favour English rather than Russian influence at the Persian court. The prince feared lest the life of the Ameer should be taken, and he knew that if his life were spared, he would, sooner or later, be replaced in office. The surest way of securing that object appeared to be to take the Ameer under Russian protection. Had the Ameer sought the privilege of asylum in the house of the Russian Legation, the Shah would have been justified, according to international law, in taking him forcibly thence ; much more was he justified in altogether disavowing the ill-judged act of Prince Dolgorouky in sending the members of his mission, and his Cossack guard, to the Ameer's house, and declaring that the Ameer was under the protection of Russia. No monarch could be expected to submit to so insulting a proceeding ; and the Shah was told by his new Minister, that unless he should assert his royal right to authority over his subject, the people of Persia would no longer look upon him as being an independent king, but as being the obedient vassal of Russia. This taunt stung the Shah to the quick, and he requested Prince Dolgorouky to withdraw the members of his mission forthwith from the house which sheltered his mother and sister. At the same time he declared his intention of sending the servants of the royal household to seize the person of the Ameer, in case the prince should refuse. The members of the Russian Legation were accordingly withdrawn, and as the British Minister also withdrew from all interference in the affair, the Ameer was left to be dealt with as the offended Shah might think proper. The king's feelings of anger were skilfully fanned by the enemies of the fallen Vizeer, and under their influence the Shah degraded him from the post of Ameer-i-Nizam, and ordered him to retire in disgrace to Kashan, under the surveillance of an escort of troops ; the officer in

26

command of which was to be responsible for his safe-keeping. But even this downfall did not satisfy the wishes of the vindictive enemies of Meerza Teki Khan. The Shah was reminded that no other government could be secure in Persia, so long as the fallen minister should live, and he was told that if he valued the security of his throne, he must consent to give the order for the death of the ex-Ameer. Still, the Shah could not be brought to consent to the capital punishment of an innocent man, and the fallen Vizeer was permitted to live for two months in retirement with his wife, amidst the cypresses and fountains that surround the splendid palace of Feen.

It was the fate of Prince Dolgorouky to be the instrument of further misfortune to the man whom he so sincerely wished to befriend. He was deeply chagrined at the results which had followed his attempt to take the ex-minister under Russian protection, and when the time approached for the arrival of a reply to the reports regarding the occurrence which he had addressed to St. Petersburg, he openly boasted that in the course of a few days he should receive instructions which would put an end to all uncertainty as to the fate of Meerza Teki Khan. All uncertainty as to his fate was, indeed, put an end to, even before the period assigned by the prince. The Ameer's enemies did not fail to report the rash boast to the Shah, and his Majesty, in order to avoid the consequences of a refusal to the demand which he anticipated from Russia, of giving a guarantee for the Ameer's life, determined to anticipate the arrival of the expected courier, and at once to cause the Ameer to be put to death. But even this measure could not be executed by Persians without recourse being had to dissimulation.

The Shah's only sister, the wife of Meerza Teki Khan, was devotedly attached to her husband, and no one had the heart to tear him from her arms. No princess educated in a Christian court and accustomed to the contemplation of the brightest example of conjugal virtues that the history of the world has recorded, could have shown more tenderness and devotion than did the sister of the Shah of Persia towards her unfortunate husband. Every day his guards took the precaution of summoning him from his room, in order that they might make sure that he had not escaped; and when he went outside to show himself, his wife was, at first, in the habit of accompanying him. Seeing, however, that this ceremony was a mere matter of form, she ceased to go forth with him, and contented herself with the precaution of tasting of every dish that was set before him. But a man was found who volunteered to put the Ameer to death without the princess being made aware of what was going to take place. One Haji Ali Khan, a clever and worthless adventurer, had been admitted into the Shah's service by the Ameer, and had been made chief of his ferashes ; a post of some importance. In order to show his zeal in the service of his new master, the Ferash-Bashi now volunteered to be the executioner of his benefactor. When he appeared at Kashan, the retainers of the ex-minister were filled with joy ; for they believed that one who had owed his advancement in life to their lord had been chosen to be the bearer of good news. They were doomed to a cruel disappointment. On the 9th of January, 1852, the ex-minister was called forth, as usual, by his guards, and on his appearing alone was seized, gagged, and dragged to an adjoining house, where he was

cast on the floor, stripped and tied. The veins in both
his arms and his legs were then opened, and he was
allowed to linger for several hours in mortal agony. He
bore his cruel fate with a resignation which was in keeping with the consistent greatness of his life. The
youthful princess, his wife, being alarmed at the absence
of her husband, was told by Haji Ali Khan that he had
gone to the bath, in order to be prepared to put on a robe
of honour which the Shah had sent to him by his hands.
When she awoke from her delusion, the heart of her
husband had for ever ceased to beat.

Thus perished, by the hands of Persians, the man
who had done so much to regenerate Persia : the only
man who possessed at the same time the ability, the
patriotism, the energy and the integrity required to
enable a Persian Minister to conduct the vessel of State
in safety past the shoals and rocks which lay in her
course. Those who, with a living imperial author,
see in every remarkable man, such as Cæsar, Charle-
magne, or Napoleon, a special instrument in the hands
of Providence for tracing out to peoples the path they
ought to follow, must be at a loss to account for the
design of Providence in raising up Meerza Teki Khan,
and permitting his fall, ere he had accomplished in a few
years the labour of centuries and stamped with the seal
of his genius a new era for his country. Had he lived
to accomplish what it was his intention to do, he would
no doubt have been ranked with the men who are held
by some people to have been specially raised up by God
for a particular mission. But his premature death,
before he had lived long enough permanently to benefit
his fellow-men, must prevent us from having recourse to

this theory for accounting for the appearance, in these latter years in Persia, of a man so remarkable as Meerza Teki Khan. His career seems rather to be illustrative of the truth of the proposition so much insisted on by the author of the *History of Civilization in England:** namely, that a people makes its own government, and that no government can force progress if the people be unsound. The Ameer's measures were distasteful to so many persons, that the Shah was compelled to listen to the cry of discontent ; consequently, the upright ruler fell, and a Vizeer was named in his place whose character was more in accordance with that of the persons he had to govern, and who permitted those he employed to imitate his own example of extorting bribes. What the Ameer had with so much difficulty effected was now at once undone. The soldiers were no longer paid, until after years of entreaty ; peculation became once more rampant in every department of the administration ; priestly influence again acquired undue ascendancy ; and Persian titles were heaped upon the great with even more prodigality than ever.

The shocking fate of Meerza Teki Khan excited, however, the greatest horror throughout Europe, and the Shah and his new Minister had to listen to the indignant protests and remonstrances called forth from foreign governments by the sentence which had been executed at Kashan. Then followed the hour of remorse. When too late the Persian king, as well as many of his subjects, became sensible of the irreparable loss their country had sustained. It is said that the king, in his grief, re-

---

* *See* Buckle's *History of Civilization in England*, pp. 115 and 146-150, vol. ii., 1861.

solved to observe each anniversary of the Ameer's death as a day of fasting and humiliation ; and the two infant daughters of the great Minister were betrothed to two sons of the Shah.

Each year that has elapsed since the death of Meerza Teki Khan has gradually added to his fame, by showing how vain is the expectation of finding another Vizeer capable of completing the work of reformation in Persia which was begun by him. The short period of his administration is now looked back upon as having been the golden era of modern Persia ; and the traveller from the west, as he pursues his tedious way across the plains of Irak, or through the lonely passes of the Elburz, if he converse with his muleteers as to the condition of the country, is sure to be told that everything now goes badly, but that things were otherwise in the time of the Ameer-i-Nizam.

CHAPTER XIV.

THE disciples of the Bāb had been little heard of during
the eighteen months that followed the conclusion of the
siege of Zinjan. It was in the summer of the year 1852
that they next forced themselves upon public notice. A
conspiracy against the life of the Shah was hatched at
Tehran, under the auspices of two priests of distinction,
and of Suleiman Khan, whose father had been master
of the horse to Abbass Meerza. Men holding the
Bāb doctrines were in the habit of· congregating, to the
number of about forty, in the house of the above-
named Khan, where their plans were concerted and
where arms of every description were collected. On the
15th of August, the Shah, who was then residing in the
neighbourhood of Tehran, at the Niaveran Palace, had
mounted his horse, and was proceeding towards the
Elburz on a hunting excursion, when four men pre-

sented themselves on his path. It is the custom for the
Persian king to ride alone, all the attendants being some
distance in front of, or behind, his Majesty; and it is a
common thing for the Shah to be addressed by those of
his subjects who have a grievance to be righted, and who
are allowed by custom to approach the sovereign and
hand to him written papers containing their petitions.
Consequently it was not thought strange when one of the
four men who appeared on this day on the king's path,
approached the horse on which his Majesty was riding,
as if for the purpose of handing a paper to the Shah.
The Bābi, as he drew near the royal person, attempted
to grasp the king's girdle, and when he found himself
repulsed, he drew a pistol from within his dress and fired
it at the Shah. His Majesty, however, had the presence
of mind to throw himself to the opposite side of his
horse, and the contents of the pistol inflicted no other
injury beyond a slight wound in the thigh. So intent
was the assassin on effecting his object, that, regardless
of the presence of the Shah's followers, who now came
up to the rescue, he drew from its sheath a formidable
dagger, with which he assailed the Shah and those who
defended him; nor did he cease his efforts until he was
himself slain. Two of his confederates were captured,
one of them having been severely wounded; the fourth
Bābi contrived to effect his escape by jumping down
a well. This occurrence was at once made known to the
dwellers in Shimran, and the report got abroad that the
king had been killed. Without waiting to hear this news
confirmed, the people in the royal camp began to disperse,
and there was a general rush towards Tehran. The
shops of the city were immediately shut, and every one

strove to lay in a supply of bread, as a provision against the stormy future. On the following day, however, men's minds were reassured by the discharge of a salute of one hundred and ten guns, to announce the safety of the king. The priests and the persons of influence amongst the people were invited to proceed to the royal camp ; and Tehran was illuminated during several nights.

The Bābi conspiracy having been discovered, ten of the conspirators were at the first put to death; some of them under circumstances of the greatest cruelty. Lighted candles were inserted into the bodies of two or three of these men, and the victims, after having been allowed to linger for some time, were hewn in two by a hatchet. The requirements of the *lex talionis* were satisfied by the steward of the Shah, acting as his representative, blowing out the brains of one of the conspirators. Amongst those who suffered death was a young woman, the daughter of a celebrated teacher of the law, and who was considered by the Bābis to be a prophetess ; on this account she had been for years detained a prisoner at Tehran. But ten victims were not enough to calm the fears of the advisers of the Shah, and a short reign of terror followed ; no one being secure against suspicion, or being denounced as a follower of the Bāb. If any one at this time imagined that the Shah's Ministers had any considerable amount of regard for their own dignity in the eyes of the world, the scene which now presented itself was well calculated to dispel the illusion. The prime minister, far from imitating the example set by Cicero in his orations against Catiline in taking to himself all the glory of having suppressed a dangerous conspiracy, was fearful

of drawing down upon himself and his family the vengeance of the followers of the Báb ; and, in order that others might be implicated in these executions, he hit upon the device of assigning a criminal to each department of the State ; the several ministers of the Shah being thus compelled to act as executioners. The minister for foreign affairs, the minister of finance, the son of the prime minister, the adjutant-general of the army, and the master of the mint, each fired the first shot, or made the first cut with a sabre, at the culprits assigned to their several departments, respectively. The artillery, the infantry, the camel-artillery, and the cavalry each had a victim assigned to them.* But the result of all this slaughter was, as might have been expected, to create a feeling of sympathy for the Bábis ; whose crime was lost sight of in the punishment which had overtaken them. They met their fate with the utmost firmness, and none of them cared to accept the life which was offered to them on the simple condition of reciting the Moslem creed. While the lighted candles were burning the flesh of one follower of the Báb, he was urged by the chief magistrate of Tehran to curse the Báb and live. He would not renounce the Báb ; but he cursed the magistrate who tempted him to do so, he cursed the Shah, and even cursed the prophet Mahomed, his spirit rising superior to the agony of his torture . . . . .

---

* " Even the Shah's admirable French physician, the late lamented Dr. Cloquet, was invited to show his loyalty by following the example of the rest of the court. He excused himself, and pleasantly said that he killed too many men professionally to permit him to increase their number by any voluntary homicide on his part."—*Glimpses of Life and Manners in Persia.* By Lady SHEIL, p. 277.

It is now time to refer to an important and interesting epoch in the history of modern Persia, and to show the position which she occupied with reference to the great European Powers immediately before the war between the nations of the West and Russia. It will enable the reader to understand more easily the motives in which originated the policy pursued by the Shah, if I show what was at this time the actual position in which the Persian prime minister found himself placed. He had on two occasions in former years been indebted for safety or protection to the good offices of the British Legation : he had, in fact, been at one time looked upon as being a British protégé. At that period the influence of the foreign missions, and their interference in the internal affairs of Persia, had not been regarded by the Shah's government with much alarm ; but a rapid change had taken place in Persian opinion in this respect, and there was nothing now so unfashionable at the court as to be connected in any way with a foreign representative. The claims of gratitude have not much weight with Persians, and, even if the Sedr-Azem had been well disposed towards those to whose influence he had owed so much, he could not but see that if he would retain his post, he must at any rate make the Shah and the courtiers understand that he had given up all intimacy with the English Minister. In order the more effectually to avert the damaging supposition that he favoured British influence at the Persian court, he took care to speak slightingly of the English government and its representative at Tehran ; and was always ready to raise difficulties and objections in the way of anything proposed by the latter. But notwithstanding his cleverness and his powers of intriguing and dissimulating, the Persian Minister did not find himself placed on a bed of roses. At one time he even spoke of resigning the high office which he held ; but if he ever seriously entertained the intention of doing so, he probably feared that it was not open to him to resign office only, but that he must make up his mind to part at the same time with office and with life.   Under these circumstances his tortuous mind suggested to him the singular idea of doing something which would induce either the Russian or the English Minister to demand his dismissal from office ; hoping that thus he might be allowed to retire into private life without being exposed to any further danger. But the possession of office, if he ever was seriously indifferent to it, reacquired in his eyes a charm which he could not resolve to dispel, and he accordingly talked no more of resigning his post.   That post now derived' additional importance, from the fact that the alliance of Persia was courted by one of the powers whose quarrel engrossed the attention of the civilized world.

Late in the autumn of the year 1853, General Bebitoff arrived at Nakhtchivan to take command of the Russian army destined to act against the Turkish forces in the Pashalic of Erzeroum ; and a messenger was despatched by him to Tehran, who was to communicate, through the Russian Minister, certain propositions from the Russian government to the Shah. A private interview with his Majesty was demanded by Prince Dolgorouky on the occasion of the arrival of the messenger at Tehran.   To this interview none of the Shah's subjects were admitted, lest the purport of the propositions should transpire : no Vizeer was there to echo the statements of the king, and no eaves-dropping page listened behind the cashmere curtains of the throne-room whilst the Russian Minister, through his dragoman, made known the wishes of his imperial master. So far the secret was kept secure, and not even to his Grand Vizeer did the Shah at first communicate what had transpired. But to the eye of jealous suspicion there are facts which explain themselves, and which do not need to be expressed in words. The Turkish ambassador was too well informed of the state of affairs at the court to which he was accredited, not to be able to draw his own conclusions from the arrival of a special Russian officer, and from the precautions which had been taken to exclude the Persian Minister from the audience given by the Shah to the stranger. His Excellency, therefore, resolved to assume a threatening demeanour, and he made known at once to the Shah his determination to quit Tehran forthwith, unless he should receive satisfactory assurances regarding the course which the Persian government intended to pursue in the conjuncture which had come about. In consequence of this sudden resolve on the part of the Turkish ambassador, the king was constrained to send for his prime minister, and to reveal to him the nature of the proposals that had been made by the representative of the Czar.

These proposals were that Persia should coöperate with Russia in the war to be waged against Turkey. A strong military demonstration must be made on the frontier of Azerbaeejan, to threaten Byazeed and Erzeroum ; and another on the frontier of Kermanshah, to threaten Baghdad and the holy cities. In the event of its being necessary that Persia should declare war against Turkey, the Shah's forces were to invade the Ottoman dominions at both points. They were to seize Kotoor, and endeavour to occupy the city of the Caliphs; and when peace should be restored in Europe, the Sublime Porte should be compelled either to leave in the hands of the Shah all the territory he might have taken, or to ransom it by the payment of a suitable sum. Further than this, the Shah was to be released from the pecuniary obligations he was under to Russia, for the balance of the money due under the Treaty of Turko-manchai, in the event of his going to war; and in the event of his not being called on actually to declare war, all the cost of his military preparations was to be deducted from his debt. Russia was also to furnish warlike stores and money, in the event of the duration of the war being protracted. These were tempting propositions for a Persian king to listen to. Should he agree to them he would be admitted to play a part in the great drama in which the chief monarchs of Christendom and the Sultan were the actors. He would be gratified by the consciousness of his being the first Persian prince of modern times who should have been able to emancipate himself from the second-rate position of a ruler whose sphere of action was confined to Asia. Furthermore, he would escape for ever from the degrading pecuniary obligations under which he was held by Russia. He would wrest from the unrighteous grasp of Turkey the strong strategical position of Kotoor; and he would endear himself to his subjects, and his memory to their children, by adding to his dominions the holy cities that contain the shrines of Ali and of Hussein. Such were the prospects to which the Shah now called the attention of his prime minister, and it devolved on that functionary to point out the alternative line of conduct that lay open to his master.

There was another way, the Vizeer said, by which the Shah might be admitted to take his place amongst the princes and rulers whose decisions swayed the affairs of the great world. If it was open to him to act with Russia against the allies, so might it be open to him to coöperate with the allies against Russia. His weight would be equally felt in either scale of the balance. If England and France should take up arms for Turkey, the allies would be as three to one, and it would be prudent for Persia to join the stronger side. She might by declaring war against Russia break up for ever the Treaty of Turkomanchai, and win back her severed provinces. By reuniting them to Persia, the Shah would endear himself to his people, and his memory to their children, as surely as he could by adding to his dominions the holy cities of the Arabian desert. The Shah was at this time a youth, and the words of his minister seemed to him those of the wisdom of age. He therefore fell in with his reasoning so far as to determine to proceed no longer in the course indicated to him by Prince Dolgorouky. Although orders had been issued for assembling a force of forty thousand men in Azerbaeejan, to be commanded by the Sirdar Azeez Khan, and a force of fifteen thousand men in Kermanshah, to be commanded by the chief of the royal body guard, it was determined to watch for the present the course of events, and not to conclude the treaty with Russia to which the Shah had given his consent.

The Russian representative could not fail to draw from this change of purpose the conclusion that the

Sedr-Azem had employed his influence to divert the Shah from his first intention. The prince was the more irritated on account of this change, inasmuch as he had already reported to the Imperial Government the full concurrence of the Shah in the views of the Czar. His government must therefore be counting to a certain extent on the assistance to be rendered by Persia in the operations about to be undertaken against Asia-Minor. Under the influence of strong feelings of disappointment, Prince Dolgorouky, at several interviews with the Sedr-Azem, endeavoured to persuade his Highness to enter into the views of Russia. These interviews, like that between Charles the Twelfth and the grand vizeer Baltazzi Mahomed on the Pruth, after the escape of Peter, afforded a picture of fiery and demonstrative earnestness on the one hand, and of imperturbable calmness on the other. The prince took occasion, at one interview, to reproach the Vizeer for the evil counsel which he had given to his master, and warned him to beware of the consequences of refusing to ratify the treaty to which the Shah had signified his assent. In his eagerness, the prince rose from his seat and approached the Vizeer, flourishing his cane in the air to give emphasis to his arguments and words, and it unluckily happened that the cane came down somewhat heavily on the Vizeer's leg. But this occurrence had not the effect of betraying the Persian Minister into a fit of anger, or of making him forgetful of his own dignity in the presence of others; he contented himself with taking the cane with which he had been struck, and throwing it to the further end of the room; and after having done so, he requested that he might be left alone. Soon after this occurrence, Prince

Dolgorouky was recalled from his post; and as the Sedr-Azem gave out that he had procured the minister's recall, his triumph was complete. In his future dealings with foreign representatives he allowed it to be seen how much his awe of them had abated.

As time wore on, news came from the West of active preparations for war, and the Shah was once more tempted to revert to his first intention of casting in his lot with Russia. He did not at first avow to the Sedr-Azem his change of plan, and it was not until he had committed himself to a specific course of action that he informed the minister of what he had done. The Sedr-Azem, however, still remained firm to the opinion he had formerly expressed, and he had again influence sufficient to induce the Shah to repudiate his engagement. But the king was naturally desirous that this vacillation in his policy should not at that time transpire, and he feared lest the pride of the Sedr-Azem should induce him to boast to foreign representatives of his having had influence enough to bring the Shah round again to his way of thinking. Accordingly when the Sedr-Azem received a visit from a foreign representative, the Shah's ferash-bashi—the executioner of the Ameer-i-Nizam—was ordered to pass by the door of the Vizeer's room, and to station himself so as to be within hearing of all that might be said. This significant hint was not thrown away upon the Sedr-Azem, who gathered from it that he might possibly go too far in withstanding the wishes of his master ; and he did not again fall into such an error.

It would appear that some rumours had reached England to the effect that the Shah of Persia had given indications of being inclined to ally himself with Russia in the war that was being waged, and the leading English journal took advantage of the appointment of a new English minister to the Persian court to give out that the said minister was going to Persia for the purpose of bringing the Shah to his knees. The passage in *The Times* newspaper to which I have alluded was of course translated and communicated to the Shah, and it is only natural to suppose that from the moment he read it he determined to preserve an attitude of firmness and independence in his dealings with the English envoy.

Meanwhile the offers which Persia had made to join the allies against Russia had been declined; the allies being sensible that they would be unable to protect Persia against the vengeance of Russia in the end, thinking it unfair to encourage a weak power to incur great risks without a reasonable hope of reaping any advantages. Their counsel to Persia was that she should remain neutral during the struggle; but this counsel little suited the temper of the excitable court of the Shah—a court which is not given to looking far into the future, and which is not too scrupulous as to the merits of the cause for which it may begin a war. The Persian king now no longer found in his minister a check upon his warlike inclinations. Several causes seem to have contributed to bring about a change in the sentiments of the Sedr-Azem. Probably the most potent of these was a conviction that it was not safe for him to thwart the wishes of the Russian party at the Persian court; and he seems to have been completely brought over to the views of that party, by some angry discussions between himself and the English Minister on matters of trifling importance.

Before the arrival at Tehran of the Hon. Charles A. Murray, who was the new representative in Persia of her Majesty's Government, some correspondence had taken place between the prime Minister and the English chargé d'affaires regarding a meerza, or Persian writer, who had been employed in the Mission, and who was much disliked by the Sedr-Azem. The Persian Vizeer had not sought to conceal the antipathy which he felt towards Hashem Khan, and he had expressed a wish that this man might not be continued in his position in the Mission, in virtue of which he was the medium of communication between the Persian Government and the British Minister. The meerza in question belonged to one of the principal branches of the tribe of Noor; of another branch of which tribe the Sedr-Azem was the chief. He had at one period been in the Persian service, but had for a long time past been unemployed; when in 1854 he was named Persian secretary to the English Mission at Tehran. The Persian Minister now asserted that Hashem Khan had never obtained a formal discharge from the Shah's service, and that he was consequently not eligible for employment under a foreign mission; the English chargé d'affaires was therefore requested not to press the question of his employment. The point of his removal from the post of Persian secretary to the Mission was yielded; not in consequence of the truth of the assertion that he had not obtained a discharge from the Shah's service, but because it was manifestly contrary to the public interests that English business should be daily transacted through a subordinate who was avowedly disliked by the Persian prime minister. When the Sedr-Azem had at first requested that Hashem

Khan might be removed from the post of Persian secretary to the English Mission, he had himself suggested, in the course of a conversation on the subject, that the meerza should be sent to Sheeraz to fill the post of agent to the English mission at that place. To this post Hashem Khan was therefore appointed, in spite of the Sedr-Azem's subsequent assertion that, as he had never obtained a formal written discharge from the Shah's service, he was incapable of holding any appointment under a foreign government.

Upon inquiries instituted by the British Minister, it appeared that it was not the custom for the Shah's servants to obtain a written discharge on their quitting the royal service, and the Sedr-Azem himself admitted that Hashem Khan, on being refused an increase of pay, had been told that he might go to where he pleased. When, however, in the autumn of 1855 the meerza was about to proceed to fill his post, the Persian prime minister unexpectedly announced to the English envoy that the Persian government would not permit Hashem Khan to hold any appointment under the British Mission; and he further intimated, in terms too plain to be misunderstood, that if Hashem Khan should attempt to quit Tehran, on his way to Sheeraz, he would be seized and detained. Mr. Murray could not submit to this interference in a matter that concerned only the government of which he was the representative, and he therefore replied that should the Persian ministers cause Hashem Khan to be arrested, they must expect the same consequences as would follow the seizure of any servant or employé of his mission. Upon this the Sedr-Azem gave orders for the arrest of the wife of Meerza Hashem, and he would not allow her to be restored to her husband; notwithstanding that the chief mujteheds, or judges, of Tehran issued a decree pronouncing it illegal to detain the wife of the meerza in captivity, or to divorce her without the consent of her husband. The Shah himself had no power to withstand the decree of the mujteheds; yet in the face of their decision, the Sedr-Azem continued to detain the wife of Hashem Khan, alleging that, as she was the sister of the Shah's wife, she was amenable to a certain extent to the domestic authority of the Shah.

Mr. Murray insisted that, in accordance with treaty engagements, the wife of the British employé, Hashem Khan, should be forthwith liberated; and he gave the Persian government a specified time for arriving at a decision, under the alternative of a suspension of diplomatic intercourse. During the period allowed to the Persian government for the purpose of coming to a decision, Mr. Murray was asked whether the matter could not be arranged in some other way than by Hashem Khan's being actually sent to Sheeraz to be agent to the British Mission at that place; he replied that he was ready to discharge that person from the English service upon the condition that his wife should be at once liberated, and that the meerza should receive a pension or employment a little more lucrative than the one he would forfeit, and, moreover, that his safety should be guaranteed. A fair opportunity was thus afforded to the Persian government of bringing this trivial quarrel to an end, had they sincerely wished to remain on good terms with the English government. But from the conduct of the Sedr-Azem in objecting to allow Hashem Khan to hold a post for which he had been the first person to suggest him;

in afterwards seizing his wife and arbitrarily detaining her, for the sole purpose of affronting Mr. Murray; and now from his refusing to take advantage of an offer by which Hashem Khan's connection with the British Mission would have been for ever terminated—one is almost forced to believe that the conduct of the Sedr-Azem was dictated by a desire to bring about a temporary rupture of diplomatic relations between the English and Persian governments.

After a short delay had been asked and conceded, for the purpose of taking into consideration Mr. Murray's proposal, the Persian government refused to agree to it. The Sedr-Azem had been taught to believe that England had at this time enough upon her hands, and that it was certain she would not go to war with Persia; there was, therefore, he thought, no great danger in breaking off friendly intercourse with the British Government. It may have been, and it probably was, the Sedr-Azem's first intention to follow up the rupture by overtures of joining Russia; but as the year 1855 wore on, there seemed less and less temptation for Persia to do so. The Sedr-Azem, however, thought that he saw a good opportunity for seizing Herat, whilst Great Britain should still be engaged in war. Mr. Murray was induced to accord a further delay to the Shah's Ministers for the purpose of their coming to a decision; the Turkish chargé d'affaires volunteering to use his influence to bring the Shah's government to a sense of just dealing. A still further delay was granted at the request of the representative of France; who, from the intimate alliance of his country with England, was entitled to be informed of the progress of the quarrel.

The Sedr-Azem now showed himself to be utterly

unscrupulous as to the means he had recourse to in order
to throw suspicion on the motives by which Mr. Murray
was actuated in demanding the liberation of the wife of
Hashem Khan. He stated openly that both that gentleman and his predecessor in charge of the English Mission, had retained the meerza in the British service
simply on account of his wife. By means of this
utterly-unfounded slander he hoped to excite public feeling against Mr. Murray. Nor was he altogether unsuccessful. Nothing is more easy than to invent and pro-
pagate stories affecting the character of others, which
those against whom they are directed may find it almost
impossible effectually to refute ; and as there seemed,
to persons unacquainted with the utter disregard of
most Persians to truth, to be a certain amount of probability in the stories set on foot by the Sedr-Azem,
these stories obtained credence in some quarters ; those
who believed them being inclined to attach blame, not
so much to any supposed breach of morality, as to the
imprudence of intriguing with a lady who was so nearly
related to the Shah. This was exactly the view of the
matter which the Sedr-Azem wished to be taken ; and he
felt sure that, if he could only gain for this story a certain
amount of belief amongst the British public, Mr. Murray
would not be supported by his Government. As to the
indignity which the propagation of this falsehood brought
upon a nobleman of the Sedr-Azem's own tribe, as well
as indirectly on the Sedr-Azem's sovereign, it was a consideration that in no way troubled his Highness.

During the time granted by Mr. Murray for the
deliberations of the Persian government as to their decision, the prime minister thought proper to send to that

gentleman a highly offensive letter, in which he insinuated
that should the British flag be struck, the Sedr-Azem
would be compelled to make certain revelations. His
Highness must have known little, indeed, of the English
character, if he really fancied that this threat would
deter Mr. Murray from carrying into execution the measure to which he had pledged himself. The British flag
was lowered at the expiration of the last delay granted
by the English Minister, and when the Sedr-Azem after
this sent two messengers—one of them of princely rank
—to the British Legation, to inquire whether there were
no means of arranging the difference that had arisen,
his messengers were told that, as preliminary measures to
any arrangement for an accommodation of the dispute,
the wife of Hashem Khan must be restored to her husband, and the Sedr-Azem must come to the British
Mission-house to withdraw his offensive letter, and
apologize for having written it.

M. Bourrée, the French minister at the Persian court,
professing to view with great solicitude the progress of a
negotiation, the unsuccessful result of which might have
the effect of driving Persia to take part with Russia
against Turkey, besought Mr. Murray to allow him to
make one more effort to reconcile him with the Persian
government; and as he feared that the Sedr-Azem might
refuse to come to the house of the British Legation for the
purpose of making an apology for the offensive letter, he
entreated Mr. Murray, for the sake of the alliance between
France and England, to be contented with a written
withdrawal of the letter and with the restoration of the
imprisoned lady. Mr. Murray could not refuse his permission to the French Minister to make the attempt, and

on the following day M. Bourrée accordingly brought to the English Minister a letter of retractation and apology from the Sedr-Azem for the offensive despatch he had written ; but instead of the lady being restored to her husband, it was proposed that she should be transferred to the house of her mother-in-law. To the latter point Mr. Murray could not consent, and the mediation of the French Minister in the matter was, therefore, at an end. But after this, and before the English Minister had completed his preparations for quitting Tehran, the Sedr-Azem seemed at one time to meditate giving way : he announced his intention of coming in person to the hotel of the English Mission. But, before proceeding to put this proposal into execution, he once more put himself into communication with M. Bourrée. His Highness's intention of proceeding to call upon Mr. Murray was, however, abandoned ; and on the 5th of December, 1855, the members of the British Mission quitted Tehran, and entered on their long journey towards the Turkish frontier.

After this the Sedr-Azem awaited with anxiety the reports of his agents in Europe as to the light in which his conduct was there viewed ; and as week after week, and month after month, passed by without his receiving from her Majesty's Government a peremptory demand for apology and reparation, his highness began to believe that the proceedings of the English Minister would be disavowed. A personal triumph of this kind would have been so gratifying to his vanity, that it would have been more than sufficient to cause him to renounce any policy to which he may have leaned of breaking with the allies and making war against Turkey. In his recklessness and exultation he thought that, under such circumstances, he might afford to gratify the national wish for the possession of Herat.

In the month of January, 1853, an agreement had been concluded between the British minister at Tehran and the prime minister of Persia, by which the Shah's government had engaged not to send troops to Herat, unless troops from the direction of Cabul, or Kandahar, or other foreign country should invade that principality. In direct contravention of this arrangement, the Sedr-Azem now instructed the Prince of Khorassan to march upon Herat; thereby affording to Great Britain an unquestionable *casus belli*.

The expedition to Herat was undertaken partly in order to gratify the national Persian desire for the possession of that place, and partly in the hope that success in the direction of Affghanistan would afford Persia advantages by the sacrifice of which reparation might afterwards be made to the English Government. Herat, after the death of Yar Mahomed Khan, had fallen under the sway of that ruler's son, Syd Mahomed; * but the new governor possessed none of the striking ability which had characterized his father, and his subjects had soon become disgusted with a ruler only remarkable for his cruelty and his excessive debauchery. Some of them had accordingly taken advantage of the absence of Syd Mahomed from Herat, upon an expedition against the tribe of Hezareh, to enter into negotiations with Prince Mahomed Yoosuf, the nephew and heir of Shah Kamran, and who was then a refugee at Meshed. The

---

* This man's name is given as Syud Mahomed in Mr. KAYE's *History of the Sepoy War*, but it is more correctly written Syd, or Cid, Mahomed.

result of these negotiations was that Prince Mahomed Yoosuf had proceeded to Herat, and obtained possession of that fortress. Syd Mahomed had been afterwards seized and imprisoned, and, in conformity with the barbarous Moslem law respecting vengeance for blood, the nephew of Kamran had avenged his death by slaying the son of Yar Mahomed.

Early in the year 1856, Prince Sultan Murad marched from Meshed at the head of an army, with which he commenced the siege of Herat. The Persian troops took the fort of Ghorian, and subsequently made Mahomed Yoosuf a prisoner. He was sent to Tehran, where he afterwards met with a melancholy fate. But the defence of Herat was continued by Isa Khan, the deputy-governor, who opposed with the greatest bravery all the assaults of the besiegers. During the progress of the operations each party attempted to blind and deceive the other—the Persian giving assurances of grace and protection, whilst besieging the town and devastating the country around it; and the Affghan boasting his loyalty and obedience to the Shah, whilst openly and heroically opposing the advance of the Persian army.

But while the Sedr-Azem was allowed to pursue his reckless course, and while the progress of the siege of Herat occupied the attention of the Shah and his subjects, preparations were being made in India for an expedition to Bushire, for the purpose of showing Persia that she could not with impunity depart from her treaty engagements with England; and in the proclamation which was issued at Calcutta, on the 1st of November, 1856, the cause of the war that was to be waged was declared to be the Persian hostile expedition against Herat.

CHAPTER XV.

Policy of the Sedr-Azem—Embassy of Ferrukh Khan to Europe—Fall of
Herat—Rules to be observed in carrying on English War against
Persia—Singular Instance of Persian Levity—War against Infidels
proclaimed at Tehran—The Sirkisikchi-Bashi—Occupation of Karrack
by British Troops—Capture of Reshire—Surrender of Bushire—
Sir J. Outram—Expedition to Burazjan—Action at Khushab—
Bombardment of Mohamra—Defeat of Persians—Expedition to Ahwaz
—Restoration of Peace—Terms of Treaty of Paris—Sultan Ahmed
Khan—Murder of Prince Mahomed Yoosuf—Fall of the Sedr-Azem—
Conclusion.

I HAVE endeavoured to show that the rupture of friendly
relations between Great Britain and Persia, arose, indirectly in the first instance, out of the unsettled state of
the political atmosphere of Europe, and from the desire
of the Persian Government to be permitted to play some
part in the drama which then occupied the stage of the
world. The Sedr-Azem was probably incapable of pursuing a consistent line of policy throughout the negotiations that preceded the war. It is considered statesman-
like in Persia to conceal one's real intentions up to the
last moment; to endeavour to take advantage of every
opening for finessing, and of every pretext for gaining
time. We are almost, as I have said, driven to believe
that the Sedr-Azem had of fixed purpose, for some
reason best known to himself, adopted a line of conduct
towards the British representative which would drive
that representative into the alternative of striking his

flag rather than of submitting to it; and our belief in this intention on the part of Meerza Agha Khan, is not shaken by the knowledge that he withdrew his impertinent letter when urged to do so by M. Bourrée. He would have been altogether unlike most Persians, had he been capable of taking up a distinct line of conduct, and consistently adhering to it from first to last. It is evident that he wavered from side to side, and was guided in his conduct and in his demands, by the advice of those whom he consulted. But if when his Highness began to annoy and insult Mr. Murray, he had any intention of following up the rupture of diplomatic relations with England, by declaring war against England's ally, the Sublime Porte, the events that had occurred in Europe had caused him to renounce any such intention; for the utmost use which he now proposed to make of the interval of non-diplomatic intercourse with England, was to gain Herat for the Shah. The peace of Paris somewhat disconcerted his calculations. There had not been wanting Europeans at Tehran to assure him that Great Britain could not afford the men or the means necessary for making war against Persia, so long as she should continue to be involved in the Crimean struggle; but now that that war was over, the Persian Minister could not but tremble as he reflected what might be the consequences of the quarrel he had brought about.

The present state of things had its advantages. The Sedr-Azem had effectually cleared himself of the suspicion that he was actuated in his conduct by a sense of gratitude towards the English for having formerly protected him. The Sedr-Azem, too, felt more secure than ever in his post, whilst the attention of the Shah was occupied by the siege of Herat; and the Minister, moreover, felt that should there be war with England, his services would become indispensable during its continuance. But war was the worst that could come of the quarrel, and anything short of war could scarcely fail to turn to the advantage of the Sedr-Azem. In case Mr. Murray's conduct should be disowned by his Government, the Persian prime minister felt that the greatest credit would redound to himself, for having withstood the pretensions of a Frankish minister, and driven him in humiliation from his post. In order the more widely to circulate the stories which the Vizeer had put into circulation regarding Mr. Murray, Ferrukh Khan had been sent on an embassy to Constantinople and to Paris, at which places he was to endeavour to put himself in communication with the English ambassadors, and to try and make them believe the Sedr-Azem's version of the origin of the quarrel at Tehran. Ferrukh Khan had also received full powers for the conclusion of an arrangement of the points in difference between the Persian Government and that of the Queen. Lord Stratford de Redcliffe, however, demanded, as one of the points to be conceded preliminary to the reëstablishment of friendly relations between the two governments, that the Sedr-Azem should be dismissed from office; and rather than accede to this demand, the ambassador plenipotentiary of Persia had resolved to continue his journey to Paris, in the hope of obtaining easier terms through the mediation of the Court of France. The Sedr-Azem was, however, well aware that there was no chance of the English Government consenting to resume diplomatic intercourse with Persia so long as the troops of that power should occupy the territory of Herat. His intention, therefore, was to retire from Affghanistan after Herat should have been taken and placed in the hands of a ruler who would of his own accord acknowledge himself to be a subject of the Shah, and who would strike coin in his Persian Majesty's name. But to effect this it was necessary in the first place to take Herat, and this the Persian troops under Prince Sultan Murad showed themselves to be unable to do. The prime minister could not afford to lose time, and he therefore despatched to the Persian camp before Herat, M. Bühler, who had been an officer in the French engineers, and who was now in the service of the Shah. The famous Affghan fortress was not, as on a former occasion, defended by an Eldred Pottinger, and it accordingly fell before the regular approaches set on foot by an European scientific officer.

But by the time Herat had fallen, it was too late for the Sedr-Azem to avoid the consequences of the rash course he had determined to pursue. Orders had been issued in India for despatching a hostile expedition to the shores of the Persian Gulf, and the English Government had now the peculiar task to perform of directing a war against a power which it had hitherto been the policy of England to sustain, and the stability of which, notwithstanding the conduct of its Minister, was still an object of concern to the Ministers of the Queen. It was no easy matter to make war on Persia without incurring the risk of bringing Persia altogether to destruction. The tribes of the southern portion of the Shah's dominions, and those of the coast of the Persian Gulf, would have been only too happy to throw off all allegiance to the

Shah, had they been in the least degree encouraged to do so by the English commanders; and had they gone over to the enemy, a general rising in Persia would have been the inevitable consequence. The Russian authorities in Georgia, also, might have consulted the tranquillity of their frontier by occupying the province of Azerbaeejan; a position which would have given Russia the command of Asia Minor. The war against Persia, therefore, had to be conducted on the principle of doing only as much mischief to the enemy as might suffice to induce him to make peace upon the terms required of him. It is singularly illustrative of Persian levity, that before the British force appeared in the Persian Gulf, the original cause of quarrel between the Sedr-Azem and Mr. Murray had altogether ceased to exist. Meerza Hashem Khan had voluntarily renounced his employment under the English Government, and all claim to any protection to which it might entitle him; whereupon he was forthwith received into favour by the Sedr-Azem, and by the Shah. His wife, the Helen of the war, was restored to him, and all the imputations which had been cast upon her character were declared by the Persian Minister himself to have been calumnies invented to serve a purpose. A suitable salary was conferred upon him, and the lady who had been so maligned, once more took her place amongst the honourable women of the land.

The question of Herat was therefore now the main point at issue between the governments of Great Britain and Persia. The capture of that fortress, which had withstood for so long a time all the power of Mahomed Shah, had filled the young king with pride and gratification; but this feeling of satisfaction was somewhat alloyed by the reflection that he was indebted for it, as he had been for so many previous military successes, to the energy and skill of his near relative, Sultan Murad Meerza. That prince, however, was allowed to remain in the government of Herat, and Isa Khan, who had so long defended the fortress, was treacherously put to death by him, after having been assured of pardon and of favour.

The problem now to be solved by the British Government of India was how to expel the Persian troops from Herat. Dost Mahomed Khan of Cabul was perfectly ready to coöperate with the English authorities, and a division of British troops might have been sent through Affghanistan. The Khan of Khelat was equally disposed to permit the passage of British soldiers through his dominions; and had the course been adopted of invading Persia from India, the Government possessed in General John Jacob, the renowned commander of the Sindh Horse, an officer than whom no one was better qualified for carrying out the project. Another course which lay open to the Government of India was to land troops at Bender-Abbass, by the permission of the Imam of Muskat, and thence to march to Yezd. This route presents no difficulties, with the exception of one rocky pass, and is daily traversed by strings of caravans; the pass between Tarem and Ghuneh, however, would make it necessary that artillery should be taken to pieces before being transported over it. But although there would be no difficulty for an invading force to overcome in reaching Yezd, the military position of such a force so far from its base of operations would be a very precarious one, and the routes

28

thence to Khorassan and Herat lie over dreary wastes of
desert. Between Yezd and Herat there are thirty stages,
and it was therefore not thought that an English army
could penetrate to Herat by this route.

On a previous occasion, the independence of Herat
had been secured by the occupation by a British force of
an island in the Persian Gulf, and as the Sedr-Azem
thought it likely that the same course would be adopted
on this occasion by the Indian Government, he gave
orders for strengthening the defences of the southern
provinces of Persia. His nephew, the Shuja-el-Mulk,
who commanded the troops in Fars, was directed to move
down to the lower country, so that he might coöperate
with the governor of Bushire; and to the prince of
Arabistan, who was considered to be one of the best officers in Persia, was committed the task of providing for
the defence of the line of the Karoon river. A jehad, or
religious war against infidels, was proclaimed at Tehran;
but this measure altogether failed to create any excitement.* There was no enthusiasm whatsoever amongst
the Persians on the subject of the war, and the general
impression that it would only be productive of disasters

* " Pendant la dernière guerre que le cabinet de Londres fit à la Perse,
le gouvernement de Téhéran, pour augmenter ses forces, donna l'ordre de
prêcher la guerre sainte dans toutes les mosquées de l'empire. Cette
résolution présenta cette particularité que l'idée première en vint d'un
Arménien catholique. Il y eut, avant qu'elle fut adoptée, les discussions
les plus curieuses. Plusieurs hommes d'état la repoussaient de toutes
leurs forces. . . . Les grands marchands étaient mécontents, les chefs
militaires trouvaient le moyen méprisable. Quant à la populace, . . .
l'annonce de ce qui allait avoir lieu la laissa complètement indifférente. . .
A Schyraz, on peut croire un instant que la populace allait s'émouvoir et
se mettre en marche, mais non pas pour attaquer les Anglais, tout au
contraire pour les aider."—*Trois Ans en Asie, par le Comte A. de Gobineau,*
pp. 201-295.

and disgrace to Persia, seems soon to have come home to
the Sedr-Azem himself. He now took occasion to supersede his nephew in the command of the field-force, by the
chief of the royal body-guard with whom he was not on
friendly terms, and whom he hoped to see disgraced in
the too-probable case of his being defeated. The
Sirkisikchi-Bashi * was the chief of the upper branch of
the Kajar tribe, and he was a man of sufficient consequence to bear all the blame of the disasters which
every one expected. The selection of such an officer to
the command in the field was prudently made; but the
far-sighted views of the Sedr-Azem were frustrated by
the slow movements of the Sirkisikchi-Bashi. Before
his Excellency's arrival at the head-quarters of the army
in the south of Persia, the disasters that had been foreseen had already taken place.

On the 4th of December, 1856, the island of Karrack
in the Persian Gulf was occupied by British troops, and
preparations were immediately made for landing a force
near Bushire. The disembarkation at Halilla Bay occupied the greater part of three days and two nights, and
no serious opposition was offered by the Persians; three
or four hundred men who appeared in the vicinity of the
bay being scattered by the fire from the English gun-
boats. The Persians had taken up an intrenched
position near Bushire, commanding the wells from
which the place is supplied with water; but on the
British line being formed, this position was abandoned.
On the 9th of December the Persians were dislodged
from the old Dutch fort of Reshire. A short but fierce
struggle took place on this occasion, and four English

---

* This officer was appointed prime minister of Persia, March 21, 1865.

officers, with a small number of non-commissioned
officers and private soldiers, were killed, or died some
hours later of the wounds they received. Brigadier
Stopford, of the 64th regiment, was shot down from his
horse while turning round to inquire why his regiment
had halted ; it had been momentarily stopped to be
dressed in line, and then the men, seeing their commander down, rushed forward to the attack. Lieutenant-
Colonel Malet, of the 3rd Bombay Light Cavalry, had
prevented one of his troopers from bayoneting a wounded
Persian ; but his humanity cost him his life, for he was
shot so soon as his back was turned, by the Persian
lying on the ground.

The defeat of the Shah's troops on this occasion
completely damped the ardour of the garrison of Bushire.
That place was exposed, on the morning of the 10th of
December, to the fire of the guns of the British ships
under the command of Sir Henry Leeke, and it did not
offer any prolonged resistance.* The governor, together
with the officer commanding the troops, came out of the
town on the day succeeding that of the struggle at
Reshire, and gave up their swords to Major-General
Stalker, who commanded the invading army. Fifty-nine
guns, together with a large quantity of ammunition and
warlike stores, were also surrendered, and the portion of
the garrison that had not escaped, grounded arms in
front of the British line. The Persian common soldiers
were on the following day escorted by the British cavalry
for some distance into the interior and then set free ; the

---

* Sir Henry Leeke proceeded to India after the capture of Bushire, and
on his way attacked, at Lingah, a large detachment of Persian troops,
which he forced to retreat from the shore.

superior officers being conveyed as prisoners to India. General Stalker then proceeded to entrench himself in a camp outside Bushire; where he was to remain inactive until the arrival of reinforcements.

On the 27th of January, 1857, Lieutenant-General Sir James Outram arrived, and assumed command of the expeditionary force. Much was expected from his well-known energy and ability; nor were such expectations left unfulfilled. On reaching Bushire, General Outram was informed that a large Persian force, said to number more than eight thousand men, had taken up an intrenched position at the town of Burazjan, forty-six miles distant. It was intended that this force should form the nucleus of a large army, to be employed in attempting to drive the British troops from Bushire. On the 31st of January, the first brigade of the second division of the invading army arrived from India, and by the 2nd of February the soldiers had landed and reached the camp. General Outram thereupon resolved to strike a blow with the object of compelling the Persian commander to evacuate Burazjan. On the evening of the 3rd of February, the main body of the British force marched from Bushire, taking with it neither tents nor extra luggage of any kind, and each man carrying his great coat, his blanket, and two days' cooked provisions; the commissariat being furnished with three days' provisions in addition. The protection of the town and camp of Bushire was provided for by a detachment of troops being left under the command of Lieutenant-Colonel Shepherd, who had also under his orders a party of seamen taken from all the ships in the harbour. The troops composing the division that now marched into

the interior under the personal command of Sir James
Outram, were her Majesty's 64th and 78th regiments,
and the 2nd European regiment of the Bombay army,
numbering between them, two thousand and two hundred
Englishmen; the 4th, 30th, and 26th regiments of the
Bombay army, and a Belooch battalion, numbering two
thousand men, including one hundred and eighteen
sappers; the 3rd regiment Bombay Light Cavalry, and
the regiment of Poona Horse, consisting together of
four hundred and nineteen men; and the third troop
of Bombay Horse Artillery, and the 3rd and 5th light
field-batteries. The number of guns in all was eighteen.
After performing in forty-one hours a march of forty-six
miles, being all the time exposed to great cold and to
deluging rain, the force reached the enemy's intrenched
position on the afternoon of the 5th of February. The
intrenchments were found to have been abandoned; the
Persians having on the preceding night evacuated their
camp with so great precipitation, that there was no time
to remove the tents, the camp equipage, and the ordnance .
stores. The spoils of the camp were being carried off
by the people of the neighbouring villages when the
British force arrived. Some of the horsemen of the
Eelkhani of Fars were still in sight, and between them
and the British cavalry a little skirmishing took place;
but the Persians eventually made off.

The Persian commander having withdrawn his men,
General Outram did not think it prudent to follow him
up the very strong passes that lie beyond Burazjan.
Accordingly, after having occupied that place for two days
and destroyed the magazines of the Persians, which were
found to contain 40,000 pounds of powder, with small-

arm ammunition and a large quantity of shot and shell, he commenced the march back towards Bushire. The returning army carried with it large stores of flour, rice and grain, which had been collected by the Persians. The march towards the shore commenced on the night of the 7th of February, and at midnight an attack was made upon the rear-guard by the Eelkhani's horse, while detachments of Persians threatened the line of march on every side. Under these circumstances the troops were ordered to halt, and were drawn up so as to protect the baggage, and to present a front to the Persian irregular cavalry, from what direction soever it might attack. Four of the Persian guns opened a heavy fire upon the column; but the British troops were ordered to lie down under arms till daybreak, and the shot passed over their heads without doing any harm. It appears that the Persian leaders had recovered from the alarm into which they had been thrown by the news of the approach of General Outram, and had even resolved to attack him in his camp on the night of the 7th, when the noise caused by the explosion of their own magazines announced to them his departure. They had then hastened to overtake him, and had tried to excite a panic amongst his troops.

When day broke on the 8th of February, the Persian force, numbering nearly seven thousand men, was discovered to be drawn up in order of battle to the northeast of the English position. The British cavalry and artillery were at once moved forward to the attack, supported by two-thirds of the infantry in two lines; the remainder of the infantry being left to protect the baggage. The fire of the artillery did great execution, and seemed completely to disconcert the Persians. The two regiments of Indian cavalry vied with each other in gathering laurels on this field. The Poona Horse succeeded in capturing the standard of the Kashgai regiment of Serbaz, and the 3rd Bombay Light Cavalry performed a still more brilliant feat of arms. The 2nd Tabreez regiment of Persian infantry was drawn up in the usual Persian loose formation, when it was charged by the British regiment above named. Referring to this exploit, it was stated afterwards, by General Jacob, who had not been present on the field of Khushab, that "a regular Persian battalion—perfectly well drilled, armed, accoutred, &c., after the best European model, composed of splendid men, who stood perfectly firm, bold, and confident in their array—was ridden over and utterly destroyed by Major John Forbes and one troop only of the 3rd regiment of Bombay Light Cavalry." * The Persian regiment was also stated to have been drawn up in a regularly formed square. But such a description of the formation of the Persian regiment in question is likely to mislead the reader, and to induce the erroneous belief that cavalry can break a perfectly-formed square of regular infantry. Had the formation of the regiment which was charged on this occasion by the 3rd Bombay Light Cavalry, been such as is understood in England by the term "a perfectly-formed square," Major Forbes, who was the leader of the charge, would never have permitted his men to rush to destruction in attempting what was impossible for them to do. But still, the array of the Persians was

---

* As the account here given of the action at Khushab somewhat differs from previously published statements regarding it, the author begs to observe that he derived his information from his brother officers who were present on that field, and from officers with whom he served at the close of the Persian expedition on the staff of Sir J. Outram.

sufficiently regular to render the exploit performed by the cavalry, a subject of just pride to themselves and to their comrades. Major Forbes brought his men up at the charge, and seeing (it is to be presumed) that the Persians were not very close together in their formation, the idea occurred to him that his horsemen might force their way through the gaps in their ranks. He, accordingly, instead of turning his men aside or bringing them to a halt, boldly led them up to the bayonets of the Persians. The momentum of the cavalry was so great that the line of the enemy scarcely stopped the horsemen for an instant; although their gallant commander paid for his decision by suffering a severe wound. The cavalry having once passed through them, the Persians could no longer offer any effectual resistance, and many of the regiment fell under the sabres of the Indians. One of the junior officers of the cavalry squadrons had now the opportunity of displaying a thoughtfulness for those around him, which was suitably acknowledged by the gift of the Victoria Cross, and which showed qualities that could not be purchased by cross or honour. The adjutant of the regiment, Lieutenant Moore, had been, with his commanding officer, foremost in the charge; his horse was impaled on the Persian bayonets, and the rider had been thrown to the ground. It was then that his perilous position was perceived by Lieutenant Malcolmson, who, amidst the clash of arms and the roar of battle, had self-possession sufficient to enable him to divine at once the only means by which his brother officer could be saved. Wheeling his Arab charger round to the spot where Lieutenant Moore was defending himself from the bayonets that were levelled at his breast, he extricated his right foot from the stirrup, which he then told Lieutenant Moore to grasp. Having assured himself that the other had done so, he applied the spur to his horse, which leaping forwards bore both the officers beyond the reach of pressing danger.

On the cavalry and artillery was thrown nearly all the burden of this day; for some delay occurred in ordering the advance of the infantry regiments, in consequence of the general commanding having been stunned by a fall from his horse. As Sir James Outram was thus unable to guide the progress of the battle, the task of giving directions fell upon General Stalker, the second in command, and upon Colonel (now Sir Edward) Lugard, the chief of the staff. It thus happened that the infantry portion of the army scarcely came into action at all, the enemy being in full retreat before ten o'clock in the forenoon. Two Persian guns were captured, and a third would have fallen into the hands of the English, had those who attempted to take it adopted the expedient of firing at the horses harnessed to it instead of at the gunners; but as fast as one man was shot down another mounted in his place, and so the gun was saved. Great astonishment was created in the minds of the Persian troops on this day by the marvellous celerity of the movements of the English artillery; and they were also greatly surprised by the unexpected effect of the new rifles, which had been partly introduced into the English army, and some of which were tried on the field of Khushab. A group of four Persian horsemen remained looking at the battle at what they considered to be a safe distance from the scene of operations; an officer of the 2nd Bombay European Regiment, wishing

to show them their danger, took an Enfield rifle from a
sergeant, and adjusting it to 900 yards, fired it at the
group of horsemen. One of the four men fell from his
horse to the ground, and the other three put spurs to
their steeds and galloped off the field.

The Persian gun-ammunition fell into the hands of
the English troops, and seven hundred Iranis were
found dead upon the field of battle. The proportion of
wounded could not be ascertained, as the small number
of General Outram's cavalry prevented a pursuit, and
gave the Persians the opportunity of carrying off their
disabled men. Many of the Shah's troops, in endeavouring to provide as effectually as possible for their
individual safety, left their arms upon the field. No
British or Indian soldiers fell into the hands of the Persians, and the latter were prevented from decapitating
the dead, as is their custom. After the termination of the
action, the English troops bivouacked for the day close
to the ground where the battle had been fought, and at
night they accomplished a march of twenty miles towards
Bushire; over a country rendered nearly impassable by
the continuous heavy rains. After a rest of six hours,
the greater portion of the infantry continued their march
to Bushire; which place they reached before midnight on
the 9th of February. The cavalry and artillery arrived
at the camp on the following morning. The loss on the
side of the British in the action at Khushab consisted of
sixteen men killed and sixty-two wounded.

It had been the intention of Sir James Outram to
send a force against the Persian fort of Mohamra on the
Karoon river, immediately after his return from Burazjan;
but, owing to the non-arrival of reinforcements which had

been expected from India, in consequence of the tempestuous weather in the Persian Gulf, it was not until the 18th of March that the general could set out from Bushire. The interval was marked by the occurrence of two events which threw a gloom over the spirits of the British troops. The first division of the force was under the command of General Stalker, under whom it had taken Bushire. That officer's health had been affected by long exposure to the climate of India, and a sense of the responsibility that now devolved upon him weighed heavily upon his mind. He had been relieved of all political responsibility by the arrival of Sir James Outram; but on the departure of that officer for Mohamra, he would find himself once more for a time in the independent command at Bushire. He wrote a note to General Outram with the object of endeavouring to dissuade him from commanding the expedition to Mohamra in person, but his Excellency's resolution in this respect remained unshaken. What now caused General Stalker most disquietude was the fact, that, although the hot weather was rapidly approaching, huts had not yet been erected for the protection of his men. On the morning of the 14th of March the idea seems to have occurred to him of seeking refuge from responsibility by committing suicide; but it is probable that he had no fixed intention of immediately putting an end to his life, since he inscribed his name on the list of persons who were on that day to dine at the staff mess, and had also invited an officer to be his guest. He told his servant to bring out his pistols, and before breakfasting he requested his aide-de-camp to load them, in order that he might wear them; immediately after breakfast, whilst he was alone in his tent, he put one of the pistols to his head, and firing it made an end of his life.

As if this occurrence were not sufficiently deplorable, it was followed three days later by another of a similar nature. Commodore Ethersey, who had succeeded Sir Henry Leeke in the command of the fleet, felt every day more and more his unfitness for the post he held. He frequently suffered from severe nervous attacks, and expressed in his diary his conviction that he should "make a mess" of the projected naval attack on Mohamra. The day after that on which General Stalker's death occurred, he sought relief by taking opium; but the dose he took was too large for the purpose of soothing him, and it excited him so much that on the next day he was reduced to imitating the melancholy example that had been set by General Stalker.

The position of the point at which Sir J. Outram intended to attack the Persians, rendered it necessary that the preliminary operations should be performed by the naval portion of the expeditionary force. Mohamra is said to have owed its origin to Alexander the Great, who, to avoid the necessity of sailing down to the Persian Gulf by the ancient channel of the Karoon, caused the canal to be dug through which that stream now flows into the Tigris.* The town was originally called Alexandria, and having been destroyed by an overflow of the river, it was rebuilt by Antiochus and called Antiochia. It was a second time overflooded, and on being restored was called Charax. The records concerning the position of this city give it a peculiar interest, as showing an instance of an oceanic delta gaining with almost unpre-

* *Travels and Researches in Chaldea and Susiana*, by W. K. LOFTUS.

cedented rapidity upon the sea.* The original site of
Charax was believed by Pliny to be only two thousand
paces distant from the shore, but, in consequence of the
rapid accumulation of mud from the great river, Charax
came in the course of time to stand fifty miles from the
sea-shore. "If we take the trouble of comparing the
historical accounts of the early Greek, Latin, and Mahomedan authors," says a modern geologist,† "the
increase of land at the delta of the Tigris and Euphrates
may be distinctly traced. Since the commencement of
our era there has been an increment at the extraordinary
rate of a mile in about seventy years, which far exceeds
the growth of any existing delta."

It has been said that the town of Mohamra, in consequence of the injury which its establishment as a free
port had done to the trade of Bussora, had been wantonly
attacked by the Turks. By the treaty of Erzeroum it
had been made over to the Persians, by whom it was
strongly fortified in order that it might be secure against
another attack. Since the rupture of diplomatic relations
between Great Britain and Persia, the fortifications of
Mohamra had been still further strengthened. Batteries,
having casemated embrasures, had been erected at the
northern and southern points of the banks of the Karoon
and the Shut-el-Arab,‡ where the two rivers join.
These, with other earthworks armed with heavy ordnance,
commanded the entire passage of the latter river; and
they were so judiciously placed, and so scientifically
formed, as to sweep the whole stream to the full

* *Travels and Researches in Chaldea and Susiana*, by W. K. LOFTUS.
† Mr. LOFTUS.
‡ The united stream of the Tigris and Euphrates is called the Shut-
el-Arab.

extent of the range of the guns up and down the river and across to the opposite shore. Indeed, everything that science could suggest appeared to have been effected by the Persians in order to prevent any hostile vessel from passing up the river to a point above Mohamra.* In addition to these precautions, their position had natural advantages; since the banks of the rivers for many miles were covered with groves of palm-trees, which afforded the best possible shelter for marksmen, and the opposite shore of the Shut-el-Arab, being Turkish territory, was not available for the erection of counter-batteries.† General Outram resolved to attack the enemies' batteries with his armed steamers and sloops of war, and so soon as the Persian fire should have slackened, to pass rapidly up the Karoon in small steamers towing boats, and then to land the force two miles up the river on the northern bank; from which point he could advance to attack the Persians in their intrenched position.

The Persian army at Mohamra consisted of nearly thirteen thousand men, under the personal command of Prince Khanlar. It consisted for the most part of Arabs, Bakhtiaris, and Beloochis, and was furnished with a suitable proportion of artillery. The British force consisted of five thousand men, and was strengthened by

---

* See despatches by Sir JAMES OUTRAM.

† I am happy to be able to record an instance of courtesy on the part of a Persian officer at Mohamra. Mr. Murray, accompanied by Dr. Dickson, physician to his mission, wished to proceed from Bussora to Bushire, after the capture of the latter town by the British, and it became necessary for him to run the gauntlet of the forts at the mouth of the Karoon river. The Persian artillerymen were at their posts, but when their commander saw that the *Hugh Lindsay* bore the flag of the British Minister, it was allowed to pass close under the batteries without a shot being fired.

twelve pieces of artillery. This division was composed of detachments of her Majesty's 14th Light Dragoons, and of the Sindh Horse ; of the 64th and 78th Regiments, commanded by Brigadier-General Havelock ; of the 23rd and 26th Regiments of the Bombay Native Army, and of a light battalion; composed of companies of different regiments ; and of the Sappers and Miners and the 3rd troop of the Bombay Horse Artillery and the 2nd light field-battery. These troops were supported by four armed steamers and two sloops of war.

On the 24th of March the steamers, having the transports in tow, moved up the river Shut-el-Arab to within three miles of the mouth of the Karoon ; but as some of the larger vessels struck on shoals, and did not reach the place of rendezvous until after darkness had set in, the attack, which had been fixed to take place at once, was necessarily deferred until the following day. During the night, a reconnaissance was made in a boat, for the purpose of ascertaining the nature of the soil of an island to the west of, and immediately opposite to, the Persian battery on the northern side of the mouth of the Karoon ; where it was wished to erect a mortar battery. The soil of the island was, however, found to consist of thick mud, and in consequence of this discovery, General Outram determined to place the mortars upon a raft. It was necessary to allow some time for the construction of this raft, and the attack on Mohamra was in consequence deferred for another day. On the 25th the raft was formed, under the superintendence of Captain Rennie of the Indian Navy, and having been armed with two 8-inch and two 5½-inch mortars, to be worked by a party of artillerymen under the command of Captain

Morgan, it was towed by the small river steamer *Comet* up the stream, and moored in a position close to the above-mentioned island. This important operation was effected during the night without its having attracted the attention of the Persians, who entertained the full confidence that no vessel could pass up the river before their batteries. During the same day the horses and guns of the artillery, a portion of the cavalry, and the infantry, were trans-shipped into boats and small steamers, to be in readiness for landing on the following morning.

At break of day on the 26th of March, the four mortars on the raft opened their fire on both the northern and the southern Persian batteries. The range of the 5½-inch mortars proved to be short, but the 8-inch shells were very efficient, bursting immediately over and inside the enemy's works; whilst from the low position of the raft, but few of the Persian guns could be brought to bear upon the mortars. At seven o'clock the several vessels of war moved up into the positions which had been assigned to them by Commodore Young, who had succeeded Commodore Ethersey in the command of the fleet. The *Semiramis*, having the *Clive* in tow, and being followed by the *Ajdaha*, entered the western channel in support of the mortar battery; the *Feroze*, the *Assaye*, the *Victoria*, and the *Falkland*, remaining in reserve until the fire of the two Persian forts should be lessened. This was soon effected; on which the vessels that had been held in reserve entered the eastern channel of the river. The *Feroze* now opened her fire on the southern Persian fort at less than point-blank range, as she passed by it to take up her position opposite to the northern fort. The division of ships in the western channel was then brought

29

to join in close attack on the two forts. So effective was now the fire from the ships, that in less than three quarters of an hour from its commencement, the Persian batteries were so far silenced as to be only able to reply from three or four guns. At a quarter before eight o'clock, the *Feroze*, which bore the pennant of Commodore Young, hoisted the rendezvous flag at the masthead, as a signal for the troop-ships to advance ; which they did in good order, although when they passed the batteries their fire had not yet ceased. Between nine and ten o'clock heavy explosions occurred in different parts of the Persian fortifications, and after the batteries had ceased firing from artillery, a fire of musketry was maintained with great perseverance, until storming parties from the *Semiramis*, *Clive*, *Victoria*, and *Falkland*, landed on shore, and drove before them the last of the enemy, taking possession of their works and guns.

The loss sustained by the British fleet at Mohamra was very small, owing to the precaution which had been taken of constructing on each vessel a breastwork of trusses of hay : only five men were killed, and eighteen wounded. Amongst the troops not a single casualty took place ; although they had to run the gauntlet of both the artillery and the musketry fire, by which some of the Indian servants on board were killed. By one o'clock the troops had landed above the Persian battery on the northern bank of the Karoon, when they formed and advanced without delay through the date-groves, and across the plain that lay between them and the intrenched camp of the Persians. The latter did not wait for the approach of the English, but fled precipitately, after having exploded their largest magazine. They left behind them their tents and baggage, their public and private stores, several magazines of ammunition, and sixteen guns. Only one troop of the Sindh Horse had by this time been enabled to land, and with it Captain Malcolm Green was ordered to follow the enemy for some distance. That officer came upon the rear-guard retreating in good order, but his numerical weakness in horsemen prevented his making any impression upon it.

The loss of the Persians was estimated at two hundred men; and seventeen of their guns fell into the hands of the British, besides large stores of provisions. The Persian artillery and the troops in the batteries had acted as well as they could have been expected to behave: they had served their guns well, and had not shrunk from exposure and labour. But the disaster of this day demanded a public punishment to be inflicted upon some of those who had composed the army of Khuzistan. Accordingly, some months later, the Khelij regiment was brought to the Shah's camp near Tehran, to be publicly disgraced. Its colonel, however, had made such good use of the time he had been in command of it, that he was enabled to save his commission and his person, by paying a handsome bribe to the prime minister. The other officers, less fortunate, had rings passed through their noses, and were thus dragged along the ranks by cords; they were then severely beaten, and thrown into prison. The major of another regiment, an Armenian called Asslan, received two thousand blows from the bastinado; though it is said that his men had fought well at Mohamra in defence of the batteries, where their colonel, Aga Jan Khan, was killed. But if the punishment now inflicted did not fall upon the right persons, the example

29—2

was the same; and the Persian Minister probably cared little what became of a commanding officer who could not afford to purchase exemption from a beating. If any one more than another deserved disgrace and punishment for this disaster to the Persian arms at Mohamra, it was the Prince Khanlar, who had been entrusted with the command of the army of Khuzistan, and who fled on the landing of the British troops, without even waiting to be defeated. But his Royal Highness could afford to pay for the exhibition of pusillanimity, and the sum of eight thousand pounds sterling produced upon the Sedr-Azem such an impression, that instead of reproaches and disgrace, Prince Khanlar received from the Shah a sword and a dress of honour!

The Persian army retreated from Mohamra to the town of Ahwaz, which is distant by about a hundred miles from the mouth of the Karoon river. Sir James Outram determined to send a small force by water to this place, for the purpose of observing the position of the enemy and of destroying, if possible, the stores said to have been collected there. On the 29th of March a flotilla, consisting of three small river steamers and three gun-boats, was despatched up the Karoon under the command of Captain Rennie. On board the vessels were three hundred soldiers of the 64th and 78th regiments, under the orders of Captain Hunt of the 78th Highlanders; and Captain Kemball, the English Political Agent in Turkish Arabia, was directed to accompany the expedition in his civil capacity. The town of Ahwaz, which is said to occupy the site of the ancient Aginis, was found to be in ruins, and not to be surrounded by defences of any kind, beyond a portion of an old stone wall. Close to Ahwaz is a natural barrier of sandstone, which stretches across the river and renders impossible the ascent of vessels drawing more than a very few feet of water : indeed the strength of the current makes the ascent of any boats a matter of difficulty. The Karoon is at this point from ninety to one hundred and forty yards in width, while the banks of the river are so high and the water under them so deep that vessels can lie close to the side. It is the more necessary to describe the condition of the Karoon river somewhat minutely, since Sir James Outram has been censured for rashness in permitting a small flotilla to ascend to a point so far away from the main army, with the possibility of its being attacked by the Persian batteries at any turn of the stream. It would seem, however, that even had the Persian commander endeavoured to intercept the return of the British vessels, he would have been unable to interfere with their free progress, since they would have been favoured by the rapidity of the current and by the height of the river banks.* As the flotilla approached Ahwaz the Persian army was discovered occupying a ridge to the left, a few hundred yards distant from the Karoon, and situated in a projecting angle, round which the river winds. The steamers were brought to anchor at about a mile and a half below the Persian position, and some horsemen, whose curiosity prompted them to approach the ships, were warned by a rifle-shot to keep at a distance. It was determined by the officer in command of the expedition to carry the town of Ahwaz, which the

---

* Captain Selby, of the Indian Navy, who had surveyed the Karoon river, was in command of one of the ships of the expedition, and acted as guide.

Persians had on the previous day abandoned; and on the forenoon of the 1st of April the troops landed on the right bank;* they advanced in skirmishing order, thereby giving the appearance of their being more numerous than in reality they were. Two gun-boats at the same time took up positions within shell-range of the Persians, and opened fire upon their camp. The Persian guns did not reply to the fire, but a few shots were discharged by their marksmen which did not take effect. By noon the British detachment was in possession of Ahwaz, and to the left of the stream the Persian army could now be distinguished in full retreat. It retired in tolerable order, being covered by the Bakhtiari horse. A British party was upon this sent across to the opposite bank of the Karoon, to set fire to the magazines that had been abandoned by the Persians; but the plundering Arabs were already at work in the deserted camp. The expedition then proceeded down the stream to Mohamra, bringing on board the ships such of the Persian stores found at Ahwaz as had not been destroyed.

So far the operations of Sir James Outram had been completely successful. Bushire and Mohamra had been taken and occupied, and the Persian forces had been defeated at Khushab and driven from Ahwaz. But had the war continued, it would have been difficult to determine a line of operations to be followed with a probability of its being attended with advantage to the British Government. General Jacob, who was second in command of the expeditionary force, and whose valuable services and great achievements on the northern frontier

* The troops landed on the *left* bank, properly speaking, of the Karoon; but to the right of the position occupied by the British vessels.

of British India made his counsel valuable, was of
opinion that since Persia had been invaded from the sea
in force, and since the British troops had obtained ,pos-
session of Mohamra, and virtually of the whole of the
Karoon river, it would be an error to abandon that district, and to restore it to Persia.* He held that the
English force should retain the province of Khuzistan ;
which, under British rule, could scarcely fail to be
restored to its former prosperity. That province is
divided from the rest of Persia by ranges of mountains
which form a complete natural barrier, and it is inhabited by tribes and people of the Arab race. It is
traversed by rivers navigable from hill to sea, and
adjoining the valley of the Euphrates, it completely
commands the outlet of that river to the ocean.
General Jacob further recommended that the port of
Bushire and the island of Karrack should be incorporated with the dominions of the Queen.* Had the
island of Karrack alone been retained permanently in
the hands of the English Government of India, its
possession would have given to that Government a
position in the Gulf of Persia which would have rendered
future breaches of treaty at Tehran unlikely of occurrence ; and the retention of Karrack would not have
entailed much cost, since the island would have been
guarded by the British squadron stationed in the Persian
Gulf, whilst it would have been governed by the officer who

---

* *Views and Opinions of General J. Jacob, C.B.* Edited by Captain
LEWIS PELLY.

† In enumerating the advantages that were likely to accrue to England
from the retention of the valley of the Karoon, General Jacob omitted to
point out the increase which British influence in Turkey would gain by the
establishment of a British province so near to the dominions of the Sultan.

represents the Indian Government at the courts of the Arab chiefs of the gulf, and who resides at Bushire. But whatever might have been the decision of her Majesty's Government with regard to the retention or otherwise of the territory conquered from Persia, had that decision been mainly influenced by considerations affecting only the future, the course actually adopted was based chiefly upon the urgent demands of the moment. The expedition to Persia had not been looked upon with favour by the English Parliament, or by the English press, and therefore a peace had been concluded at Paris before Mohamra had been taken. The expedition to Ahwaz formed the concluding act of the war.

Ferrukh Khan, the Persian ambassador to the court of France, had concluded a treaty in the name of his master, which had been signed on the part of England by Lord Cowley at Paris on the 4th of March, 1857. Intimation of this event was given to Sir James Outram at Mohamra, by despatches which reached him on the 4th of April, and the ratifications of the Treaty were exchanged at Baghdad in the following month. By this treaty it was agreed that the forces of her Majesty the Queen should evacuate the Persian territory, subject to certain conditions being fulfilled. The principal one of these was that the Shah of Persia should take immediate measures for withdrawing from the territory, and city, of Herat, and from every other part of Affghanistan, the Persian troops and authorities then stationed therein; such withdrawal to be effected within three months from the date of the exchange of the ratifications of this treaty. His Majesty the Shah further agreed to relinquish all claims to sovereignty over the territory and city of Herat, and the countries of Affghanistan, and never to demand from the chiefs of Herat, or of the countries of Affghanistan, any marks of obedience, such as the coinage, or the " Khotbeh,* " or tribute.

His Persian Majesty further engaged to abstain thereafter from all interference with the internal affairs of Affghanistan. He promised to recognize the independence of Herat, and of the whole of Affghanistan, and never to attempt to interfere with the independence of those states.

In case of differences arising between the government of Persia and the countries of Herat and Affghanistan, the Persian Government engaged to refer them for adjustment to the friendly offices of the British Government, and not to take up arms unless those friendly offices should fail of effect.

The British Government, on their part, engaged at all times to exert their influence with the states of Affghanistan, to prevent any cause of umbrage being given by them, or by any of them, to the Persian Government ; the British Government engaging, if appealed to by the Persian Government in the event of difficulties arising, to use their best endeavours to compose such differences in a manner just and honourable to Persia.

In the case of any violation of the Persian frontier by any of the Affghan states, the Persian Government had the right, if due satisfaction were not given, to undertake military operations for the repression and punishment of the aggressors ; but it was to be distinctly understood that any military force of the Shah

* " Khotbeh " refers to the public announcement of dependence on the Shah, by praying for him in the mosques.

which might cross the border for such purpose, was to
retire within his own territory as soon as the object
should be accomplished, and that the exercise of this
right was not to be made a pretext by Persia for the
permanent occupation, or the annexation, of any town
or portion of the Affghan states.

In respect to the establishment and recognition of
consuls, and the restrictions of trade, each of the contracting parties was to be in the dominions of the other
on the footing of the most favoured nation.

On the ratifications of this treaty being exchanged,
the British Mission was to return to Tehran, where it
was to be received with certain specified apologies and
ceremonies.   The Sedr-Azem was to write, in the Shah's
name, a letter to Mr. Murray, expressing his regret at
having uttered and given currency to the offensive imputations upon the honour of her Majesty's Minister, and
requesting leave to withdraw his offensive letter to that
gentleman ; and two letters were sent from the Persian
minister for foreign affairs, one of which contained a
rescript from the Shah respecting the imputation upon
Mr. Murray.

Another stipulation of the treaty was, that the agreement entered into between Great Britain and Persia in
the year 1851, for the suppression of the slave-trade in
the Persian Gulf, should continue in force for ten years
from the month of August 1862.

Such were the principal terms of the treaty agreed
to at Paris between the plenipotentiaries of England and
of Persia. Great Britain had not wished to gain anything
by the war, and accordingly she was willing to grant
peace upon the conditions that the independence of Aff-

ghanistan should be secured, and that suitable apology should be made for the affronts which had been offered to the representative of the Queen at the Persian court. The terms demanded from Persia were so light that they might have been secured at a less cost than that involved in the capture of Bushire and of Mohamra. It is probable that the seizure and retention of the island of Karrack, and the blockade of Bushire would have had the effect of producing the evacuation of Herat by the troops of the Shah, and of bringing the Persian court to apologize for its conduct previously to the suspension of diplomatic relations at Tehran. As it was, the capture of Mohamra and the defeat of the Shah's troops at Khushab had no effect whatever on the negotiations for peace at Paris; for it was immediately after the capture of Bushire that the Sedr-Azem had sent instructions to Ferrukh Khan to conclude peace upon any terms whatsoever. The success which had attended the British arms at Khushab on the 8th of February was not known at Paris on the 4th of March, and it was not until long after peace had been made that Mohamra fell. The Sedr-Azem, on listening to the paragraphs of the treaty, which a secretary had brought from Paris, exclaimed, when he came to a pause, " Is that all ? " and on being told that there was nothing more, he uttered a fervent " Alhamdulillah ! "—Praise be to God !—for he had fully expected that one of the clauses insisted on by England would contain a demand for his own dismissal from office.

But, although Persia lay at the mercy of Great Britain, and would have been obliged to accept any terms offered to her, it very soon became a cause of sincere

satisfaction to her Majesty's Government, that nothing
had been allowed to retard the conclusion of peace. No
sooner had the ratifications of the treaty been exchanged
at Baghdad, than news reached Sir James Outram at
that city, of the outbreak of the mutinies in India. He
hurried back to Bushire, and ere his arrival at that place,
General Havelock had already put to sea with the two
famous regiments * that so soon afterwards stemmed the
tide of rebellion in Bengal. The second Bombay European Regiment had also departed for India ; where, in the
Western Presidency, its presence was as much required as
was that of the other two English battalions further east.
The 3rd Bombay Light Cavalry was also released from
service in Persia, and with the 14th Light Dragoons and
a body of the Bombay Artillery, which had also formed
portions of the Persian force, it took a prominent part in
the subsequent war in India. Every loyal officer and
man was urgently required in Hindostan, and had the
Persian war continued, India would have been deprived
of the services, when she most wanted them, of Sir James
Outram, Sir Henry Havelock, Sir George Le-Grand
Jacob, Sir Edward Lugard, and others. But for the
timely arrival of British troops from the shore of the
Persian Gulf, the mutineers must have been allowed to
keep the field for a time almost unopposed ; and it is impossible to assign any limits to the proportions which the
mutiny might in such case have assumed.

General Jacob remained at Bushire in command of a
native Indian force, with which he was to hold that place
until Persia should have fulfilled the conditions imposed
upon her by the Treaty of Paris. It has been said that

* The 64th and 78th regiments.

one of these conditions was, that Herat should thenceforth be independent. It was to be governed thereafter
by an Affghan Prince, and the selection of the new
governor became an object of importance to the Persian
court. By the 8th article of the Treaty of Peace, the
Persian government had engaged to set at liberty without
ransom, immediately after the exchange of the ratifications of the Treaty, all prisoners taken during the operations of the Persian troops in Affghanistan. Amongst
those prisoners was Mahomed Yoosuf, the nephew and
heir of the late Prince Kamran of Herat. Prince Mahomed
Yoosuf had defended Herat against the troops of the Shah,
and had been sent as a prisoner to Tehran in the spring
of the year 1856. There he had been brought into the
Shah's presence with a rope round his neck, and after
having been reproached with his so-called rebellious
conduct, had been pardoned by the king and set free
within the walls of the capital. But it was not the intention of the Persian government to permit the independent
Sedozye prince to return to his principality, and they took
advantage of a warning regarding the contents of the
coming treaty to make away with Mahomed Yoosuf
whilst he should still be in the power of the Shah.

On the 10th of April, 1857, a courier arrived at
Tehran from Paris, bearing despatches in which Ferrukh
Khan informed his government of the terms of the treaty
which he was about to conclude ; and as the signed agree-
ment would follow in the course of a few days, the Sedr-
Azem had no time to lose in deciding on the fate of
Mahomed Yoosuf. His Highness was aware that that
Affghan prince would feel that, should he recover his
power, he would owe its possession to the measures taken

by the English Government, and he, therefore, determined
to place upon the throne of Herat, a ruler who would owe
his advancement to the good-will of the Persian government. He found a man suited to this purpose in the
person of Sultan Ahmed Khan, a Barukzye, and who
was the nephew and son-in-law of Dost Mahomed Khan.
The terms upon which Sultan Ahmed Khan was to receive
the aid of Persian influence and Persian gold, to enable
him to establish himself at Herat, were these :—He was,
of his own accord, to strike coin in the name of the Shah,
and to cause the " Khotbeh," or prayer for the Suzerain,
to be read for the Persian king in the mosques of Herat.
Thus, although Persian troops should no longer remain
on Affghan soil, and though by Treaty the Shah should
renounce all pretensions to sovereignty over Herat, his
coin would still be the current coin of that principality,
and every Affghan who should attend at the mosques,
would know that his immediate ruler acknowledged the
Shah of Persia to be his Suzerain. In the powerlessness
of Sultan Ahmed Khan, if not in his good-faith, the Sedr-
Azem saw a guarantee for the fulfilment of his part of
the stipulation. Sultan Ahmed accordingly lost no time
in hurrying eastwards, in order that he might receive
possession of Herat from Prince Sultan Murad. In his
anxiety to communicate personally with that general
he forgot the circumstance that the prince was as yet
ignorant of the terms of the agreement that had been
concluded at Tehran ; and he also overlooked the fact
that the Persian commander and his soldiers had at
last tasted a much longed-for fruit, which, like that
found by the Lotus-eaters, made them forget the way
to their homes. Hastening to the tent of the Persian

SULTAN AHMED KHAN. 463

commander, the Barukzye Sirdar was informed by the guards that his Royal Highness was asleep; and when he pushed them aside, and they still barred his way, he wounded one of them with his dagger. The noise of the scuffle awoke the prince, who, on learning what had taken place, gave orders that the Affghan intruder, whose coming he had little looked for, should be severely bastinadoed. But notwithstanding this unto- ward commencement of sovereignty, Sultan Ahmed Khan persevered in the course to which he had pledged himself; nor did he ever seek to evade the terms upon which he had agreed to hold Herat. Coin was struck in the Shah's name, and the customary prayer was read for his Persian Majesty in the mosques of the city, in the same manner as would have been done had the Persian troops held the principality; and Sultan Ahmed Khan continued volun- tarily to acknowledge himself to be the vassal of the Shah until the day came when he died at his post, as his capital was about to fall into the hands of the foe against whom he had so long and so bravely defended it.

More terrible was the death, and less brilliant the career of the Sedozye claimant to the throne of Herat. On the 11th of April, 1857, the day succeeding that of the arrival at Tehran of the copy of the proposed treaty of Paris, Mahomed Yoosuf was seized, and the Sedr- Azem took advantage of a blood-feud to put an end to the dangerous rivalry of this Affghan prince to the new governor of Herat. Shah Kamran had been put to death by his Vizeer Yar Mahomed Khan, and Mahomed Yoosuf, the nephew of Kamran, had, in accordance with Affghan usage and Moslem law, avenged his death by slaying Syd Mahomed, the son of Yar Mahomed Khan. The relatives of Syd Mahomed were, in turn, ready to kill Mahomed Yoosuf; but they could not venture to do so so long as that prince should be living under the Shah's protection at Tehran. They were now, however, urged to demand the blood of their feudal foe, and the hapless Yoosuf was dragged to a mound in front of the Kasr-i-Kajar palace, and there clumsily hacked to pieces by the sabres of the relatives of Syd Mahomed. On the 13th of April the signed treaty was received from Paris, and was at once accepted by the Shah's government and ratified by his Majesty.

Peace had not been restored one hour too soon for the interests of Persia. Tabreez, the chief city of the kingdom, had lately been in open insurrection; the southern provinces were agitated and paralyzed by the presence of a British force; and in Khorassan the Turkomans were overrunning whole districts and carrying the inhabitants into captivity. It was the study of the Sedr-Azem to conceal this state of things from the knowledge of the Shah, and to cause his Majesty to believe that his numerous subjects were blessed with prosperity and contentment. But even the absolute power of a Grand Vizeer is unable at all times to exclude the discontented or the honest from the hearing of the sovereign, and so many murmurs reached the ears of the king that his Majesty at length determined to dismiss his Minister from office, and to assume in his own person the chief direction of the administration of his country.

That his Majesty's unceasing efforts have since then been directed solely towards securing the well-being of all classes of his subjects, and towards accomplishing the difficult task of providing for the furtherance of justice throughout his wide dominions, it would be unfair to deny. It will be the lot of some future writer to tell the English students of Oriental story that another name has been added to the list of exceptional Eastern monarchs; but it is not my intention to attempt to trace the course of Persian history through the years that have elapsed since the downfall of the late Sedr-Azem.

In conclusion, I shall only state that if the picture presented in these pages of the condition of Persia be not an inspiriting one, it is at least drawn with impartiality. It would have been a gratifying task to tell of a prospect of the coming triumph of civilization throughout Central Asia, but had I ventured to hold out so delusive a hope to the reader, I should have been guilty of paltering with that truth which ought to be as jealously watched over by the historian as was the Ark of God by the Jewish priest of old.

THE END.

30

LONDON :

PRINTED BY SMITH, ELDER AND CO ,

OLD BAILEY, E.C.

.

www.ingramcontent.com/pod-product-compliance
Lightning Source LLC
Chambersburg PA
CBHW031814270326
41932CB00008B/417